THE INTER-AMERICAN SYSTEM

The Royal Institute of International Affairs is an unofficial body which promotes the scientific study of international questions and does not express opinions of its own. The opinions expressed in this publication are the responsibility of the author.

The Institute gratefully acknowledges the comments and suggestions of the following who read the manuscript on behalf of the Research Committee: C. J. Child, Professor R. A. Humphreys, Miss Daphne Kirkpatrick.

The Inter-American System

GORDON CONNELL-SMITH

Issued under the auspices of the
Royal Institute of International Affairs

OXFORD UNIVERSITY PRESS
LONDON NEW YORK TORONTO
1966

Oxford University Press, Ely House, London W.1

GLASGOW NEW YORK TORONTO MELBOURNE WELLINGTON
CAPE TOWN SALISBURY IBADAN NAIROBI LUSAKA ADDIS ABABA
BOMBAY CALCUTTA MADRAS KARACHI LAHORE DACCA
KUALA LUMPUR HONG KONG

Printed in Great Britain by
Butler & Tanner Ltd, Frome and London

To
Sarah and Nicholas Connell-Smith

CONTENTS

PREFACE

THIS book, which covers the period from the beginnings of the inter-American system to the celebration of its seventy-fifth anniversary (14 April 1965), was substantially finished in the summer of 1964. After that the cut-off point became a moving frontier. Finally, when I was just about to send off the manuscript, the Dominican crisis occurred. In view of this I added one or two footnotes and altered very slightly my final paragraph; but I believe—and hope readers will agree—that neither the Dominican crisis nor United States intervention was surprising in the light of my analysis. A postscript attempts to relate the implications of these events to the main body of the book.

The study is based upon documents—principally those of the Organization of American States, the Pan American Union, and the United States Department of State—and a survey of the work of others in this field. But I was given facilities in the Pan American Union building which enabled me to observe the day-to-day working of the Secretariat, and to talk to leading officials and representatives of the member states to the OAS. I attended many meetings of the OAS Council during the year 1961–2, and the Ninth Meeting of Consultation of American Foreign Ministers in July 1964. I visited Inter-American Specialized Organizations, namely the Pan American Institute of Geography and History and the Inter-American Indian Institute in Mexico City. I also discussed the inter-American system with numerous people who have been intimately concerned with its development.

My research was supported by a grant from the Rockefeller Foundation, supplemented by another from the Royal Institute of International Affairs. I would like to express my appreciation of the generosity of both these bodies.

I am deeply indebted to Professor Robin Humphreys of University College London, who first suggested that I should write a book on the inter-American system, and has shown me innumerable kindnesses ever since; and to Professor Lewis Hanke of Columbia University, who did so much to smooth my path when I first began my research in the United States. Among other United States scholars, I am particularly grateful to Dr Bryce Wood of the Social Science

Research Council for many stimulating ideas as well as for generously reading my manuscript and making some valuable criticisms.

I wish to record my appreciation of the consideration shown me by many distinguished and busy men who discussed inter-American relations with me. I would mention specifically Mr Dean Rusk, United States Secretary of State, and Dr Alberto Lleras Camargo, former President of Colombia and first Secretary General of the Organization of American States. At the Pan American Union, I profited from several useful discussions with Dr William Sanders, Assistant Secretary General of the OAS, who was also good enough to help me in other ways. I had most interesting talks with the ambassadors to the OAS of Brazil and Mexico, Drs Ilmar Penna Marinho and Vicente Sánchez Gavito, and derived considerable benefit from my meetings with Dr William Manger, former Assistant Secretary General of the OAS, and Mr John C. Dreier, former United States ambassador to the organization. In Mexico City I had illuminating discussions with Drs Antonio Gómez Robledo and Luis Quintanilla, both of whom have rendered distinguished service to their country within the inter-American system. My talks with the prominent Mexican scholars, Dr Cosío Villegas and Dr Francisco Cuevas Cancino, at the Colegio de México also enabled me to clarify a number of important points.

My warm thanks are also due to Mr Arthur Gropp, the Librarian, and his Staff at the Columbus Memorial Library, Washington, D.C., who did so much to further my work, and whose good fellowship and hospitality made my stay among them so pleasant. While I am indebted to many people in the Pan American Union building, I must mention specifically Miss Helen Kaufmann and Sr Jorge Grossmann, whose work was greatly increased by my persistent inquiries, but who met them with unfailing patience. I am also indebted to Dr E. Taylor Parks of the State Department's Historical Division for his kindness in facilitating my work on the department's records in the United States National Archives.

During the final preparation of my manuscript for press, I was fortunate enough to receive much wise counsel and very many helpful suggestions from Miss Katharine Duff, which I record with deep gratitude. I would also like to thank warmly Dr Howell A. Lloyd, my colleague at the University of Hull, who most kindly read my manuscript and made a number of valuable comments and suggestions.

My wife, Wendy Connell-Smith, not merely endured the writing of this book. I gratefully acknowledge her invaluable assistance at every stage in its preparation.

While expressing my appreciation of the very important help I have received, I must claim as entirely my own all errors which this book may contain, and take sole responsibility for all judgements not specifically attributed to persons named in the text or footnote references.

In conclusion, I would like to mention my very young fellow-travellers in the western hemisphere. Since their first years were so much influenced by my writing this book, it seems appropriate that I should dedicate it to them.

G. C-S.

University of Hull
July 1965

ABBREVIATIONS

AJIL	*American Journal of International Law* (New York, &c., American Soc. of Internat. Law, 1907–).
Ann. OAS	*Annals of the Organization of American States* (Washington, PAU, 1949–58).
B. PAU	*Bulletin of the Pan American Union* (1893–1948, replaced by *Ann. OAS*).
Docs Am. For. Rel.	*Documents on American Foreign Relations, 1962,* ed. R. P. Stebbins (New York, Council on Foreign Relations, 1963).
DSB	*Department of State Bulletin* (1939–).
For. Aff.	*Foreign Affairs* (New York, Council on Foreign Relations, 1922–).
For. Int.	*Foro Internacional* (México, D.F., Colegio de México, 1960–).
For. Rel. US	US Dept of State, *Foreign Relations of the United States, Diplomatic Papers* (1861–).
GAOR	*General Assembly Official Records* (UN).
HAHR	*Hispanic American Historical Review* (Baltimore, Md, 1918–22; Durham, N.C., 1926–).
IA-ECOSOC	Inter-American Economic and Social Council.
IAEA	*Inter-American Economic Affairs* (Washington, 1947–).
Int. Concil.	*International Conciliation* (New York, Carnegie Endowment, 1907–).
Int. Conf. Am. States	*The International Conferences of American States,* ed. J. B. Scott (New York, Carnegie Endowment, 1931); *First Supplement,* 1933–40 (Washington, Carnegie Endowment, 1940); *Second Supplement,* 1942–54 (Washington, PAU, 1958).
Int. Org.	*International Organization* (Boston, Mass., World Peace Foundation, 1947–).
JIAS	*Journal of Inter-American Studies* (Gainesville, Univ. of Florida, 1959–).
PAU	Pan American Union.
Pol. Sci. Q.	*Political Science Quarterly* (Acad. of Pol. Sci. of the City of New York, 1886–).
RIIA, *Survey*	Royal Institute of International Affairs, *Survey of International Affairs* (London, 1925–).
SCOR	*Security Council Official Records* (UN).
Stebbins, *US in World Affairs*	R. P. Stebbins, *The United States in World Affairs, 1951–* (New York, Council on Foreign Relations, 1952–).
YBUN	*Yearbook of the United Nations.*

ABBREVIATIONS

AJIL	*American Journal of International Law* (New York, &c., American Soc. of Internat. Law, 1907–).
Ann. OAS	*Annals of the Organization of American States* (Washington, PAU, 1949–58).
B. PAU	*Bulletin of the Pan American Union* (1893–1948, replaced by *Ann. OAS*).
Docs Am. For. Rel.	*Documents on American Foreign Relations, 1962*, ed. R. P. Stebbins (New York, Council on Foreign Relations, 1963).
DSB	*Department of State Bulletin* (1939–).
For. Aff.	*Foreign Affairs* (New York, Council on Foreign Relations, 1922–).
For. Int.	*Foro Internacional* (México, D.F., Colegio de México, 1960–).
For. Rel. US	US Dept of State, *Foreign Relations of the United States, Diplomatic Papers* (1861–).
GAOR	*General Assembly Official Records* (UN).
HAHR	*Hispanic American Historical Review* (Baltimore, Md, 1918–22; Durham, N.C., 1926–).
IA-ECOSOC	Inter-American Economic and Social Council.
IAEA	*Inter-American Economic Affairs* (Washington, 1947–).
Int. Concil.	*International Conciliation* (New York, Carnegie Endowment, 1907–).
Int. Conf. Am. States	*The International Conferences of American States*, ed. J. B. Scott (New York, Carnegie Endowment, 1931); *First Supplement*, 1933–40 (Washington, Carnegie Endowment, 1940); *Second Supplement*, 1942–54 (Washington, PAU, 1958).
Int. Org.	*International Organization* (Boston, Mass., World Peace Foundation, 1947–).
JIAS	*Journal of Inter-American Studies* (Gainesville, Univ. of Florida, 1959–).
PAU	Pan American Union.
Pol. Sci. Q.	*Political Science Quarterly* (Acad. of Pol. Sci. of the City of New York, 1886–).
RIIA, *Survey*	Royal Institute of International Affairs, *Survey of International Affairs* (London, 1925–).
SCOR	*Security Council Official Records* (UN).
Stebbins, *US in World Affairs*	R. P. Stebbins, *The United States in World Affairs, 1951–* (New York, Council on Foreign Relations, 1952–).
YBUN	*Yearbook of the United Nations.*

Introduction

THE inter-American system has been in existence for seventy-five years, ever since the First International Conference of American States established 'The International Union of American Republics' in 1890. The system includes certain treaties and agreements between the American nations; numerous inter-American institutions created to further common objectives and the observance of agreed principles; and a form of multilateral diplomacy through which the American states conduct a part of their international relations.

The Organization of American States dates from the adoption of its charter at the Ninth International Conference of American States in May 1948. Until then, the inter-American system had possessed no constituent document, its continuation being provided for by resolutions passed at the international conferences. In 1948 the OAS was established as the central organization through which the inter-American system operates. It has its own subordinate organs, but there are many inter-American institutions which, although related to it, are not under its authority. The Organization of American States is therefore not a new name for the much older inter-American system; the latter is 'a term of more general and wider-embracing scope'.[1]

Although representing only a fraction of inter-American diplomacy, the inter-American system affects—at times significantly—bilateral relations between the American states. It has frequently provided a convenient, sometimes even necessary, framework within which bilateral agreements (mainly between the United States and individual Latin American countries) have been concluded, notably in the field of defence. The inter-American label has tended to make such agreements more acceptable to the Latin American countries concerned. It has helped the United States, and Latin American governments co-operating with her, in the face of anti-(North) Americanism and criticism of the latter's subservience to their powerful neighbour.

In this study, incidentally, the term 'inter-American relations' is

---

[1] M. Canyes, *The Organization of American States and the United Nations.* 4th ed. (1958), p. 13. On this point see also J. C. Dreier, *The Organization of American States and the Hemisphere Crisis* (1962), pp. 10–11.

employed predominantly to describe relations between the United States and the countries of Latin America. These are, of course, the most important international relations between the members of the inter-American system. How far it is accurate to speak of 'Pan America' as consisting of two entities, the United States and Latin America, is debatable. Even the accuracy of the term 'Latin America' is open to question; some Latin Americans have preferred 'Indo-America'. But within the inter-American system the division between the 'one' and the 'twenty' has been very marked.

The inter-American system has been the subject of extravagant claims. A former Director General of the Pan American Union described it as 'a system of international cooperation without parallel in universal history'.[2] A Mexican diplomat and man of letters has written: 'Cooperation is the contribution of America to international affairs. In contrast to the systems of universal domination and of the balance of power, there was conceived and developed in America the system of cooperation that is based upon common action, mutual aid and mutual respect.'[3] A United States professor of government has said that it is not only 'the world's oldest, best-organized, and most effective of all existent regional arrangements', but ' . . . an arrangement without parallel in the history of Great Power and small-states relations'.[4] Sumner Welles, one of the most distinguished (North) Americans to have worked in the field of inter-American relations, saw the inter-American system in 1942 as a 'cornerstone of the world structure of the future'.[5] Not surprisingly, speeches at inter-American conferences and on such public occasions as Pan American Day abound with exaggerated accounts of its achievements.

On the other hand, critics of the inter-American system, largely, but by no means exclusively, Latin Americans, have often been extravagant too. Pan Americanism has been denounced, for example, as 'that strait jacket . . . within which, like the insane, twenty republics of Latin America argue among themselves'.[6] Other Latin

---

[2] Dr Leo S. Rowe, quoted in T. H. Reynolds, *The Progress of Pan-Americanism: a Historical Survey of Latin-American Opinion* (1942), p. 9.

[3] A. Reyes, quoted in B. Wood, *The Making of the Good Neighbor Policy* (1961), p. 328.

[4] J. L. Mecham, *The United States and Inter-American Security, 1889–1960* (1961), pp. vii ff.

[5] Quoted in R. A. Humphreys, 'The Pan American System and the United Nations', *International Affairs*, xxii/1 (1946), p. 75.

[6] J. J. Arévalo, *The Shark and the Sardines* (1961), p. 104.

American critics of the inter-American system have referred to it as an association of 'the elephant and the ants'; 'the cat and the mice'; and 'the wolf and the lambs'.[7] There is a general criticism that the inter-American system is a mere rubber stamp for approving United States policies. Yet there has been a feeling in the United States that the inter-American system has not always provided her with the support to which she is entitled. In times of crisis (as, for example, over Castro's Cuba) demands have grown for unilateral action under the Monroe Doctrine to safeguard United States interests. There has been criticism in both Latin America and the United States of the gap between the extravagant claims made for the inter-American system and its modest achievements.

Of course the inter-American system, like all such international organizations, has achieved far less than has been claimed for it, and the realities of international relations in the western hemisphere are very different from the ideals expressed in the Charter of the Organization of American States and other inter-American documents. But that is not to say the inter-American system has failed in its purposes nor that inter-American relations have not been importantly affected by its existence. How far and in what ways it has been of value to both the United States and the countries of Latin America will be considered in this book.

Numerous studies have been made of the inter-American system, whose usefulness to the present writer will be evident in the pages which follow. The majority of the authors have been specialists in international law or political scientists, much concerned with discussing juridical issues and analysing the structure of the inter-American system. The approach in this book is different in that, while by no means ignoring juridical and structural problems, it lays much more stress upon the political and economic environment (both hemispheric and world) in which the inter-American system has been operating.

This study is one of international organization: the oldest international organization of its kind in the world which, since it embraces one very powerful and twenty comparatively weak nations, should throw some light upon similar international relationships. A comparison between the inter-American system and Soviet relations with the countries of Eastern Europe would be even more fruitful for this purpose. Regrettably, this must lie outside the scope of the

---

[7] See, for example, G. Wythe, *The United States and Inter-American Relations: a Contemporary Appraisal* (1964), p. 34.

B

present work. But the inter-American system is not merely one of coexistence between the powerful and the weak; it involves countries differing widely in such respects as their social systems, cultures, economic philosophies—and racial composition, a matter of great significance in the international community today.

This study is also concerned with the subject of regionalism: relations between a regional body and the United Nations. The Organization of American States is, in fact, the only effective regional agency within the meaning of Chapter VIII of the United Nations Charter. The question of competence between the world organization and the inter-American system in the field of international peace and security is of great importance for the future of both. The experience of the OAS in this context has been illuminating. However, the determining factors in the resolution of this question hitherto have not been the juridical arguments, concerned with interpreting charters and distinguishing between 'disputes' and 'acts of aggression'. Behind these has been the power struggle between the United States and the Soviet Union, with which the inter-American system has become increasingly involved.

The Soviet challenge in the western hemisphere is new. But the power factor has always shaped the development of the inter-American system: the power of the greatest nation in the hemisphere. The United States was responsible for launching the Pan American movement, and a judgement on the success or failure of the inter-American system would be largely a vindication or criticism of her Latin American policy.[8] This is, therefore, in a very real sense a study of United States foreign policy, of particular interest since Latin America has been something of a laboratory in its development. The United States has carried over into the United Nations and her international relationships in other regions something of the attitudes and techniques she acquired earlier in the inter-American system. Whether the experience of building up a system of international relations with twenty small nations whose combined strength was far exceeded by her own has been sound preparation for the role the United States has played in world affairs since the end of the Second World War is another matter. In recent years the situation has been somewhat modified, with the United States having to adjust her relations with the other members of the inter-American system in the light of extra-continental developments.

[8] This is well illustrated by Mecham's book (see above, p. 1, n. 4).

An account of the inter-American system is also of interest in studying United States foreign policy because of its close association with the most fundamental dogmas in this field: isolationism and the Monroe Doctrine. Moreover, all three major aspects of United States foreign policy may be seen clearly in action: concern for her national security, with the region in the proximity of the Panama Canal being particularly sensitive; the promotion of her foreign trade, since Latin America is an important field of overseas investment and source of raw materials; and a sense of mission which has led her to try to promote in Latin America her own ideas of democracy and private enterprise. Furthermore, although Latin America has generally been given a low priority in United States diplomacy, it has provided a show-case of her foreign policy: evidence that her relations with weak nations are fundamentally different (that is, more altruistic) than the traditional relationships between great and small powers, and the present relationships within the communist world. The inter-American system thus has played an important role in sustaining the self-image which the United States projects to the world in her struggle against international communism; a role whose value has been considerably enhanced by the extension of the struggle to the western hemisphere.

This study sets out first of all to examine the foundations of the inter-American system: to distinguish the myths from the realities, without forgetting that myths have a tendency, in international as well as domestic politics, to be more influential than realities. Next (Chapters II to IV) comes an account of the development of the system from the First International Conference of American States to the end of the Second World War, taking in the first phase of meagre achievement, the evolution of the Good Neighbour policy, and the wartime partnership. After a brief survey of inter-American relations since the end of the Second World War (Chapter V), there is a description of the three major documents appertaining to the Organization of American States signed at the Inter-American Conference for the Maintenance of Continental Peace and Security, and the Ninth International Conference of American States (Chapter VI). There follows (in Chapters VII and VIII) an account of the work of the OAS in maintaining international peace and security, and its role in other fields. Finally, the concluding chapter attempts to assess the work of the inter-American system, and to show the trends within it and the world environment which are likely to shape its future.

I The Foundations of the Inter-American System : Myths and Realities

The Origins

The concept of a distinctive 'system' embracing the United States and the countries of Latin America long antedates the establishment of their international organization. The idea that the peoples of the western hemisphere stand in a special relationship to one another setting them apart from the rest of the world possessed adherents at least as early as the beginning of the nineteenth century.[1] The origins of this 'Western Hemisphere Idea' may indeed be considered inherent in the essentially European conception of a 'New World' which the colonizers took with them to America. A distinctive American system, however, could be established only after political independence had been achieved. For the American colonies were a subordinate part of the European system of international relations.

It is not surprising, therefore, to find that the United States, the first American nation to emerge from the European empires in the western hemisphere, took the lead in developing the concept of an American system. It has been said that '... the concept of an American system ... was an idea inherent in the American situation. It was the logical summing up of the political experience of the United States since independence. . . .'[2] President Monroe's famous Message of 2 December 1823 postulated the existence of a separate American system and declared the latter to include the whole of the western hemisphere not then under effective European control. But even before 1823 there were influential advocates of the 'Western Hemisphere Idea' in the United States, notably Thomas Jefferson, the former President, and Henry Clay, the expansionist of 1812 and later Secretary of State under John Quincy Adams.

Writing to Alexander von Humboldt in 1813 and speaking of the

---

[1] A. P. Whitaker, *The Western Hemisphere Idea: its Rise and Decline* (1954), p. 1.
[2] L. Bornholdt, 'The Abbé de Pradt and the Monroe Doctrine', *HAHR*, xxiv/2 (1944), p. 220.

governments he felt would emerge from the independence movements in Spanish America, Jefferson declared:

> History . . . furnishes no example of a priest-ridden people maintaining a free civil government. . . . But in whatever governments they end, they will be *American* governments, no longer to be involved in the never-ceasing broils of Europe. The European nations constitute a separate division of the globe; their localities make them part of a distinct system; they have a set of interests of their own in which it is our business never to engage ourselves. America has a hemisphere to itself. It must have a separate system of interest which must not be subordinated to those of Europe.[3]

But the most ardent advocate of an American system during the period of the Spanish American wars of independence was Henry Clay. In March 1818 Clay declared to the House of Representatives that whatever forms of government the new nations of Spanish America established, 'these governments will be animated by an American feeling, and guided by an American policy. They will obey the laws of the system of the New World, of which they will compose a part, in contradistinction to that of Europe.'[4] Two years later Clay proposed the creation of a "system of which we shall be the centre, and in which all South America will act with us" in promoting inter-American commerce and at the same time establishing "the rallying point of human wisdom against all the despotism of the Old World".[5]

Two points in these statements by United States leaders are particularly noteworthy. First, there is the view expressed by both men that the most important characteristic of the governments of the newly independent nations of Spanish America was that they would be American governments, part of an American system. Even if, for example, they were dictatorships, they would be American dictatorships, having no links with extra-continental powers. This viewpoint has, generally speaking, been shared by United States governments ever since. Latin American dictators who have co-operated within the inter-American system have not usually incurred the hostility of their powerful neighbour. But the United States has always opposed attempts by Latin American governments to enter into relations with countries outside the western hemisphere which might threaten her interests.

---

[3] Quoted in Whitaker, *Western Hemisphere Idea*, p. 29.
[4] Quoted in D. Perkins, *A History of the Monroe Doctrine* (1955), p. 4.
[5] Whitaker, p. 32.

The second point arises from Jefferson's assertion that 'America has a hemisphere to itself'. What Jefferson meant by the word 'America' is difficult to establish. We know that Jefferson, like Clay, was an expansionist; so was John Quincy Adams, who advised Monroe to reject Canning's well-known overtures. Adams saw in the British proposals an attempt to prevent United States expansion into parts of Spanish America, especially Cuba, whose future was of great concern to both Jefferson and himself. He was at this time quoted by Addington, the British chargé d'affaires in Washington, as saying that Monroe was anxious to give Canning's proposals the most deliberate consideration, since they were 'of such magnitude, such paramount consequence as involving the whole future policy of the United States, as far at least as regarded their own hemisphere'.[6] The appropriation by United States citizens of the adjective 'American', not surprisingly resented by Latin Americans, has encouraged a proprietary attitude towards the hemisphere already present in 1823.

The importance of the Monroe Doctrine in the development of the inter-American system could scarcely be overemphasized. Gaston Nerval was guilty of little exaggeration when he declared that 'the story of the Monroe Doctrine is the story of inter-American relations'.[7] As this study will seek to show, the Monroe Doctrine has provided the ideological basis of the inter-American system and yet has been a major obstacle to its effective development. The Doctrine has been an obstacle fundamentally because of its unilateral character as the national policy of the strongest power in the western hemisphere limiting the freedom of action of its weaker neighbours. It could well be called 'a hemispheric projection of the national policy of isolation'.[8] Latin American efforts to have it transformed into an alliance were quickly rebuffed. The Latin Americans were not invited to co-operate in setting up an American system. On the contrary, Monroe declared there already existed a political system in 'America' essentially different from the political system of the allied (i.e.

[6] C. K. Webster, ed., *Britain and the Independence of Latin America, 1812–1830* (London, 1938), ii. 503. In fact the day after Addington's despatch was written Monroe sent his famous Message to Congress.

[7] Gaston Nerval, *Autopsy of the Monroe Doctrine: the Strange Story of Inter-American Relations* (1934), p. v. 'Gaston Nerval' is the pseudonym of the Bolivian writer Raúl Díez de Medina. For an illuminating discussion of 'Bolivarismo y Monroísmo' see Antonio Gómez Robledo, *Idea y experiencia de América* (1958), ch. v.

[8] Whitaker, *Western Hemisphere Idea*, p. 24.

European) powers. Therefore 'we [i.e. the United States] should consider any attempt on their part to extend their system to any portion of this hemisphere as dangerous to our peace and safety'. The non-colonization portion of Monroe's Message represented another aspect of the warning against an extension of the European system in the western hemisphere.

It is not easy to decide what Monroe meant by the word 'system'. The term could apply to forms of government, systems of alliances, and principles of foreign policy such as the balance of power. Although the United States had already recognized the royalist government of Iturbide in Mexico and was soon to extend recognition to the Empire of Brazil, Monroe undoubtedly had in mind republican institutions as the essential difference between America and Europe. He seems to have been referring to the monarchical form of government when he said: 'nor can anyone believe that our southern brethren, if left to themselves, would adopt it of their own accord'. On the other hand, the President was anxious above all to isolate the western hemisphere from the European balance of power and this, rather than the forms of government adopted by the new Spanish American nations, was his main concern.

Thus, the United States was responsible for predicating the existence of a separate American system, but not for initiating inter-American co-operation. The separation of the American system from that of Europe was proclaimed in the interests of the United States, not of developing closer international relations within the hemisphere.

Internationalism in the western hemisphere had its leading advocates in Spanish America. Of these, much the most celebrated was Simón Bolívar, so often acclaimed as the 'father of Pan Americanism'. The name of Bolívar is invoked by supporters and critics of the inter-American system alike: for example, a President of the United States launching a new programme of inter-American co-operation;[9] Guatemalan[10] and Cuban[11] delegates at inter-American conferences denouncing United States policies towards their countries. Perhaps only the word 'non-intervention' has been used more frequently than Bolívar's name at Pan American gatherings. Yet Simón Bolívar's plans for international co-operation in the western

---

[9] See below, p. 175, n. 84.
[10] Tenth Inter-American Conference (1954), *Docs, Plen. Sess.*, Doc. 95 (English), SP-23, p. 13.
[11] Eighth Meeting of Consultation, *Actas y documentos*, OEA/Ser. F/III. 8, p. 183.

hemisphere were far different from the American system postulated by Monroe. Bolívar wanted a Spanish American grouping with Great Britain, an extra-continental power, as its protector against the other European powers *and* the United States. But the Bolívar myth persists, for its value to all concerned with promoting Pan Americanism and good relations between the United States and Latin America is obvious.[12] The name of James Monroe, on the other hand, is seldom mentioned at inter-American conferences—again, for reasons obvious to every student of inter-American relations.[13] Yet the inter-American system owes its origins to the concept of Monroe, not to that of Bolívar.

The idea of a Pan Latin American grouping has long had its advocates. Some of these have desired to see Latin America freed of its dependence upon the United States and in closer relations with Europe and other regions of the world. Others have considered that ties between the United States and a unified Latin America would be stronger and more fruitful than the present association of the American republics. Dependence of individual Latin American countries upon the United States and rivalries between them[14] have been prominent factors limiting the growth of Pan Latin Americanism. There are indications, however, such as the Montevideo Treaty of 1960,[15] that larger, stronger units may emerge in Latin America in the foreseeable future. These developments will be discussed later in the study.

The Position of Canada and the European Dependencies

Another interesting aspect of Monroe's role in the development of the inter-American system is shown in the fact that the latter has not come to embrace the whole of the western hemisphere. The President had said in his message that 'with the existing colonies or dependencies of any European power we have not interfered and shall not interfere'. And, although the no-transfer principle had already qualified this protest of self-denial, and the United States for long

---

[12] It is natural that Latin Americans should stress the role of Simón Bolívar in developing the inter-American system and that the US, anxious to encourage them to regard the OAS as their own and not an instrument of her policies, should do so too.

[13] In any case the US has generally been anxious that the Doctrine should not be discussed at inter-American conferences, since it is her national policy. See below, p. 64.

[14] Including, notably, rivalry for Washington's favours.

[15] See below, p. 278, n. 16.

believed that political links between 'existing colonies' and Europe would eventually weaken and dissolve, Canada and other parts of the hemisphere have remained outside the inter-American system.

The case of Canada is of particular interest. Although the idea of her eventually joining the inter-American system was accepted at an early date, the United States for a long time opposed inviting her to do so because of her ties with Great Britain.[16] Between the two world wars there was some Latin American support for Canadian membership, but the United States did not favour even a Mexican proposal that Canada should send an observer to the Seventh International Conference of American States.[17] During the period of the Second World War and afterwards there was a growing sentiment in favour of Canada's admission among members of the inter-American system. And at the Ninth International Conference the name 'Organization of American *States*' was adopted specifically to facilitate Canada's subsequent membership, now desired by the United States.[18] But, although Canada is included in the region covered by the Inter-American Treaty of Reciprocal Assistance and is a member of such bodies as the Pan American Institute of Geography and History and the Inter-American Statistical Institute, she has not joined the OAS. The present (April 1965) state of inter-American relations is not such as to encourage her to seek membership.

The continued existence of European dependencies in the western hemisphere has been of special concern to the countries of Latin America.[19] One of the many Latin American criticisms of the Monroe Doctrine has been that it did not protect them from European territorial encroachments during the nineteenth century when these did not threaten United States interests. Today, the countries of Latin America are more 'anti-colonial' than is the United States, who numbers the colonial powers in question among her important allies and whose position on the issue accords with Monroe's dictum on 'existing colonies'. As well as a general Latin American desire to end all colonialism in the western hemisphere, there have been specific claims laid to several of the European dependencies. The matter is further complicated by the granting of independence to Jamaica and Trinidad and Tobago, for this raises the present possibility of their

---

[16] D. G. Anglin, 'United States Opposition to Canadian Membership in the Pan American Union: a Canadian View', *Int. Org.*, xv/1 (1961), pp. 1–20. This contains references to works on wider aspects of the question of Canada and the inter-American system.   [17] *For. Rel. US, 1933*, iv. 127–9.
[18] See below, p. 198.   [19] See below, p. 197, n. 8.

joining the Organization of American States and the future prospect of a territory claimed by a Latin American country doing so.[20]

The Bonds of Unity

So far, then, the inter-American system has come to include only the United States and the twenty republics of Latin America. The ideological basis of this system, as we have already noted, is the 'Western Hemisphere Idea', of which the Monroe Doctrine has been the most effective expression. This predicates a special relationship, setting its members apart from the rest of the world. What are the bases of this special relationship and how far in practice has the system been isolated from international society as a whole? Plainly, there was the negative factor of separation from Europe. But exponents of the 'Western Hemisphere Idea' have affirmed more positive bonds of unity, arising from historical experience, geographical propinquity, and the sharing of common ideals and institutions.

These claims form a mixture of myth and reality. The historical experience shared by all the countries of the inter-American system was, of course, that of being at one time colonies of European powers and (with the exception of Brazil) of fighting for independence. The course of events after independence was very different. In the words of a former Secretary General of the Organization of American States: 'An empire was destroyed in the south, while one was built in the United States. A process of integration made the United States; a process of disintegration divided the twenty nations to the south.'[21] Again, the idea that the Americas form a continental unit distinct and separate from the rest of the world is an illusion. Although the western hemisphere is a continental island, and North and South America are connected by land, normal communications between them are not overland.[22] And by air Washington is closer to Moscow than to Buenos Aires, while Rio de Janeiro is further from the centre of the North American continent than any European capital except Athens.[23] Nevertheless, the concept of the countries of the western hemisphere as neighbours has been a powerful one, though it has a political rather than a geographical validity.

The sharing of common political ideals and institutions is considered the third major bond of unity between the United States and

---

[20] See below, p. 298.　　[21] C. Dávila, *We of the Americas* (1949), p. 17.
[22] The still uncompleted Pan American Highway was meant to bring the members of the inter-American system into closer physical relations.
[23] R. A. Humphreys, *The Evolution of Modern Latin America* (1946), p. 161.

the countries of Latin America. Joseph Byrne Lockey, in his essay 'The Meaning of Pan-Americanism', said:

The fact that all American states have cherished from the beginning of their existence a common political ideal, the ideal of popular, representative government, has been and is a powerful bond of union between them. The practice of American governments, to be sure, is not always in accord with the rule. But governments pass; ideals endure.[24]

More recently, Mecham has declared: '. . . even though the Latins falter in establishing permanent, stable, and truly popular, representative, republican governments, they are at one with the United States in striving toward the same objective. There may be a difference between the Americas in progress but not in purpose'.[25] But the members of the inter-American system have claimed more than common ideals. In spite of such aberrations as the short-lived Mexican monarchy of Iturbide and the more durable Empire of Brazil, the general adoption of republican forms of government in Latin America (with constitutions roughly modelled on that of the United States) gave an appearance of common political systems. The tendency to identify the republican form of government with freedom (and democracy) has been general in the Americas, where this freedom has been contrasted with the tyranny of extra-continental systems such as monarchy, fascism, and international communism. In 1936 'the existence of a common democracy throughout America' was proclaimed in the 'Declaration of Principles of Inter-American Solidarity and Co-operation' adopted at the Inter-American Conference for the Maintenance of Peace held at Buenos Aires. The Charter of the Organization of American States reaffirms that 'the solidarity of the American States and the high aims which are sought through it require the political organization of those States on the basis of the effective exercise of representative democracy' (Article 5(d)). Here the gap between ideal and actuality remains very wide, as is also true of the concept of 'the historic mission of America' in the field of human rights.

The Monroe Doctrine and the Latin American Demand for Non-Intervention

The principles proclaimed by international organizations are, of course, largely the expression of aspirations, and the fact that the

---

[24] *Essays in Pan-Americanism* (1939), p. 21.
[25] *The United States and Inter-American Security*, p. 475.

inter-American system illustrates this general characteristic is not in itself a damaging criticism. But recent, more serious efforts to realize some of these aspirations have come into conflict with the most cherished principle of the inter-American system: non-intervention.

This principle has been described, with justification, as the *American* Doctrine of Non-Intervention[26] and the cornerstone of the inter-American system. A Mexican critic of the system has declared: 'The principle of non-intervention perhaps represents the greatest conquest of Pan Americanism. No other international principle has had such deep roots in the juridical conscience of the American states or had greater importance in the life of the hemisphere.'[27] Unfortunately, strict adherence to the principle of non-intervention is an insurmountable obstacle to the implementation of other important principles such as representative democracy and human rights.[28] Non-intervention is a negative principle; the fulfilment of many Latin American aspirations today involves positive action—in fact, intervention. Again, the principle of non-intervention is fundamentally the expression of national sovereignty, itself setting limits upon effective international organization.

But non-intervention in the experience of the inter-American system has not been merely a general principle that all members shall refrain from intervening in one another's affairs.[29] It has evolved specifically as a means of obtaining from the United States a binding pledge not to intervene in the affairs of the other American republics. At the very outset—at the First International Conference of American States, before such events as the 'taking' of the Panama Canal, the Roosevelt Corollary to the Monroe Doctrine, and the Platt Amendment[30]—the Latin American countries tried unsuccessfully to persuade the United States not to intervene diplomatically on behalf of her nationals residing in their territories. Thus what S. F. Bemis described as 'the Latin American ultimate conception of non-intervention'[31] was mooted at the inception of the inter-American system.

[26] e.g., A. Van Wynen Thomas and A. J. Thomas, Jr, *Non-Intervention: the Law and its Import in the Americas* (1956), *passim*.
[27] J. Castañeda, *Mexico and the United Nations* (1958), p. 179.
[28] M. M. Ball, 'Issue for the Americas: Non-Intervention v. Human Rights and the Preservation of Democratic Institutions', *Int. Org.*, xv/1 (1961), pp. 21–37.
[29] Indeed, interventions have been a constant feature of international relations among the countries of the Caribbean region. See below, p. 223.
[30] See below, pp. 47 ff.
[31] *The Latin American Policy of the United States: an Historical Interpretation* (1943), p. 234.

This is of particular significance since, as will be shown in the next chapter, the principal objective of the United States in initiating the Pan American movement was to gain support for her policy of limiting extra-continental influence in the western hemisphere. In other words, a system which was promoted to prevent extra-continental intervention became at once concerned with the question of intervention by the promoting power. And ever since, it has been the major aim of the United States within the inter-American system to bar extra-continental influence inimical to her interests from the western hemisphere, while the Latin American countries, generally speaking, have been concerned, above all, to limit United States intervention in their affairs. This difference is highlighted in the Monroe Doctrine which, while expressing the determination of the United States to forbid extra-continental intervention in the hemisphere, has been strongly associated with her own interventions in Latin America.

The United States claims that the Monroe Doctrine has protected Latin America from outside aggression; that, in the words of the Clark Memorandum,[32] it was 'an unbought, freely bestowed, and wholly effective guaranty of their freedom, independence, and territorial integrity against the imperialistic designs of Europe'.[33] This interpretation has not been acceptable to most Latin Americans, who consider the Doctrine to have given less than effective protection against Europe and none whatever against the United States herself. On the contrary, they have seen it as an expression of United States hegemony employed to justify that country's own intervention. It is noteworthy that while external threats have from time to time induced a considerable measure of inter-American co-operation, they have never really united the western hemisphere. And, generally speaking, the power of the United States has been a bigger (and ever-present) threat to the genuine independence of Latin America than has that of any extra-continental country or group of countries. Indeed, the unequal distribution of power in the hemisphere has so far limited their freedom of action as to make the Latin American countries in varying degrees satellites of their northern neighbour. Not unnaturally, the United States has striven to maintain the imbalance of power in the western hemisphere by preventing extra-hemispheric

---

[32] See below, p. 78.
[33] J. W. Gantenbein, ed., *The Evolution of our Latin-American Policy: a Documentary Record* (1950), p. 407.

powers from intervening to challenge her hegemony. She has rejected the idea that it might be legitimate for a Latin American country to seek the support of an extra-hemispheric power in a dispute with her, and has jealously watched the development of relations with extra-continental powers by Latin American countries.

From the Latin American point of view, on the other hand, the presence in the hemisphere of extra-continental power to offset that of the United States would seem on the surface to be highly desirable. In the words of one United States scholar, the Latin American countries 'can find protection against the northern neighbor only by using his enemies across the oceans as a balance against him'. In this writer's opinion, 'the temptation to do this will be almost irresistible notwithstanding the extraordinary dangers involved'. For, he goes on:

Political integration of the hemisphere in terms of isolation from the Old World would inevitably mean hegemony for the United States and insecurity for the others. Only by preventing this type of integration and by preserving a transoceanic and triangular political pattern with North American [*sic*] can they balance its strength and obtain equality of security with the United States.[34]

Until very recently there has been no extra-continental power which the Latin American countries could use in this way. Britain, so influential in the western hemisphere during the nineteenth century, was an imperial power making her own encroachments upon Latin American territory, until she began to withdraw from the region in favour of the United States. The challenges to United States hegemony in the twentieth century, from the Axis powers in the 1930s and earlier 1940s and from the communist countries since the end of the Second World War, have not been such as to secure wide support in Latin America, though the twenty republics have been less than wholehearted in opposing them.

The Latin American countries have been anxious, nevertheless, to maintain, and where possible strengthen, their relations with other regions of the world. They welcomed the establishment of the League of Nations, of which, in marked contrast to the United States, they all became members at one time or another. Later, they all became founder members of the United Nations and participated increasingly in the affairs of other parts of the world. The relationship of the

[34] N. J. Spykman, *America's Strategy in World Politics: the United States and the Balance of Power* (1942), p. 360.

inter-American system to the world organization is a recent problem. But the American republics have never really been isolated from the rest of the world, though the extent of their extra-continental international relations has been a matter of difference between the United States and the countries of Latin America.

A second course open to the Latin Americans for strengthening their position *vis-à-vis* the United States would be to form a grouping among themselves. Efforts to this end during the nineteenth century resulted in miserable failure,[35] and not until the last few years have more serious attempts been made. The form these attempts have taken is noteworthy. Steps towards economic integration were stimulated not within the inter-American system, but by the United Nations Economic Commission for Latin America, a body itself created in the face of United States discouragement. Only subsequently was the economic integration of Latin America associated with the inter-American system as one of the aims of the Alliance for Progress. Another important development in closer inter-Latin American relations may be seen in the refusal of six Latin American countries (Argentina, Bolivia, Brazil, Chile, Ecuador, and Mexico) to support the resolution adopted at the Eighth Meeting of Consultation of Foreign Ministers at Punta del Este in January 1962 to exclude Cuba from the inter-American system.[36] The potential significance of their abstention is enormous. For the United States was extremely anxious to obtain inter-American solidarity on the Cuban issue and the six included such important countries. Even the subsequent reduction of 'the six' to one (Mexico) has not destroyed the possible long-term effects of this event on inter-American relations. But the formation of a Latin American grouping of comparable strength with the United States seems a very remote prospect.

The third course open to the countries of Latin America—and, given such factors as their individual weakness, their inability so far to form a strong grouping among themselves, and their economic dependence upon the United States, virtually the only course hitherto open to them—has been to join with their powerful neighbour in the inter-American system. In so doing they might hope both to safeguard themselves against any extra-continental threats and to exert collective pressure upon the United States to exercise her enormous power with restraint.

[35] See below, pp. 36–39.
[36] See below, p. 178.

The One and the Twenty

For the most important single feature of the inter-American system is that it embraces one great power and twenty small ones; the world's wealthiest country and twenty countries of differing but far lower levels of economic development. The wide margin of political and economic power enjoyed by the United States over any or all of her southern neighbours has been the key factor in inter-American relations. An effective inter-American system has been possible only to the extent the United States has been prepared to limit her use of this wide margin of power.[37] Such restraint has not been easy since, given the vast disparity of power, not only action but, in certain circumstances, inaction on the part of the United States has had a profound effect on the fortunes of the other American republics.

How far has the United States exercised such restraint? There is no doubt she has done so to a greater extent since the development of the Good Neighbour policy in the 1930s. But there are no solid grounds for supporting claims, made so frequently since the inception of the inter-American system, that international relations within the hemisphere have been fundamentally different from those elsewhere because the United States has not acted like the European great powers. The United States is 'a member of the competitive system of national states, with a behaviour pattern characteristic of an ambitious and dynamic national state'.[38] The Panama Canal and the Guantánamo Bay base in Cuba bear witness to the precedence her own security takes over the sovereign rights of small states lying within her sphere of influence.

The self-image of the United States in the field of foreign policy is such an important factor in her relations with Latin America—and therefore in the development of the inter-American system—that it warrants closer examination. Bemis well illustrates this self-image in his study of the Latin American policy of the United States, where he constantly marks the contrast between the restraint exercised by his own country and the policies of imperialist powers. Two passages may suffice as examples. Of United States policy towards Mexico just after the end of the First World War Bemis says: 'restraint [was] exercised . . . under conditions which would have brought about immediate intervention by any other great power'. While in Cuba,

---

[37] In the 1960s the US has been called upon not merely to exercise restraint in the use of her power, but to use her economic power to give massive aid to her Latin American neighbours on their terms.

[38] R. W. Van Alstyne, *The Rising American Empire* (1960), p. 9.

c

during the period of the Platt Amendment, Bemis considers United States 'occasional interventions, abundantly supported by treaty right, were reluctant and temporary. . . . This forbearance shows lack of a fundamental advancing urge like that of the imperialist powers of the Old World in Asia and Africa'.[39]

Lockey, in his essay 'Pan-Americanism and Imperialism', makes the point that in her relations with Latin America 'Pan-Americanism was the choice of the United States rather than imperialism'.[40] The question of imperialism in relation to United States policy in the western hemisphere has two aspects. There is the claim (as expressed, for instance, in the Clark Memorandum) that the Monroe Doctrine saved the countries of Latin America from the imperialist designs of the European powers; and the assertion that the United States did not herself pursue an imperialist policy towards her southern neighbours. Both claims make an assumption about the peoples of Latin America which is hardly complimentary: that they are among the backward peoples of the world who, in the normal course of events, would have been colonized. The truth is that, when the United States makes self-flattering comparisons between herself and the European great powers, she is contrasting her own behaviour towards Latin America with theirs in Asia and Africa—not towards their smaller European neighbours.

Racial Discrimination and Economic Imperialism

This focuses attention upon an element in relations between the United States and Latin America to which insufficient emphasis has been given and which, in the world and hemispheric environments of the 1960s, is of growing importance for the inter-American system: the racial question. Although of greater significance today, it has always been an important factor in inter-American relations that the United States is not only a great power, but a 'white' power; while the countries of Latin America are not only small powers, but, with few exceptions, small powers with largely non-white populations. This is especially true of most of the Latin American countries nearest to the United States,[41] the racial factor being of special significance for the latter's relations with Mexico.[42] The fact that the United States has

[39] *Latin American Policy of US*, pp. 214, 278–9.
[40] *Essays*, p. 158.
[41] Moreover, the expansionist urge was most powerful among the southern states.
[42] D. M. Dozer, *Are We Good Neighbors?: Three Decades of Inter-American Relations, 1930–1960* (1959), pp. 179–83, 220.

a Negro minority unable to exercise its full civil rights has further complicated this question, weakening her moral position in the inter-American system as wel as in the world at large. Despite recent efforts by the United States government to remedy this situation, and the existence of racial discrimination in Latin America—where the Indian often enjoys very few rights indeed—this factor still has considerable importance in inter-American relations.

Today a very large proportion of politically conscious people everywhere regard racial discrimination as the worst form of repression. Latin Americans, like other 'non-Europeans' in the post-war world, have been following the racial problem in the United States with great interest even when their own fellow-countrymen have not suffered personal humiliations there on account of the colour of their skin. Over thirty years ago, Clarence Haring expressed the view that 'the Anglo-Saxon prejudice against men of color is a constant factor of disturbance in the relations between citizens of the United States and those of many Latin American countries, and it works infinite harm to the cause of international fraternity'.[43] Much more recently, Frank Tannenbaum has declared the treatment of Latin Americans as inferiors to be the most serious source of United States difficulties in Latin America.[44] The racial question is likely to become more prominent in inter-American relations as social revolution undermines the present dominant position of 'white' élites in much of Latin America.

The emergence of the United States as a world power (which was closely connected with her promotion of the Pan American movement) brought a determination to take over responsibility for good order in Latin America; a sentiment which found expression in the Roosevelt Corollary to the Monroe Doctrine. For Theodore Roosevelt, the dominant position of the United States in the western hemisphere was exactly like that of 'the English speaking race' in South Africa. Both were in the interests of civilization. Also in the interests of civilization was his taking of the Panama Canal; Colombia was not a responsible power to be dealt with as he would have dealt with a small European power.[45] In the words of Hubert Herring, Theodore Roosevelt 'made it clear how he would deal with refractory Latin Americans: he would "show those Dagos that they will have to

[43] *South America looks at the United States* (1928), pp. 73–74.
[44] 'The United States and Latin America', *Pol. Sci. Q.*, lxxvi/2 (1961), p. 163.
[45] H. K. Beale, *Theodore Roosevelt and the Rise of America to World Power* (1956), pp. 32–33.

behave decently" '.⁴⁶ Racial issues in foreign affairs were of great concern to him, as his private correspondence shows.

Nor was the racial factor absent from the rather different imperialism of Woodrow Wilson, which displayed another aspect of the white man's burden: that of the missionary, dealing with immature peoples and 'teaching them to elect good men'. This attitude is well illustrated by a letter from Wilson's Secretary of the Interior to his Secretary of State, Lansing, in 1919: 'And now a word as to Mexico. I wish somehow that you could be given a free hand in this matter. I know it would be a stiff hand, an authoritative hand, and that is what these people need. They are naughty children who are exercising all the privileges and rights of grown ups'.⁴⁷ Even Franklin Roosevelt's liberal remark, 'They think they are just as good as we are and many of them are',⁴⁸ betrays an innate sense of superiority which has shown itself from the beginning in the United States attitude towards Latin America.

As the world environment has become increasingly unfavourable to colonialism, so has the racial question, so intimately linked with it, become more acute. The challenge to foreign political control has been accompanied by a growing attack on racial discrimination. Both were greatly stimulated by the Second World War and its aftermath. Repercussions have been felt within the inter-American system. Haiti submitted a draft resolution to the Mexico City Conference in 1945 calling for 'abolition of any policies or action having a character of racial discrimination in the relations amongst the American Republics'. In the event a much watered-down version was adopted.⁴⁹ But Panama, not surprisingly, has been most concerned to raise the question of racial discrimination, since she has had the specific grievance of such discrimination in the Panama Canal Zone exacerbating her nationalist feeling about United States presence there. The outlook of United States citizens in the zone (the 'Zonians') bears an unhappy resemblance to the traditional attitude of white settlers in Africa and elsewhere towards the 'natives'.

The Panamanian delegation to the Tenth Inter-American Conference endeavoured to have the anti-communist resolution adopted

⁴⁶ *A History of Latin America from the Beginnings to the Present* (N.Y., 1961), p. 800.
⁴⁷ Quoted in R. F. Smith, 'The United States and Latin-American Revolutions', *JIAS*, iv/1 (1962), p. 95.
⁴⁸ Quoted in Wood, *Good Neighbor Policy*, p. 359.
⁴⁹ *Report of the Delegation of the United States of America to the Inter-American Conference on Problems of War and Peace* (1946), pp. 22, 109, 355–6.

there amended to include a phrase calling for the elimination of all forms of racial discrimination.[50] This was not accepted by the United States, but the words 'without any discrimination' were added to the 'Declaration of Caracas'.[51] It is noteworthy that the separate resolution on racial discrimination (XCIV) adopted at Caracas stressed the fact that such discrimination 'promotes the continuation of a favorable climate for the action of communist propaganda'. And it recommended: 'That the American States adopt or strengthen, wherever it is deemed necessary, legal and educational measures to make effective the abolition of racial discrimination, thus fulfilling the American concept of the rights of man and as one of the ways to fight international communism.' Prejudice and discrimination in the United States against 'people of mixed blood' have been described as 'an "Achilles' heel" for Communist propaganda in Latin America as in most of the underdeveloped areas of the world'.[52]

With the growing challenge from international communism following the Cuban revolution the questions of imperialism and racial discrimination became more prominent within the inter-American system. The United States charged the Cuban government both with providing a beachhead for Soviet imperialism and with denying human rights to its citizens. This naturally provoked counter-charges against the United States of imperialism and denial of rights to her own Negroes. At the Seventh Meeting of Consultation of Foreign Ministers, for example, the Cuban delegation denounced both the position of Negroes in the southern United States and racial discrimination in the Panama Canal Zone.[53] At the Eighth Meeting of Consultation the Cuban President denounced the military base at Guantánamo as established by force, without the consent of the Cuban people.[54]

Since the end of the Second World War the United States has been increasingly on the defensive against charges of racial discrimination (mainly within her own territory) and of imperialism in Latin America (and elsewhere). Since its critics (and not only communists) condemn imperialism as the economic exploitation of supposedly inferior peoples, the two are closely linked. Latin American

[50] Tenth Inter-American Conference, *Diario* (1954), p. 415.
[51] See below, p. 163.
[52] T. W. Palmer, Jr, *Search for a Latin American Policy* (1957), p. 124.
[53] Seventh Meeting of Consultation, *Actas y documentos*, OEA/Ser. F/III. 7, p. 323.
[54] Eighth Meeting of Consultation, *Actas y documentos*, OEA/Ser. F/III. 8, pp. 191–2.

nationalism[55] has been predominantly a protest against United States domination and what has been denounced as economic exploitation. In spite of considerable economic development in some of them, the countries of Latin America, generally speaking, are still over-dependent upon a small number of primary products and, in many cases, upon the United States market for their sale. Moreover, Latin America is a major area of United States private investment. Her economic interest in the region has traditionally coloured, if not largely determined, her attitude towards it. It has been well observed that 'the main business of United States diplomats in Latin America before 1939 was the defense of the economic interests of their co-citizens'. And the diplomats themselves very often have had business connections in the region.[56]

A Low Priority Area for Diplomats

In view of the crucial role generally played by the United States ambassador in the affairs of at least the smaller Latin American countries, the need for men of high quality in such diplomatic posts is obvious. Yet the history of inter-American relations furnishes over-many examples of a striking insensitiveness on the part of the United States envoys in Latin America and of the administrations which appointed them. The first United States minister to Mexico, Joel Poinsett, was recalled on the insistence of the Mexican government for meddling in Mexican politics; while it has been said of Poinsett's successor, Anthony Butler, that his sole qualifications for the post were 'an acquaintance with Texas and a strong desire to see the United States obtain it'.[57] And more recently there was the case of Spruille Braden in Argentina in 1946,[58] and the role of John E. Peurifoy in Guatemala in 1954.[59] Reference to the Guatemalan crisis

[55] What has been called, paradoxically, 'continental nationalism' as distinct from the nationalism of individual countries. This may be compared with Arab nationalism, though the latter is much more highly developed.

[56] Wood, *Good Neighbor Policy*, pp. 333–4. Wood points out significantly (pp. 341–2), that none of the Good Neighbour team (Roosevelt, Hull, Welles, and Duggan) 'entered office in 1933 on leave from positions in law firms or business enterprises, and it is unlikely that any of them anticipated going to such positions at the end of their public service'.

[57] Cited in G. H. Stuart, *Latin America and the United States* (1955), p. 136.

[58] See below, pp. 141–2.

[59] 'The activities of our "pistol-packing" Ambassador John E. Peurifoy were considered successful in the United States at the time, but they left a vivid impression in Latin America of a type of "Big Stick" diplomacy that is feared and disliked' (H. L. Matthews, ed., *The United States and Latin America* (1959), p. 163).

brings to mind that John Foster Dulles, United States Secretary of State at the time, showed himself singularly careless of Latin American feelings.[60]

The truth is that the United States has always regarded Latin America as a low priority area for her diplomats,[61] in spite of the assertion which at least used to be made in the instructions given to her delegates to inter-American conferences that 'among the foreign relations of the United States as they fall into categories, the Pan American policy takes first place in our diplomacy'.[62] Sumner Welles, an outstanding figure among United States diplomats concerned with the inter-American system, wrote on this point:

> Three years after I entered the foreign service of the United States I asked to be transferred to a post in Latin America. It was not difficult to secure compliance with my request, but it was hard to prevent my superiors from entering a notation upon my efficiency record that my judgment and mental stability should receive especial scrutiny. In those remote days assignment to Latin-American posts was usually reserved for those who required disciplinary action, or for those who had proved themselves misfits or incapable.[63]

Another outstanding exception, like Welles strongly associated with the Good Neighbour policy—and who also requested a diplomatic appointment in Latin America (Mexico), was Josephus Daniels.[64] It is none the less illustrative of the United States attitude towards Latin America that Daniels was appointed, since, as Secretary of the Navy, he had ordered the occupation of Vera Cruz in 1914.[65] Moreover, Franklin Roosevelt was then Assistant Secretary of the Navy, and claimed to be the author of a constitution imposed upon Haiti;[66] so the President's credentials for improving inter-American relations were hardly reassuring! At all events, the difficulty experienced by the Kennedy administration in filling the post of Assistant Secretary of State for Inter-American Affairs seems to suggest that Latin America was still not a region much sought after by United States career

[60] See below, pp. 161–2.
[61] For criticisms of the poor quality of US diplomats in Latin America see, for example, D. G. Munro, *Intervention and Dollar Diplomacy in the Caribbean, 1900–1921* (Princeton UP, 1964), p. 544; and W. F. Sands, *Our Jungle Diplomacy* (Univ. of North Carolina Press, 1944), pp. 193, 233 ff.
[62] e.g. *For. Rel. US, 1938*, v. 54.
[63] *Where Are We Heading?* (1946), p. 182.
[64] E. D. Cronon, *Josephus Daniels in Mexico* (1960), pp. 8–9.
[65] Ibid. p. 15.
[66] Bemis, *Latin American Policy of US*, p. 193.

diplomats.[67] In marked contrast, Washington is the most important ambassadorial assignment for Latin Americans.

All this reflects the disproportionate power of the United States which has made her policy the major influence determining the fortunes of the inter-American system. This study will show how her initiative brought the Pan American movement into being after the failure of internationalism in Latin America; and how the ideological basis of this movement was the national policy of the United States aimed at preventing extra-continental intervention in the western hemisphere: the Monroe Doctrine. The major result of the First International Conference of American States was the establishment of a permanent Pan American institution situated in Washington under the direction of the United States Secretary of State.

Seventy-Five Years On

The first phase in the history of the inter-American system was characterized by meagre achievement. The dominant position of the United States ensured that Pan American conferences never dealt with the major political issues of the hemisphere, while her own interventions caused increasing resentment. For a long time the United States resisted attempts by Latin American countries to modify the composition of the Governing Board of the Pan American Union and to secure from her a pledge of non-intervention. During this phase all serious threats to Latin American security from outside the continent vanished. At the same time Article 21 of the League of Nations Covenant was virtually an acceptance by the signatories of the Monroe Doctrine: a pledge not to deal with 'American questions'. The Latin Americans, with no prospect of extra-continental support to strengthen their position, therefore endeavoured to obtain assurances of their security from the United States within the inter-American system.

The second phase began when the administration of Franklin D. Roosevelt, after certain limited steps by its two immediate predecessors—and some trial and error on its own part—acquiesced in Latin American demands for a non-intervention pledge. There is no doubt that to the Roosevelt administration this undertaking meant giving up unilateral armed intervention. Along with unqualified acceptance of the non-intervention principle (at Buenos Aires in 1936), the members of the inter-American system adopted that of consultation in situations where previously the United States had acted unilaterally.

[67] See *NYT*, internat. ed., 16 June 1961, 'A Post Goes Begging'.

Soon it became clear that, in Latin American eyes, non-intervention involved much more than mere abstention from sending in the United States marines. The deteriorating world situation encouraged the Roosevelt administration to make further efforts to improve relations with its southern neighbours and to strengthen the inter-American system.

The period of the Second World War brought the twenty-one American republics into a more intimate relationship and a proliferation of new inter-American agencies. But this new intimacy created problems threatening the continuation of the Good Neighbour policy. Moreover, plans for forming a new world organization in which the United States took a leading part cast doubt upon the future of the inter-American system. With the adoption of the United Nations Charter the American regional organization had to be formalized and its relations with the world body defined. The existence of the United Nations and the role of the Organization of American States as 'within [it] . . . a regional agency' struck a severe blow at the isolationist core of the 'Western Hemisphere Idea'.

Since 1945 both the world and hemispheric environments have been unfavourable to the inter-American system. It is indisputable that inter-American relations generally have deteriorated during this period even though there have been striking institutional developments including, of course, the adoption of the Charter of the Organization of American States. In the first place, the United States emerged from the Second World War as one of the 'super-powers' and much the stronger of the two. This made the imbalance of power within the inter-American system even more marked than before. Outside the hemisphere the United States assumed commitments and concluded alliances which struck another blow at the 'Western Hemisphere Idea' and aroused misgivings in Latin America of possible involvement in these extra-continental commitments.[68] Within the United Nations, the United States was one of the permanent members of the Security Council, while the countries of Latin America, although always having two non-permanent seats there, were among the smaller powers seeking to exert their influence through the General Assembly. Thus the existence of the United Nations with full American participation underlined the different status in international affairs of the United States and the countries of Latin America.

[68] See, for example, Castañeda, *Mexico & the UN*, p. 190.

The world environment has had increasing influence upon the situation within the western hemisphere. The Latin American countries looked to the United States for substantial assistance in their economic development when the war was over. It soon became clear their hopes were not going to be fulfilled, and, in particular, that the United States was to give priority to the economic recovery of Western Europe. So Latin Americans complained bitterly of what they called United States 'neglect' in favour of other regions of the world; they shared increasingly with the peoples of Asia and Africa what came to be known as 'the revolution of rising expectations'. They also shared the growing nationalism of these peoples; a nationalism in their case directed against the United States.

The Cold War imposed greater strains upon inter-American relations. The United States became even more committed in other regions and, while Latin America seemed to be remote from the struggle against international communism, she gave it low priority, especially in the matter of economic aid. At the same time, Latin American fear of being involved in United States extra-continental commitments helped to induce a perceptible growth of neutralism south of the Rio Grande. In any case, Latin American governments were more concerned with their own growing economic and social problems.

The situation became worse when the communist challenge directly threatened the western hemisphere. The United States had the greatest difficulty in obtaining Latin American support against the Guatemalan government of Jacobo Arbenz when she denounced it as communist. Instead of inter-American solidarity in the face of a common threat there developed further the concept of reciprocity: economic aid as the price of political support. Even the vastly more serious challenge of Cuba failed to create a truly united front among the members of the inter-American system. Apparently many Latin Americans continued to fear the possibility of United States intervention more than international communism. In the meantime the Alliance for Progress, designed to meet the communist challenge and to transform inter-American relations, has yet to prove adequate for its tasks. Like the defence of the western hemisphere against the intervention of international communism, it has been over-much a United States rather than a truly inter-American effort.

Thus, briefly, has the story of the inter-American system so far unfolded. United States action brought it into being; her Latin

American policy at first prevented it from achieving anything significant; then her policy of restraint gave it a fresh start. At the end of the Second World War her global commitments and policies jeopardized its future, as did her subsequent preoccupation with international communism in the hemisphere. Since the Cuban revolution she has made a new effort to make it more meaningful. Over the same period, the role of Latin America has been, by comparison, a negative one. This reflects the different power status, and therefore interests and aims, of the parties. For, put simply (this study will be concerned at a later stage with the complexities), the United States has viewed the inter-American system as an instrument for reinforcing her own policies; the Latin American countries as a means of persuading the United States to modify those policies. This is far from the whole story, but it is fundamental to any realistic analysis of the inter-American system.

The One and the Twenty Again

The essential conflict between the 'one' and the 'twenty'—the clash between the interests of the great power and those of the smaller ones—has shown itself in all the major fields of international relations in the western hemisphere. The United States has 'great power' interests to which those of the smaller powers within her sphere of influence must in the last resort necessarily be subordinated. For her own security the United States maintains the base at Guantánamo in Cuba and control of the Panama Canal, both offensive to Latin American nationalism; she is concerned to support friendly governments in countries of strategic importance to her, regardless of their character. More often than not, the most co-operative governments have been dictatorships, and it is hard to disagree with the contention that 'one of the most powerful reasons for the perpetuation of dictatorial regimes in America is the decided moral and material support which they have been historically furnished by the United States'.[69] Such governments generally have been the readiest to grant favourable concessions to United States business interests (and, more recently, to follow her anti-communist policies) and, lacking popular support, have been more amenable to United States pressure. This suggests that, while paying lip-service to the encouragement of representative democracy in Latin America, the United States has a strong interest in just the reverse, especially since there is so much

[69] Castañeda, *Mexico & the UN*, p. 184.

popular feeling against her in Latin America. In practice, the United States attitude towards furthering democracy in Latin America has fluctuated according to her immediate policy objectives. But in any case, she has always been concerned primarily with procedural democracy, especially the holding of elections—which only too often have proved farcical.[70]

The countries of Latin America, on the other hand, depend for their security upon the United States—her power to shield them from extra-hemispheric attack and her restraint to secure them against aggression of her own. They know that any international action within the hemisphere authorized by the OAS will be in effect action by the United States. At the same time, they know that in the last resort the United States will act unilaterally if she feels her vital interests are threatened. As President Kennedy warned after the abortive invasion of Cuba in April 1961:

> Any unilateral American intervention, in the absence of an external attack upon ourselves or an ally, would have been contrary to our traditions and to our international obligations. But let the record show that our restraint is not inexhaustible. Should it ever appear that the inter-American doctrine of noninterference merely conceals or excuses a policy of non-action—if the nations of this hemisphere should fail to meet their commitments against outside Communist penetration—then I want it clearly understood that this Government will not hesitate in meeting its primary obligations, which are to the security of our Nation.[71]

This was, in effect, a reminder that the Monroe Doctrine is still in existence, as the *New York Times*, for example, noted in an editorial the following day.[72]

In the economic field the division of the members of the inter-American system into the 'one' and the 'twenty' has been perhaps even more marked. On this point Dr William Manger, formerly Assistant Secretary General of the OAS, declared:

> There could be nothing more dangerous for the inter-American regional organization than for a situation to develop whereby one country would find itself on one side of an issue and all the others on the other side. And yet, that is exactly what is happening in the economic field, in which the

---

[70] See T. P. Wright, Jr, 'Free Elections in the Latin American Policy of the United States', *Pol. Sci. Q.*, lxxiv/1 (1959), pp. 89–112.

[71] 'The Lesson of Cuba: Address by President Kennedy', *DSB*, xliv/1141 (1961), p. 659.

[72] *NYT*, internat. ed., 21 Apr. 1961.

United States invariably finds itself opposed by every other American republic on every economic issue that presents itself.[73]

As the most highly industrialized country in the world, the United States has been concerned with fostering the most favourable conditions for her private overseas investment, a large proportion of which is in Latin America. This had been a major reason for her initiating the Pan American movement in the first place. The countries of Latin America, on the other hand, have been anxious above all to secure high and stable prices for their products and substantial government loans from the United States to assist their economic development. The unsuccessful attempt to reconcile the two sets of interests in the Economic Agreement of Bogotá[74] is only one instance of the difficulty of furthering inter-American co-operation in the increasingly important economic field.

Along with this divergence of economic interests there has been a clash of economic philosophies. In spite of increasing government intervention in practice, the United States remains dedicated in principle to private capitalism as the decisive factor in the economy, while in Latin America the tradition of state enterprise is strong. This difference, taken with the widespread unpopularity of United States 'big business' in Latin America, is what has made fruitful inter-American economic co-operation so difficult. But the question goes deeper than mere economic philosophies since, of course, the concept of private enterprise in the United States is not merely one of an effective means of economic progress, but a way of life and the basis of a culture. Not only is democracy identified with capitalism, but so are virtues, such as hard work and thrift, which are greatly admired in the United States. These standards, typically those of the 'middle class' in highly industrialized societies, are not widely acceptable in Latin America where no middle class of comparable significance yet exists.[75] The divergence on economic questions is therefore closely linked with one in the cultural field, the Latin Americans deriving some compensation for their inferiority to the United States in the political and economic sphere from a conviction of their higher spirituality: Rodó's Ariel compared with his (United States) Caliban.

Another field in which this division into 'one' and 'twenty' is of

---

[73] *Pan America in Crisis* (1961), p. 72.
[74] See below, pp. 267-8.
[75] On this question, cf. C. Véliz, 'Obstacles to Reform in Latin America', *World Today*, xix/1 (1963), pp. 18-29, and J. J. Johnson, *Political Change in Latin America* (1958).

particular significance is that of international law. As the United States delegates to the Seventh International Conference of American States were instructed:

> It should be borne in mind that there is a vast difference between the conception of this Government and that of other first-class Powers, including Great Britain, France, Germany, Italy and Japan, and that of Latin American countries and certain small European Powers, as regards many fundamental principles of International Law.[76]

A study of the inter-American system reveals how concerned the Latin American countries have been to create juridical safeguards against the use by the United States of her overwhelming power; the store they have set by the Pan American principle of the juridical equality of states. As Lilliputians, they have sought to tie up the United States Gulliver with a mass of juridical knots. This has naturally provoked United States criticism of excessive Latin American legalism. John C. Dreier, for ten years United States representative on the OAS Council, has remarked that: 'Juridical disputation is the language of inter-American politics, and the tangled web of juridical precedents and institutional procedures in the OAS provides ample opportunity for carrying on such disputation *ad infinitum*'.[77] The principle of non-intervention represents the major juridical achievement of the Latin Americans in their endeavour to restrain United States power.

However, within the inter-American system, the Latin American countries have been concerned not so much to strengthen international law as to change it. This is hardly surprising since international law has been created in the main by the great powers, which alone can in practice enjoy many of the rights in theory possessed by all nations. The emergence of large numbers of new sovereign states since the end of the Second World War has been accompanied by a growing challenge to some traditional rules of international law, for 'the immense majority of new states did not participate in the process of formation and development of the numerous juridical institutions and rules of law that were consolidated and systematized during the nineteenth century'.[78] More specifically: 'It is felt that many of the

---

[76] *For. Rel. US, 1933*, iv. 65.
[77] 'The Organization of American States and United States Policy', *Int. Org.*, xvii/1 (1963), p. 38.
[78] Castañeda, 'The Underdeveloped Nations and the Development of International Law', *Int. Org.*, xv/1 (1961), p. 39.

most important norms in international law were developed and perpetuated by a few Western European powers and the United States, all of whom shared a large community of interests, and that these rules were often forced on much of the rest of the world.'[79] Often the independence of the new states has been qualified by treaties, upon whose 'sanctity' the interested great powers have insisted, but which were, in fact, imposed upon the former because of their weakness. Within the western hemisphere the perpetual treaties under whose terms the United States maintains the base at Guantánamo in Cuba and administers the Panama Canal Zone are outstanding examples.

Since the end of the Second World War the Latin American countries have challenged many of the traditionally accepted principles of international law, and have been involved in controversies over such matters as the extent of territorial waters, claims to Antarctica, and the European colonies and 'occupied territories' in the western hemisphere.[80] They have not received the support of the United States on these issues. From the beginning of the inter-American system the Latin American countries have sought to persuade the United States to subscribe to doctrines which would have the effect of curtailing rights she claimed under international law; to create a special American international law. The United States, understandably, has been extremely reluctant to do this, and has always opposed the establishment of an Inter-American Court of Justice. On the whole, the United States has stood by her rights as a great power in the face of Latin American efforts to reduce them.

It would appear legitimate to speak of the 'twenty', confronting the United States on certain fundamental issues within the inter-American system, as constituting 'Latin America'. But there are strict limits to the use of the term even in this context. Quite apart from obvious differences between the Latin American republics in size, resources, ethnic composition of their populations, social structure, political forms, and degrees of economic development, relations between them have not been intimate. Physical obstacles such as great mountain ranges, deserts, and jungles have been an important factor limiting the growth of Latin American unity, and trade between these countries still amounts to only some 10 per cent of their total foreign commerce. Disputes between individual Latin American

---

[79] C. N. Ronning, *Law and Politics in Inter-American Diplomacy* (1963), p. 157.
[80] These issues are discussed by Prof. Ronning, chs. vi–viii.

countries, largely concerned with frontiers,[81] have prevented closer co-operation to secure concessions from the United States. This study will consider how far the inter-American system has brought them into closer and more harmonious relations; how far, in other words, the Pan American movement has actually helped to foster Pan Latin Americanism. Certainly, during the last decade, the Latin American countries have become increasingly conscious of sharing certain common problems and aspirations. Reference has already been made to recent efforts at more effective co-operation between groups of them.

Latin American Attitudes

Following this consideration of the United States approach to the inter-American system and that of Latin America as a whole, a brief examination will now be made of the attitudes of three of the largest Latin American republics, all of them among the six countries which did not support the United States position at the Punta del Este Meeting in January 1962: Argentina, the country with traditionally the strongest ties with Europe; Brazil, the biggest and potentially greatest of the Latin American countries; and Mexico, the immediate neighbour of the United States, who has suffered most from the latter's intervention. Then some attention will be paid to Cuba, to show the important role that island has played in the fortunes of the inter-American system.

Argentina, it is generally agreed, has been the least co-operative of the Latin American countries within the inter-American system; and she had previously declined to take part in the Hispanic-American conferences. The traditional Argentine position has been much criticized, and with some justification. But its significance lies in the fact that it has been based upon an understandable rejection of the isolationist core of the 'Western Hemisphere Idea'. A system of closer ties within the hemisphere at the expense of those with Europe had no appeal for Argentina when James G. Blaine launched the Pan American movement at the First International Conference of American States. Geographically remote from Washington, her economic interests and the culture of her ruling class were linked with Europe. It is hardly surprising her delegation took the lead in

---

[81] See below, ch. vii, *passim*, and, for historical background, G. Ireland, *Boundaries, Possessions, and Conflicts in South America* (1938); and *Boundaries, Possessions, and Conflicts in Central and North America and the Caribbean* (1941).

rejecting a proposed customs union and strongly denounced the idea of limiting relations with Europe.[82] There have been other reasons for her policy: ambitions to lead a group of smaller South American countries, jealousy of the United States, and rivalry with Brazil are among them. But her geographical position and historic ties with Europe would seem to provide the strongest motives for a traditional reluctance to commit herself too closely to a purely American grouping. She has been the leading exponent of the idea of strong extra-continental ties to limit the power and influence of the United States.

After the Second World War, during the Perón era, Argentina aspired to take a 'Third Position' between the United States and the Soviet Union, but failed to create a lasting 'justicialist' bloc.[83] Following Perón's overthrow in 1955, President Frondizi greatly improved relations with the United States, granting unprecedented concessions to the latter's oil interests.[84] However, Argentina did not support the United States position at Punta del Este, a main factor in Frondizi's removal by military coup not long afterwards. The new Argentine government, although strongly anti-communist and, therefore, supporting the United States policy towards Cuba, annulled the oil contracts made during Frondizi's presidency.[85] It is unlikely Argentina will co-operate really closely with the United States within the inter-American system, whatever the character of her government.

Brazil, traditionally, has been more friendly towards the United States than has Argentina. As a non-Spanish speaking nation in the western hemisphere, Brazil has long had something in common with the United States, for whom she has been a main 'bulwark' in Latin America. But Brazil has the potential of a great power, and, with a population and resource endowment far greater than those of Argentina, has firmer hopes of becoming the leader of Latin America. It is understandable that, as she grows in power, she will want to be more independent of the United States, and she has given many signs of wishing to develop her strength as soon as possible. The emergence of Brazil is the biggest challenge to the concept of the 'one' and the 'twenty'. Of course Brazil is as yet far from being a great power, and

[82] See below, p. 43.
[83] G. Pendle, *Argentina* (1963), pp. 155 ff.
[84] S. G. Hanson, 'The End of the Good-Partner Policy', *IAEA*, xiv/1 (1960), p. 67.
[85] Stebbins, *US in World Affairs 1963* (1964), pp. 302–3.

is over-dependent upon the United States for economic and financial aid, the more so since her development plans have induced persistent inflation and balance of payments crises. But, in recent years, she has shown determination to follow an 'independent' foreign policy, based upon widening her international relations outside the western hemisphere,[86] and for long resisting United States pressure to support stronger measures against Cuba. Brazil's position, especially since it involved closer co-operation with Mexico,[87] was a key factor, within the hemisphere,[88] in encouraging the exercise of restraint by the United States in the Cuban crisis. The overthrow of President Goulart by military coup in April 1964 led to a stronger anti-communist policy internally and to Brazil severing diplomatic relations with Cuba. At the Ninth Meeting of Consultation of American Foreign Ministers Brazil supported sanctions against the Cuban government.[89] Yet it seems probable that, before too long, she will once again seek to follow an independent foreign policy, for this is the hallmark of the power Brazil aspires to be in the foreseeable future.

The role of Mexico in the inter-American system has been, over the whole period, the most significant one of any Latin American nation. With the greatest experience of United States intervention, Mexico understandably has seen the inter-American system primarily as an instrument for restraining the United States in the exercise of her power through the strict application of the principle of non-intervention. Mexican jurists played a leading part in formulating this principle[90] and Mexico has been particularly concerned to maintain it. This study will show Mexico's key position at crucial stages in the development of the inter-American system. It was the non-recognition of a Mexican government by the United States, and the consequent denial of representation to Mexico on the Governing Board of the Pan American Union, which brought about a modification of that body's composition at the Fifth International Conference of American States. It is not surprising that a Mexican Foreign Minister,

---

[86] J. H. Rodrígues, 'Nueva actitud exterior del Brasil', *Foro Int.*, ii/3 (1962), pp. 408–22.

[87] A. Garciá Robles, 'Las relaciones diplomáticas entre México y el Brasil', *Foro Int.*, iv/3 (1964), pp. 347–78.

[88] Extra-continental factors were even more important, of course.

[89] See below, pp. 185–6.

[90] L. Quintanilla, 'La política internacional de la Revolución Mexicana', *Foro Int.*, v/1 (1964), pp. 2 ff., calls the principle of non-intervention the *Doctrina Carranza*. He points out also that Carranza opposed collective intervention.

Genaro Estrada, subsequently formulated the doctrine that recognition of a government should be automatic without reference to its origins. Efforts by the Coolidge administration to improve relations with Mexico were the first steps of a change in United States Latin American policy, and Mexico was deeply concerned with events in Nicaragua which brought the intervention issue to a head at the Sixth (Havana) Conference in 1928.

At the Seventh International Conference of American States, generally considered as marking a turning point in the fortunes of the inter-American system, Dr Puig Casauranc, the Mexican Foreign Minister, was the chief spokesman of the Latin American demand for 'non-intervention'. It is interesting to note Cordell Hull (head of the United States delegation at Montevideo) recording in his *Memoirs* that when Dr Puig attacked United States corporations in a speech calling for a moratorium on debts,[91] Saavedra Lamas of Argentina 'came to the rescue'.[92] For Mexico's policy has over the whole period been more difficult for the United States to deal with than has that of Argentina.

In the development of the Good Neighbour policy launched at Montevideo the role of Mexico was outstanding. It was the Mexican delegation which initiated the Additional Protocol Relative to Non-Intervention at the Inter-American Conference for the Maintenance of Peace held at Buenos Aires in 1936.[93] In a subsequent radio broadcast the head of her delegation declared this had been Mexico's principal objective at the conference.[94] More importantly Mexico's resistance to her pressures, following the expropriation of the oil properties in 1938, served notice on the United States that non-intervention meant a great deal more to Latin America than mere abstention from unilateral military action on her part.[95] At Mexico City in 1945 Foreign Minister Ezequiel Padilla voiced what was to be the increasingly stronger demand of the Latin Americans in the post-war period that the inter-American system should concern itself with the economic and social problems of the continent.

[91] This speech is an example of the lead often given by Mexico as champion of socio-economic matters at inter-American conferences. Incidentally, it was Mexico who proposed the establishment of an inter-American bank at the First International Conference of American States.

[92] *The Memoirs of Cordell Hull* (1948), i. 335–6.

[93] Inter-American Conference for the Maintenance of Peace (Buenos Aires, Dec. 1936), *Proceedings* (*Stenographic Reports*) (1937), p. 84.

[94] *Informe de la Delegación de México a la Conferencia Interamericana de Consolidación de la Paz* (1938), p. 303.   [95] See below, p. 104.

The role of Mexico at the Ninth International Conference of American States again was an outstanding one. The Charter of the OAS, for example, was largely the comprehensive document her delegation proposed, and her influence was important in preventing the establishment of an Inter-American Defense Council. As the firm opponent of collective as well as unilateral intervention, Mexico refused to support Mr Dulles's anti-communist resolution at the Tenth Inter-American Conference, and has since steadfastly opposed resolutions at Meetings of Consultation and in the OAS Council which might justify intervention against Cuba. Even at the height of the Cuban crisis in October 1962, when the OAS Council passed a resolution supporting measures to secure the withdrawal of Soviet rockets from the island, the Mexican delegate (together with the Bolivian and Brazilian delegates) declared that this should not be taken to justify an armed attack on Cuba. Since then Mexico has maintained that the nature of the Cuban government is an internal matter, thereby rejecting the United States view that Dr Castro's alignment with international communism is itself a threat to the hemisphere. Moreover, Mexico firmly opposed the convocation of the Ninth Meeting of Consultation of American Foreign Ministers on the grounds that the acts allegedly committed by Cuba against Venezuela did not constitute aggression, and refused to implement the sanctions which it imposed.

It is even more significant that Mexico has emerged as the principal supporter among the Latin American countries (other than Cuba) of United Nations primacy in the field of international peace and security. She has maintained that the world organization should deal with the problem of Cuba, and suggested that the question of the validity of the main resolution of the Ninth Meeting be referred to the International Court of Justice.[96] In taking this position, Mexico has demonstrated both her concern for maintaining a strict juridical interpretation of treaties[97] in instances where these have undoubtedly been strained, and a long-standing sympathy for Cuba. But, by taking an 'independent' position on this crucial issue, she has staked a claim to leadership in Latin America which cannot but provoke the jealousy—and perhaps before long emulation—of Brazil and

---

[96] See below, p. 186.

[97] Mexico's critics allege that she herself has violated her obligations under the Rio treaty by not carrying out the decisions of the Ninth Meeting of Consultation. See, for example, A. P. Whitaker, 'Cuba's Intervention in Venezuela: a Test of the OAS', *Orbis*, viii/3 (1964), p. 535.

Argentina, formerly associated with her in 'the six'. It is worth re-marking that Mexico has been able to pursue this policy because of her internal stability as compared with her major rivals for leadership among the Latin American countries. This has very important implications for the inter-American system.

The Problem of Cuba

It is perhaps almost appropriate that the future of the inter-American system should appear in the 1960s to depend so much upon relations between the United States and Cuba since these relations have played such an ominous (though insufficiently appreciated) role in its past. The possibility of annexing Cuba was an important factor in United States reaction to Canning's proposals in 1823 (and thus in the formulation of the Monroe Doctrine) and to the Congress of Panama in 1826. The fact that Cuba was not eventually annexed is cited as strong evidence of United States abstention from the imperialism characteristic of other great powers. It is doubtful, however, whether the self-image of the United States as liberator of Cuba is accepted by many other than her own citizens. For Cuban sovereignty was from the first severely limited by the perpetual treaty giving the United States the right of intervention in the island's internal affairs, and what amounted to a veto in its international relations. Cuba became effectively a satellite of her powerful neighbour.[98]

The United States intervened many times in Cuba between the signing of the treaty and the abrogation of the Platt Amendment[99] (which bestowed the right to do so) in 1934. By this last date Cuba had played an important role in the evolution of the Good Neighbour policy itself illustrating the real status of the island at the time. The United States was anxious to be rid of the Machado government in 1933, but wanted to avoid armed intervention to achieve this. Machado's removal was effected, but he was eventually replaced by a government which did not meet with United States approval. Consequently, by a policy of not recognizing this new government, the Roosevelt administration finally brought about its downfall. The significant result of United States action was to pave the way for the dictatorship of Fulgencio Batista. In this episode Latin Americans have seen both the power of the United States to intervene success-fully without resorting to actual armed invasion and her preference

[98] See below, pp. 47–48.   [99] Ibid.

for a dictator over a more democratic government of which she does not approve.

Such a view of United States relations with Cuba may not be wholly justified, but the fact remains that Cuba has never been truly free to determine her own destiny. Perhaps this was inevitable in view of her proximity and therefore strategic importance to such a great power. Certainly no power strong enough to prevent it would acquiesce in the establishment of a hostile government so close to its frontiers. The Monroe Doctrine proclaimed that the United States could not view the extension of an extra-continental system to any part of the western hemisphere as otherwise than endangering her peace and security. The alignment of Cuba with the Soviet Union clearly was the most serious challenge yet to the Monroe Doctrine.

The Future of the Inter-American System

The challenge to the inter-American system was a different one, which threatened its whole future by emphasizing its basic inner contradictions, revealing in so doing how erroneous has been the widely held idea that the Monroe Doctrine has been 'Pan-American-ized'. The Cuban crisis brought into relief the essential divergence of interests between the United States and Latin America in supporting the inter-American system. Of what value to the United States was the OAS if it could not be mobilized to meet the greatest challenge ever offered to her? On the other hand, in the absence of a direct threat of armed attack, were the Latin Americans to jeopardize the cherished principle of non-intervention which for them represented the most valuable attribute of the OAS? The United States was able to obtain OAS endorsement of her actions to secure the removal of Soviet missiles from Cuba; though, as we have noted, with reservations on the part of Bolivia, Brazil, and Mexico. But she has not succeeded in obtaining hemispheric endorsement for the position that the continued existence of a Cuban government aligned with the Soviet Union is not to be tolerated. Even the exclusion of Cuba from the OAS was not fully supported. This meant, as the Brazilian delegation at Punta del Este suggested, that the other members of the inter-American system would have to find a way of coexisting with the Castro government. This, the United States firmly refused to do: 'communism is not negotiable in this hemisphere'.

Yet events in recent years have made it increasingly clear that the inter-American system is fundamentally a form of coexistence. The post-war world revealed the natural partners of the United States to be the countries of Western Europe, not those of Latin America. At the same time Latin Americans were coming to realize that they shared certain common interests with the emerging countries of other continents. Therefore, while it has been possible for the United States to build a 'Good Neighbourhood' by accepting the principle of non-intervention in the affairs of the countries of Latin America, it proved vastly more difficult to create a partnership in the western hemisphere. Yet, although the post-war world accentuated the differences between the United States and Latin America, both parties demanded more of the inter-American system than before. The United States wanted to use it as an instrument for combating international communism; the Latin Americans in tackling their economic and social problems. Neither was satisfied with the outcome, though the United States had notably more cause for satisfaction than Latin America.

In the spring of 1965 the future of the inter-American system as an effective international organization was in doubt. The years since the end of the Second World War brought new forces in international relations and new alignments of powers, challenging institutions built up under quite different circumstances. As the oldest international association of its kind it is understandable that the inter-American system should experience the shock of such challenges; that its inherent problems and contradictions should be aggravated under the new conditions. But if an analysis reveals the inter-American system to be in many ways an artificial creation and its proclaimed foundations very largely mythical, it still represents a political reality in the western hemisphere. A system of relationships has been brought into existence; it will persist in some form. The question is how important it will be in hemisphere and wider international relations.

In the final chapter of this study an attempt is made to assess the achievements of the inter-American system; to see how far it has fulfilled its purposes and furthered the interests of its members. There is also an attempt to assess its future prospects in the light of recent developments within the hemisphere and outside it. Before such assessments are possible, however, it will be necessary to trace the history of the inter-American system through its various phases from the First International Conference of American States to the most recent developments in the Cuban problem. The first phase, in which a beginning was made but achievements were limited, is the subject of the following chapter.

2   The First Phase

The Hispanic-American Conferences

The history of the inter-American system begins with the First International Conference of American States (officially styled 'The International American Conference'), held in Washington from 2 October 1889 until 19 April 1890. For this was the first meeting of what is now called the Inter-American Conference. It resolved to establish the International Union of American Republics, modest forerunner of the present Organization of American States, and the Commercial Bureau of the American Republics, later to be renamed the Pan American Union. Over sixty years earlier, however, there had been held the first, and most important, of several Hispanic-American conferences which occupy a significant place in the story of internationalism in the western hemisphere. This was the famous Congress of Panama (22 June–15 July 1826), so closely linked with the name of Simón Bolívar. The others were the First Congress of Lima (11 December 1847–1 March 1848); the 'Continental Congress', held at Santiago de Chile (September 1856); and the Second Congress of Lima (14 November 1864–13 March 1865).

These Hispanic-American conferences had several important features. First, they represented efforts by the participating countries to unite in the face of external threats to their independence. These threats came first from Spain and her potential allies; this was the case in 1826 and 1847. Then, fear of United States expansionist tendencies, manifested by the Mexican War and the filibustering activities of William Walker in Central America, became an important factor in bringing about the Continental Congress.[1] Finally, threats from Europe again during the period of the American Civil War[2]

---

[1] See W. R. Manning, ed., *Diplomatic Correspondence of the United States: Inter-American Affairs, 1831–1860* (1932–9), x. 776, for the comments of the US Minister to Peru on the 'Continental Treaty'.

[2] In 1861 Spain regained possession of Santo Domingo and in the following year seized the Chincha Islands from Peru. Her rather pathetic attempt to recapture something of her former empire brought Spain subsequently into war with Chile, Ecuador, and Bolivia, as well as Peru. Much more serious was the intervention of England, France, and Spain in 1862 to force Mexico to pay her debts to their nationals, for this was only the prelude to Napoleon III's attempt to impose a monarchy upon that country.

stimulated the holding of the Second Congress of Lima. The background to what proved the last of these 'political' conferences[3] illustrates the dilemma facing the countries of Latin America at that
time: if the United States was strong enough to enforce the Monroe
Doctrine, her power could be a threat to their independence, while
if she was too weak to do so, they were likely to be threatened from
Europe.

A second important feature of these conferences was the limited
participation in them; they were attended by only a few Spanish
American countries, with some extra-continental representation at
the Congress of Panama.[4] The most notable absentee—and this, above
all, sets them apart from the International Conferences of American
States—was, of course, the United States. Now there was a fundamental difference between Bolívar's plans for international co-operation and the American system conceived by Monroe and some of his
prominent fellow-countrymen. First, the America of the Liberator's
great design was, undoubtedly, Spanish America. Then there was his
desire for the protection of Great Britain, even against the United
States—the very antithesis of the exclusion of extra-continental
intervention purposed by the Monroe Doctrine. But Bolívar's predilection for Britain and coolness towards the United States were not
the reason why the latter failed to take part in the Hispanic-American
conferences. For the government of Colombia invited the United
States to send representatives to the Panama Congress, and Mexico
and Central America also sent her invitations. Moreover, by the time
the first Hispanic-American conference had ended, Bolívar's influence
was waning; so, incidentally, was his interest in the great design.

The decisive factor was the policy of the United States, who had
no intention of entering into an alliance with the countries of Latin
America, and diplomatically rebuffed overtures to this end made
by five of them.[5] President John Quincy Adams, who nevertheless
proposed the sending of delegates to Panama, assured the House of
Representatives that the assembly would be merely consultative.[6]
However, Congressional opposition caused such delay that the
delegates appointed never arrived at Panama to take part in the

---

[3] A number of technical and juridical conferences were held between the Second
Lima Congress and the First International Conference of American States.
[4] Great Britain had an agent there and the Netherlands an unofficial—and
apparently uninvited—observer.
[5] Bemis, *John Quincy Adams and the Foundations of American Foreign Policy*
(1949), p. 404.
[6] Gantenbein, p. 40.

proceedings. But it is clear no great opportunity of launching an inter-American system was thereby lost. The instructions of Secretary of State Henry Clay to the delegates show United States determination not only to maintain her neutrality as between Spain and her former colonies, but to prevent any attempt by the latter to liberate Cuba.[7] Both were understandable objectives of United States foreign policy; they provided no basis for close co-operation with the Latin Americans.

The Hispanic-American conferences, as has already been noted, were concerned, above all, with the question of security against external aggression. Since the United States was adamant on maintaining complete freedom of action in this field no inter-American system could be established for that purpose. As the United States grew in power and was able to make good the promise contained in President Monroe's Message, she had still less reason to ally herself with the countries of Latin America. When, in the last two decades of the nineteenth century, she initiated the Pan American movement it was with quite different objectives in view. Nor, for a very long time indeed, did the inter-American system include an alliance for collective security.

Although the most notable, the United States was by no means the only absentee from the early conferences. Neither of the other two non-Spanish-speaking American countries attended any of them. Haiti was ignored, but Brazil was invited to the Congress of Panama, though (like the United States) not by Bolívar. Argentina, rival of Brazil and aspiring to leadership of the Spanish American nations, likewise took no part in any of these gatherings, thus beginning a long tradition of opposition to closer international ties within the hemisphere. Of the remaining Spanish American countries only some were represented at each of the conferences. The achievements of the Hispanic-American conferences would therefore have been limited in scope even had all the treaties and agreements adopted at them been ratified. In fact, none of them came into effect.

A third important feature of these conferences, then, was the enormous gap between what has been described as the 'extremely highly developed vision of the necessities of international organization'[8] possessed by some Latin Americans and their achievements. Inability to unite to meet threats from external aggression was

---

[7] International American Conference, *Reports of Committees and Discussions Thereon*, Vol. IV, *Historical Appendix: The Congress of 1826, at Panama, and Subsequent Movements toward a Conference of American Nations* (1890), pp. 113–50.
[8] J. P. Humphrey, *The Inter-American System: a Canadian View* (1942), p. 34.

complemented by failure to create machinery for solving disputes among themselves. This was an even harder task, of course, for, as external threats receded, nationalism proved a stronger force than internationalism. So, although the importance of establishing the principle of arbitration of inter-American disputes was fully realized, no arbitration agreement was put into effect and no inter-American conferences were called to solve the bitter boundary disputes, or to end conflicts such as the Paraguayan War (1864–70) and the War of the Pacific (1879–83).

The significance of the Hispanic-American Conferences in the development of the inter-American system lies in the fact that when the United States came to promote her quite differently motivated Pan American movement towards the end of the nineteenth century, she was able to build upon the idea of international co-operation associated with the earlier efforts. Moreover, the ideals of Simón Bolívar were proclaimed as the symbol of inter-American solidarity.

The First International Conference of American States (*Washington, 1889–90*)

The United States initiated the Pan American movement in the 1880s for three main reasons. First, the great increase in her economic production following the Civil War made her anxious to extend her foreign trade; Latin America was an obvious field for such an extension, especially since the United States had an unfavourable trade balance with her southern neighbours. Secondly, European economic and financial interests were firmly entrenched in Latin America, and, in the view of some influential North Americans, should be countered for political as well as economic reasons. Thirdly, but by no means least in importance, conflicts such as the Paraguayan War and the War of the Pacific showed the urgent need for establishing inter-American peace machinery, both to forestall possible European intervention and to bring about conditions of stability necessary for a considerable increase of United States trade in the region. The promotion of peace and prevention of war figured prominently in Blaine's first efforts to hold a Pan American conference.[9]

James G. Blaine is one of the most important figures in the history of the inter-American system. A great admirer of Henry Clay, he was

---

[9] In the judgement of R. H. Bastert, 'A New Approach to the Origins of Blaine's Pan American Policy', *HAHR*, xxxix/3 (1959), p. 380, the origins of Blaine's Pan American policy are to be found in the 'existence or the menace of these wars'.

Secretary of State in the short-lived Garfield administration and again under Benjamin Harrison. He described the foreign policy of the Garfield administration as having two objects: 'First, to bring about peace and prevent future wars in North and South America; second, to cultivate such friendly, commercial relations with all American countries as would lead to a large increase in the export trade of the United States. . . .'[10] The two objectives were closely linked. Blaine was concerned with the bigger question of curbing European influence and intervention in Latin America, particularly that of Britain. He denounced English capital, for example, as being behind Chile's war against Peru and declared before the House Committee on Foreign Affairs during its investigation of United States efforts to end that war:

> I think it will be demonstrated in the very near future that the United States will have to assume a much more decided tone in South America than the one which I took and which was rescinded, or else it will have to back out of it, and say that it is a domain that does not belong to us, and we surrender it to Europe.[11]

Such were the sentiments of the man who was to preside over the First International Conference of American States.

In November 1881 Blaine issued invitations to all the other American governments to take part a year later in a congress at Washington 'for the purpose of considering and discussing the methods of preventing war between the nations of America'. This was the only subject to be discussed. The War of the Pacific was then taking place, but Blaine hoped it would have ended by the time the congress met. But the congress did not meet. Garfield's assassination brought Blaine's political rival, Chester Arthur, to the presidency and, three months later, Frederick T. Frelinghuysen to the State Department. In the following August Frelinghuysen withdrew the invitations (which some nations had already accepted), ostensibly on the grounds that the War of the Pacific had not ended, but clearly as part of a general reversal of Blaine's Latin American policy.

Between 1881 and Blaine's return to office under Harrison in 1889, however, other influences were at work promoting the Pan American movement in the United States. In Congress, among others, was future President William McKinley; outside it publicists such as Hinton Rowan Helper and William Eleroy Curtis.[12] Helper was

---

[10] Quoted in Lockey, *Essays*, pp. 52–53.   [11] Ibid. p. 62.
[12] Whitaker, *Western Hemisphere Idea*, pp. 77–79.

responsible for getting the first bill proposing an inter-American conference introduced into Congress in 1880 and another bill he inspired
in 1882 resulted in a commercial commission being sent to tour Latin
America in 1884. Curtis, who was appointed secretary to this commission, later became the first Director of the Commercial Bureau of
the American Republics. In May 1888 an Act of Congress authorized
the United States President to arrange what was to be the First International Conference of American States. Although the invitations
were issued under the Democratic administration of Grover Cleveland
(who did not himself favour the Act), by the time the conference met
the Republicans were back in office and Blaine, as Secretary of State
once more, presided over it.

Invitations had been sent to all the Latin American states and also
to Hawaii, which Blaine, during his first tenure of office, had declared
to fall within the scope of the Monroe Doctrine. The original bill had
included Canada, but the Act of Congress did not do so. Hawaii failed
to accept the invitation in time to be represented at the conference;
the Dominican Republic declined to attend because the United States
had not ratified a treaty of arbitration and commercial reciprocity
signed in 1884. So all the Latin American countries except the Dominican Republic were represented at the First International Conference
of American States.

The agenda for the conference,[13] approved by the United States
Congress and included in the invitations, consisted mainly of commercial matters, though it was proposed to consider a plan for the
arbitration of all disputes between the American states. United States
concern to increase her trade with Latin America was shown also in
the composition of her delegation and the provision of a '6,000-mile,
"de luxe" railroad excursion, conducted by the United States
government for the benefit of the visiting delegates, and with the
apparent object of casting considerable light on the industrial might
of the United States on display in all the great cities east of the
Mississippi'.[14] This tour, which took place before the delegates got
down to serious business, was ostentatiously boycotted by the Argen-
tinian representatives whose opposition was in no small measure
responsible for the failure of the United States to attain her major

---

[13] The agenda for the first six International Conferences of American States
and the conventions and resolutions adopted at them are contained in *The International Conferences of American States, 1889–1928*, ed. J. B. Scott (1931).

[14] T. F. McGann, 'Argentina at the First Pan American Conference', *IAEA*,
i/2 (1947), p. 27.

commercial objectives. Indeed, the Washington conference took little effective action on any of the chief items on the agenda. In particular, the proposal for a customs union was rejected and no firm arbitration treaty was adopted. The only tangible result of significance was the establishment of institutions from which the inter-American system was to develop.

Yet the First International Conference of American States must be regarded as an event of considerable importance. It reveals at the outset the basic factors influencing inter-American relations and the difficulties limiting effective international organization in the hemisphere. The divergence of interests between the United States as a great power and the Latin American countries as small ones was well brought out in the debate on 'Claims and Diplomatic Intervention'. The Conference voted to recommend that:

1. Foreigners are entitled to enjoy all the civil rights enjoyed by natives, and they shall be accorded all the benefits of said rights in all that is essential as well as in the form or procedure, and the legal remedies incident thereto, absolutely in like manner as said natives.

2. A nation has not, nor recognizes in favor of foreigners, any other obligations or responsibilities than those which in favor of the natives are established in like cases by the constitution and the laws.[15]

This recommendation, substantially the Calvo Doctrine, ran contrary to international law, which required states to maintain a certain minimum standard of conduct in their treatment of foreigners irrespective of how they treated their own citizens.

It received the affirmative votes of all the Latin American countries except Haiti, who abstained on the grounds that, while agreeing with Part 2 of the recommendation, her constitution did not allow full property rights to foreigners.[16] The United States voted against it. Her delegate on the committee declared: 'I can not concur in any opinions which diminish the right or reduces [*sic*] the power of a nation by diplomatic reclamation, which is the manifestation of its moral strength and vitality, to protect the rights and interests of its citizens.'[17] William Henry Trescot took his stand on international law, denying, incidentally, the existence of an 'American international law'.

---

[15] International American Conference, *Reports of Committees*, ii. 938.
[16] *Rapport adressé au Gouvernement d'Haïti par Mr. Hannibal Price délégué à la Conference Internationale Américaine tenue à Washington, États-Unis du 2 octobre 1889 au 19 avril 1890* (1890), pp. 18–27.
[17] *Reports of Committees*, ii. 937h.

This division on the question of diplomatic intervention was essentially a conflict of interests between the great power, seeking to expand economically, and the small powers fearful that such expansion would lead to intervention when disputes arose between them and the great power's business concerns. Thus was posed at the very first international conference of American states the intervention question which has dominated the inter-American system ever since.

There was a similar conflict of views on a resolution to condemn 'the right of conquest'. The United States objected to this on the grounds that it would apply in cases where a country had acquired territory as indemnification for an aggression committed against it.[18] She obviously had some of her own acquisitions in mind.[19] One of her delegates, Mr Carnegie, was particularly concerned that the resolution might lead to a consideration of past cessions. This was another significant issue upon which the United States took one stand and all the Latin American countries—except in this case Chile—the other.[20] Chile abstained because of her own recent conquests at the expense of Bolivia and Peru. Eventually a compromise recommendation on the right of conquest was linked with the proposed arbitration treaty.

An ominous feature of the First International Conference of American States was the stand taken by Argentina. In opening the debate on the proposed customs union, her delegate, Dr Sáenz Peña, gave a powerful exposition of his country's policy not only on the subject under discussion, but on the inter-American system as a whole. He stressed the economic ties between Latin America and Europe, concluding with a personal plea against an exclusively American association: 'Let America be for mankind.'[21] Since United States policy was concerned fundamentally with limiting the extra-continental ties of the Latin American countries, Argentina, with the closest such ties, was bound to be unco-operative. But Argentina's stand represented a wider Latin American view: opposition to the United States adding economic domination to the political primacy she had already established in the western hemisphere.[22]

Another significant feature of this conference was its failure to conclude a firm treaty of pacific settlement of inter-American disputes.

[18] Ibid. pp. 1132–5.
[19] The US maintained that Mexico had been the aggressor in 1846.
[20] *Reports of Committees*, ii. 1131, 1139.
[21] Ibid. i. 131.
[22] Cf. the views of José Martí, the Cuban patriot, quoted in R. N. Burr and R. D. Hussey, *Documents on Inter-American Cooperation*, Vol. II, *1881–1948* (1955), pp. 37–41.

For while it approved a Plan of Arbitration, adopting the latter 'as a principle of American international law for the settlement of the differences, disputes or controversies that may arise between two or more of them', the treaty subsequently signed by eleven of the states never came into effect. Not one of the signatories ratified the treaty by the agreed date. Thus did the first Pan American conference follow the unhappy precedent of the earlier Hispanic-American ones. This failure to adopt an effective arbitration treaty was only the first of many. The American Treaty on Pacific Settlement, signed at the Ninth International Conference in 1948, has not been fully ratified (1965).

The Establishment of Institutions

The most important result, then, of the First International Conference of American States—and here it differed from the Hispanic-American conferences—was the establishment of institutions. It created an international association under the title of 'The International Union of American Republics' for the prompt collection and distribution of commercial information. This association was to be represented in Washington by an agency called 'The Commercial Bureau of the American Republics' under the supervision of the United States Secretary of State.[23] Both institutions were to continue in existence for ten years in the first instance, but would be renewed for further such periods unless a majority of the members of the Union decided otherwise. The Bureau was set up by November 1890, and, as we have seen, its first director was William E. Curtis, who had done a great deal to promote the Pan American movement in the United States. Curtis, incidentally, was unpopular with the Latin American delegates because of a book he had written on *The Capitals of Spanish America* after a very brief tour of them. Blaine had nominated him chief secretary of the First International Conference, and, when the Argentine delegation contrived to eliminate him by insisting there should be two secretaries speaking both English and Spanish (Curtis spoke no Spanish), made him 'executive officer'.[24] Curtis's appointment as Director of the Bureau reflects the United States domination which for a long time gave that institution the appearance of a colonial office and was the cause of rising Latin American dissatisfaction.

[23] The date upon which the resolution to establish the International Union of American Republics was unanimously passed, 14 Apr. 1890, is commemorated in Pan American Day.

[24] McGann, *IAEA*, i/2 (1947), p. 29.

However, all the then existing American republics except Chile and the Dominican Republic agreed to join the International Union; the latter adhered in 1892 and the former in 1899. Cuba and Panama were to join soon after acquiring independent status.[25] At first the Bureau was concerned mainly with publishing the *Bulletin of the Bureau of the American Republics*, whose first issue appeared in October 1893. But on 1 April 1896, at the invitation of Richard Olney, the United States Secretary of State, the diplomatic representatives of the countries belonging to the International Union of American Republics met 'for the purpose of consulting and taking such action as may be advisable respecting the future operations of the Commercial Bureau of the American Republics'. It was agreed that a committee of five should be appointed by the Secretary of State to consider the Bureau's future.[26] The report of this committee was adopted with some amendments at a second meeting of the 'Representatives of the Governments composing the International Union of American Republics' held at the Department of State, Washington, on 4 June 1896.[27] As a result, the scope of the Bureau's activities was enlarged to cover all matters concerned with the economic life and growth of the American republics instead of the mere collection and dissemination of commercial information. A permanent executive committee to supervise the administration of the Bureau was created, consisting of the United States Secretary of State as chairman and four other persons chosen by lot among the Latin American members. It would meet normally once a month.[28]

The Second Conference (Mexico City, 1901–2)

Two important international developments took place before another International Conference of American States was held. First, there were new and ominous manifestations of United States predominance in the western hemisphere, including the Spanish-American War which marked her emergence as a world power and Britain's retreat before her opposition in the Venezuelan crisis of 1895. United States success in supporting a Latin American country against an extra-continental power was due to the fact that, in Richard Olney's arrogant words, 'To-day the United States is practically sovereign on

---

[25] W. H. Kelchner, 'The Development of the Pan American Union', *B. PAU*, lxiv/4 (1930), p. 335.
[26] International Bureau of the American Republics, *Minutes of the Executive Committee*, i. 1–21.
[27] Ibid. pp. 159–68. [28] Ibid. pp. 115–23.

this continent, and its fiat is law upon the subjects to which it confines its interposition.'[29] This new assertion of the Monroe Doctrine could hardly be reassuring to the Latin Americans.[30] The second important development was the First Hague Peace Conference (18 May–29 July 1899), at which the Convention for the Pacific Settlement of International Disputes was adopted, creating the Hague Permanent Court of Arbitration. Two American republics, the United States and Mexico, were represented at this conference. Their participation is a reminder that the inter-American system has never been truly separated from other developments in the field of international organization and indeed has been linked specifically with attempts on a wider scale to codify international law.

The Second International Conference of American States met in Mexico City from 22 October 1901 until 31 January 1902; once again the initiative came from the United States. The conference programme had been prepared by the Executive Committee of the Bureau on instructions from a meeting of diplomatic representatives of members of the Union.[31] It included arbitration, commercial matters, and the reorganization of the Bureau. All the independent republics sent delegates, but Venezuela withdrew from the conference before it ended, and the Brazilian delegate, who died on 18 December, was not replaced.

The question of arbitration was again both prominent and controversial, and, as a compromise, three agreements were adopted. Sixteen of the delegations signed a protocol of adherence to the Hague Conventions, whose principles were to be recognized as a part of American international law; of these, the Convention for the Pacific Settlement of International Disputes provided a system of purely voluntary arbitration. Seventeen signed a treaty, linked with the Hague Conventions, agreeing to the arbitration of pecuniary claims. Nine signed, and six subsequently ratified, a treaty of compulsory arbitration which, however, like its unratified predecessor at Washington, was little more, in effect, than an undertaking to agree to arbitrate. The United States was not among the signatories of this last treaty. Nor did her delegation sign a convention on the rights of aliens, which sought,

---

[29] Gantenbein, p. 348.

[30] Concern over the implications of the Doctrine was expressed at a 'rather pathetic' Congress (it was attended only by representatives of Ecuador, Santo Domingo, and Mexico and one delegate representing three states of Central America) which met in Mexico City in 1896 (Perkins, p. 189).

[31] International Bureau of the American Republics, *Minutes of the Executive Committee*, ii. 182–4, 199–210.

like the similar document at the First Conference, to restrict the use of diplomatic pressure on behalf of aliens: that is, to prevent what the Latin Americans interpreted as intervention.

A significant decision of the Second International Conference was to reorganize the Bureau, now called the 'International Bureau of the American Republics'. Detailed provision was made for its management by a Governing Board consisting of the United States Secretary of State as Chairman and the diplomatic representatives of the other American governments accredited to Washington. Provision was made for holding the Third International Conference, which, according to another resolution at Mexico City, was to meet

within five years, in the place which the Secretary of State of the United States of America and the diplomatic representatives accredited by the American Republics in Washington, may designate for the purpose, and in accordance with what at the meeting of the said representatives may be resolved, regarding the programme and other necessary details, for all of which they are hereby expressly authorized by the present Resolution.

Another interesting outcome of the conference was the establishment of an International Sanitary Bureau in Washington (December 1902), the first of what are now called the Specialized Organizations.[32]

The Third Conference (Rio de Janeiro, 1906)

The interval between the Second and Third International Conferences provided striking new evidence of United States power and ambition. Although there was an attempt by Great Britain and Germany (later joined by Italy) to coerce Venezuela by armed force to pay her debts (1902), clearly the greater threat to Latin American independence now came from the United States. European influence in the western hemisphere was waning. Britain, in particular, was anxious to conciliate the United States, as could be seen in her hasty retreat from the Venezuelan imbroglio and in the Hay–Pauncefote treaties, under which she gave up her rights to share in controlling an Isthmian canal. The United States, on the other hand, took the Canal, established protectorates over Cuba and Panama, and proclaimed the Roosevelt Corollary to the Monroe Doctrine during those years. In view of the importance of relations between the United States and Cuba for the future of the inter-American system the terms under which the island became formally independent in 1902 should be

[32] See below, pp. 207-8.

recalled. The strategic and other requirements of the United States were set out by Secretary of State Elihu Root in what came to be known as the Platt Amendment. In addition to giving the United States the right to intervene in Cuba, under circumstances clearly to be determined by herself, it stated

That the government of Cuba shall never enter into any treaty or other compact with any foreign power or powers which will impair or tend to impair the independence of Cuba, nor in any manner authorize or permit any foreign power or powers to obtain by colonization or for military or naval purposes or otherwise, lodgment in or control over any portion of said island.[33]

As a result, the United States enjoyed the control of Cuba which the Platt Amendment denied to 'foreign' powers.

In 1904, the year after taking the Panama Canal route, Theodore Roosevelt proclaimed that:

Chronic wrongdoing, or an impotence which results in a general loosening of the ties of civilized society, may in America, as elsewhere, ultimately require intervention by some civilized nation, and in the Western Hemisphere the adherence of the United States to the Monroe Doctrine may force the United States, however reluctantly, in flagrant cases of such wrongdoing or impotence, to the exercise of an international police power.[34]

Some important implications of Roosevelt's attitude towards Latin America have already been discussed.[35] The divergence of interests— and therefore viewpoint—between the United States as a great power and the countries of Latin America as small powers is well illustrated by comparing the Roosevelt Corollary with the Drago Doctrine.[36] Following the Anglo-German blockade and bombardment of Venezuela, the Argentine Foreign Minister, Luis M. Drago, had proposed that the United States should subscribe to the principle that 'public debt gives no place for armed intervention, and less still to the material occupation of the soil of American nations by a European power'. Roosevelt's corollary likewise pronounced against European interven-

---

[33] Gantenbein, p. 488.   [34] Ibid. p. 362.   [35] See above, pp. 15–16.
[36] Whitaker, *Western Hemisphere Idea*, pp. 86 ff., calls it 'Drago's Economic Corollary to the Monroe Doctrine' and describes it (p. 88) as a new departure in Argentine foreign policy. He asserts that 'if the United States had accepted it, perhaps the whole future history of United States–Argentine relations and of inter-American relations in general might have been changed for the better'. But, of course, the US instead extended the scope of the unilateral Monroe Doctrine with the Roosevelt Corollary.

tion in the western hemisphere, but not against intervention as such. On the contrary, it claimed for the United States a monopoly of the right (and the assumption of a duty) of intervention in the Americas. It is not surprising that the Argentine newspaper *La Prensa* (8 December 1904) described the Roosevelt Corollary as 'the most serious and menacing declaration against South American integrity which has come out of Washington'.[37] In the following year the United States took over control of the Dominican Republic's customs, the first in a series of interventions in Central America and the Caribbean region which lasted until the Good Neighbour policy ended them.

Thus the background of relations between the United States and Latin America against which the Third International Conference took place was unpropitious. Secretary of State Elihu Root, as chairman of the Governing Board of the International Bureau, tried therefore to ensure that no controversial political issues would be included in the conference's agenda. In the event, the main items in the programme were: the reorganization of the Bureau on a more permanent basis; adherence to the principle of arbitration of inter-American disputes; the extension for a further five-year period of the treaty on the arbitration of pecuniary claims signed at the Second Conference; a resolution referring to the Second Peace Conference at The Hague the question of the forcible collection of public debts; and the creation of a committee of jurists to prepare, for consideration by the next conference, codes of public and private international law. In an attempt to avoid a repetition of the heated disagreements over this matter which had occurred at the opening sessions of the first two conferences, the Governing Board also agreed upon the regulations of the Third Conference. Further to avoid such disagreements, the deliberations of the conference were to be confined to the subjects contained in the programme 'except when by a vote of two-thirds of the delegations the conference decides to take into consideration a new matter submitted by one delegation and seconded by another'. Secretary Root instructed the United States representatives that the function of the conference was to deal with matters of common interest and not subjects of controversy. He told them to oppose changes to the rules drawn up by the Governing Board and any attempt to raise questions not contained in the programme.[38]

---

[37] Quoted in T. F. McGann, *Argentina, the United States, and the Inter-American System, 1880–1914* (1957), p. 223.

[38] *For. Rel. US*, *1906*, pt. 2, p. 1567.

Elihu Root was not himself a member of the United States delegation to the Third Conference, but he visited it and addressed it in
conciliatory terms.[39] However, his well-known statement that 'We
neither claim nor desire any rights or privileges or powers that we do
not freely concede to every American republic' could hardly offset the
Roosevelt Corollary and the interventions it sought to justify. Root
noted, with approval, that no political questions were to be discussed,
no controversies settled, and no judgement passed upon the conduct
of any state. By avoiding such issues there would be more harmony
than otherwise; but there would also be little achievement, and the
conference would fail to reflect the true state of inter-American
relations.

The Third International Conference of American States was held
at Rio de Janeiro from 23 July to 27 August 1906. It was attended by
delegations from all the republics (now including Panama as well as
Cuba) except Haiti and Venezuela. The question of pecuniary claims
and the forcible collection of debts was prominent. The United States
delegates reported that the extent to which force was admissible for
the collection of public debts overshadowed in interest all other topics
before the conference.[40] Eventually, it was decided (as the United
States wanted) to invite the Second Hague Conference to examine
the question of the compulsory collection of public debts.[41] A convention provided for the appointment of an International Commission
of Jurists, composed of one representative from each of the signatory
states, to draft codes of public and private international law. Unlike
a similar proposal at the Mexico City conference[42] which failed for
want of ratification, this convention was ratified and the commission
held its first meeting in Rio de Janeiro, in June–July 1912.

A resolution of the Third Conference continued the International
Union of American Republics and the Bureau for a further period of
ten years. The purposes, organization, and functions of the Bureau
were reformulated and new regulations laid down for its administra-

[39] Gantenbein, pp. 59–62.
[40] *Report of Delegates of the US* (1907), p. 12.
[41] In the view of J. P. Humphrey, p. 64: 'The reference of the problem of the
forcible collection of public debts to the Hague Peace Conference was a significant
recognition of the fact that there are certain questions that can be effectively dealt
with only by a universal body.' In addition, I believe the desire of the US to
refer this question to the Hague Conference illustrates her determination to uphold
her rights under 'general' international law rather than make an agreement with
the Latin American countries limiting those rights.
[42] The commission proposed at Mexico City, however, would have included two
European jurists as well as five Americans.

tion. The delegation of Ecuador tried unsuccessfully to have the chairmanship of the Governing Board made elective rather than always filled by the United States Secretary of State.[43] The conference did not act upon a recommendation by the Governing Board's Committee on Reorganization of the International Bureau of the American Republics that a convention be concluded as a basis of the Bureau. The Governing Board was authorized to designate the place at which the Fourth International Conference should convene, the meeting to be held within the following five years, and to provide for the drafting of the programme and regulations.

The Fourth Conference (*Buenos Aires, 1910*)

Two significant events occurred in the year following the Rio conference: the Second Peace Conference at The Hague and a conference of Central American states in Washington. At The Hague the Latin Americans sought in vain to have the Drago Doctrine accepted as international law. The United States, on the other hand, was successful in securing the adoption of her own proposal that the renunciation of force for the collection of public debts should be contingent upon the acceptance of arbitration. This was a blow for the Latin Americans, since it actually recognized the right to use armed force, and, although most of them signed the convention embodying the United States proposal, ten did so with reservations. Few ratified it.[44]

The Washington conference, meeting under the sponsorship of the United States and Mexico, adopted measures for the peaceful settlement of disputes between the Central American states far in advance of the agreements made (but not fully ratified) at the International Conferences. These included the establishment of a Permanent Court of Justice to which the signatories agreed to submit all disputes and controversies between them which they could not settle through diplomacy. This court did not last long, however, and the role of the United States in bringing about its demise is noteworthy. When the Bryan–Chamorro Treaty was ratified in 1916, giving the United States rights to construct a canal through Nicaraguan territory and the lease for a naval base on the Gulf of Fonseca, Costa Rica and El Salvador appealed to the court on the grounds that these concessions infringed their rights. The court upheld their appeals but

---

[43] Third International American Conference, *Minutes, Resolutions, Documents*, pp. 157–62.

[44] J. B. Scott, ed., *The Hague Conventions and Declarations of 1899 and 1907* (New York, 1918), pp. 89 ff.

Nicaragua, supported by the United States, ignored its decision and this virtually dissolved the court. Clearly, the United States was not prepared to accept arbitration in practice when she considered her important interests were at stake.[45] The five Central American republics also agreed in 1907 not to recognize new governments set up in any of them by revolution until they had been sanctified by free elections. This was the Tobar Doctrine which, although the United States did not sign the agreement, was the basis of her recognition policy towards Central America for over a quarter of a century.

The Fourth International Conference of American States met in Buenos Aires from 12 July until 30 August 1910. All the republics except Bolivia were represented. This conference was on the whole harmonious, but achieved very little. Of course, the careful preparation of the programme and exclusion of controversial matters were again largely responsible. For relations between the United States and her southern neighbours had not improved since the Third Conference. An attempt by the Brazilian delegation to introduce a motion praising the Monroe Doctrine had to be withdrawn because it aroused criticism of recent encroachments by the United States.[46]

At Buenos Aires Latin American concern was expressed over United States domination of the Governing Board of the Bureau. There were two particular complaints. First, since they were represented on the board by their accredited diplomats in Washington, any Latin American government not recognized by the United States was deprived of representation. This complaint was hardly rectified by a provision at the Fourth Conference that 'any Republic having no representative accredited before the Government of the United States of America may designate a member of the Governing Board to represent it in the "Union of American Republics", and in this case said representative will have a vote for each representation'. The second complaint concerned the chairmanship of the Governing Board. Some delegations felt—as the delegate of Ecuador had done at the previous conference—that the equality of members demanded that this position should be made elective. In the event, however, it was agreed that the American republics had conferred the chairmanship upon the United States Secretary of State.

At the Fourth Conference the 'International Union of American

---

[45] Nor did the US accept the decision of an arbitration commission on the Chamizal issue between herself and Mexico in 1911. See below, p. 184.

[46] A. Alvarez, *The Monroe Doctrine: its Importance in the International Life of the States of the New World* (1924), pp. 193–6.

Republics' was renamed 'Union of American Republics' and the International Bureau became the 'Pan American Union'. The latter now had its seat in the Building of the American Republics in Washington, erected largely through funds provided by Andrew Carnegie who had been a United States delegate to the First Conference. The existence of the Pan American Union was continued for another ten years by resolution; once again a recommendation to ensure its permanence and continued development through a convention was not acted upon. The Fifth Conference was provided for along the same lines as the two previous ones; but it was destined not to be held until 1923. Meanwhile, international relations in the western hemisphere were importantly affected by the First World War.

Inter-American Relations before the First World War

At the outbreak of the First World War the Pan American movement had not achieved a great deal. Four International Conferences had been held (as well as a much larger number of special and technical ones) and many resolutions and recommendations had been passed at them. But few of these agreements had been ratified and those, on the whole, the less important ones. Little progress had been made towards establishing effective machinery for the peaceful settlement of inter-American disputes, a major purpose of the Pan American movement. At the same time, it is of interest that efforts in this field were linked with the wider conferences at The Hague. When hostilities began in Europe there existed no inter-American machinery for dealing with possible external aggression. No such threat had arisen since the First International Conference, and the United States, powerful enough to sustain the unilateral Monroe Doctrine, had no reason to enter into defence commitments with the countries of Latin America. Nor by now did the Latin American countries want the United States to make such a commitment. For them, apprehension over United States intervention had already replaced any fear of extra-continental aggression. Their main objective was to restrain their powerful neighbour, who was in process of making the Caribbean her exclusive preserve and the countries in the region her satellites. Although this was what Bemis has called a 'Panama Policy', it was resented throughout Latin America.

The Latin American countries had not found the inter-American system much help in restraining the United States. They had failed at the outset to persuade her to accept the Calvo Doctrine, which would place her nationals in their territories on the same footing as natives. The United States claimed the right of diplomatic intervention on behalf of her citizens and of using armed force to collect public debts if arbitration was refused. Moreover, the International Conferences were not allowed to become vehicles for criticizing United States policies. This management of the conferences was helped by United States domination of what was now the Pan American Union. As we have seen, not only was the United States Secretary of State chairman of the Governing Board, but the other members were diplomatic representatives whose main function was to cultivate good relations with the host nation. The Latin American countries obviously occupied a subordinate position in an organization which so often proclaimed the absolute equality of its members. Thus, although the inter-American system had institutions, these were unsatisfactory to the Latin Americans, who were beginning to demand changes.

Clearly, the inter-American system was of much greater value to the United States. 'According to the Latin-American view', it has been said, 'the United States ministered Pan American good-will in order to allay the ill-will engendered by its practices of intervention.'[47] Certainly the United States was anxious to present her own national policy of excluding unwelcome European influence from the western hemisphere as being that of 'Pan America'. It was in her interests to propagate the 'Western Hemisphere Idea' and to portray relations between herself and the countries of Latin America as being fundamentally different from those between ambitious great powers and small ones in other regions of the world. But the façade of inter-American solidarity was beginning to crack in the face of the realities of international relations in the hemisphere. Pan Americanism seemed no more than a cloak for what many Latin Americans called 'Yankee Imperialism'.

Theodore Roosevelt, who had done so much to increase Latin American fear and suspicion of the United States, was followed by William Howard Taft and dollar diplomacy—and further interventions. Then came Woodrow Wilson, who denounced dollar diplomacy and the misuse of the Monroe Doctrine, but proved the greatest interventionist of all.[48] 'The years from 1913 to 1921', wrote a United

---

[47] Mecham, p. 72.
[48] For a critical Latin American view of Wilson as an interventionist, see R. A. Martínez, *De Bolívar a Dulles: el panamericanismo, doctrina y práctica imperialista* (1959), p. 126.

States historian, 'witnessed intervention by the State Department and the navy on a scale that had never before been contemplated, even by such alleged imperialists as Theodore Roosevelt and William Howard Taft.'[49] Wilson's 'missionary interventionism' and recognition policy introduced a further unfortunate element into the Latin American policy of the United States. It is difficult to take seriously Wilson's proposed Pan American Pact which 'envisaged the creation of a true regional security system in America . . . [and] was intended to multilateralize the hitherto jealously guarded Monroe Doctrine'.[50] For the idea of an American League of Nations, transforming the Doctrine into a defensive alliance among all the American countries, which was proposed by President Brum of Uruguay in April 1920, was opposed by the United States.[51] And the fate of the League of Nations Covenant in the United States Senate is also indicative of the prospects for Wilson's project had he pursued it.

At all events, when the United States entered the First World War her relations with Latin America had not been transformed for the better as President Wilson's early speeches had promised. There had been the occupation of Vera Cruz, the Pershing expedition against Pancho Villa, and the occupation of the Dominican Republic, Haiti, and Nicaragua by the United States marines. Inter-American solidarity was unimpressive in the First World War. Eight Latin American countries declared war on Germany, but only Brazil and Cuba played anything approaching an active part. Although five others severed diplomatic relations with Germany the neutrals remaining included such important countries as Argentina, Chile, and Mexico.

It is perhaps worth noting that there was held in Washington, from 24 to 29 May 1915, the First Pan American Financial Conference, attended by representatives of all the American republics except Mexico and Haiti.[52] Called by the government of the United States, its main purpose was to discuss economic and financial problems arising out of the state of war then existing in Europe. It established the International High Commission, later called the Inter-American High Commission, for the purpose of studying the establishment of a gold standard value, of bills of exchange, the uniform classification of

---

[49] A. S. Link, *Woodrow Wilson and the Progressive Era, 1910–1917* (1954), p. 93. The essential continuity of US policy in the Caribbean region during the presidencies of Roosevelt, Taft, and Wilson is well brought out in Munro, *Intervention and Dollar Diplomacy in the Caribbean, 1900–1921*.

[50] Whitaker, *Western Hemisphere Idea*, pp. 123–4.

[51] Brum's plan was encouraged by Wilson's suggestion. See Burr & Hussey, ii. 79.

[52] *Int. Conf. Am. States*, 1st Suppl., pp. 396, 472–4.

merchandise, customs regulations, consular certificates and invoices, port charges, uniform regulations for commercial travellers, legislation on trade-marks, patents and copyrights, a uniform low postage rate, and the arbitration of commercial disputes. This body, which existed until 1933, invites comparison with the Inter-American Financial and Economic Advisory Committee set up after the outbreak of the Second World War.[53] What is more important, its tasks remind us that, while concerned from the outset with commercial matters, the inter-American system had not yet begun to deal with the more fundamental economic problems.

From the First World War there emerged the League of Nations, whose existence had important implications for the inter-American system. The League's origins were linked in a significant manner with the Monroe Doctrine, and so were American attitudes, both north and south of the Rio Grande, towards it. For Latin Americans the Monroe Doctrine had long since become the symbol of United States intervention, and, while the concept of a League of Nations appealed to their idealism, the establishment of such an organization seemed also to offer the hope of some measure of protection against the United States which hitherto they had lacked. At the same time—and quite naturally—the very reasons which made the League attractive to Latin Americans aroused hostility among influential elements in the United States. The latter were opposed to both increased United States involvement in Europe and any limitation of the Monroe Doctrine as assuring United States hegemony in the western hemisphere.

In a vain attempt to make it acceptable to these elements, Article 21 was written into the League Covenant: 'Nothing in this Covenant shall be deemed to affect the validity of international engagements such as treaties of arbitration or regional understandings like the Monroe Doctrine, for securing the maintenance of peace.' This reference to the Doctrine is highly ambiguous, for the Monroe Doctrine was not a 'regional understanding', whatever that term might mean.[54] It is not surprising that the United States Senate proposed the following very specific reservation to Article 21:

The United States will not submit to arbitration or to inquiry by the assembly or by the Council of the League of Nations, provided for in said

---

[53] See below, p. 112.
[54] It is described as an 'inept phrase' in the instructions to the US delegates to the Fifth International Conference, repeated in *For. Rel. US, 1928*, i. 578.

treaty of peace, any questions which in the judgment of the United States depend upon or relate to its long established policy commonly known as the Monroe Doctrine; said doctrine is to be interpreted by the United States alone and is hereby declared to be wholly outside the jurisdiction of said League of Nations and entirely unaffected by any provision contained in the said treaty of peace with Germany.[55]

If Article 21 proved unsatisfactory to the United States Senate, it was profoundly disturbing to Latin America. Argentina and Mexico stated in adhering to the League of Nations Covenant that they did not recognize the Monroe Doctrine as a regional understanding.[56] El Salvador sent a note to the State Department on 14 December 1919, pointing out that Article 21 had 'awakened warm discussions throughout the whole American Continent, due no doubt to its brevity and lack of clearness', and requesting 'the authentic interpretation of the Monroe Doctrine as it is understood in the present historical moment and in its future application by the Government of the United States'. The reply was far from definitive.[57] Obviously, the League of Nations would not form an adequate counterpoise to United States domination in the western hemisphere.

Nevertheless, the existence of the new, wider international organization, and the fact that all the Latin American countries were at some time members while the United States was not, were important for the development of the inter-American system.[58] Questions such as the relative merits of the regional, as compared with the wider organization and the relationship between them were now raised. By their adherence to the League the Latin American countries were registering a protest against the United States conception of an exclusive inter-American system based upon the Monroe Doctrine. Moreover, membership of the League of Nations enhanced the stature of Latin American countries in international affairs and made them less ready to accept United States tutelage. Within the League the Latin Americans felt less inferior than in the United States-dominated inter-American conferences.[59]

[55] Quoted in P. M. Brown, 'The Monroe Doctrine and the League of Nations', *AJIL*, xiv/1–2 (1920), p. 209.
[56] Seventh International Conference of American States, *Minutes and Antecedents with General Index* (1933), Plen. Sess., Antecedents, p. 206.
[57] RIIA, *Survey, 1925* (1928), ii. 403–4.
[58] For an account of Latin American relations with the League during its early years, see W. H. Kelchner, *Latin American Relations with the League of Nations* (1930).
[59] S. P. Duggan, 'Latin America, the League, and the United States', *For. Aff.*, xii/2 (1934), p. 283.

Yet the position of Latin America relative to the United States was actually weakened as a consequence of the First World War. The League proved disappointing as an instrument for offsetting the political preponderance of the United States, while Latin America's economic dependence upon its northern neighbour was greatly increased. Hitherto, although United States economic penetration of Central America had been considerable, South America's trade was still largely with Great Britain and Germany. The First World War and the post-war depression in Europe enabled the United States to transform this situation so that she acquired economic as well as political ascendancy over Latin America. Thus whatever benefit the South American countries had derived from the division of influence over them between Europe and the United States was now lost.[60] Truly, 'at the end of World War I, the United States found itself in an unprecedented position in its relations with the twenty countries of Latin America'.[61] This obviously would exacerbate the essentially 'great power–small powers' relationship between the United States and Latin America.

The Fifth Conference (Santiago de Chile, 1923)

The Fifth International Conference of American States met at Santiago de Chile from 25 March to 3 May 1923, and was attended by delegations from all the republics except Bolivia (for the second successive time), Mexico, and Peru. Mexico refused to participate because, her government not being recognized by the United States, she had been deprived of representation on the Governing Board of the Pan American Union, which had approved the conference's programme. This programme, containing the largest number of items of any International American Conference up to that time, included the reduction and limitation of military and naval expenditures; the rights of aliens; measures tending towards a closer association of the republics of the American continent with a view to promoting common interests (that is, Uruguay's proposals for an American League of Nations); and questions arising out of an encroachment by a non-American power on the rights of an American nation (in other words, the Monroe Doctrine). Once again, the conference was to consider organizing the Pan American Union on the basis of a convention. In Lloyd Mecham's view: 'The inclusion of so many political subjects

---

[60] See RIIA, *Survey, 1927* (1929), pp. 402–3.
[61] Wood, *Good Neighbor Policy*, p. 3.

on a conference agenda indicated that the Latin Americans were un-willing to accept the Anglo-American concept of inter-American association.' He declares that: 'This agenda surely represented the most serious attack to date on the United States' conception of Pan Americanism.'[62] However, although she did not vigorously oppose these topics being included in the programme, the United States was determined to prevent any effective action being taken on them contrary to her interests.

The debate at Santiago on disarmament centred mainly upon the comparative naval strengths of Argentina and Brazil, but nothing substantial was decided. The question of the rights of aliens—still an important subject of disagreement between the United States and the Latin Americans—was referred to the Commission of Jurists at Rio de Janeiro; so was a proposal by Costa Rica for establishing a Permanent Court of American Justice. The items concerned with an American League of Nations and the Monroe Doctrine were disposed of by referring them (for study) to the Governing Board of the Pan American Union. However, a bitter attack on the Monroe Doctrine was made by Colombia,[63] and a number of other delegates took the opportunity to ask for it to be defined. They were rewarded only with a statement by the head of the United States delegation that his country regarded it as 'original and essentially national'.[64] The uni-lateral character of the Doctrine and United States determination not to 'Pan Americanize' it were strongly underlined later in the same year by Secretary of State Charles Evans Hughes when he said: 'as the policy embodied in the Monroe doctrine is distinctively the policy of the United States, the government of the United States reserves to itself its definition, interpretation, and application'.[65]

The Latin Americans had some limited success in modifying the organization of the Pan American Union. With its seat in Washington, its membership limited to their diplomatic representatives there, the Secretary of State its Chairman, and another United States citizen its Director General, the Pan American Union did indeed resemble a colonial office. The absence of Mexico from Santiago gave special point to Latin American dissatisfaction. Costa Rica ('representing a number of other Delegations') proposed that members of the Union

---

[62] Mecham, p. 95.
[63] Fifth International Conference of American States, *Actas de las sesiones de las Comisiones de la Conferencia*, pp. 185–95; *Report of Delegates of USA* (1924), p. 6.
[64] Ibid. *Actas de las sesiones*, p. 199.
[65] Gantenbein, p. 387.

should appoint any representatives they wished to the Governing Board, but the United States ('and various other Delegations') opposed such a change.[66] As a compromise it was agreed that, although the composition of the Governing Board would remain the same, an American republic, which for any reason had no diplomatic representative in Washington, might make a special appointment to it. For 'the Governments of the American Republics enjoy, as of right, representation at the International Conferences of American States and in the Pan American Union'. The chairmanship of the Governing Board, hitherto held *ex officio* by the Secretary of State, was henceforward to be elective. It was reported that fourteen states had threatened to resign from the Union unless the rule was changed.[67] This concession was more apparent than real, however, for the Secretary of State continued as Chairman, though now he was formally elected by the other members of the Board.

At the Fifth International Conference the Union of American Republics and the Pan American Union were continued by resolution on much the same lines as before; once again they were not put on the basis of a convention. But their scope was widened by the establishment of four permanent commissions to co-operate with the Pan American Union for the following purposes: the development of economic and commercial relations between the American republics; the study of all matters relating to the international organization of labour in America; the study of questions relating to hygiene in the countries of the continent; and the development of intellectual co-operation, with special reference to co-operation between universities. The Santiago Conference was the first to consider the rights of women, and it also recommended that social problems be included on the agenda of future conferences.

A noteworthy achievement of the Fifth International Conference was the Treaty to Avoid or Prevent Conflicts between the American States, usually known as the Gondra Treaty,[68] which marks a first, though limited, step towards setting up effective inter-American peace machinery. This treaty embodied the principle of a 'cooling-off

---

[66] Fifth International Conference of American States, *Verbatim Record of the Plenary Sessions* (1923), pp. 484–5; see also *Report of Delegates of USA*, p. 4. For discussion among members of the US delegation on the Costa Rican proposals, see US Nat. Archives, Records of the US Delegation to the Fifth International Conference, E 126, no. 12, Meeting of American Delegation, 10 Apr.

[67] S. G. Inman, *Building an Inter-American Neighborhood* (1937), p. 8.

[68] Named after Dr Manuel Gondra, head of the Paraguayan delegation, who proposed it after a deadlock had occurred in the committee discussing disarmament.

period'[69] since the signatories agreed not only to submit to a commission of inquiry all controversies which could not be settled through diplomatic channels or submitted to arbitration under existing treaties, but also not to mobilize or commit any hostile act until six months after the commission had made its report. Two permanent commissions were to be established, at Montevideo and Washington, to receive and transmit requests for convoking commissions of inquiry. However, since the disputants themselves were to appoint the latter, there could be an infinite delay in the proceedings.

Of more immediate consequence for the future of the inter-American system was a resolution to continue work on the codification of American international law and for a reorganized Commission of Jurists to meet for that purpose at Rio de Janeiro in 1925. The commission of jurists created by the Third Conference had accomplished little. An interesting debate took place at Santiago on whether or not there existed such a thing as 'American international law'.[70] The Chilean jurist Alejandro Alvarez claimed that the American nations had adopted both principles and practices which constituted a body of international law distinctive from that of Europe. The technical adviser to the Argentine delegation, on the other hand, not only denied the existence of American international law, but doubted whether it was desirable there should be such a thing.[71] However, the Commission of Jurists met in 1927, and from its deliberations emerged the document destined to arouse the strongest feeling against the United States at the Sixth International Conference the following year: a draft code on the rights and duties of states which included a clause declaring that 'no state has the right to intervene in the internal affairs of another'.

The Sixth Conference (*Havana, 1928*)

Between the Fifth and Sixth International Conferences of American States tension over the intervention issue was growing. Under the aegis of the Monroe Doctrine the United States was using her political hegemony to safeguard and further her growing economic interests in the western hemisphere, and her economic power to promote political ends. The political instability of the countries of Central America and

---

[69] Cf. Secretary of State Bryan's famous 'cooling-off' treaties which he concluded with ten of the Latin American countries (Bemis, *Latin American Policy of US*, p. 196).

[70] This question is considered further below, pp. 310–11.

[71] Extracts from both arguments are reproduced in Burr & Hussey, ii. 81–87.

F

the Caribbean region, together with their economic and strategic importance and geographical proximity to the United States, made them particularly vulnerable to what has euphemistically been called 'protective imperialism'.[72] In the absence of any external threat to the security of the hemisphere clearly it was the interests of the United States which were to be protected—against any unfavourable circumstances arising within the Latin American countries.

Latin American indignation was strongly aroused by United States intervention in Nicaragua in 1926 after her marines had been withdrawn from that country in the previous year. In Nicaragua the United States employed the policy of non-recognition[73] to force one president of whom she disapproved out of office before landing marines to support another whom she favoured. It is of interest that Secretary of State Kellogg alleged that Bolshevism was connected with the efforts of the rival candidate Sacasa to unseat the man favoured—and substantially assisted—by his government. This idea seems to have been stimulated by Sacasa's stay, as a refugee, in Mexico, with whom the United States had lately been involved in a long dispute over oil rights. Nicaragua was far from being a special case, however. On 25 April 1927 President Calvin Coolidge made the speech in which he declared: 'it is . . . well established that our Government has certain rights over and certain duties toward our own citizens and their property, wherever they may be located. The person and property of a citizen are a part of the general domain of the nation, even when abroad.'[74] The insistence of the United States on what she maintained was her right of intervention under international law—a right possessed equally by the European powers, but which she forbade them to exercise in the western hemisphere—and her only too frequent exercise of this right in the Caribbean region and Central America made the Latin Americans anxious to have 'non-intervention' accepted as a principle of 'American international law'. Hence the very close link between the codification of American international law and the intervention issue.

United States intervention in Nicaragua gave special point to the second session of the International Commission of Jurists held at Rio de Janeiro (18 April–20 May 1927). A draft code of international

[72] Bemis, *Latin American Policy of US*, pp. 224, &c.

[73] Shortly before the Fifth International Conference there had been held a second conference of Central American Republics in Washington which reaffirmed the non-recognition policy enunciated at the first. See above, pp. 51–52.

[74] Gantenbein, p. 117.

law prepared by the American Institute of International Law (an international organization composed of the national societies in each of the American republics) contained a provision prohibiting the occupation of any part of an American republic's territory by another state, even temporarily or with its consent. An attempt by the organizing committee of the Commission of Jurists to exclude the provision from discussion served only to provoke the political debate it had sought to avert. A clause was finally included in the draft code forbidding intervention by one state in the internal affairs of another.[75] The representatives of the United States accepted this clause apparently in the belief that intervention in internal affairs did not apply to measures taken for the protection of foreign lives and property.[76] Other proposals condemning intervention were dropped when the United States delegates made reservations. But the intervention issue was now before the Sixth Conference and in view of its fundamental character in relations between a great power (which alone could enjoy the 'right' of intervention) and small ones (whose independence was threatened by such intervention), nothing less than the future of the inter-American system as an effective international organization was at stake.

The United States had been disturbed by the criticism she had met at Santiago and since then. In his instructions to her delegates to the Sixth International Conference,[77] the Secretary of State warned them that:

The past year has seen the development of a vigorous anti-American propaganda throughout Latin America based on charges of "imperialism" and characterized by violent criticism of the relations existing between the United States and Mexico and the American policy in Nicaragua . . . it is not improbable that . . . certain delegates may attack the policy of the United States Government towards Latin America with special reference to its relations with Mexico, Nicaragua, Panama and Haiti.

He also advised them 'that an effort may be made to suggest the formation of an American League of Nations or a League of Latin American Nations, or the creation of an American Permanent International Court, projects upon which the United States would not look with sympathy'. The delegates were to counter any such moves

---

[75] International Commission of Jurists, *Sessions held at Rio de Janeiro, Brazil, April 18th to May 20th, 1927, Public International Law: Projects to be Submitted for the Consideration of the Sixth International Conference of American States* (1927), Project II, art. 3, p. 8.

[76] RIIA, *Survey, 1927*, pp. 425–6.   [77] *For. Rel. US, 1928*, i. 534–85.

as far as possible. On intervention they were told: 'This Government could not, of course, undertake to limit or bind its action in future unknown contingencies regarding the measure of protection which it might deem it incumbent upon it to exert on behalf of American citizens and property endangered by revolution or other civil turmoil in a foreign country.' Any suggestion to invite representatives of the League of Nations or unofficial observers from Spain or other European countries to attend the Sixth Conference should be opposed. Evidently, the United States government had reason to believe some Latin American countries were likely to raise these issues.

The instructions show also that the United States feared the Monroe Doctrine was likely to be raised again, even though 'in the view of this Government, that Doctrine has no place in the discussions of the Conference as it is essentially a national policy of the United States'. They reaffirmed the quite untenable position to which the United States had so stubbornly clung, that the Monroe Doctrine was not incompatible with the national sovereignty of the Latin American countries. But the United States delegates were advised in interpreting the Doctrine: 'It may be observed that the United States is uninfluenced even by the willingness or desire of any American State to yield any transfer of its territory or to submit to any form of political control or influence of a non-American State.' Another revealing passage reads:

Recent efforts, which there is no occasion to criticize so long as they are kept within their proper sphere, to bring Latin American States into closer contact with non-American Powers make it important that there should be no sacrifice through such endeavors of essential American interests. There should be no yielding to the suggestion of the control or influence of non-American Powers in the settlement of political questions of a distinctively American nature, or of the establishment by non-American Powers of territorial or political rights over American territory.

With all these thorny topics apparently in the offing, the United States delegates were reminded, as their predecessors at the Fifth Conference had been, that:

It should be borne in mind that the function of these Pan American Conferences is to deal so far as possible with non-controversial subjects of general interest, upon which free and full discussion may be had with the purpose and probability of arriving at agreement and cooperation . . . you will bear in mind that the present Conference has not been called to sit in judgment on the conduct of any nation, or to attempt to redress alleged wrongs.

The United States was well aware, then, of increasing Latin American resentment and expected serious opposition at the Sixth International Conference. Therefore the Coolidge administration took steps to strengthen its position. The President himself, accompanied by Secretary of State Kellogg, journeyed to Havana to give an inaugural address; the United States fielded an impressive delegation headed by the distinguished former Secretary of State Charles Evans Hughes; and she reverted to her traditional policy of opposing the inclusion of 'political' subjects on the agenda. In the event the United States was unable to prevent discussion of controversial aspects of her Latin American policy, but Hughes and his colleagues found the opposition less formidable than they had anticipated. In the words of one contemporary historian, 'When it came to the point, almost every Latin American delegation found good reasons for not joining battle.'[78] A basic weakness of the Latin American position was, of course, that the countries were divided among themselves and so did not present a united front. This point was made by Hughes two months after the Havana conference, when he declared there was not 'an entity known as Latin America on the one side, dealing with an entity known as the United States on the other. . . . There is, properly speaking, no concert of Latin American States'.[79]

While common fear of the United States was still not strong enough to cause the Latin American republics to co-operate effectively and continuously with one another, there were individual reasons for weakness at Havana. Most of the countries of Central America and the Caribbean region were either occupied by the United States marines (Haiti and Nicaragua) or enduring some form of client status which made firm opposition impossible. Cuba was negotiating for the repeal of the Platt Amendment and a reduction in the United States tariff on sugar. Chile and Peru were anxious not to offend the arbitrator of their dispute over Tacna and Arica. The fact that Argentina was the leading spokesman for Latin American freedom from United States domination must have deterred Brazil and Chile, resentful of Argentine pretensions to South American leadership, from supporting the cause with warmth.

The Sixth International Conference of American States was held

[78] RIIA, *Survey, 1927*, p. 429.
[79] Ibid. pp. 429–30.

at Havana from 16 January until 20 February 1928.[80] All twenty-one American republics were represented. The programme was divided into eight sections: the organization of the Pan American Union; matters of an inter-American juridical nature; problems of communications; intellectual co-operation; economic problems; social problems; reports on treaties, conventions, and resolutions adopted at previous conferences; and future conferences. Discussion on the reorganization of the Pan American Union and matters of an inter-American juridical nature brought out the greatest conflicts of interest between the United States and the Latin Americans.

The Havana Conference had before it a resolution adopted at Santiago for organizing the Pan American Union on the basis of a convention prepared by the Governing Board. Up to this point, as we have seen, the Pan American Union had been operating under a series of resolutions which could be modified at any time without the need of ratification by the member states. When the proposed convention was discussed at Havana three main controversial questions arose: economic (as distinct from commercial) problems; political matters; and the composition of the Pan American Union.

The preamble to the convention recognized the juridical equality and complete independence of the American republics and expressed their desire to promote 'the increasing conciliation of their economic interests'. Dr Pueyrredón, head of the Argentine delegation, had wanted to include a declaration against excessive barriers to inter-American trade. He was, in fact, attacking the tariff and sanitary police policies of the United States, which were particularly disadvantageous to Argentina. Hughes strongly opposed this proposal and Pueyrredón received only limited support from other Latin American delegations. Indeed his own government decided, for the sake of good relations with the United States, not to support his stand, and he resigned. But Argentina did not ratify the convention which, significantly, her delegation signed with an expression of regret that the economic principles it upheld in the discussion had not been included. This attempt by Latin Americans to have fundamental economic questions dealt with by the inter-American system, and United States opposition to it, foreshadowed what was later to be a major field of discord in which it would be more accurate to speak of 'an entity known as Latin America'.

---

[80] For an account of the conference, see J. B. Scott, 'The Sixth International Conference of American States, held at Habana, January 16–February 20, 1928: a Survey', *Int. Concil.* (June 1928), pp. 275–349.

The matter of political questions and the Pan American Union had been stimulated by earlier proposals for a closer political association along the lines of the League of Nations. United States opposition to the discussion of political matters and to an American League of Nations has already been demonstrated. Nor were the Latin Americans willing to give functions of a political character to a body dominated by the United States. In fact, Mexico proposed that the Pan American Union should be specifically forbidden to exercise political functions and this was embodied in a clause of the convention.

Mexico, with a particular interest in this question, also proposed a number of changes in the composition of the Pan American Union: the Governing Board should be composed of the representatives whom the governments might deem it convenient to appoint; the offices of Chairman and Vice-Chairman should rotate annually among the members of the Board; the office of Director General should also rotate annually among the various republics; this official should not accept from any government other offices or commissions than those of a purely educational nature; and the Governing Board should decide which posts on the staff of the Pan American Union should be held by Latin Americans.[81]

Hughes, who had of course presided over the Governing Board during his own term of office as Secretary of State, denied that this gave undue influence to the United States; but he accepted in principle the right of the members of the Governing Board to elect someone other than the United States Secretary of State to the chairmanship.[82] He opposed the idea of rotation for both the Chairman and the Director General, however, and it was abandoned. On the matter of the Governing Board it was decided that: 'The government of the Pan American Union shall be vested in a Governing Board composed of the representatives that the American governments may appoint. The appointment may devolve upon the diplomatic representatives of the respective countries at Washington.' The Director General would continue to be appointed by the Governing Board, and himself would appoint, with the Board's approval, the staff of the Pan American Union, 'endeavoring as far as possible to distribute the positions among the nationals of the countries members of the Union'.

---

[81] Humphrey, p. 207; see also *La participación de México en la Sexta Conferencia Internacional Americana: informe general de la delegación de México* (1928), pp. 20–22.

[82] Sixth International Conference of American States, *Minutes and Reports of Committees* (Havana, 1928), pt 1, 1C–2M, Minutes Jan. 23, 1928, Second Session, Comm. 1, pp. 5–6.

These changes in the organization of the Pan American Union were included in the convention adopted by the Sixth International Conference. They were also embodied in a much shorter resolution pending ratification of the convention. In the event, the latter was not ratified.

It was agreed that the Director General should in future attend the International Conferences as an adviser at the expense of the Union. He was attending the Sixth Conference as a member of the United States delegation, Hughes explained, because there was no appropriation available for him to represent the Union.[83] The records of the United States delegation to the Fifth Conference reveal, however, that the Director General (Leo S. Rowe) was actively engaged as one of its members. It is of interest that Dr Rowe expressed the view, in a discussion among the United States delegates of changes in the organization demanded by the Latin Americans, 'that without the Secretary of State as presiding officer, the organization would run great danger of falling to pieces'.[84]

The most crucial issue at Havana arose, as has already been noted, from the proposal of the Rio Commission of Jurists containing the non-intervention clause.[85] This was because United States interventions and insistence on her right to intervene—under circumstances to be determined by herself—were the major cause of her unpopularity with her southern neighbours and the chief obstacle preventing the development of effective inter-American co-operation. An attempt by the Peruvian rapporteur of the conference committee on public international law (whose country, significantly, was seeking United States support in its dispute with Chile over Tacna and Arica) to replace the Rio proposal with an earlier (1916) statement on the rights and duties of states formulated by the American Institute of International Law provoked a bitter discussion. This latter formula, which Hughes found acceptable, did not unequivocally condemn intervention and so was unsatisfactory to many of the Latin American delegations. In the absence of agreement, a sub-committee recommended

---

[83] *Minutes and Reports of Committees* (Havana, 1928), pt 1, 1C–2M, Minutes Jan. 23, 1928, Second Session, Comm. 1, p. 7.

[84] US Nat. Archives, Records of the US Delegation to the Fifth International Conference, E 126, no. 12, 11 Apr. 1923, Notes on first portion of meeting of the Delegation, 9 Apr. 1923.

[85] The minutes of the debate on intervention in Commission II (Public International Law and Frontier Police) of the Sixth Conference are contained in Sixth International Conference of American States, *Diario* (1928), pp. 485–505, 527–9, 532–40.

shelving the matter until the Seventh International Conference, but in the plenary session—just before the compromisers planned the adjournment—the delegation of El Salvador moved that the non-intervention clause be approved.

The debate which followed has been described as 'so productive of ill feeling and bad language that the minutes of the meeting had to be re-written'.[86] During it Hughes made his well-known defence of the United States position:

> Let us face the facts. The difficulty, if there is any, in any one of the American Republics, is not of any external aggression. It is an internal difficulty, if it exists at all. From time to time there arises a situation most deplorable and regrettable in which sovereignty is not at work, in which for a time in certain areas there is no government at all . . . . What are we to do when government breaks down and American citizens are in danger of their lives? Are we to stand by and see them killed because a government in circumstances which it cannot control and for which it may not be responsible can no longer afford reasonable protection? . . . . Now it is a principle of international law that in such a case a government is fully justified in taking action—I would call it interposition of a temporary character—for the purpose of protecting the lives and property of its nationals. I could say that that is not intervention. One can read in text books that that is not intervention. . . . Of course the United States cannot forego its right to protect its citizens. International law cannot be changed by the resolutions of this Conference. . . . The rights of nations remain, but nations have duties as well as rights.[87]

The United States case as Hughes presented it was virtually un-answerable, but it either ignored or glossed over the most important aspects of the intervention issue. First, it was not really a matter of rights under international law, but of power; for the United States alone could enjoy such rights. Secondly, it was not a simple matter of the breakdown of government; the United States had on occasion intervened either without such breakdown having taken place or with the purpose of overthrowing a government of which she did not approve. Thirdly, her 'interpositions' had not always been of a truly 'temporary character'.

Nevertheless, Hughes confounded further the outspoken opponents of intervention by calling upon the chairman of the Nicaraguan delega-tion, whose country was the outstanding example at this time of

---

[86] Inman, *Building an Inter-American Neighborhood*, p. 9.
[87] *Report of Delegation of USA* (1928), pp. 14–15.

United States intervention, to support him. This the Nicaraguan dutifully did. Moreover, the Cuban delegation warmly supported the United States. In words which were to be re-echoed with some irony more than thirty years later, Dr Ferrara of Cuba warned that the principle of non-intervention, which was supposed to guarantee freedom and the right of self-determination, might well become the very means by which tyranny would be perpetuated.[88] But there was irony enough at the time, for the Machado government then in power in Cuba was itself to be overthrown by United States pressure.[89] Although, with what proved to be two temporary exceptions (for both reversed their position at the next International Conference), the Latin Americans as a whole clearly were opposed to intervention in principle, only thirteen delegations stood out unreservedly for the Rio proposal. In any case the United States was determined not to accept it. With no agreement possible, therefore, it was decided to refer the matter to the Seventh Conference.

The Havana Conference considered a number of projects concerning arbitration and conciliation, and adopted a resolution accepting the former in principle and agreeing to hold a special conference on the subject within one year. The Sixth Conference also condemned acts of aggression, but neither defined aggression nor provided for sanctions against aggressors. Eight of eleven conventions adopted at Havana codified branches of international law: the status of aliens, treaties, diplomatic officers, consular agents, maritime neutrality, asylum, the duties and rights of states in the event of civil strife,[90] and private international law (the Bustamente Code). The much larger number of resolutions covered a vast field of inter-American economic, social, and cultural activity. One of them created the Pan American Institute of Geography and History; another the Inter-American Commission of Women. For the first time, the conventions and resolutions adopted by an International Conference were not signed as separate instruments but included in the Final Act.

There were notable omissions from the achievements of the Sixth International Conference. Nothing was actually done to strengthen the inter-American peace machinery, although it was resolved to hold a special conference for that purpose. Costa Rica's proposal for establishing a Permanent Court of American Justice was again not accepted;

---

[88] The Castro government made the same point with specific reference to the Trujillo dictatorship in the Dominican Republic. See Ronning, *Law & Politics*, pp. 65–66.

[89] See below, p. 81.

[90] See below, p. 223.

nor was a draft treaty on good offices, mediation, and conciliation, submitted by the Rio Commission of Jurists. This draft contained the important proposal that the Governing Board of the Pan American Union should act as a council of conciliation. Acceptance would have given that body conciliatory powers similar to those possessed by the Council of the League of Nations. However, it ran counter to the decision of the Sixth Conference that the Governing Board should not be assigned political functions.

The Conference on Conciliation and Arbitration (Washington, 1929)

The International Conference of American States on Conciliation and Arbitration (Washington, 10 December 1928–5 January 1929), listed as the first of the 'special conferences', may then be considered as an extension of the work undertaken at Havana. All the American republics except Argentina sent delegations. The conference adopted two major peace instruments: the General Convention of Inter-American Conciliation, and the General Treaty of Inter-American Arbitration with the Additional Protocol of Progressive Arbitration. The first of these added conciliatory functions to the commissions provided by the Gondra Treaty and empowered the permanent commissions to perform these functions, without first being requested to do so, until the *ad hoc* commissions had been established; but the latter still needed the co-operation of both disputants. All states present signed the convention, and eighteen subsequently ratified it.

The General Treaty of Inter-American Arbitration was the first such treaty since the Second International Conference, if renewals of the pecuniary-claims agreements are excepted. The signatories bound themselves to submit to arbitration all questions of a juridical character, which included the interpretation of a treaty; any question of international law; the existence of any fact which, if established, would constitute a breach of an international obligation; and the nature and extent of the reparation to be made for the breach of an international obligation. These, it is noteworthy, were matters declared to be suitable for arbitration in the Optional Clause of the Statute of the Permanent Court of International Justice. Controversies within the domestic jurisdiction of any of the parties and not controlled by international law, and those affecting third parties, were excluded from the treaty. A basic weakness was that, unlike the Conciliation Convention, the arbitration treaty made no provision for a permanent commission which could act on the initiative of one of the parties to a dispute. The co-operation of both disputants was required in setting up arbitration machinery. In other words, the treaty amounted only to a promise to agree to arbitration. We have already noted the failure of both the Fifth and Sixth International Conferences to act on Costa Rica's proposal for a Permanent Court of American Justice.

The United States, who opposed the establishment of such a court, ratified the General Treaty of Inter-American Arbitration with a reservation which robbed it of any obligatory character. Other American republics made exceptions and reservations which greatly weakened what was already a modest enough treaty. The Additional Protocol of Progressive Arbitration was intended to establish a procedure whereby parties to the treaty could formally abandon, wholly or in part, reservations made by them or exceptions from arbitration stipulated in the treaty. Such action would progressively extend the scope of this peace instrument.

Returning to the Havana Conference, this is generally considered to have been an immediate triumph for Hughes and the United States policy he succeeded in defending, but at the same time the low-water mark of the Pan American movement.[91] It is also regarded as a turning-point in the history of inter-American relations, when 'the authorities at Washington saw that the time had come when they would either have to change their ways radically or be left alone with their Hemisphere idea'.[92] How far this judgement of the significance of the Havana Conference is a valid one may be deduced from the following chapter. Certainly, the Sixth Conference has been taken as a convenient point at which to end one phase in the history of the Pan American movement. What at that point had the inter-American system achieved?

Conclusion

There had been a great deal of activity. Numerous Pan American conferences and congresses had been held on a wide range of topics including those concerned with commerce, intellectual co-operation, public health and sanitation, the protection of children, and the status of women.[93] There was already an imposing list of inter-American

[91] e.g. Dreier (*Int. Org.*, xvii/1 (1963), p. 41): 'it became clear that although Mr. Hughes had won the battle of Havana, the United States had lost the war of non-intervention'.
[92] Whitaker, *Western Hemisphere Idea*, p. 130.
[93] *Int. Conf. Am. States*, 1st Suppl., App. A.

organizations.[94] The inter-American system, through these conferences and organizations, was undoubtedly helping to develop more
intimate if not necessarily more harmonious relations in the western
hemisphere.

On more fundamental issues, however, the record was meagre. The
absence of inter-American machinery for mutual defence, noted by
some writers,[95] was hardly surprising since this had never been a
purpose of the system and no external threat had yet arisen to make
it one. But the settlement of inter-American disputes had been a
major objective from the beginning and the failure either to establish
adequate peace instruments or to resolve controversies such as those
over Tacna-Arica and the Chaco were serious. Moreover, though
replete with agreements about such things as trade-marks and copyrights, the inter-American system had not yet come to tackle the real
economic problems of the hemisphere.

The Latin Americans could feel only disappointment with the inter-
American system. Had the League of Nations been effective it would
have offered them more security than an exclusively American association which, for all the professions of equality and complete independence, was thoroughly dominated by their great neighbour. Unable
to offset the power of the United States through extra-hemispheric
links, the Latin American countries had been unsuccessful, too, in
restraining her within the system.

The United States was dominant as never before in the western
hemisphere. The European powers had accepted the Monroe Doctrine
and the League of Nations was chary of touching 'American' questions.
The United States enjoyed all the rights of a traditional great power
under international law and, in addition, those she had assumed in
the western hemisphere under the Monroe Doctrine. But the exercise
of all this power made nonsense of the self-flattering comparisons
with international relations in other regions which American statesmen were so fond of making at Pan American gatherings. The gap
between ideals and actuality had grown too wide by 1928 to be hidden
beneath platitudes about inter-American solidarity. Latin American
resentment was mounting. Only a change in United States policy
could make Pan Americanism meaningful for the other twenty members of the inter-American system. The question, then, was how

[94] Ibid. App. B; and R. D. Masters, *Handbook of International Organizations
in the Americas* (Washington, Carnegie Endowment for Internat. Peace, 1945).
[95] e.g. Mecham, pp. 110–11.

much, in terms of changing her attitude and modifying her objectives, the United States was prepared to pay to improve relations with her southern neighbours and to create an effective international association in the western hemisphere.

3 The Good Neighbour Policy and a New Look for the Inter-American System

WE saw in the previous chapter how, after the First World War, the United States enjoyed an unprecedented position of strength relative to her Latin American neighbours. No non-American power nor the newly formed League of Nations could challenge the Monroe Doctrine. Seemingly, therefore, the United States could afford to modify a Latin American policy the main proclaimed object of which had been to prevent extra-continental intervention in the western hemisphere. Certainly there was no longer any justification for employing the marines to forestall European interventions in the Caribbean region. Yet, apparently, it was some years before the United States began to contemplate changing her policy, and even then it was events within the hemisphere which forced a reappraisal upon her.

It is easy to understand United States complacency. The marines had not been used merely to forestall European intervention, and they had been sent in so frequently as to seem—to the United States —part of the natural order of things. As Bryce Wood has put it:

> It should not be surprising that a certain sense of the normality, and even the propriety of calling on the Marines, should have persisted beyond 1920, independently of the nature of the formal justification for such action; it was an habitual, nearly automatic response to "disturbed conditions" or "utter chaos" in a Caribbean country.[1]

Here again the self-image of the United States was involved. She did not recognize the incompatibility of what she considered her rights with the national sovereignty—and, indeed, self-respect—of her smaller neighbours, just as she refused to face the fact that even in its 'original' form the Monroe Doctrine relegated the Latin American countries to something less than truly independent status. The exercise of her hegemony was rationalized into the fulfilment of treaty obligations (for she had secured rights of intervention by treaty in certain cases), the duty to maintain order and promote good

[1] *Good Neighbor Policy*, p. 5.

government, and so on. All this was powerfully aided by the ambiguous term 'American' which made hemispheric questions appear United States domestic concerns with which she might properly deal as she saw fit. Convinced of her own good intentions—and she genuinely had no desire to acquire the territory of her neighbours—she felt no need to change her policy towards them until Latin American opposition forced her to do so.

For the Latin American countries, the absence of any extra-continental challenge to the Monroe Doctrine meant a weakening of their position *vis-à-vis* the United States. The only conceivable threat to their security now came from the latter, who gave little sign of exercising more restraint in the use of her enormous power. We have seen something of the growing Latin American resentment at United States interventions, and how the situation in Nicaragua brought matters to a head at the Havana Conference. Nicaragua was, in fact, a turning-point in the history of inter-American relations, for it brought about the first attempts by the United States to rethink the intervention issue.

Repercussions of United States Intervention in Nicaragua

The Nicaraguan affair had certain features which produced a deep crisis where other interventions had not done so. In the first place, there were the United States motives for intervening, mainly political and not merely for the protection of the lives and property of her nationals; then there was the fact that the involvement was not confined to Nicaragua, for it was intimately related to a quarrel with Mexico; thirdly, the difficulties experienced by the United States in carrying out her wider objectives made the period of intervention a prolonged one; and this in its turn brought mounting criticism in the United States and, significantly, concern to the State Department at its international repercussions outside the hemisphere.

When civil conflict broke out in Nicaragua in 1926 relations between the United States and Mexico were already strained because of the Mexican government's plans to expropriate foreign-owned land. These plans, and a campaign to restrict the activities of the Mexican clergy, aroused strong feeling in the United States, where they were denounced as 'Bolshevism'. Moreover, Mexican support for the Liberal faction in Nicaragua was interpreted as part of a plan to dominate Central America. Early in 1927 Secretary of State Kellogg actually presented a memorandum to the Senate Committee on

Foreign Relations entitled 'Bolshevist Aims and Policies in Mexico and Latin America'. For a short time war with Mexico seemed possible, but this possibility provoked such concern in the United States that the Coolidge administration was forced to take up a less threatening attitude. In the autumn Dwight Morrow was sent as ambassador to Mexico, an appointment which has been described as marking the real beginning of the Good Neighbour policy.[2]

However, the civil war continued in Nicaragua where United States prestige demanded that the Conservative government should not be overthrown by the Liberals. President Coolidge sent Henry L. Stimson as his special representative to Nicaragua for the purpose of obtaining a settlement satisfactory to the United States. This eventually involved not merely supervising elections and training a National Guard to keep order when the marines were eventually withdrawn, but also 'the dropping of bombs on bandits who were called Nicaraguan patriots elsewhere than in Washington'.[3] In attempting to carry out Woodrow Wilson's famous dictum of 'teaching the Latin Americans to elect good men', the State Department's own education was furthered more than the cause of democracy. In the end United States intervention paved the way for the dictatorship of Anastasio Somoza, commander of the National Guard.

The long and unsatisfactory involvement in Nicaragua provoked increasing criticism in the United States and questioning of the various motives which the State Department and Administration put forward to explain and justify it. Intervention became occupation; the supervision of elections proved vastly more difficult than anticipated; guerrilla operations against the alleged bandits were costly and frustrating; and the protection of the lives and property of United States citizens was jeopardized by the hostility aroused by the presence of the marines. Finally Stimson, who had become Secretary of State in the Hoover administration, announced that the marines would be withdrawn immediately after the presidential election in 1932. In the meantime, a new element had entered into the situation. At an early stage there had been criticism in Europe and Latin America of what was described as United States imperialism. By the autumn of 1931 Stimson, opposing Japanese intervention in Manchuria, clearly was embarrassed by the continued presence of United States marines in Nicaragua. As for landing forces in the larger Latin American countries, Stimson declared: If we landed a single soldier

[2] Matthews, p. 152.   [3] Wood, *Good Neighbor Policy*, p. 26.

G

among those South Americans now . . . it would put me in absolutely wrong in China, where Japan has done all of this monstrous work under the guise of protecting her nationals with a landing force.'[4] Later on, when the United States became more involved in world affairs generally, her relations with Latin America were to be affected increasingly by broader considerations of foreign policy.

The Hoover Administration

More was done to improve inter-American relations during the administration of Coolidge's successor, Herbert Hoover,[5] who came to the presidency with some experience of Latin American affairs as a former Secretary of Commerce and chairman of the Inter-American High Commission.[6] Moreover, Hoover had already demonstrated his concern to improve inter-American relations by embarking on a goodwill tour as president-elect which took him to ten of the Latin American countries at the end of 1928. During his tour he stressed the good neighbour concept and repudiated that of 'big brother'. In office, Hoover took a number of steps to make good his promise.

During Hoover's presidency, the State Department was less ready than hitherto to champion the cause of private citizens with grievances against Latin American governments and limited its action to protect them in case of revolution. Woodrow Wilson's recognition policy was abandoned as far as it had been applied to Latin America as a whole, though Central America was still treated as a special case. In 1930 there was published the Clark Memorandum on the Monroe Doctrine, which had been drawn up near the end of the Coolidge administration by Under-Secretary of State J. Reuben Clark. This document was, in effect, a repudiation of the Roosevelt Corollary, of which it declared 'it is not believed that this corollary is justified by the terms of the Monroe Doctrine, however much it may be justified by the application of the doctrine of self-preservation'. Thus the Clark Memorandum denounced only intervention under the cloak of the Monroe Doctrine, not intervention as such. Furthermore, it did nothing to change the character of the Doctrine, which remained a unilateral policy of the United States.

Under Hoover's administration United States policy in the Caribbean region underwent a noticeable change. The marines were with-

---

[4] Wood, *Good Neighbor Policy*, p. 45.
[5] See A. DeConde, *Herbert Hoover's Latin-American Policy* (1951).
[6] See above, pp. 55–56.

drawn from Nicaragua in 1932 and plans were made in the same year to evacuate Haiti. In the previous year the United States had acted with restraint when the Dominican Republic defaulted on a loan in breach of treaty obligations. In 1932 also the Hoover administration declined to help United States bankers when the government of El Salvador defaulted on a loan. Its abstention from intervening in the Panamanian revolt of January 1931 was perhaps more significant, since the United States had the right to intervene under the 1903 treaty.[7] These instances of United States restraint in the sensitive Central American and Caribbean area illustrate Herbert Hoover's contribution to the development of a new Latin American policy.

Unfortunately, however, Hoover's administration provided the Latin Americans with a new grievance in the Smoot-Hawley Act which raised the United States tariff to the highest level in its history. The political effect of this tariff far exceeded its impact on trade relations between the United States and Latin America as a whole, although certain countries were particularly affected by it. More significantly, the failure of the United States to do anything positive to alleviate Latin American economic distress caused by the world economic depression offset to no small extent Hoover's efforts to improve inter-American relations. At all events, the changes which took place in United States Latin American policy during the Hoover administration did not arouse much sympathy south of the Rio Grande. Only bolder, more imaginative action would persuade Latin Americans there was a real change of attitude towards them in Washington.

The Launching of the Good Neighbour Policy

Franklin D. Roosevelt eventually succeeded in convincing the Latin Americans that such a change had taken place. Ironically, his main experience of Latin America before becoming President was an active part in two of Wilson's interventions.[8] However, during the 1928 election campaign, when he ran for Governor of New York State, Franklin Roosevelt wrote an article for *Foreign Affairs*[9] in which he criticized United States interventions in the Caribbean

---

[7] It also refrained from intervening in Cuba, with unhappy consequences for the Roosevelt administration. See below, p. 81.

[8] See above, p. 19.

[9] 'Our Foreign Policy: a Democratic View', *For. Aff.*, vi/4 (1928), pp. 573–86. In this article (p. 581), Roosevelt also advocated US co-operation with the League of Nations.

region and demanded the renunciation 'for all time' of 'arbitrary intervention in the home affairs of our neighbors'. A passage in the article is worth quoting at this stage for the suggestion it makes of 'collective intervention':

> It is possible that in the days to come one of our sister nations may fall upon evil days; disorder and bad government may require that a helping hand be given her citizens as a matter of temporary necessity to bring back order and stability. In that event it is not the right or the duty of the United States to intervene alone. It is rather the duty of the United States to associate with itself other American Republics, to give intelligent joint study to the problem, and, if the conditions warrant, to offer the helping hand or hands in the name of the Americas. Single-handed intervention by us in the internal affairs of other nations must end; with the cooperation of others we shall have more order in this hemisphere and less dislike.

During the 1932 presidential election campaign Roosevelt denounced the Hoover administration's tariff policy, and his subsequent appointment of Cordell Hull, a leading supporter of lower tariffs, as Secretary of State, seemed to lend substance to Latin America's hopes that it, too, might have a 'new deal'. In his inaugural address on 4 March 1933 the new president pledged the United States to pursue the policy of a good neighbour in her international relations. Roosevelt specifically applied the good neighbour concept to Latin America in a speech made during the celebration of Pan American Day on the following 12 April.

> The essential qualities of a true Pan Americanism [he said] must be the same as those which constitute a good neighbor, namely, mutual understanding and, through such understanding, a sympathetic appreciation of the other's point of view. It is only in this manner that we can hope to build up a system of which confidence, friendship, and good will are the cornerstones.[10]

Clearly much had to be done to convince Latin Americans that this was the beginning of a new relationship between them and the United States. The marines were still in Haiti, although arrangements had been made for their evacuation in 1934; Haiti, the Dominican Republic, and Nicaragua were still financial protectorates; the independence of Panama and Cuba was restricted by treaties in favour of the United States; the latter's recognition policy denied the Central American republics the right of revolution (though the

---

[10] Gantenbein, p. 160.

United States did not always enforce this policy); the United States continued to insist upon the unilateral character of the Monroe Doctrine; and she still claimed the right of intervention even though she was limiting her exercise of this right. To these long-standing Latin American grievances had been added a high tariff policy in the face of the world economic depression. How far was the Good Neighbour prepared to go in meeting these grievances and thus transform the traditional Latin American policy of the United States?

Cuba: From Machado to Batista

The Roosevelt administration was soon given an opportunity to discover some of the implications of its promised new deal for Latin America. What Bryce Wood has called 'The Cuban Experience',[11] played a most important part in the evolution of the Good Neighbour policy[12] as well as in the unhappy history of relations between Cuba and the United States. Interestingly, the Cuban situation confronted the Roosevelt administration precisely because Stimson had refused to intervene after President Machado amended the Cuban constitution in order to prolong the life of his dictatorship. The United States government was anxious lest Machado's oppressive measures should provoke a revolution making intervention necessary; the answer to the problem was to force him to change his ways or bring about his removal. Thus the Good Neighbour embarked upon a course of interfering in Cuban domestic politics in order to avoid what it interpreted as 'intervention', and Sumner Welles was sent as ambassador to Havana in May 1933.

Officially, Welles was to mediate between Machado and his opponents; the United States government denied there was any coercion. But the knowledge that the United States could land troops or withdraw recognition from the Cuban government sufficed to bring about the desired result. In August Machado gave way and left Cuba. Welles's triumph lasted for less than a month, however, for the Céspedes government he had sponsored was overthrown after an army mutiny led by Sergeant Fulgencio Batista, and replaced by that of Dr Ramón Grau San Martín. This development was a severe blow to Welles's prestige, and he was determined to bring about Grau's downfall. The man who has been considered (not unjustly) the great

---

[11] *Good Neighbor Policy*, chs ii & iii.
[12] See also E. D. Cronon, 'Interpreting the New Good Neighbor Policy: the Cuban Crisis of 1933', *HAHR*, xxxix/4 (1959), pp. 538–67.

exponent of the Good Neighbour policy now strove to persuade Roosevelt to land United States troops in Cuba. Welles wanted these troops, not to protect the lives and property of his fellow-countrymen, but to sustain a counter-revolution. He called this 'limited intervention' to avoid the necessity of 'full intervention'. He declared:

> The disadvantages of this policy as I see them lie solely in the fact that we will incur the violent animosity of the extreme radical and communist groups in Cuba who will be vociferous in stating that we have supported the Céspedes Government because that Government was prepared to give protection to American interests in Cuba and that our policy is solely due to mercenary motives.[13]

But Roosevelt and Hull believed the disadvantages of acting upon Welles's recommendation would be nothing less than the destruction of the Good Neighbour policy they were beginning to implement. Nevertheless, in view of the unsettled conditions in Cuba some thirty United States warships of various kinds were sent to the island and its vicinity. The administration refused to land troops, however, in spite of further efforts by Welles to have it do so.[14]

Although he failed to persuade his government to intervene with armed forces, Welles was successful in ensuring that it did not accord recognition to Grau. He and Adolf A. Berle, Jr, then serving under him in Havana, emphasized the instability of the Cuban government and its lack of popular support; also that its continuance was prejudicial to United States commercial interests. In the meantime Welles maintained what he himself described as an 'anomalous' relationship with Batista,[15] 'that extraordinarily brilliant and able figure' as he later described him,[16] and encouraged him to bring to power a new government to replace Grau. Eventually, though after Welles had left Havana to resume the post of Assistant Secretary of State, Grau resigned. Welles, whose personal prestige had been such an important factor in the whole episode, finally triumphed.

But vastly more important matters than Welles's prestige were at stake in the Cuban experience. The United States had practised non-intervention in only the very narrowest sense of not actually landing troops. There had been a considerable show—and therefore threat—

---

[13] *For. Rel. US, 1933*, v. 398.
[14] In his book, *The Time for Decision* (1944), p. 196, Welles refers to 'innumerable demands for American armed intervention, especially from certain people representing commercial interests', but makes no mention of his own!
[15] *For. Rel. US, 1933*, v. 472.   [16] *Time for Decision*, p. 197.

of force; there had been intermeddling in the domestic affairs of Cuba to an extent that had made a mockery of that country's national sovereignty; non-recognition had been employed as an effective weapon to bring down a government of which the United States (in the person of Sumner Welles) did not approve. If the Roosevelt administration thought this interpretation of non-intervention would be acceptable to the Latin Americans it was soon disillusioned. Before the Cuban experience was over, the Seventh International Conference of American States had begun at Montevideo.

The Seventh Conference (Montevideo, 1933)

The Grau government was planning to send a delegation to Montevideo and there were other embarrassments awaiting the United States there. From Mexico, where sympathy for the Cuban government was strong, Josephus Daniels sent Washington a translation of a memorandum by the Foreign Minister proposing that the Monroe Doctrine be modified so as to prohibit American as well as European intervention in the affairs of the members of the inter-American system.[17] Daniels, who had been encouraging Roosevelt and Hull to refuse Welles's requests to intervene in Cuba, shared the Mexican government's sympathy with Grau and its view that the Monroe Doctrine should be 'Pan Americanized'. He warned Hull against exaggerated reports of communism in Cuba and argued in favour of converting the Doctrine into a general hemispheric policy.[18] But the Secretary of State accepted Welles's advice against recognizing the 'radical' Grau government and was opposed to any discussion of the Monroe Doctrine at the Seventh Conference. Like his predecessors, he hoped it would not be raised.

Outstanding from the Sixth Conference was the draft project on the Rights and Duties of States which had been submitted through the Pan American Union by the American Institute of International Law. The instructions to the United States delegates to the Seventh International Conference reveal the State Department's objections to this draft. One of the articles, for example, 'without some qualification, would strike directly at the Platt Amendment and our Conventions with Haiti and Santo Domingo. It would also prevent the landing of troops in any country for the protection of American nationals during the frequent revolutions in Latin American

---

[17] *For. Rel. US, 1933*, iv. 20–27.
[18] Cronon, *Josephus Daniels in Mexico*, pp. 70–73.

countries.'[19] It is clear from these instructions that when they were drafted the United States government had no intention of adhering to the proposed Convention on the Rights and Duties of States unless it was greatly modified.

The outlook for the Seventh Conference was discouraging. It had already been postponed once, and there had been suggestions of a further postponement from the ABC powers[20] and Colombia. The World Economic Conference in London had been a failure, and President Roosevelt publicly poured cold water on Latin American hopes of economic concessions by stating that: 'Unsettled conditions, such as European commercial-quota restrictions, have made it seem desirable for the United States to forgo immediate discussions of such matters as currency stabilization, uniform import prohibitions, permanent customs duties, and the like.'[21]

Apart from United States involvement in Cuba, there were two serious disputes between Latin American countries: the Leticia issue between Colombia and Peru, and the Chaco War between Bolivia and Paraguay. These two disputes revealed only too clearly the inadequacy of the inter-American peace machinery, and, as a consequence, involved the League of Nations in 'American questions'. In neither case had both parties ratified the appropriate inter-American agreements, while all four had subscribed to the League of Nations Covenant. So after *ad hoc* attempts at mediation by fellow members of the inter-American system had failed, the League of Nations assumed jurisdiction over the disputes. The United States, not without some misgiving about setting precedents prejudicial to the Monroe Doctrine, acquiesced in this; the problems were intractable, and neither concerned the Caribbean region, where she was particularly sensitive to extra-continental 'interference'. Incidentally, the relationship of the inter-American system to other international organizations was raised at the Montevideo Conference.

On the agenda at Montevideo[22] was a proposed addition to the inter-American peace machinery. To the annoyance of the United States, Argentina, with, as we have noted, the poorest record of co-operation within the inter-American system, had initiated an Anti-War Treaty of Non-Aggression and Conciliation.[23] It was signed at

---

[19] *For. Rel. US, 1933*, iv. 67.   [20] Argentina, Brazil, and Chile.   [21] Hull, i. 319.
[22] The agenda, and the conventions, recommendations, resolutions, and motions adopted by the Seventh and Eighth International Conferences of American States and the Inter-American Conference for the Maintenance of Peace are contained in *Int. Conf. Am. States*, 1st Suppl.   [23] Translation of text, ibid, pp. 496–9.

Rio de Janeiro on 10 October 1933 on behalf of herself, Brazil, Chile, Mexico, Paraguay, and Uruguay. The treaty, comprising seventeen articles, condemned wars of aggression and the settlement of territorial questions by resort to violence; declared that any differences arising between the signatories would be submitted to peaceful settlement; and made provision for the establishment of conciliation commissions to deal with disputes. The parties bound themselves not to recognize territorial changes effected by other than pacific means, and undertook to exercise against any states resorting to force the political, juridical, or economic measures authorized by international law. But diplomatic or armed intervention would take place only in accordance with treaties of which they were signatories. The Anti-War Treaty was open to all states,[24] and the Latin Americans naturally wanted to secure adherence by the United States.

The Seventh International Conference of American States met at Montevideo from 3 to 26 December 1933.[25] All the American republics except Costa Rica were represented, ten, including the United States, by delegations led by their foreign ministers.[26] It is of interest that the delegations of Cuba and El Salvador represented governments not recognized by the United States. The conference programme included the organization of peace; problems of international law; political and civil rights of women; economic and financial problems; social problems; intellectual co-operation; transportation; and results of previous conferences and plans for future ones. A special topic was included by the Committee on Initiatives: the establishment of an International American Bank.[27] The outstanding issues at Montevideo were intervention, tariffs, and the Chaco War; of special significance for the future was the relationship between the inter-American system and other international organizations.

This last question was raised before the conference got down to its agenda, when the desirability of admitting representatives of non-American states or organizations was considered. There was support

[24] Not merely American ones. In fact, eleven non-American states signed and six ratified the Anti-War Treaty. *Inter-American Peace Treaties and Conventions* OEA/Ser. X/2 (English) (PAU, 1961), p. 33.

[25] For an account of the conference, see C. Dávila, 'The Montevideo Conference: Antecedents and Accomplishments', *Int. Concil.* (May 1934), pp. 121–58.

[26] This was the first time a US Secretary of State had led his country's delegation since the First International Conference.

[27] The Seventh Conference recommended the creation of an Inter-American Bank (Resolution XXXVIII), but no action was taken until 1940. See below, p. 112, n. 7.

for inviting Spain and Portugal to send observers, and it was also suggested that representatives from the League of Nations might be present. Although Hull successfully opposed admitting non-American representatives to the Seventh Conference, the League Commission then endeavouring to end the Chaco dispute was invited to attend the closing session. It was warmly applauded by the delegates and its work in connection with the Chaco war was acknowledged in resolutions included in the Final Act. In one of these, introduced by Cordell Hull, Bolivia and Paraguay were reminded of their obligations under the League of Nations Covenant to submit their dispute to peaceful settlement.[28] The Seventh Conference resolved to entrust to its successor not only 'the determination of the principles that must guide the admission of observers of organizations or of non-American States to the International Conferences of American States, as well as of their character and prerogatives', but also the study of 'the activities and methods of cooperation with other parts of the world by the Pan American Organization'.

The tariff question proved more complex than a straightforward grievance of Latin America against the United States when it was discussed at Montevideo. United States duties (and sanitary regulations) affected only a few states, mainly Argentina, Uruguay, Cuba, and Mexico; the United States had grievances against Latin American governments because of the operation of their tariff policies against her; and there were serious tariff disputes among Latin American countries themselves. Of particular importance was the very large part played by customs duties in the revenues of certain Latin American countries. So when Hull proposed a reduction of tariff barriers through bilateral and multilateral treaties, this proved a much less attractive proposition than the Latin Americans had anticipated.

The most important speech on economic matters came from the head of the Mexican delegation, Dr J. M. Puig Casauranc, who warned the Conference that the basic issues for the hemisphere now were not political, but economic and social. The future of the inter-American system, he declared, would depend upon whether it tackled problems of social justice and brought purchasing power to the masses of people in the hemisphere.[29] In the course of his speech Puig proposed a moratorium on debts and the reduction of interest

[28] Hull (i. 336–7) describes President Roosevelt and himself as being anxious to bolster the authority of the League of Nations.

[29] See F. B. Pike, 'Can We Slow Our Loss of Latin America?', *IAEA*, xv/1 (1961), p. 3.

rates. According to Hull the Mexican Foreign Minister 'was applauded wildly as he dramatized the distressed debtors oppressed by conscienceless corporations in Wall Street'.[30] There is no doubt Puig was Hull's *bête-noire* at Montevideo, for he also denounced the Monroe Doctrine and urged recognition of the Grau government in Cuba. However, Puig's economic and financial proposals were shelved for consideration by the 'dormant' Inter-American High Commission.[31] But the Mexican Foreign Minister had struck a prophetic note which would be re-echoed in his country's capital in 1945 and become ever louder in the post-war period.

The Mexican delegation also took the initiative in producing a peace code, bringing together into a single instrument the various treaties and agreements for the prevention and peaceful settlement of disputes, and proposing an American Court of International Justice. In December 1933 none of the numerous inter-American peace treaties had been ratified by all the American republics, and Argentina, sponsor of the latest, had not ratified any of them. It was resolved at Montevideo to submit the peace code through the Pan American Union to member governments. The Seventh International Conference adopted an Additional Protocol to the General Convention of Inter-American Conciliation under which the signatories undertook to establish permanent commissions of investigation and conciliation to replace the *ad hoc* commissions of the Gondra Treaty. It also called upon those states which had not done so to adhere to and ratify the Gondra Treaty, the Pact of Paris,[32] the two Washington treaties of 1929, and the Anti-War Treaty.

The most notable result of the Seventh International Conference of American States was the adoption of the Convention on the Rights and Duties of States. We have already seen how crucial the intervention issue had become in inter-American relations and how the United States was beginning to modify her position even as Charles Evans Hughes was defending it at Havana.[33] But, as the instructions to her delegates confirm, the United States was not prepared to relinquish the right of intervention she enjoyed under international law, even though she had become very reluctant to send her armed forces into the territory of her small neighbours. She would have liked to convince the Latin Americans of her good intentions without

[30] Hull, i. 335.
[31] *For. Rel. US, 1933*, iv. 163. See above, pp. 55–56.
[32] Or Kellogg-Briand Pact, signed in 1928 and open to all states.
[33] And even Hughes preferred to call it 'interposition of a temporary character'.

giving up the freedom to act when she felt her vital interests demanded it. She discovered at Montevideo how strongly the Latin Americans wanted a firm 'non-intervention' commitment. In spite of Havana, the strength of Latin American feeling on this issue seems to have surprised the Secretary of State and his fellow delegates. Hull recorded that one of the latter 'almost exploded' when criticism of the United States became violent, while, for himself, it was one of the most uncomfortable and disagreeable experiences he had ever had at a public meeting.[34]

Dr Puig Casauranc rejected Hughes's defence of the Monroe Doctrine and the value of the Clark Memorandum. 'The indisputable fact', he said, 'is that that Doctrine bothers us, it separates rather than unites us, it pains us. The absolutely indisputable fact is that, as long as there is no result (*sic*) of an agreement or reciprocal obligation, even though this be a favor, this Doctrine is an annoyance and a humiliation.'[35] Not surprisingly, the Cuban delegate made a critical speech in which he roundly denounced the Platt Amendment:

> Cuba was born with the congenital vice of intervention. But that intervention represented in the Platt Amendment has been the substitute for the annexation of Cuba to the United States. In making this declaration here I am fully conscious of what I am saying and of the meaning which I give to it. For two years I was in touch with the archives of the State Department in Washington and with other private archives, registering old documents in the preparation of a treatise on the history of North American Diplomacy in Cuba. In the perusal of these studies, my investigations brought to light some of the private papers of Mr. Platt, whose name the famous amendment bears. In one of his notes to a certain Mr. Atkins, in May, 1901, Senator Platt confesses that the Platt Amendment is a substitute for the annexation, because there was a "foolish joint resolution" which kept the United States from annexing Cuba; in other words, because there was a "joint resolution" the Platt Amendment was necessary, or there would be no Cuban Republic. That is what the author of the Platt Amendment said.[36]

Of Sumner Welles's activities in Cuba, the delegate said:

> it is impossible to maintain silence when it is affirmed that the United

---

[34] *Memoirs*, i. 334. Hull was referring to criticism made in Plenary Session. The speeches quoted here were made in committee.
[35] Seventh International Conference of American States, *Minutes and Antecedents with General Index*, 2nd Cttee, Problems of International Law, p. 111.
[36] Ibid. p. 105.

States of America did not wish to intervene in Cuba, because it is not so. If by intervention we understand the last stage of intervention, properly speaking, the actual, physical occupation of a country, the subjugation of a people, perhaps then the statement would have been correct: but if it is not intervention to consent that in a defenceless country a representative of the United States of America should raise a people in insurrection against the Government, if it is not intervention to consent that Minister Wells (*sic*) patronize a revolution in Cuba against the country's vital interests . . . if it is not intervention to surround the defenceless island with an awe inspiring fleet and try to impose upon it a Government, to which we do not want to consent; if that is not intervention, then Gentlemen, there is no intervention in America! (applause).[37]

He also took occasion to denounce the statement made in support of intervention by the Cuban delegation at Havana:

My country, today under the rule of a most liberal government, must make a definite declaration that Cuba is positively against intervention, and that the men who made the declaration in Havana did not represent the spirit of the Cuban people who are against intervention. Intervention is not only the "curse of America" but, as a Cuban internationalist has said, it is the "curse of curses" of my country, the cause of all the evils of the Cuban Republic.[38]

It is of interest that one of the delegates of Nicaragua, who had spoken up for Hughes at Havana, declared he had come to Montevideo as a point of honour to support the principle of non-intervention.[39]

The Monroe Doctrine was strongly criticized by the delegate of Haiti, another of the smaller nations which had considerable experience of United States intervention:

The Monroe Doctrine is nothing more than the expression of the desires of a single State of the Continent. Its abusive interpretation has caused the smaller nations of this hemisphere to shed so many tears and so much blood. These smaller nations have been impoverished and enslaved by Uncle Sam at the selfsame moment that our "dear relative" has proclaimed before the civilized world the right of the smaller countries to govern themselves. In short, let us consider the anxiety and the perpetual disquietude of these small nations exposed, as they are, to the violences and humiliations of foreign intervention.[40]

---

[37] Ibid. Minutes of 9th Cttee, Economic Problems, 5th Sess. (13 Dec. 1933), pp. 103–4. [38] Ibid. 2nd Cttee, Problems of International Law, p. 105. [39] Ibid. pp. 123–4. [40] Ibid. p. 106.

Cordell Hull decided to accept the Convention on the Rights and Duties of States, though he did so with a reservation which referred to statements and policies of the Roosevelt administration and 'the law of nations as generally recognized and accepted'. The most important article of the convention was the one affirming that 'no state has the right to intervene in the internal or external affairs of another'. In a telegram to the Acting Secretary of State in Washington, informing him that he had voted for the convention (with reservation), Hull declared: 'the demand for unanimous affirmative vote was very vociferous and more or less wild and unreasonable.'[41]

The acceptance of this convention is an important milestone in the history of the inter-American system; it marks the beginning of a process not yet fully worked out. Hull expressed regret (in his reservation) that there had not been time 'within which to prepare interpretations and definitions of these fundamental terms that are embraced in the report'. In fact, only years of experience would reveal the full implications of the terms, the most important of which, 'intervention', it has so far proved impossible to define satisfactorily. The United States reservations were important. After all, it was under 'the law of nations as generally recognized and accepted' that she had always claimed the right of intervention and rejected the Calvo Doctrine, now virtually included as Article 9 of the Convention. Again, United States treaty rights to intervene were safeguarded by Article 12: 'The present Convention shall not affect obligations previously entered into by the High Contracting Parties by virtue of international agreements.'

We have already seen that the Roosevelt administration's interpretation of 'intervention' was, at this stage, a very narrow one: the actual employment of armed force. Only with such a narrow definition could it have protested that it was not intervening in Cuba in 1933. Two days after the Montevideo Conference ended, President Roosevelt declared that 'the definite policy of the United States from now on is one opposed to *armed*[42] intervention'. In the same speech he said:

The maintenance of law and orderly processes of government in this hemisphere is the concern of each individual nation within its own borders first of all. It is only if and when the failure of orderly processes affects the other nations of the continent that it becomes their concern; and the

---

[41] *For. Rel. US, 1933*, iv. 201.   [42] My italics.

point to stress is that in such event it becomes the joint concern of a whole continent in which we are all neighbours.[43]

Once again,[44] Roosevelt seemed to be visualizing some form of collective intervention, another aspect of the question which was to become of greater significance later on. It is noteworthy that Article 8 of the Convention on the Rights and Duties of States forbids any state to intervene. Not until fifteen years later was 'or group of states' added to this most important of all inter-American principles. Indeed, at Buenos Aires in 1936, 'any state' became 'any one state'.[45]

Among the less striking achievements of the Seventh Conference was a comprehensive resolution (LXX) on the codification of international law. This provided for the continuation of the International Commission of Jurists; the establishment of a Commission of Experts to organize and prepare the work of codification; the creation by each government of a national commission to codify international law; and for the Pan American Union to set up a juridical section of a purely administrative character to serve as a general secretariat in this work of codification. Little headway had been made up to 1933 with the codification of international law in the western hemisphere. Resolution LXX stressed that this task 'must be gradual and progressive, it being a vain illusion to think for a long time of the possibility of carrying it out completely'. Moreover,

in this connection the necessity of coordinating this work with the work of codification being done by the League of Nations must be taken into account as far as possible, since international law tends to universalize its rules as the interdependence of the civilized community becomes more and more confirmed and consolidated.

Implementing the Good Neighbour Policy

In the years immediately following the Seventh Conference the Roosevelt administration took further steps to establish itself as the Good Neighbour in Latin American eyes. One of the most important of these was the negotiation of a new treaty with Cuba, abrogating the hated Platt Amendment, which was eventually signed on 29 May 1934. Under its terms, the United States no longer possessed the right of intervention; there were no restrictions on the freedom of Cuba to contract foreign loans; and Cuba was no longer forbidden to enter into alliances which might impair her sovereignty. But the

---

[43] Quoted in RIIA, *Survey, 1933* (1934), p. 351.
[44] See above, pp. 79–80.   [45] See below, p. 97.

United States was to retain her naval base on leased territory at Guantánamo Bay and her close economic links with the island. Would this prove the opening of a new period in the relations between the United States and Cuba? Miss Katharine Duff, who thought it would, nevertheless uttered a warning that now has a prophetic ring:

> The question of American economic domination remained, however, unsolved, and might yet have considerable influence on the policy of the United States, if the Cuban attempt at social revolution were successful, or if the Cubans were ever in a position to act upon the saying of their national hero José Martí that 'a people economically enslaved but politically free will end by losing all freedom; but a people economically free can go on to win its political freedom'.[46]

Certainly, the close economic ties between Cuba and the United States made almost impossible the re-shaping of the former's economy. The United States sugar subsidy helped to perpetuate a situation prejudicial to vast numbers of Cubans, for whom it limited the possibility of owning land, provided only seasonal employment, and meant higher prices for imports from the United States.[47]

Another act of the Good Neighbour was to withdraw the last detachments of marines from Haiti in August 1934, over three months in advance of the date agreed the previous year. Negotiations were also begun on the subject of United States financial control, and in July 1935, agreement was reached for the Haitian government to purchase the National Bank of Haiti from the National City Bank of New York. As we noted, the delegates of Haiti and Cuba had (not unnaturally) been strong critics at Montevideo of United States intervention. It was not, incidentally, until some years later that the United States relinquished her remaining special rights in Haiti and the Dominican Republic. In the meantime a new treaty was signed with Panama (2 March 1936) which, although still restricting that country's sovereignty in a number of ways, specifically ended the right of intervention hitherto enjoyed by the United States. However, it was not ratified until 1939.

In January 1934 the recognition policy (Tobar Doctrine) applied by the United States to the five Central American republics since

---

[46] K. Duff, 'Relations between Cuba and the United States (1898–1934)', in RIIA, *Survey, 1933*, pp. 392–3.
[47] P. C. M. Teichert, 'Latin America and the Socio-Economic Impact of the Cuban Revolution', *JIAS*, iv/1 (1962), pp. 111–12.

1907 was ended. This came about as a result of a revolution in El Salvador in December 1931. The new, Martínez government was immediately recognized by Mexico and several South American countries. The United States and the four other Central American republics, acting in accordance with the 1923 treaty,[48] did not grant it recognition. But Costa Rica soon gave notice that she would not be bound by the treaty beyond its term of ten years, and the day following its expiry (2 January 1934) she recognized Martínez. El Salvador, who had already pointed out that her ratification of the 1923 treaty had been subject to a reservation on the recognition question, likewise declared her intention to terminate the treaty on 1 January 1934. By the end of that month all the other Central American governments had recognized Martínez. In the following April a new Treaty of Central American Fraternity, looking forward to the political union of Central America at some future date and omitting any provision regarding non-recognition of revolutions, was signed at Guatemala City. Meanwhile, United States recognition of the Salvadoran government on 26 January 1934 confirmed the breakdown of the special recognition policy in Central America.

The implementation of Cordell Hull's economic proposals proved less fruitful than his acceptance of non-intervention in improving inter-American relations. We have already noted that while United States tariff policy had been a highly controversial political issue at Havana and subsequently, its effect on Latin American trade as a whole had been limited. The consequences of tariff reductions were therefore bound to disappoint the Latin Americans, who, as we have also seen, were not eager to reduce their own customs duties. Although the United States concluded bilateral agreements under the Reciprocal Trade Agreements Act with eleven Latin American governments between June 1934 (when the Act was passed) and 1 January 1940, there is little evidence to show that these significantly increased trade between the countries concerned. Nor did the Export-Import Bank, created in 1934, achieve a great deal in stimulating Latin American economic development and inter-American trade in its first years of operation.

Some reference has already been made to the growing influence of the world situation upon the inter-American system. The Reciprocal Trade Agreements Act itself was concerned with world, not merely hemispheric trade. United States opposition to Japanese intervention

---

[48] See above, p. 62, n. 73.

in Manchuria, we noted, had made her more conscious of her own armed interventions in the Caribbean region, and League of Nations efforts to settle certain inter-American disputes had been officially welcomed at Montevideo. Concern over the inadequacy of the inter-American peace machinery was complemented in the years following the Seventh International Conference by growing anxiety over the failure of the League of Nations to maintain peace in other regions of the world. In the autumn of 1935 Italy invaded Ethiopia; in the following March Hitler announced the remilitarization of the Rhineland and Germany's repudiation of the Locarno Treaty; civil war broke out in Spain a few months later. The western hemisphere was beginning to feel the effects of Axis trade and cultural penetration.

The Buenos Aires Conference (1936)

In the meantime, the end of the Chaco War provided an additional reason for holding a special inter-American peace conference. President Roosevelt, in letters to the presidents of the other American republics on 30 January 1936, declared that 'with the conclusion of the Chaco War and with the reestablishment of peace throughout this Continent, there would appear to be offered an opportunity for helpful counsel among our respective governments which may not soon again be presented'.[49] He therefore proposed an extraordinary inter-American conference to determine how the maintenance of peace among the American republics might best be safeguarded. The ineffectiveness of the inter-American peace instruments, which the Chaco War had underlined and to which the gaps in ratification by the signatories bore further witness, formed the basis of Roosevelt's appeal. But the need to strengthen inter-American co-operation in the face of the growing threat to peace outside the hemisphere was very much in his mind, as the ensuing conference revealed.

It is significant that the Inter-American Conference for the Maintenance of Peace should have been held at Buenos Aires. Argentina had ratified none of the inter-American peace instruments except her own Anti-War Treaty; she was the most consistent opponent of the United States within the inter-American system; she had the biggest grievance of any Latin American country against United States economic policy—the operation of the latter's sanitary regulations against her meat; she had the closest ties, economic and cultural, with Europe; and, at this time, she was a firm supporter of the League

---

[49] *Int. Conf. Am. States*, 1st Suppl., p. 130.

of Nations, of whose Assembly her Foreign Minister, Dr Saavedra Lamas, was President. Thus Argentina was the most difficult Latin American republic to win over with the Good Neighbour policy. Cordell Hull had made special efforts to cultivate Saavedra Lamas's co-operation at Montevideo;[50] he was willing, in the same cause, to have Buenos Aires as the meeting-place for this conference. But Hull was to record later that the eyes of the Argentine Foreign Minister were 'more on the dying League than on the living Pan American idea'.[51]

When the Buenos Aires Conference met, sixteen Latin American countries were members of the League which, in spite of its weakness, they still valued to some extent as a counterpoise to the United States. It is worth noting that Franklin Roosevelt, in his letters to the other American presidents, was careful to avoid giving the impression that he was proposing measures which would supplant the League. The steps he was suggesting, he said, 'would advance the cause of world peace, inasmuch as the agreements which might be reached would supplement and reinforce the efforts of the League of Nations and of all other existing or future peace agencies in seeking to prevent war'. But the Roosevelt administration certainly was not anxious for closer co-operation between the inter-American system and the League of Nations. Indeed, it could hardly afford to be, since there was strong anti-League feeling among some influential supporters of closer inter-American ties—and this was a presidential election year. The links between isolationism and the 'Western Hemisphere Idea' have already been stressed. There was also the specific matter of United States neutrality policy. As members of the League of Nations, most of the Latin American countries had recently been placed under an obligation to take part in sanctions against Italy for her aggression in Ethiopia.

Roosevelt's initiative met with a favourable response, but the replies showed differing views of the possible role of a reinforced inter-American peace system. The Presidents of Argentina, Chile, and Mexico stressed the interdependence between regional and wider international organizations; the Presidents of Haiti, Honduras, El Salvador, and Venezuela generally approved the idea of reinforcing the work of the League of Nations. Three countries, Colombia, the Dominican Republic, and Guatemala, favoured establishing an American League of Nations. The Guatemalan President included in his reply a proposal he had already made to the United States the previous December: a General Treaty of American Solidarity and Mutual Co-operation providing for the creation of an Association of American Republics whose members would defend any one of them against acts of aggression or of intervention by any foreign power. During subsequent consideration of the agenda several countries proposed a regional League, the most comprehensive plan coming from Colombia. The Colombian project involved the end of Article 21 of the League Covenant recognizing the Monroe Doctrine, the status of which was also affected by the Guatemalan treaty. Cuba, Ecuador, Panama, and Peru joined Colombia and Guatemala in proposing an inter-American Court of Justice.

The agenda finally adopted by the Governing Board of the Pan American Union was divided into six sections: the organization of peace; neutrality; the limitation of armaments; juridical problems; economic problems; and intellectual co-operation. The principal concern of the conference was ostensibly the improvement of the inter-American peace machinery and the prompt ratification of existing peace instruments. But various countries had special matters they wanted discussed. Argentina, for example, was anxious to raise again United States sanitary restrictions and the subject of intervention; the United States was particularly interested in the question of neutrality.

The Inter-American Conference for the Maintenance of Peace took place from 1 to 23 December 1936. It was attended by delegations from all twenty-one American republics and its opening session was addressed by President Roosevelt. Its main importance in the history of the development of the inter-American system[52] lies in its adoption of two major, and inter-related documents: the Convention for the Maintenance, Preservation and Reestablishment of Peace, and the Additional Protocol Relative to Non-Intervention. The first of these agreements introduced into the inter-American system the principle of consultation; the second reinforced the principle of non-intervention and linked it with consultation. The two documents were negotiated and presented to the conference simultaneously as joint proposals.

For Latin Americans, the more important of these agreements— and an end in itself—was the Additional Protocol Relative to Non-

---

[52] In the view of F. Cuevas Cancino, *Roosevelt y la buena vecindad* (1954), p. 218, the Buenos Aires Conference marks the real beginning of a new phase for the inter-American system.

Intervention. Mexico's initiative in pressing for its adoption, and subsequent declaration that it had been her principal objective at the Buenos Aires Conference, have already been noted.[53] This, incidentally, raises the question of whether plans had already been laid for expropriating United States oil properties in Mexico. On the basis of available information, however, one cannot add to Bryce Wood's observation that 'such foresight seems improbable although its possibility cannot be excluded'.[54] Article 1 of the Additional Protocol reads:

> The High Contracting Parties declare inadmissible the intervention of any one of them, directly or indirectly, and for whatever reason, in the internal or external affairs of any other of the Parties.
> The violation of the provisions of this Article shall give rise to mutual consultation, with the object of exchanging views and seeking methods of peaceful adjustment.

This meant that the United States was accepting a broader interpretation of the principle of non-intervention without the reservations she made at Montevideo. In itself, this was a victory for the Latin Americans. Cordell Hull spoke to the conference of 'this hour of your great triumph',[55] though he gave it little importance in his *Memoirs*.[56]

But the Additional Protocol was no mere repetition of the Montevideo pledge with some elaboration and no United States reservation. Reference has already been made to the phrase 'any one state', which implies collective action of some kind. This must be read in conjunction with the principle of consultation. Together they introduced the concept of 'collective responsibility' by all the American republics in situations which previously would have led to intervention by any one of them. Certainly the United States has assumed an essential element of reciprocity in the Additional Protocol and the interrelated convention: that is to say, she agreed to the principle of non-intervention on the understanding that the Latin Americans accepted the principle of collective responsibility. How far the Latin American countries interpreted these agreements in the same way time would show.

Consultation was to take place in the field of peace and security. This principle was embodied in the Convention for the Maintenance,

[53] See above, p. 31.
[54] *Good Neighbor Policy*, p. 121. Wood's comment also applies to the Bolivian expropriations of 1937.
[55] Inter-American Conference for the Maintenance of Peace, *Proceedings*, p. 84.
[56] Hull, i. 500.

Preservation and Reestablishment of Peace. Article 1 of this Convention called for consultation 'for the purpose of finding and adopting methods of peaceful cooperation' should the peace of the American republics be menaced. Article 2 called for consultation without delay to seek 'a method of peaceful collaboration' in the case of war or a virtual state of war between American states; while

in the event of an international war outside America which might menace the peace of the American Republics, such consultation shall also take place to determine the proper time and manner in which the signatory states, if they so desire, may eventually cooperate in some action tending to preserve the peace of the American Continent.

While the principle had thus been established, no machinery of consultation was provided; nor were the signatories committed to take any subsequent action. As regards the first deficiency, the United States delegation had proposed the creation of a Permanent Inter-American Consultative Committee composed of the foreign ministers of the twenty-one republics. Argentina, in particular, opposed this as leading towards the political organization of the hemisphere and conflicting with the obligations of Latin American members of the League of Nations. For similar reasons, the United States was unsuccessful in persuading the other American republics to adopt her neutrality policy.[57] It is of interest that, during the discussion of the United States proposal for a neutrality treaty, a Uruguayan delegate declared:

It is a truth that it would not be very pleasant to prove once more, but it is the truth that we are more closely linked to the European Continent, and to some of these countries very strongly indeed, than we are to the American Continent. The countries of the River Plate basin, for example, due to their connection with certain European countries, in a cultural and economic way, because of the content and volume of their relations, cannot lightly enter into a system which, in a more or less veiled manner, would perhaps oblige them to break their relations with them and be victims of consequent reprisals.[58]

In view of its importance in the development of the inter-American system—and its relevance to Latin American reluctance to go further at Buenos Aires—brief consideration should be given at this stage to the question of how the Monroe Doctrine was affected by the acceptance of non-intervention and consultation in 1936. From the Latin

[57] See below, p. 312.   [58] *Proceedings*, p. 257.

American standpoint, the Doctrine represented the very antithesis of these two principles: they had not been consulted in its formulation or interpretation, and it was closely associated with United States intervention. Therefore, acceptance of non-intervention and consultation should have had important implications for the Monroe Doctrine. One (Peruvian) delegate at the Buenos Aires Conference saw in the new agreements:

the complete transformation of the Monroe Doctrine . . . in other words . . . the Monroe Doctrine vanishes, we see it disappear without noisy farewells, to be replaced by this cooperative formula of our America, in which we affirm and declare that the defense of our Continent is entrusted to our own countries, our own means and resources.[59]

Like so many pronouncements on the demise of the Monroe Doctrine this one was premature, but the speech is important as reflecting Latin American desire for an end of the Doctrine, not its 'Pan Americanization'. This was underlined by the fate of a Brazilian 'Project for an Inter-American Pact for Collective Security', which Mecham declared would have made the Doctrine 'the common doctrine of all the American republics' (p. 129). The Latin Americans had no wish to give their support to the Monroe Doctrine; nor, for that matter, had the United States any intention of sharing with them its interpretation and application.

The Buenos Aires Conference also sought to strengthen the inter-American peace machinery with two new instruments: the Treaty on the Prevention of Controversies, and the Inter-American Treaty on Good Offices and Mediation. The first provided for permanent bilateral mixed commissions to eliminate, as far as possible, the causes of future controversies between the signatories; the second for a permanent panel of eminent citizens (to be prepared by the Pan American Union), to one of whom the parties to a controversy might have recourse for the exercise of good offices and mediation. The conference (like the Seventh International Conference) called upon those states which had not done so to adhere to or ratify existing peace instruments. Projects for an Inter-American Court of Justice (strongly supported by the Central American states) and a League of American Nations were postponed once more for consideration by the next International Conference. The United States delegation abstained from voting on a resolution recommending 'Coordination of Pacific Instruments with the Covenant of the League of Nations'.[60] It

---

[59] Ibid. p. 90.   [60] So did Costa Rica.

would not support a resolution which, in spite of its broad terms, might involve United States co-operation with the League.

The Convention to Coordinate, Extend, and Assure the Fulfillment of the Existing Treaties Between the American States, also adopted at the Buenos Aires Conference, came out of its committee on neutrality. It provided machinery for the co-ordination of existing peace instruments and envisaged the general objective of a common neutrality policy. The instruments concerned were the Treaty to Avoid and Prevent Conflicts (Gondra Treaty, 1923); the Pact of Paris (1928); the General Convention of Inter-American Conciliation (1929); the General Treaty of Inter-American Arbitration (1929); and the Treaty of Non-Aggression and Conciliation (1933). The signatories to the new convention agreed to have recourse to one or more of these peace instruments if involved in a controversy which they could not solve by diplomatic negotiations. Should hostilities nevertheless break out, the High Contracting Parties would 'through consultation, immediately endeavor to adopt in their character as neutrals a common and solidary attitude, in order to discourage or prevent the spread or prolongation of hostilities'. Moreover,

they may consider the imposition of prohibitions or restrictions on the sale or shipment of arms, munitions and implements of war, loans or other financial help to the states in conflict, in accordance with the municipal legislation of the High Contracting Parties, and without detriment to their obligations derived from other treaties to which they are or may become parties.

Although this convention referred to 'a common and solidary attitude' of neutrality, every government retained its freedom to act in accordance with its domestic legislation and in conformity with its multilateral treaties. It was stated specifically in a separate article that 'Nothing contained in the present Convention shall be understood as affecting the rights and duties of the High Contracting Parties which are at the same time members of the League of Nations.' Moreover, while the governments undertook to consult, the convention contained no provision for determining the aggressor in any conflict; nor did it cover the question of equality of treatment in applying embargoes and other restrictions. The conference referred to the Committee of Experts in charge of the Codification of International Law a Bolivian project on the definition of an aggressor and the application of sanctions, after discussion had revealed differences among the delegations on these matters. Behind the convention was an attempt by the United States to have the Latin American countries adopt a more specific policy of neutrality based on her own neutrality legislation; an attempt which was thus unsuccessful.

Another interesting document emanating from the Buenos Aires Conference was the Declaration of Principles of Inter-American Solidarity and Co-operation. The conference declared:

1. That the American Nations, true to their republican institutions, proclaim their absolute juridical liberty, their unqualified respect for their respective sovereignties and the existence of a common democracy throughout America;

2. That every act susceptible of disturbing the peace of America affects each and every one of them, and justifies the initiation of the procedure of consultation provided for in the Convention for the Maintenance, Preservation and Reestablishment of Peace, signed at this Conference; and

3. That the following principles are accepted by the American community of Nations:

a) Proscription of territorial conquest and that, in consequence, no acquisition made through violence shall be recognized;

b) Intervention by one State in the internal or external affairs of another State is condemned;

c) Forcible collection of pecuniary debts is illegal; and

d) Any difference or dispute between the American nations, whatever its nature or origin, shall be settled by the methods of conciliation, or unrestricted arbitration, or through operation of international justice.

This declaration shows how far the aspirations if not the achievements of the inter-American system had progressed by 1936. Of particular interest is the inclusion of 'a common democracy' for the first time.

The Buenos Aires Conference achieved little in the fields of disarmament and the codification of international law. Nor did the work of its committee on economic problems add much to what had been resolved at Montevideo. In this field we have already noted Argentina's concern with United States sanitary regulations, the interpretation of which placed severe restrictions on her exports of meat to that country. The Roosevelt administration was, in the event, unable to overcome the opposition of domestic interests to the liberalizing of these regulations, which might have improved its relations with Argentina.[61] At Buenos Aires, as we have seen, Hull

[61] See Wood, 'The Department of State and the Non-National Interest: the Cases of Argentine Meat and Paraguayan Tea', *IAEA*, xv/2 (1961), pp. 3–32.

found Argentine opposition once more the main stumbling-block to Latin American acceptance of such of the United States objectives as support for her neutrality legislation.[62] A large number of conventions and resolutions emerged from the committee on intellectual co-operation.

United States Policy (*1936–8*)

During the two years which elapsed between the Buenos Aires Conference and the Eighth International Conference of American States there were developments both inside and outside the western hemisphere of great significance for the inter-American system. The United States was made aware of the wider implications of 'non-intervention', while the deteriorating international situation in Europe and the Far East enhanced the need for closer inter-American co-operation.

There had been important changes in United States thinking on the intervention question even before the Buenos Aires Conference. We saw how the State Department interfered in Cuban domestic politics in order to avoid having to send in the marines. It was soon evident that such interference was incompatible with the Latin American concept of a 'good neighbour' and perhaps only Welles's personal involvement prevented the United States from recognizing the Grau government. At all events, the Roosevelt administration decided to follow up its policy of non-intervention (in the sense of not sending armed forces into the territory of the small neighbours of the United States) by what Bryce Wood has called the policy of non-interference: 'The policy of noninterference renounced any and all techniques of influence for the pursuit of certain former policy objectives. These latter objectives were the spread of democratic institutions in Latin America and the avoidance of situations usually described as instability, chaos, or anarchy'.[63] Although the United States still desired both democratic institutions and stability in Latin America, a policy of non-interference forbade direct measures to achieve them.

The pitfalls of non-interference were evident as soon as the Roosevelt administration tried to pursue this policy. They are inherent in United States power and Latin American weakness. The

---

[62] I am not, of course, suggesting that Argentina would have reversed her stand on these questions had she received satisfaction over the meat question.

[63] *Good Neighbor Policy*, p. 137.

United States could abstain from sending in the marines; she could not divest herself of the influence her power gave her, had she wished to do so. That being the case, lack of action on her part could often be as decisive as positive measures: non-recognition of a government, for example, even when the United States was not actually using this as an instrument of policy. Moreover, in circumstances of instability and civil conflict, there were groups in Latin American countries urging the United States to interfere, and accusing her of consciously aiding their rivals by not doing so. Nicaragua provided the Roosevelt administration with experience of such difficulties; it was much criticized by some Latin Americans for not preventing the seizure of power by General Somoza. Moreover, the maintenance of friendly relations with tyrants such as Somoza, Batista, and Trujillo aroused considerable indignation in Latin America. Incidentally, the Roosevelt administration also faced domestic criticism of the policy of non-interference, though this was more often concerned with 'radical' governments which these critics felt the United States should remove from power.

While wishing to avoid both armed intervention and interference in the affairs of its neighbours, the Roosevelt administration was, of course, determined to safeguard United States interests in the western hemisphere. In particular, it had not abandoned the policy of supporting United States commercial interests should these be denied justice in their dealings with Latin American governments. In its view, non-intervention did not include abstaining from diplomatic representations in such cases. At Montevideo, as we noted, the United States had entered a reservation to the Convention on the Rights and Duties of States, which had included what was virtually the Calvo Doctrine. At Buenos Aires the question of diplomatic intervention was referred to the Committee of Experts established at Montevideo.

The United States evidently did not consider acceptance of the Additional Protocol at Buenos Aires deprived her of the right of diplomatic reclamation. Her pledge not to intervene 'directly or indirectly' meant she would not employ armed force or the threat of armed force 'for any purpose whatever'. The Latin Americans interpreted 'non-intervention' more broadly. Even at the First International Conference of American States, as we saw, they sought to have the United States accept the Calvo Doctrine. Since then, as United States economic penetration of Latin America had increased, so had the support given by United States administrations to their nationals. There had been a significant retreat from the more extreme forms of such support since Coolidge's presidency. Much more was expected from the 'Good Neighbour': he should stop insisting on international arbitration of disputes between United States citizens and corporations and Latin American governments. On the other hand, the Roosevelt administration believed the Good Neighbour policy was a two-sided one; that the concessions it had made would evoke reciprocity. We have already noted this with regard to 'collective responsibility' in the field of peace and security. The United States government also expected reciprocity in the treatment of its nationals; it certainly did not contemplate accepting the Latin American position in 1936.

Events in the next two years extended this conflict of viewpoints from the realm of conference committees into that of practical politics. For in March 1937 the government of Bolivia annulled the petroleum concession of the (United States-owned) Standard Oil Company of Bolivia and confiscated its properties; and, almost exactly a year later, the Mexican government expropriated United States (and British and Dutch) oil companies. During these disputes, the United States came to abandon her insistence on international arbitration, since the Latin American governments concerned made it plain they would not agree to this, and to develop new techniques for influencing their policies. One of these, which later became more useful, was granting or withholding government loans and technical assistance. The most important factor determining the Roosevelt administration to pursue a policy of moderation in these disputes was the deterioration of the world situation. The interests of the oil companies had to be subordinated to the growing national interest of security. It was particularly important for the United States to have the collaboration of Mexico, who was, in fact, being forced through the companies' boycott to sell an increasing amount of oil to the Axis powers. Even so, the disputes were not finally settled until after the Second World War had broken out.

The Eighth Conference (Lima, 1938)

They were thus in their early stages when the Eighth International Conference of American States met at Lima (9–27 December 1938). By this time the world situation had become much more serious and the Axis powers were gaining ground in Latin America through trade and propaganda. The main business of the Lima Conference, at which all the American republics were represented, was to develop more effective inter-American co-operation in the face of this growing extra-continental challenge. Undoubtedly the implementation of the Good Neighbour policy had lessened Latin American fear and suspicion of the United States, which had always limited the scope of the inter-American system. Even so, the Declaration of Lima, the most important achievement of the Eighth International Conference, was hardly convincing testimony of continental solidarity. Once again, Argentina took the lead in diluting United States proposals for closer co-operation to meet threats from outside the hemisphere. Her Foreign Minister stressed the ties of the River Plate countries with Europe and, indeed, recalled with approval Sáenz Peña's speech on similar lines at the First International Conference of American States.[64] He objected to the Declaration being directed only against 'non-American' threats and this word was changed to 'foreign' in deference to Argentina's wishes.

The Declaration of Lima finally read (after a preamble):

The Governments of the American States Declare:

First. That they reaffirm their continental solidarity and their purpose to collaborate in the maintenance of the principles upon which the said solidarity is based.

Second. That faithful to the above-mentioned principles and to their absolute sovereignty, they reaffirm their decision to maintain them and to defend them against all foreign intervention or activity that may threaten them.

Third. And in case the peace, security or territorial integrity of any American Republic is thus threatened by acts of any nature that may impair them, they proclaim their common concern and their determination to make effective their solidarity, coordinating their respective sovereign wills by means of the procedure of consultation, established by conventions in force and by declarations of the Inter-American Conferences, using the measures which in each case the circumstances may make advisable. It is understood that the Governments of the American Republics will act independently in their individual capacity, recognizing fully their juridical equality as sovereign states.

Fourth. That in order to facilitate the consultations established in this and other American peace instruments, the Ministers for Foreign Affairs of the American Republics, when deemed desirable and at the initiative of any one of them, will meet in their several capitals by rotation and without

---

[64] Eighth International Conference of American States, *Minutes of the Plenary Sessions* (1938) First Plenary Session, pp. 15–16. See above, p. 43.

protocolary character. Each Government may, under special circumstances or for special reasons, designate a representative as a substitute for its Minister for Foreign Affairs.

Fifth. This Declaration shall be known as the "Declaration of Lima".

It is difficult to challenge the judgement of Dr William Manger on the key third article, that: 'Words more vague, obscure and ambiguous, expressed with greater circumlocution could hardly have been devised'.[65]

Although the Declaration of Lima provided for consultation through meetings of foreign ministers, these could have been held under the terms of the agreements made at Buenos Aires. Unlike the latter, however, the Declaration of Lima was not a formal convention. Thus it did not require ratification, doubtless an advantage since Argentina, Bolivia, Peru, and Uruguay had not yet ratified the Buenos Aires Consultation Pact. In fact, the Lima Conference (incidentally, the shortest of the International Conferences) adopted no conventions or formal treaties. Much of its work was repetition. The Declaration of American Principles, for example, added little to the comparable declaration at Buenos Aires; indeed, there was no reference to 'the existence of a common democracy throughout America', which would have had a particularly odd ring in the hall from which the national deputies had been ejected by the Peruvian dictator.[66] Nothing further was done at Lima to improve or coordinate inter-American peace instruments, though various projects were referred to the International Conference of American Jurists (the former International Commission of American Jurists). These included the Mexican peace code and a United States draft; the creation of an Association of American Nations; and the problem of defining the terms 'aggressor' and 'sanctions'. While the conference declared its 'firm purpose' to establish an American Court of International Justice, discussion of plans to create one produced no agreement to do so. The United States was still opposed to such a court as well as to an American League of Nations.[67]

On the question of co-operation with other international organizations (raised at Montevideo), the Lima Conference resolved:

1. To recommend to the Pan American Union as well as to other Pan American organizations that they cooperate with international bodies

---

[65] *Pan America in Crisis*, p. 42.
[66] Mecham, p. 139.   [67] *For. Rel. US, 1938*, v. 60–61.

in other parts of the world, within the limits imposed by their organic statutes and without affecting the integrity of the international organization of the twenty-one American Republics.

2. To recommend to the Pan American Union and to other Pan American organizations that, in order to establish a mutually advantageous interchange they make available to other international bodies the information they have at their disposal; exchange points of view and, as much as possible, coordinate the investigations they may carry on in the fields of economic, social, cultural and juridical activity.

3. To recommend to the Pan American Union, as the permanent secretariat of the International Conferences of American States, that it make known to other international bodies the conclusions of the conferences and the measures adopted to make them effective.

4. To request the Governing Board of the Pan American Union to adopt the measures deemed necessary for the greatest possible development of these cooperative relations.

But observers from such organizations and from non-American states were not admitted to the Lima Conference.

The matter of pecuniary claims and diplomatic intervention— a topical one in view of the recent oil expropriations in Bolivia and Mexico—was referred back to the Committee of Experts for further study and report. Among other resolutions, the American republics agreed to apply the procedure of consultation to important economic, cultural, and other questions, and to curb the activities of foreign minorities. There was the usual large number of resolutions on commercial matters, communications (including the Pan American Highway), the rights of women, and so on. All these subjects, though making their contribution to the development of closer inter-American relations, were of course subsidiary to the main purpose of the conference. Of the latter Hull said on his return to the United States: 'the American republics made it clear to all the world that they stand united to maintain and defend the peace of this hemisphere.'[68]

In fact, only a modest foundation for continental solidarity had been laid at Lima. Given the state of inter-American relations a decade earlier, this was no mean achievement; but it was not enough. The Roosevelt administration could hardly be satisfied with Latin America's response to the Good Neighbour policy.[69] The truth was, however, that Latin Americans did not acknowledge any obligation

---

[68] Mecham, p. 148.
[69] Another difficulty was that of being a Good Neighbour to Latin American countries between whom there was rivalry, notably Argentina and Brazil. This is

of reciprocity. In abstaining from interventions which had been affronts to their sovereignty, and acquiescing in their attempts to free themselves from economic vassalage (as they saw it) to her large corporations, the United States was only behaving as the Good Neighbour she professed to be. In so doing, the United States was winning goodwill. By the end of 1938 she wanted more than that: in fact, positive support for a policy of continental solidarity in the face of the growing challenge from outside the hemisphere. She did not get this at Lima.

So in 1939 the United States began to evoke reciprocity (where she had previously anticipated it), and to use specific economic inducements to gain particular objectives. This 'evocation of reciprocity', as Bryce Wood calls it,[70] was necessary if she was to obtain the degree of support she wanted in the limited time which the international situation suggested was at her disposal. For the Latin Americans, the biggest threat to whose independence had traditionally come from their northern neighbour, did not readily accept that a greater menace was arising from the Axis powers. It would take the outbreak of hostilities and positive measures by the United States to make possible something approaching continental solidarity on the foundations laid by the Good Neighbour policy of restraint.

On the Eve of the Second World War

Before examining how the Good Neighbours fared as wartime partners, let us summarize very briefly the achievements of the inter-American system on the eve of the Second World War. In the field of peaceful settlement of inter-American disputes, which had been a major objective from the beginning, progress had not been encouraging. There was no lack of peace instruments, but reservations and failures to ratify rendered them largely inoperable. They failed to cope with the serious boundary disputes which were the major cause of friction between Latin American countries.[71] Indeed, in only one case (the dispute between the Dominican Republic and Haiti in 1937–8) was use made of them.[72] Moreover, as we have seen, the inter-American peace procedures were established outside the Pan

---

discussed by Bryce Wood, 'External Restraints on the Good Neighbor Policy', *IAEA*, xvi/2 (1962), pp. 3–24.   [70] *Good Neighbor Policy*, pp. 309 ff.

[71] For a useful summary of the inter-American peace structure on the eve of the Second World War and a brief account of its application to inter-American disputes during the previous decade, see Mecham, pp. 149–80.

[72] M. M. Ball, *The Problem of Inter-American Organization* (1944), p. 48.

American Union and its Governing Board. A proposal that the latter should act as a council of conciliation was not accepted by the Sixth International Conference.[73] Nor did the conferences themselves often take the initiative in attempting to settle existing inter-American disputes. It is of interest that in this field the League of Nations took a hand in the western hemisphere, as did the Permanent Court of International Justice in certain legal issues between American republics.

For most of the fifty years since the opening of the First International Conference of American States, the question of inter-American co-operation in the field of hemispheric security against extra-continental aggression had not arisen. The Monroe Doctrine, unchallenged from outside the hemisphere, had become the symbol of United States hegemony within it. While fostering Latin American support for her own policy of limiting European influence in the Americas, the United States jealously maintained the unilateral character of the Monroe Doctrine. As the world situation deteriorated, however, and a threat to her security developed, the United States sought the positive support of her neighbours to meet it. This did not involve what has been described as the Pan Americanization of the Monroe Doctrine. It did mean that the defence of the hemisphere became a major concern of the inter-American system. As we have just seen, modest steps towards collective security had been taken at Buenos Aires and Lima.

There had been much more activity in other spheres, but on fundamental economic and social problems only the smallest beginnings had been made, although economic development was already becoming linked with security in the months before the Second World War broke out. As far as the structure of the inter-American system was concerned, in Professor Ball's judgement, 'no effective attempt whatever seems to have been made, to date, to bring about a real integration of the work of the different inter-American agencies'.[74] The war period was to cause major developments in many fields; it would bring a new intimacy to inter-American relations, and new problems; it would occasion far-reaching changes in the structure of the inter-American system; more important, perhaps, it would transform international society and the environment within which the system would operate when the war was over. To developments within the inter-American system during the Second World War we shall turn in the following chapter.

[73] See above, p. 71.   [74] Ball, *Inter-American Organization*, pp. 4–5.

I

4   Developments during the Second World War

I N the previous chapter an attempt was made to describe the development of a new United States policy towards Latin America and the effect this had upon the inter-American system. The Good Neighbour policy greatly improved inter-American relations, dissipating to a considerable extent the ill-will so evident at the time of the Sixth International Conference of American States. It gave the inter-American system a 'new look' by establishing two fundamental and related principles: non-intervention and consultation. But there has been a tendency to exaggerate the degree of inter-American co-operation achieved by the Good Neighbour policy before the outbreak of the Second World War and the strength of the wartime partnership it is credited with having made possible. Some indication has been given of the difficulties the Roosevelt administration experienced in evolving and implementing the Good Neighbour policy. The limited response its efforts to build up continental solidarity evoked from Latin America has also been shown. This chapter will endeavour to appraise the development of the inter-American system during the Second World War.

The disinclination of the Latin Americans fully to support the policy of the United States is understandable. In the first place traditional fear of United States power had not been superseded by a greater fear of the threat from outside the hemisphere;[1] in the second place, Latin American countries had important ties—especially economic ones—with Europe. In this last respect, Argentina's interests in particular were in conflict with those of the United States, and her reluctance to co-operate, therefore, was logical. Quite apart from the use of economic aid as a means of securing support for her policies, the United States would have to take steps to lessen Latin American dependence upon European markets if she was to achieve a substantially greater degree of continental solidarity. In the months

---

[1] Cf. Bemis, *Latin American Policy of US*, p. 356: 'At Lima nobody was nervous any longer about the "Colossus of the North"; it was the new Colossus of Europe that they feared.'

between the Lima Conference and the outbreak of war in Europe the Roosevelt administration made a start in this direction. The President himself, in a speech on Pan American Day, promised support to Latin America against economic pressure from the Axis powers 'so that no American nation need surrender any fraction of its sovereign freedom to maintain its economic welfare'.[2] Little had been done, however, by September 1939.

The Panama Meeting (1939)

Shortly after the outbreak of hostilities in Europe, the United States took the initiative in calling a Meeting of Consultation.[3] The 'First Meeting of Ministers of Foreign Affairs of the American Republics for Consultation under the Inter-American Agreements of Buenos Aires and Lima' took place in Panama City from 23 September until 3 October 1939. Its programme,[4] approved by the Governing Board of the Pan American Union, contained three items: neutrality, protection of the peace of the western hemisphere, and economic co-operation. In fact, it was concerned to maintain the peace of the hemisphere through a policy of neutrality, and to safeguard the economies of the American states against the effects of dislocation which inevitably would follow war in Europe. All members of the inter-American system were represented at the Panama Meeting.

In pursuit of the first objective, the Panama Conference adopted a 'General Declaration of Neutrality' reaffirming the neutrality of the American states, but leaving 'to each one of them to regulate in their individual and sovereign capacities the manner in which they are to give it concrete application'. As part of the same resolution the conference voted to establish, for the duration of the European war, an Inter-American Neutrality Committee, composed of seven experts in international law designated by the Governing Board of the Pan American Union, 'with a view to studying and formulating recommendations with respect to the problems of neutrality, in the light of experience and changing circumstances'.

In the United States-sponsored Declaration of Panama, the members of the conference claimed 'as of inherent right' that the

---

[2] W. L. Langer and S. E. Gleason, *The Challenge to Isolation, 1937–1940* (1952), p. 133.
[3] *For. Rel. US, 1939*, v. 15–16.
[4] The programmes, and the conventions, recommendations, resolutions and motions adopted by the First and Second Meetings of Consultation of American Foreign Ministers are contained in *Int. Conf. Am. States*, 1st Suppl.

waters for a distance of approximately 300 miles from their shores should be 'free from the commission of any hostile act by any non-American belligerent nation, whether such hostile act be attempted or made from land, sea or air'. This was creating American international law with a vengeance![5] Of course the neutral zone was not respected by the belligerents. Further measures to strengthen neutrality included a resolution calling for another Meeting of Consultation 'in case any geographic region of America subject to the jurisdiction of any non-American state should be obliged to change its sovereignty and there should result therefrom a danger to the security of the American Continent'. To combat subversive ideologies in the western hemisphere, the conference resolved 'to recommend to the Governments represented therein, that they take the necessary measures to eradicate from the Americas the spread of doctrines that tend to place in jeopardy the common inter-American democratic ideal'.

The second major concern of the Panama Meeting, economic co-operation, was of particular importance to the Latin American countries, who put forward numerous proposals in this field.[6] But Sumner Welles, head of the United States delegation, was unable to agree to anything specific at this stage. The conference resolved to create an Inter-American Financial and Economic Advisory Committee to study ways of reducing the economic consequences of the war for the American states and of increasing inter-American economic co-operation. It would consist of twenty-one experts, one from each nation, to be installed in Washington not later than 15 November 1939.[7]

The Havana Meeting (1940)

It was recommended that another Meeting of Foreign Ministers should be held at Havana on 1 October 1940 'without prejudice to an

[5] A number of South American governments had wanted a declaration by the American republics during the First World War that the belligerent nations must refrain from committing hostile acts within a reasonable distance from their shores. Reference was made to this in the preamble to the Declaration of Panama.

[6] Latin American concern with economic questions is illustrated 'by the remark of a Cuban commentator that, although the purpose of the Panama Conference was to consider general issues of neutrality and security, "the majority of the Cuban delegation was composed of sugar experts" ' (Wood, *Good Neighbor Policy*, p. 311).

[7] An early project of this committee was the drafting of a convention establishing an inter-American bank, which was opened to signature on 10 May 1940. But it never received the required number of ratifications to come into operation.

earlier meeting if this should be found necessary'. The Second Meeting of Consultation actually met from 21 to 30 July 1940. For in the meantime the international situation had become much more threatening after German occupation of Denmark, Norway, Belgium, Luxembourg, the Netherlands, and much of France. This made more urgent the question—already raised at Panama—of the possible transfer of colonies in the western hemisphere belonging to countries overrun by the Germans. In response to this situation the United States, in effect, reiterated one of the oldest principles of her foreign policy: the no-transfer rule of 1811. A joint resolution of Congress, passed on 17–18 June 1940, stated:

> That the United States would not recognise any transfer, and would not acquiesce in any attempt to transfer, any geographic region of this hemisphere from one non-American power to another non-American power; and . . .
>
> That if such transfer or attempt to transfer should appear likely, the United States shall, *in addition to other measures*, [author's italics] immediately consult with the other American republics to determine upon the steps which should be taken to safeguard their common interests.

At Havana Secretary of State Hull was anxious to obtain support for this resolution, but he found the Latin Americans less enthusiastic. Argentina, as usual, was in the vanguard of the opposition,[8] but, in Hull's own words: 'Another group of delegates argued, in effect: "Your Government sends you down here to commit us to what we've sworn we would never agree to on account of its many abuses— and that's the Monroe Doctrine . . ." '.[9] Latin American objections to the United States resolution were twofold: first, such action was provocative and therefore threatened their neutrality; and, secondly, if anything had to be done in this matter, it should be with the object of ending all colonialism in the western hemisphere. Eventually the United States had her way. The Second Meeting of Foreign Ministers adopted the Act of Habana Concerning the Provisional Administration of European Colonies and Possessions in the Americas. Should a change of sovereignty over any such territories be threatened the

[8] For the initial position of Argentina see Telegram from the US ambassador in Buenos Aires (Armour) to Sec. of State, 20 July 1940, *For. Rel. US, 1940*, v. 235–7. It is of interest that Argentina proposed unofficially after the German violation of Danish and Norwegian neutrality that the American states should assume the status of non-belligerency. The US was not prepared to agree to this. For further details, and a consideration of Argentina's motives in proposing it, see Langer & Gleason, *Challenge to Isolation*, pp. 608–10.

[9] *Memoirs*, i. 824.

American republics would create an emergency committee to administer them. The Havana Meeting also adopted a convention embodying the essential features of the Act and establishing the Inter-American Commission for Territorial Administration, to be composed of representatives of every ratifying state. This commission would take over from the emergency committee established by the Act. Moreover, the latter had said that: 'Should the need for emergency action be so urgent that action by the committee cannot be awaited, any of the American Republics, individually or jointly with others, shall have the right to act in the manner which its own defense or that of the continent requires.' This, in practice, would mean action by the United States.

The Act of Habana is of some interest for the further light it throws on the relationship between the Monroe Doctrine and the inter-American system. In Mecham's view, in accepting the Act, 'the Latin-American nations were formally endorsing the United States' implementation of the no-transfer principle of the Monroe Doctrine'. And he goes on: 'It would be difficult to present more convincing evidence of Latin America's new confidence in the integrity of the United States.'[10] Latin American reluctance to endorse the position already taken up by the United States on this question has already been noted. More importantly, this matter well illustrates the desire of the United States to have 'inter-American' support for the principles embodied in the Monroe Doctrine, a quite different thing from formulating a Pan American policy in co-operation with the other members of the system. This again was true of Resolution XV of the Final Act adopted at Havana.

Resolution XV, entitled 'Reciprocal Assistance and Cooperation for the Defense of the Nations of the Americas', declared:

That any attempt on the part of a non-American State against the integrity or inviolability of the territory, the sovereignty or the political independence of an American State shall be considered as an act of aggression against the States which sign this declaration.

In case acts of aggression are committed or should there be reason to believe that an act of aggression is being prepared by a non-American nation against the integrity or inviolability of the territory, the sovereignty or the political independence of an American nation, the nations signatory to the present declaration will consult among themselves in order to agree upon the measure it may be advisable to take. . . .

---

[10] *The United States and Inter-American Security, 1889–1960*, p. 188.

Although this cannot seriously be held to have 'confirmed the abandonment by the United States of its pretension to act as the sole guardian of the Monroe Doctrine',[11] it certainly 'brought the American republics perceptibly nearer towards the establishment of a genuine system of regional security'.[12] More specifically, Resolution XV provided an inter-American framework for the numerous bilateral reciprocal-assistance agreements subsequently negotiated between the United States and various Latin American countries. For it stated that: 'All the signatory nations, or two or more of them, according to circumstances, shall proceed to negotiate the necessary complementary agreements so as to organize cooperation for defense and the assistance that they shall lend each other in the event of aggressions such as those referred to in this declaration.'

The Havana meeting also dealt with the peaceful solution of conflicts within the hemisphere. In Resolution XIV, it recommended to the Governing Board of the Pan American Union:

that it organize, in the American capital deemed most suitable for the purpose, a committee composed of representatives of five countries, which shall have the duty of keeping constant vigilance to insure that States between which any dispute exists or may arise, of any nature whatsoever, may solve it as quickly as possible, and of suggesting, without detriment to the methods adopted by the parties or to the procedures which they may agree upon, the measures and steps which may be conducive to a settlement.

On 4 December 1940 the Governing Board designated Washington as the seat of the Inter-American Peace Committee (as it came to be called) and selected as members two countries from the north (the United States and Mexico), two from the south (Argentina and Brazil), and one from Central America and the Antilles (Cuba).[13] This committee was destined to play an important role in the inter-American peace machinery during the post-war period, but it never functioned during the war years.

The question of foreign subversive activities was also discussed at Havana, and Resolution VII, 'Diffusion of Doctrines tending to place in Jeopardy the Common Inter-American Democratic Ideal or to threaten the Security and Neutrality of the American Republics', recommended measures to combat them. These included: effective

[11] Humphrey, p. 183.
[12] Humphreys, *Evolution of Modern Latin America*, p. 157.
[13] PAU, *Minutes of Governing Board*, vol. xxxi, pt 3, pp. 420–1.

prohibition of political activity by foreign individuals, groups, or parties; strict supervision of the entry of foreigners into the territory of any American state; effective police supervision of the activities of foreign groups in the hemisphere; and the creation of an emergency penal system for the enforcement of such measures as might be necessary.

Resolution XXV, on economic and financial co-operation, strengthened the Inter-American Financial and Economic Advisory Committee and expanded its work. The committee was instructed, *inter alia*, to consider ways of increasing domestic consumption and mutual exchange among the American nations of commodities formerly exported outside the hemisphere, and to create 'instruments of inter-American cooperation' for storing, financing, and marketing such commodities. It was also to develop commodity arrangements with a view to assuring equitable terms of trade for both producers and consumers; and to recommend methods of improving the standard of living of the peoples of the Americas, including public health and nutrition, and the distribution of part of their surpluses as a humanitarian and social-relief measure. In the meantime, it was to consider 'the desirability of a broader system of inter-American cooperative organization in trade and industrial matters'. Incidentally, just before the Havana meeting, there had been considered in Washington a project for setting up 'a Pan-American trade cartel under the leadership of the United States which would serve as a central planning and action agency to control the trade of all the Western Hemisphere nations with the outside world'.[14] However, this plan was opposed in both the United States and Latin America, and came to nothing.

At Havana the United States had obtained the agreement of the other members of the inter-American system in principle, while remaining free to take specific measures mainly through bilateral arrangements with individual states. Significantly, neither the Convention for the Administration of Colonies nor the Declaration of Reciprocal Assistance required unanimous action for its implementation. One or more signatories could act under them, and this in practice meant the United States and those Latin American countries willing to support her. But, Professor Whitaker pointed out:

It must . . . be recognized that while the abandonment of the rule of unanimity made for more effective action, this advantage was gained at the

¹⁴ Dozer, p. 72.

risk of sowing dissension in Pan American ranks. As a matter of fact, considerable dissension did arise in the course of the next eighteen months and this was due mainly to the new policy towards the war that was gradually developed after the Havana meeting by the United States, independently and without resort to Pan American consultation.[15]

For while 'the guiding principles' of inter-American policy remained 'neutrality and non-involvement in the war', he went on, 'the United States moved slowly but surely towards non-belligerency and all-out aid to the enemies of the Axis'.

Hemisphere Defence and Economic Assistance

From the outbreak of war in Europe, the United States had been more and more preoccupied with problems of hemisphere defence. She neither anticipated nor even desired any sizeable military contribution by the Latin American countries, but she did want base facilities and also co-operation against the subversive activities of Axis agents and sympathizers in Latin America. In view of the role of the military in most Latin American countries it was important to co-operate with it on political grounds, and this involved the supply of arms not strictly geared to the defence of the western hemisphere. The United States increased the number of her service missions in Latin America, eventually replacing those previously furnished by European countries, and extended the provision of facilities for training Latin American officers in her own military academies and training schools.[16]

The United States did not find it easy to obtain the facilities she required, for two main reasons. First, the Latin Americans were apprehensive over the growing United States involvement in the war, which threatened their neutrality; secondly, there were considerations of national sovereignty. They were reluctant—understandably in the light of their experience—to permit United States armed forces on their soil. In Brazil, for example, whose north-eastern 'bulge' was the most vulnerable region of South America, three years of delicate discussions preceded permission to station United States forces. The United States encountered considerable opposition in Panama to her plans for constructing bases outside the Canal Zone. The negotiations have been described as 'certainly among the least edifying in the

[15] Whitaker, ed., *Inter-American Affairs, 1941* (1942), pp. 36–37.
[16] E. Lieuwen, *Arms and Politics in Latin America* (1961), pp. 190 ff.

history of the Good Neighbor Policy'.[17] While they were in progress
the Panamanian government was overthrown, though the United
States denied any responsibility for this. Even so, they dragged on well
into 1942 with Panama seeking new concessions and firm assurances
that United States troops would be withdrawn at the end of the war
in Europe. In the case of Mexico there was the additional complica-
tion of the unsettled oil question. The long-standing boundary dispute
between Ecuador and Peru, which flared up again in the spring of
1941, not only threatened the peace of the hemisphere; it delayed
United States efforts to secure the use of the strategically important
(Ecuadoran) Galápagos Islands. The most co-operative Latin
American government was, significantly, that of the Dominican
Republic. President Trujillo's offer of 4 December 1939 has been
described as 'virtually a blank check for the forces of the United States
to make use of the territory of the Dominican Republic as they saw
fit'.[18]

Inter-American economic co-operation, though as we have seen
the subject of general agreements reached at Panama and Havana,
depended in practice, as did defence measures, on initiatives taken by
the United States. Broadly speaking, the Roosevelt administration
aimed at strengthening the economies of the Latin American countries
(as well, of course, as that of the United States) and weakening the
economic position hitherto enjoyed south of the Rio Grande by the
Axis powers. These objectives involved obtaining strategic raw
materials from Latin America, needed by the United States and
increasingly difficult for the Latin American producers to sell elsewhere; ensuring the Latin Americans a supply of manufactured goods
at reasonable prices; and developing 'new lines of Latin American
production for which a new or complementary market can be found
in the United States or in other republics of the Western Hemisphere'.
For the latter purpose, the Financial and Economic Advisory Committee set up in June 1940 an Inter-American Development Commission. Also established by the Committee were an Inter-American
Coffee Board, to stabilize the coffee market in the interests of both
producers and consumers, and the Inter-American Maritime
Technical Commission to deal with problems of shipping. There were
numerous bilateral agreements between the United States and indi-

---

[17] Langer and Gleason, *The Undeclared War, 1940–1941* (1953), p. 615. For
an account of military collaboration between the US and Latin America prior
to Pearl Harbour, including negotiations for bases, see pp. 596–624.
[18] E. O. Guerrant, *Roosevelt's Good Neighbor Policy* (1950), p. 155.

vidual Latin American countries which included the granting of credits, provided almost entirely at this stage by the (United States) Export-Import Bank. On the eve of the Havana Conference President Roosevelt had requested Congress to increase the lending authority of the Export-Import Bank by $500 millions 'to the end that the Bank may be of greater assistance to our neighbors south of the Rio Grande, including financing the handling and orderly marketing of some part of their surpluses'.[19]

In addition to these measures, the Roosevelt administration set up in August 1940, the Office for Coordination of Commercial and Cultural Relations between the American Republics, later called the Office of the Coordinator of Inter-American Affairs (CIAA). Its object was to promote 'hemisphere defense, with particular reference to the commercial and cultural aspects of the problem'. The co-ordinator was Nelson A. Rockefeller, who had presented to the Secretary of Commerce in the previous June a paper on *Hemisphere Economic Policy* proposing a degree of planning which, however, had proved unacceptable to the administration though the President had at first favoured a 'cartel' project based on it.[20] The work of CIAA covered a wide range of activities, including economic development, technical assistance, transportation, education, sanitation, and public health, as well as cultural exchanges. Opinions of its achievements vary. The money it cost the United States has been described as representing 'a phenomenally large investment in goodwill'.[21] The value of the investment in those terms is debatable, but there is no doubt the United States was anxious to limit Axis influence in Latin America and increase goodwill towards herself. For Latin Americans had become apprehensive over the shift of United States policy away from strict neutrality and resentful of her pressures to align them with her. On the eve of Pearl Harbour the United States had not achieved the degree of co-operation from Latin America she could have wished for, although it may have been 'in a world of human frailty . . . perhaps as much as could have been expected from a community of twenty independent countries'.[22]

[19] Langer & Gleason, *Challenge to Isolation*, p. 695.
[20] Ibid. pp. 632–5.
[21] Dozer, p. 116.
[22] Langer & Gleason, *Undeclared War*, p. 624. They were, in fact, referring to Latin American support for the United States following the Japanese attack. It is astonishing that Mecham, p. 208, should assert that 'when war came to the Americas the respective states were able to glide smoothly and naturally into their predetermined roles as cobelligerents'.

The Wartime Partnership

Two days after the Japanese attack on Pearl Harbour the United States informed the other American republics of her desire to hold, at the earliest possible moment, a consultative meeting in conformity with Resolution XV adopted at Havana.[23] The Third Meeting of Consultation of Ministers of Foreign Affairs of the American Republics took place in Rio de Janeiro from 15 to 28 January 1942. Already the nine Central American and Caribbean countries (Costa Rica, Cuba, the Dominican Republic, Guatemala, Haiti, Honduras, Nicaragua, Panama, and El Salvador) had declared war on the Axis powers, while Colombia, Mexico, and Venezuela had severed diplomatic relations with them. The remaining Latin American countries had proclaimed their non-belligerency and affirmed their faith in the principle of continental solidarity. However, it is important to note that ten American countries were at war while eleven were not. Moreover, the ten belligerents had signed the Declaration of the United Nations on 1–2 January 1942, two weeks before the Rio meeting opened—without any reference to the inter-American system.

The most important United States objective at Rio de Janeiro was the adoption of a resolution by which all the American republics would sever relations with the Axis powers.[24] This proved impossible to achieve, for Argentina and Chile[25] refused to subscribe to such a document. For the sake of unanimity a weaker resolution, merely recommending breaking off relations, was adopted. In his *Memoirs*, Cordell Hull recorded his anger that Sumner Welles, who headed the United States delegation, had accepted this formula which, in the Secretary of State's view, was 'the equivalent of a surrender to Argentina'.[26] Chile's unwillingness to break off relations with the Axis powers was not unreasonable in view of her long and vulnerable coastline; she made an unsuccessful attempt to obtain economic and military aid from the United States as a condition of making the break. Argentina's policy corresponded with her traditional attitude, now reinforced by the pro-Nazi sympathies of her government.[27] By

---

[23] Hull, *Memoirs*, ii. 1143.   [24] *For. Rel. US, 1942*, v. 23.
[25] It is interesting to note that Chile cabled to the Chairman of the Governing Board of the PAU on 9 Dec. 1941 (presumably after receiving the US memorandum on the subject) requesting consideration of the advisability of holding a Meeting of Consultation (*Int. Conf. Am. States*, 2nd Suppl., p. 3).
[26] Hull, ii. 1149. Welles rebuts Hull's criticism in his *Seven Major Decisions* (1951), pp. 101–25.
[27] Senator Tom Connally, Chairman of the Senate Foreign Relations Committee, did not help matters by suggesting that the Argentine people might change

the end of the Rio meeting all the Latin American republics except Argentina and Chile had severed diplomatic relations with the Axis powers.

In addition, the Meeting recommended the severance of commercial and financial relations with the Axis powers. It established an Inter-American Defense Board in Washington to study and recommend to the American governments measures necessary for the defence of the continent. Another new agency created at Rio was the Emergency Advisory Committee for Political Defense, composed of seven members, to study and coordinate measures against subversive activities. There was to be an Inter-American Conference on Co-ordination of Police and Judicial Measures. The Inter-American Neutrality Committee became the Inter-American Juridical Committee, with expanded scope. A number of resolutions aimed at increased economic co-operation were also adopted.

Of special significance was the inclusion of a resolution (XXV) on post-war problems. The Third Meeting of Foreign Ministers resolved:

1. To request the Governing Board of the Pan American Union to con-voke an Inter-American Technical Economic Conference charged with the study of present and post-war economic problems.
2. To entrust the Inter-American Juridical Committee with the formula-tion of specific recommendations relative to the international organiza-tion in the juridical and political fields, and in the field of international security.
3. To entrust the Inter-American Financial and Economic Advisory Com-mittee with a similar function in the economic field, to make the necessary preparations for the Inter-American Technical Economic Conference, referred to in the first paragraph of this Resolution.
4. To request the Pan American Union to appoint an Executive Com-mittee to receive such projects as the American nations may present, and to submit said projects, respectively, to the Inter-American Juridical Committee and to the Inter-American Financial and Economic Ad-visory Committee.
5. To request the Pan American Union to direct this Executive Com-mittee to submit the recommendations of the Inter-American Juridical Committee to the Governments of the American Republics so that the conclusions reached may be adopted at a subsequent Meeting of Ministers of Foreign Affairs.

---

their President if he did not change his policy (see D. H. Popper, 'The Rio de Janeiro Conference of 1942', *Foreign Policy Reports*, xviii/3 (1942), p. 30).

6. To request the Pan American Union to determine, in agreement with the Governments of the American Republics, the date and place of meeting of the Inter-American Technical Economic Conference, referred to in the first paragraph of this Resolution.

Two further resolutions of the Rio meeting are of particular interest. One of these (XXII) was an endorsement of the Good Neighbour policy, declaring 'that the principle that international conduct must be inspired by the policy of the good neighbor is a norm of international law of the American Continent'. The other, headed 'Support and Adherence to the Principles of the "Atlantic Charter" ', expressed 'satisfaction with the inclusion in that document of principles which constitute a part of the juridical heritage of America in accordance with the Convention on Rights and Duties of States approved at the Seventh International Conference of American States, held at Montevideo in 1933' (XXXV). On the day after the Rio meeting ended a Protocol of Peace, Friendship and Boundaries was signed by Ecuador and Peru.[28] The ABC powers and the United States had taken the opportunity to work out a compromise procedure for settling the boundary dispute between these two countries.

Although strongly desiring the Latin American countries to sever diplomatic and commercial relations with the Axis powers, the United States did not want the remaining non-belligerents to make declarations of war. The Inter-American Defense Board was established for political rather than military reasons: to give the Latin Americans a sense of participation in a joint effort to ensure the security of the hemisphere. The work of the Board would in any case be limited by the different degrees to which its members were involved in the war. Brazil and Mexico declared war later in 1942, thus bringing the total number of belligerents up to twelve; while Bolivia and Colombia did so the following year. But, for most of the war period, the remaining South American countries went no further than severing diplomatic relations; Chile did not do even this until a later stage, and Argentina remained neutral much longer. For this reason, and because of the dominant role necessarily played by the United States, military co-operation was conducted essentially on a bilateral basis. Even before the Inter-American Defense Board was set up in Washington the United States had established joint defence

---

[28] This did not end the matter, however, for Ecuador felt she had been forced to make a disadvantageous agreement for the sake of inter-American unity. See below, pp. 238–9.

commissions with Mexico and Brazil, and further negotiations with Latin American countries, including Lend-Lease arrangements, were conducted bilaterally. Although there was some co-operation in air and naval patrolling against Axis submarines, the United States bore by far the main burden of hemisphere defence. According to an official statement more than 100,000 United States troops were stationed in Latin America during the Second World War.[29] Only Brazil and Mexico sent armed forces overseas, though it must be stated that the United States discouraged a number of offers to do so by other Latin American countries because of the difficulties involved in administering small contingents.

Truly 'inter-American' military co-operation was therefore very limited. Lend-Lease aid was furnished to eighteen Latin American countries,[30] totalling some $475 millions, of which over 70 per cent went to Brazil, who contributed an expeditionary force and provided special facilities for air transport. Otherwise the main purpose of Lend-Lease was to strengthen existing Latin American governments against possible overthrow by Axis-sponsored revolutions and make them more co-operative in granting facilities required by the United States. Specifically, this involved fostering the goodwill of the military leaders in these countries, a policy which laid the United States open to criticism of supporting dictatorships.

While the United States did not seek active military support from her southern neighbours, she was anxious for their co-operation in combating Axis subversion in the hemisphere. The Emergency Advisory Committee for Political Defense was much more active than the Inter-American Defense Board. It comprised seven members, nominated by the governments of Argentina, Brazil, Chile, Mexico, the United States, Uruguay, and Venezuela. In theory, the members of the committee represented the American nations as a whole; in practice they did, of course, consult their own governments and receive advice from them. The Emergency Advisory Committee held its first meeting at Montevideo on 15 April 1942, and elected as its chairman Dr Alberto Guani, the Uruguayan Foreign Minister. Most of the American states co-operated with the committee in taking measures to control pro-Axis subversion within their own frontiers. The committee's publication of reports[31] on widespread Nazi

---

[29] *DSB*, xxviii/718 (1953), p. 466.
[30] Argentina and Panama (who was given aid under special provisions for the protection of the Panama Canal Zone) did not receive Lend-Lease funds.
[31] They were actually memoranda submitted by the US.

espionage activities in Chile and Argentina[32] had important repercussions. In Chile it helped bring about a severance of diplomatic
relations with the Axis powers in January 1943. In the case of
Argentina, the committee's persistent denunciations—and the anom-
aly of her serving on it—caused her withdrawal just after the termination of her membership had been recommended by that body.[33]

The main objectives of United States economic policy towards
Latin America had been formulated between the outbreak of war in
Europe and the Rio Meeting. After Pearl Harbour they remained
fundamentally the same: to ensure an increasing supply of strategic
raw materials; to strengthen the economies of the Latin American
countries in the interest of the war effort; and to eliminate Axis concerns in the western hemisphere. The Rio Meeting provided for co-
operation between the Inter-American Financial and Economic
Advisory Committee and national commissions from each country to
promote the 'economic mobilization' of the resources of the Americas.
A number of wartime specialized conferences were held, though not
the Inter-American Technical Economic Conference to study present
and post-war economic problems called for in Resolution XXV of the
Final Act at Rio.[34] But, as with military co-operation, most economic
co-operation was on a bilateral basis.

Procuring strategic raw materials was particularly important because it involved not merely ensuring supplies for United States war
industries and denying such materials to the Axis powers, but also
the economic stability of Latin American countries which were so
dependent upon their export. Financial assistance was given to Latin
American countries mainly through the Export-Import Bank and
technical assistance through the Institute of Inter-American Affairs,
a subsidiary of the Office of the Coordinator of Inter-American
Affairs. Created in March 1942 for the purpose of improving the
health and welfare of the Latin American peoples in collaboration
with their governments, this institute promoted technical programmes
as well as projects for health, sanitation, and food supply. The
United States also took steps to improve transport facilities, including
an abortive attempt to complete the Inter-American Highway from

[32] Emergency Advisory Committee for Political Defense, *Annual Report Submitted to the Governments of the American Republics, July, 1943* (Montevideo, 1943),
pp. 85–129.

[33] Ibid. *2nd Ann. Rep.*, pp. 6–10.

[34] The long delay in holding this conference caused increasing discontent among
the Latin Americans.

the Mexican-Guatemalan border to Panama City. She was successful in bringing about the elimination of Axis-owned airlines in Latin America. But she was unable to supply the Latin Americans with sufficient manufactured goods during the war period, and no civilian supplies were furnished under Lend-Lease.

Meanwhile, in accordance with Resolution XXV of the Rio Meeting, the Governing Board of the Pan American Union had appointed an Executive Committee on Post War Problems which published towards the end of 1944 a report entitled *Pan American Postwar Organization, Observations and Suggestions of the Executive Committee.* Among its suggestions for strengthening the inter-American system was that there should be greater coordination between the Pan American Union and the various inter-American agencies. It also recommended eliminating some wartime agencies and preserving others. The Inter-American Juridical Committee submitted two reports to the Executive Committee (in 1942 and 1944) which, however, stressed the importance of a world organization. By the end of 1944, following the Dumbarton Oaks Conference, the question of regionalism in relation to a general international organization had become an important one in planning the future of the inter-American system.

New Stresses and Strains

Long before the end of 1944, however, inter-American co-operation was running into difficulties. A year earlier a revolution occurred in Bolivia which the United States government believed to be the work of pro-Axis forces plotting in Argentina. This almost led the United States to publish an indictment of Argentina and impose heavy economic sanctions upon her. Such a unilateral step undoubtedly would have strained relations between the United States and other Latin American countries. It was averted by Argentina's belated severance of diplomatic relations with the Axis powers at the end of January 1944. The Emergency Advisory Committee for Political Defense, obviously pressed by the United States, resolved on 24 December 1943:

> To recommend to the American Governments which have declared war on the Axis Powers or have broken relations with them, that for the duration of the present world conflict they do not proceed to the recognition of a new government instituted by force, before consulting among themselves for the purpose of determining whether this government complies

K

with the inter-American undertakings for the defense of the Continent, nor before carrying out an exchange of information as to the circumstances which have determined the establishment of the said government.[35]

A further resolution, on 5 January 1944, applied this formula to the new government of Bolivia and recommended that consultation and exchange of information should be conducted through regular diplomatic channels.[36] The United States opposed a consultative meeting which might have produced criticism of the 'Guani Doctrine'[37] as a form of intervention. Argentina, who denounced the recommendation as exceeding the committee's authority and as constituting intervention in the internal affairs of another country, recognized the Bolivian government on 3 January 1944. The United States and the other Latin American countries did not do so until changes had been made in that government and it had taken certain steps to fulfil its obligations to hemisphere security and the United Nations. As one of these steps the Bolivian government 'turned over to the United States for secret deportation, eighty-seven persons selected by United States intelligence agencies as the most dangerous Axis agents in the country'.[38] The Bolivian affair did not enhance the prestige of the United States, for she had virtually forced a policy of non-recognition upon the other Latin American countries (except Argentina), while paying lip-service to the principle of consultation.

Relations between the United States and Argentina soon deteriorated still further, producing more strain on the inter-American system. When President Ramírez was overthrown and replaced by General Farrell in February 1944, the United States refused to recognize the new Argentine government. The other Latin American countries, except Bolivia, Chile, and Paraguay, followed suit, though Ecuador joined these three 'recalcitrants' after a revolutionary change of her own government in June 1944. The United States wanted to take stronger action against the rulers of Argentina, of whom, incidentally, Colonel Juan Perón was becoming the outstanding— and, from the United States point of view, most provocative—figure. President Roosevelt himself condemned the Argentine government for repudiating 'solemn inter-American obligations'. He accused it of being under Nazi-Fascist influence and using Nazi-Fascist methods.

---

[35] Emergency Advisory Committee for Political Defense, *2nd Ann. Rep.*, p. 79.
[36] Ibid. p. 92.
[37] So called after the name of the committee's chairman.
[38] L. Duggan, *The Americas: the Search for Hemisphere Security* (1949), p. 107.

There was considerable domestic pressure in the United States for strong action against Argentina. In the event, the Roosevelt administration's fulminations did not prove a prelude to serious economic sanctions[39]—still less to something more drastic. It had become clear that the other Latin American countries did not support this threatening attitude towards Argentina. Moreover, there was growing resentment of United States pressure to get them into line through bilateral diplomatic channels instead of calling a Meeting of Consultation as some Latin American governments wanted.[40] It was essentially a quarrel between the United States and Argentina in which the other Latin American countries were anxious not to have to take sides. The United States was embarrassed by a request made by Argentina to the Governing Board of the Pan American Union for a Meeting of American Foreign Ministers to consider the issue.

The problems of Bolivia and Argentina were symptomatic of a general weakening of the wartime partnership between the United States and Latin America now becoming increasingly evident. But a deterioration in inter-American relations was inherent in the partnership itself. For while the Good Neighbour had refrained from intervention in the affairs of the Latin Americans, the wartime partner was more and more involved in them. The military bases, the FBI agents searching for subversives,[41] the corps of administrators and business men directing all kinds of co-operation: these represented massive intervention. During the war Latin America became ever more conscious of United States economic power which, whether applied in the form of aid or sanctions, gave the policy of partnership the character of dollar diplomacy. An outstanding consequence of United States aid (economic and military) was to strengthen Brazil, whose contribution to the war effort was by far the most important of any Latin American nation, at the expense of Argentina, the most unco-operative. There was also the question of providing Latin American governments with weapons which might be used against democratic opposition groups or against each other. It is not surprising that the great increase of United States activity in Latin America, although

---

[39] Such sanctions, to be effective, required the co-operation of Great Britain, who was not willing, for reasons of trade and investments in Argentina, to give it.

[40] For instance, in Jan. 1944, Mexico had proposed a Meeting of Foreign Ministers to consider the question of recognizing the Bolivian government, and, in the following August, she proposed a similar meeting to consider the problem of Argentina.

[41] During the war about 1,000 enemy aliens were deported from Latin America to custody in the US (Mecham, p. 233).

often of a beneficent nature, failed to engender Latin American affection for her.

United States future policy towards Latin America was brought into doubt by the resignation of Sumner Welles from his post as Under Secretary of State in August 1943. After an inauspicious start in Cuba,[42] Welles had come to be recognized as the chief architect of the Good Neighbour policy. His resignation was generally interpreted as the result of personal differences with Secretary Hull rather than differences over policy, but it was regarded with misgivings in Latin America. Moreover, Welles was subsequently very critical of Hull's handling of the Argentine problem.[43] The next two years saw several changes in the office of Assistant Secretary of State in charge of relations with the other American republics. Undoubtedly there was a lack of consistency in United States Latin American policy during that period.[44] In the year Welles resigned, it was strongly attacked in a magazine article by a Republican Senator as one of 'hemispheric handout'.[45] The Senator's attack provoked much adverse comment in Latin America as well as in the United States.

Another important factor weakening inter-American co-operation was the disappearance of the threat to the security of the western hemisphere. For while the United States was still engaged in a great war in other parts of the world, the Latin Americans were becoming more concerned over post-war economic problems and how their powerful neighbour intended to assist in solving them. Their economies had been distorted by the war. The United States procurement programmes had increased the already heavy dependence of Latin American countries on the production of a few key raw materials, for which demand would inevitably fall when the war was over. Even when new production lines had been developed these would not be competitive in peace-time conditions. Some Latin American countries had accumulated substantial dollar reserves because the United States had been unable to supply the goods they wanted to purchase. They were anxious about the availability and prices of these things when wartime controls were lifted, and the United States was unwilling to commit herself to post-war planning in this field. Soon the

[42] See above, pp. 81 ff.
[43] In his *Seven Major Decisions*, p. 110, Welles described Hull as having a 'violent antipathy to Argentina' which became 'an obsession'.
[44] It had already suffered considerably from the clash of personalities and disagreements between various agencies of the US government. See, for example, Langer & Gleason, *Challenge to Isolation*, pp. 278-9.
[45] Burr & Hussey, ii. 154.

Latin Americans were complaining of the sacrifices they had made to supply the United States with war materials at low prices. Between the concept of 'handouts' on the one hand and 'sacrifices' on the other there was ample scope for ill-feeling.

If the Latin Americans feared the United States would neglect their economic problems they had a different apprehension over the military bases built during the war years. They began to suspect the United States of seeking to retain them when the war was over, and such a course had its advocates in the United States Congress.[46] As early as 1943 the Merritt Report had recommended that steps should be taken to obtain the use after the war of the air bases the United States had built in Latin America. This aroused vigorous protests in Ecuador, for the Galápagos Islands were specifically mentioned. Brazil likewise made plain her opposition to the continued use of bases on her soil and there were acrimonious exchanges with Panama over the bases outside the Canal Zone before the United States finally gave way.

Post-War Problems: The Mexico City Conference

Difficulty arose also from the growing United States involvement in plans for establishing a world organization. Specifically, the Latin American countries resented United States failure to consult them prior to the Dumbarton Oaks Conference, where provisional plans for the world organization were formulated. And when the conference's proposals were made known they were dissatisfied with the status of regional agencies, which, although they were to be recognized and even encouraged, were subject to important restrictions by the Security Council without whose authorization they could not take enforcement action.[47] The Dumbarton Oaks proposals and the circumstances under which they were drawn up emphasized the growing divergence of interests between the United States as a great power, now preparing to take a leading part in world affairs commensurate with her strength, and the Latin American countries as small powers, apprehensive over the dominant position in the United Nations which the great powers were allocating to themselves. The Latin Americans were aware that within the United States administration there was a conflict of views between those who wished to

---

[46] Dozer, pp. 134–6.
[47] It should be noted that, at this point, the inter-American system contained no provision for the imposition of sanctions.

maintain and strengthen the inter-American system and those who took the 'universalist' standpoint. Further resentment was caused early in 1945 when the United States, who had not pressed them to do so earlier, suddenly informed Chile, Ecuador, Paraguay, Peru, Uruguay, and Venezuela that they would have to declare a state of belligerency against Germany and Japan in order to be invited to the San Francisco Conference establishing the new world organization.

The Latin Americans thus had a number of reasons for desiring a Meeting of Consultation with the United States. They wanted to reach a settlement of the Argentine problem; to consider the future of the inter-American system in the light of the Dumbarton Oaks proposals and the growing United States preoccupation with the world organization; and above all, to discuss their post-war economic problems. The United States recently had shown little inclination to consult with her neighbours, and actually had opposed a meeting to discuss Argentina. Aware of the growing deterioration in her relations with Latin America, she finally agreed in December 1944 to a conference the following February in Mexico City. But, in order to exclude Argentina, it was to be a meeting of those American countries who had co-operated in the war effort. To make this procedure acceptable to the Latin American countries, the United States agreed to consider the Argentine problem after the main topics had been dealt with. The agenda of the conference was arranged through direct diplomatic negotiations instead of by the Governing Board of the Pan American Union of which, of course, Argentina was a member. El Salvador was at first excluded from the conference because her government was not recognized by a majority of the other American governments, but during the proceedings recognition and admission were granted.

The Inter-American Conference on Problems of War and Peace, held in Mexico City (21 February–8 March 1945), is classified as one of the 'special' conferences.[48] Of its status it has been said, however: 'there can be no doubt that, from a juridical point of view, the Mexico City Conference was a purely diplomatic Conference of Allies, outside of the Inter-American System'. But the same writer considered that Argentina's subsequent adherence to the conference's Final Act gave the meeting a retroactive competence to deal with the reorganiza-

---

[48] The other two previous 'special' conferences were the International Conference of American States on Conciliation and Arbitration (see above, pp. 71–72) and the Inter-American Conference for the Maintenance of Peace (see above, pp. 94–102).

tion of the inter-American system.[49] The agenda of the Mexico City Conference was as follows:

1. Further cooperative measures for the prosecution of the war to complete victory.
2. Consideration of problems of international organization for the maintenance of peace and collective security.
   a) World organization;
   b) The further development of the inter-American system and its coordination with the world organization.
3. Consideration of the economic and social problems of the Americas.
   a) Economic cooperation during the war and in the transition period;
   b) Consideration of methods to develop such cooperation for the improvement of economic and social conditions of the peoples of the Americas, with a view to raising their standard of living.
4. Pursuant to the desires of the Governments consulted, whenever the foregoing topics are disposed of, consideration would be given to the resolution adopted by the Governing Board of the Pan American Union at its meeting on Monday, January 8, relative to the request of the Argentine Government.

The Director General of the Pan American Union (Dr Leo S. Rowe) attended the conference as an 'Honorary Member', and the General Secretariat of the League of Nations and the International Labour Office were represented by observers.

The work of the conference on the first item of the agenda was concerned mainly with continuing and increasing existing cooperation. Two resolutions dealing with war problems recommended the surrender of war criminals (VI) and called for the elimination of centres of subversive influence (VII). The wartime Inter-American Defense Board was to function pending the establishment of a permanent military agency (Resolution IV), but the Inter-American Financial and Economic Advisory Committee was replaced by the permanent Inter-American Economic and Social Council (Resolution IX, 7). This last change was part of the reorganization of the inter-American system. The Latin American countries by now were much more interested in post-war problems than in the war effort.

The Latin Americans had a great deal to say about the world organization, for they objected to many features of the Dumbarton

[49] Josef L. Kunz, 'The Inter-American Conference on Problems of War and Peace at Mexico City and the Problem of the Reorganization of the Inter-American System', *AJIL*, xxxix/3 (1945), pp. 527–8.

Oaks proposals. Since the United States was one of the sponsors of these proposals, however, her delegation at Mexico City refused to support the numerous amendments desired by most of the Latin American countries. Nor would Secretary of State Stettinius (who had succeeded Hull in December 1944) commit himself before the San Francisco Conference to a declaration favouring autonomy for the inter-American system. Under United States pressure, the Mexico City Conference gave the Dumbarton Oaks proposals a general endorsement as constituting 'a basis for, and a valuable contribution to the setting up of, a General Organization. . . .' But the same resolution (XXX) also contained

the following points regarding which a consensus exists among the American Republics represented in this Conference that did not participate in the Dumbarton Oaks conversations:

a) The aspiration of universality as an ideal toward which the Organization should tend in future;
b) The desirability of amplifying and making more specific the enumeration of the principles and purposes of the Organization;
c) The desirability of amplifying and making more specific the powers of the General Assembly in order that its action, as the fully representative organ of the international community may be rendered effective, harmonizing the powers of the Security Council with such amplification;
d) The desirability of extending the jurisdiction and competence of the International Tribunal or Court of Justice;
e) The desirability of creating an international agency specially charged with promoting intellectual and moral cooperation among nations;
f) The desirability of solving controversies and questions of an inter-American character, preferably in accordance with inter-American methods and procedures, in harmony with those of the General International Organization;
g) The desirability of giving an adequate representation to Latin America on the Security Council.

The main purpose of these points was to reduce the dominant role of the great powers. Latin American concern over the future of the inter-American system was also evident. The Secretary General of the conference was charged with transmitting this resolution and the observations of individual Latin American governments to all the nations invited to the San Francisco Conference and to the conference itself.

The most significant resolutions adopted at Mexico City concerned the future of the inter-American system: 'Reciprocal Assistance and American Solidarity' (VIII) and 'Reorganization, Consolidation and Strengthening of the Inter-American System' (IX). Resolution VIII, known as the Act of Chapultepec,[50] contained some important innovations in the field of inter-American peace and security. It declared that: 'The security and solidarity of the Continent are affected to the same extent by an act of aggression against any of the American States by a non-American State, as by an act of aggression of an American State against one or more American States'.[51] Such aggression against one or more of them would be considered aggression against them all. The Act of Chapultepec provided for sanctions (including the use of armed force) in principle, though without laying down any procedure through which they would be adopted. The pledge to use sanctions was restricted to the duration of the war,[52] but the Act of Chapultepec looked forward to the conclusion of a treaty embodying these obligations in permanent form. On the insistence of the United States delegation, the Act of Chapultepec contained the proviso that:

The above Declaration and Recommendation constitute a regional arrangement for dealing with such matters relating to the maintenance of international peace and security as are appropriate for regional action in this Hemisphere. The said arrangement, and the pertinent activities and procedures, shall be consistent with the purposes and principles of the general international organization, when established.

Since under the Dumbarton Oaks proposals no enforcement action might be taken by regional agencies without prior authorization by the Security Council of the world organization, a crucial issue was involved here for the future of the inter-American system.

Resolution IX of the Final Act at Mexico City provided for some far-reaching changes in the inter-American system. The International Conferences of American States were to meet normally at four-year intervals instead of five as hitherto and 'shall be the inter-American organ entrusted with the formulation of general inter-American

---

[50] After the castle in Mexico City where it was signed.

[51] This was an advance upon the Havana declaration, which had been limited to aggression by a non-American state against an American state.

[52] The US administration was able to undertake these obligations in wartime under the President's executive powers. The treaty which was adumbrated for the post-war period would, of course, require 'the advice and consent' of the Senate.

policy and the determination of the structure and functions of inter-American instruments and agencies'. The next International Conference would be at Bogotá in 1946. There were to be regular annual Meetings of the Ministers of Foreign Affairs (called by the Governing Board of the Pan American Union), except in those years when there was an International Conference of American States. The next regular Meeting would be in 1947. The Meetings 'shall be charged with taking decisions on problems of great urgency and importance concerning the inter-American system and with regard to situations and disputes of every kind which may disturb the peace of the American Republics'.

The Governing Board of the Pan American Union would be composed 'of one *ad hoc* delegate designated by each of the American Republics, which delegates shall have the rank of Ambassadors and shall enjoy the corresponding privileges and immunities, but shall not be part of the diplomatic mission accredited to the government of the country in which the Pan American Union has its seat'. The Chairman of the Governing Board was to be elected annually and would not be eligible for re-election for the term immediately following. The constant re-election of the United States representative (no longer the Secretary of State) was thus made impossible and the chairmanship was opened to Latin Americans. The Director General and Assistant Director General of the Pan American Union were to be chosen by the Governing Board for a term of ten years; they would not be eligible for re-election, nor could they be succeeded by persons of the same nationality. These measures represented a considerable modification of the policy of the United States, whose opposition to such changes at previous conferences has been noted.

The functions of the Governing Board were to be enlarged. In addition to its existing ones it was to

take action, within the limitations imposed upon it by the International Conferences of American States or pursuant to the specific direction of the Meetings of Ministers of Foreign Affairs, on every matter that affects the effective functioning of the inter-American system and the solidarity and general welfare of the American Republics;

to call the regular Meetings of Ministers of Foreign Affairs and special meetings when requested, 'to consider exclusively emergency questions. In the latter case the call shall be made upon the vote of an absolute majority of the Board;' and to supervise the inter-American agencies 'which are or may become related to the Pan

American Union, and . . . receive and approve annual or special reports from these agencies'. Moreover, the Governing Board, 'availing itself of all Pan American agencies that it deems appropriate', was 'charged with preparing, beginning May 1, 1945, a draft charter for the improvement and strengthening of the Pan American system. The Governing Board shall submit the draft to the Governments of the Continent prior to December 31, 1945.'

The third topic on the agenda of the Mexico City Conference (consideration of the economic and social problems of the Americas) aroused most interest among the Latin American delegates as the opening speech by the Mexican Foreign Minister, Ezequiel Padilla, underlined.[53] The Latin Americans were eager to receive concrete assurances from the United States of assistance over the difficult period of transition from war to peacetime trading conditions. They received from Assistant Secretary Clayton what Professor Whitaker described as

general (rather too general) assurances of aid from the United States. . . . On the other hand, they were specifically urged to lower their trade barriers —which to them meant placing their newly developed industries in competition with the older, larger, and more efficient industries of the United States. The net result of the address and the discussion that followed it was to stress the essentially bilateral character of "inter-American" economic relations and the dichotomy between economically "colonial" Latin America and the economically mature United States.[54]

The United States formula for improving living standards in Latin America was one of expanding economies based on discarding tariffs, the encouragement of private capital, and the banning of state enterprises. Most of the Latin Americans regarded United States policy as designed to expand her own trade and investment and did not accept it as being in their interests.[55] The Economic Charter of the Americas and the various other resolutions adopted at Mexico City contributed nothing practicable to the solution of Latin America's economic problems. The Inter-American Technical Economic Conference was fixed for 15 June 1945 at Washington. It was over three years since the decision to hold this conference had been taken at Rio de Janeiro; many years of further delay were to come. In brief, as Lloyd Mecham

[53] Inter-American Conference on Problems of War and Peace, *Diario* (1945), pp. 25–26.
[54] *Inter-American Affairs, 1945*, pp. 12–13.
[55] Cf. L. Enríquez, 'A Latin Looks at Chapultepec', *The Inter-American*, iv/4 (1945), pp. 16–17.

has put it: 'With respect to meeting Latin-American desires on the economic front, it must be recorded that the Mexico City conference was short on concrete programs but long on glowing generalities.'[56]

As agreed beforehand, the Argentine question was considered after the other major items. Evidently the United States had now decided to make her peace with Argentina before the United Nations conference at San Francisco; the other Latin American countries were also anxious that unity should be re-established by Argentina's adherence to the decisions taken at Mexico City. So Resolution LIX of the Final Act declared:

... that the Conference hopes that the Argentine Nation will cooperate with the other American Nations, identifying itself with the common policy these nations are pursuing, and orienting its own policy so that it may achieve its incorporation into the United Nations as a signatory to the Joint Declaration entered into by them.

... that the Final Act of this Conference shall be open to adherence by the Argentine Nation, in accordance with the criteria of this resolution, and to authorize His Excellency Dr. Ezequiel Padilla, President of the Conference, to communicate the resolutions of this assembly to the Argentine Government through the Pan American Union.

The Argentine Government responded by adhering to the Final Act; declaring war against the Axis powers; and agreeing to take immediately

the measures necessary for a state of belligerency, as well as those required to put to a definite end, all activity of persons, firms and enterprises of whatever nationality, that might endanger the security of the State or interfere with the war effort of the United Nations or threaten the peace, welfare and security of the American nations.[57]

This settlement of the Argentine problem, involving a complete reversal of United States policy towards the Farrell government over the previous year, served its immediate purpose of patching up inter-American unity before the San Francisco Conference. But the fundamental differences between the United States administration and the Argentine government had not been removed, and it was only a matter of time before the problem arose again in an acute form.

A number of other noteworthy resolutions were adopted at the

---

[56] Mecham, p. 266.
[57] PAU, *Minutes of Special Meeting of Governing Board . . . March 31, 1945,* App. B, p. 2.

Mexico City Conference. Resolution XXXIX recommended the Inter-American Juridical Committee immediately to draft an Inter-American Peace System, coordinating existing agreements for the prevention and pacific solution of inter-American controversies. The same body was requested to prepare, for consideration and approval by the Ninth International Conference, an Inter-American Charter of Social Guarantees.[58] It was asked to draw up also a draft Declaration of the International Rights and Duties of Man (XL) and to study a project presented by the delegation of Guatemala entitled 'Defense and Preservation of Democracy in America Against the Possible Establishment of Anti-Democratic Regimes in the Continent' (XXXVIII). These subjects would raise very important issues indeed if they were followed up seriously. There was a resolution on racial discrimination (XLI); and a Tribute to Canada (XXII) which could be interpreted as a gesture designed to encourage that country to join the inter-American system. The Declaration of Mexico (XI) restated the principles of the inter-American system along the lines of those made at Buenos Aires and Lima, but emphasized such matters as the rights of man, the social obligations of states, and the importance of economic co-operation.

The Mexico City Conference has generally been considered among the more successful inter-American conferences, especially in view of the difficult situation facing the American nations. Of course some of the problems, such as the future of the military bases built by the United States in Latin American countries and that of the European colonies in the western hemisphere,[59] were not discussed by the conference. Laurence Duggan, a leading member of the State Department 'team' who developed the Good Neighbour policy,[60] made the interesting observation that:

Desire to bar Soviet influence from the Americas was one of the reasons for the success of the Mexico City Conference. It was an intangible factor, something no delegate frankly stated, and the importance of this factor relative to the direct Latin American desire for political and economic co-operation with the United States it is impossible to fix. It was strongest

---

[58] It is noteworthy that the Inter-American Juridical Committee was enjoined to collaborate with the ILO in this project.

[59] This matter had become increasingly important to the Latin Americans during the war period, especially to Guatemala and Argentina, who pressed their particular claims (and entered reservations embodying them) at major inter-American meetings.

[60] See Wood, *Good Neighbor Policy*, pp. 340 ff.

in the delegates from countries of static feudalistic society. It was certainly decisive in gaining the support of reactionaries who had previously been cool to inter-American co-operation, and may have been the most important single reason for the wide area of agreement on matters previously highly controversial.[61]

The attachment of the Latin American governments to the inter-American system, apparent at Mexico City (and again at San Francisco) may well have been prompted in large part by antipathy towards the Soviet Union. There were other obvious factors: the usefulness of the inter-American system as an instrument for restraining the United States in the exercise of her power had been demonstrated in the recent past, while hopes of increased inter-American economic co-operation (that is, United States economic aid) were complemented by fears that these would be prejudiced should the United States adopt a 'universalist' rather than a 'regional' policy.

But the Mexico City Conference, though comparatively successful, did not settle very much; a great deal of its work was of a provisional character. The reorganization of the inter-American system was to be carried out by the Ninth International Conference, to which other important political questions had been referred. Concrete economic matters were to be the subject of the Inter-American Technical Economic Conference, scheduled for June 1945. The Act of Chapultepec was not merely provisional pending the conclusion of a collective-security treaty. Both it and the treaty would be subject to decisions on regional arrangements to be made at the San Francisco Conference where, indeed, the place of the inter-American system as a regional grouping within the world organization would be determined.

The United Nations Charter

The difficult position of the United States at Mexico City as one of the sponsors of the Dumbarton Oaks Conference has been noted. Obviously, she could not support Latin American criticism of the proposals made there, and she was unwilling to present their points of view at San Francisco. The United States administration (which, between the two conferences, had been changed by the death of Franklin Roosevelt and the succession of Harry S. Truman to the presidency) was divided on the issue of regionalism.[62] Other considerations included the fear that firm adherence to 'legitimate regional

[61] *The Americas*, p. 117.
[62] See R. B. Russell and J. E. Muther, *A History of the United Nations Charter: the Role of the United States 1940–1945* (1958), pp. 694–8.

arrangements' might invite 'the formation of a lot of dangerous new "regional spheres of influence" '.[63] In particular, the United States wished to avoid giving the Soviet Union any justification for building a sphere of influence in Eastern Europe and a 'bloc' in the United Nations. However important this factor, within the United Nations the United States and the countries of Latin America belonged to different groups of nations with conflicting interests. One group consisted of the great powers, determined to have a preponderant voice in the new world organization, and the other of the small powers, anxious to limit great power domination. Thus the San Francisco Conference was to emphasize the basic divergence of interests between the United States as a great power and the other American republics as small ones.

This dichotomy was particularly evident in the opposition of the Latin American countries, along with other small powers, to the proposed great power veto in the Security Council. The United States naturally joined the other great powers in preventing any significant modification of the veto provision. She therefore opposed also the Latin American demand for recognition in the United Nations Charter of the juridical equality of states, now one of the basic principles of the inter-American system. For this principle was incompatible with the privileged position held by the five permanent members of the Security Council; so the vaguer term 'sovereign equality' was adopted. The United States likewise joined the other great powers in resisting any enlargement of the authority of the General Assembly at the expense of the Security Council, a change also supported by many Latin American countries. For reasons deriving from her status as a great power (and her relations with other great powers, especially the Soviet Union), the United States opposed a permanent seat on the Security Council for Latin America. The latter had to be content with two non-permanent seats. One significant issue on which the United States and the countries of Latin America were in agreement (as a 'bloc' in the eyes of the Soviet Union) was in ensuring the admission of Argentina to the conference. Russia's opposition to Argentina's admission provided another reason for the Latin American countries to distrust her.[64]

[63] A. H. Vandenberg, Jr, ed., *The Private Papers of Senator Vandenberg* (1952), p. 187.
[64] This account of divergences between the US and the Latin American countries at San Francisco is based mainly upon ch. i of J. A. Houston, *Latin America in the United Nations* (1956).

In numerous other attempts to modify the Dumbarton Oaks proposals, Latin American countries had further disappointments. But they have been credited with being mainly responsible for what was the most far-reaching modification made at San Francisco: Article 51 of the Charter. We have already noted that the Act of Chapultepec contained provisions for sanctions, including the use of armed force, to meet armed aggression; and that the Dumbarton Oaks proposals required that 'enforcement action' should not be taken by regional agencies without the authorization of the Security Council. We have also noted the desire of the Latin American countries to preserve and even strengthen the inter-American system, while the United States government was divided on the issue of regionalism versus universalism. At Mexico City, however, the United States had joined with the other members of the inter-American system in agreeing in principle to strengthen their regional organization and to sign a collective-security pact. So eventually at San Francisco, with Latin American support, the United States delegate, Senator Vandenberg,[65] made a proposal which emerged as Article 51 of the United Nations Charter.[66] The Inter-American Treaty of Reciprocal Assistance was to become the first defence pact having this article as its juridical basis.

Nevertheless, the Dumbarton Oaks proposals on regional arrangements were incorporated as Chapter VIII of the Charter. This said *inter alia* that 'no enforcement action shall be taken under regional arrangements or by regional agencies without the authorization of the Security Council' (Art. 53), and that 'the Security Council shall at all times be kept fully informed of activities undertaken or in contemplation under regional arrangements or by regional agencies for the maintenance of international peace and security' (Art. 54). A reading of Articles 51–54 shows clearly that while the right of individual or collective self-defence may be exercised without authorization by the Security Council (and continued until the Council takes over), this applies only in cases of *armed attack*. Otherwise, enforcement action may be taken only with the authorization of the Council. The problems arising from this distinction will be discussed at a later stage.

The Argentine Question

In persuading the Latin Americans to accept the Vandenberg compromise the United States reiterated her promise to conclude a

[65] Vandenberg was the US representative on the conference commission dealing with regionalism, whose chairman, incidentally, was Alberto Lleras Camargo, later the first Secretary General of the OAS.   [66] See below, p. 217.

defence pact with them. On 29 August 1945 the Governing Board of the Pan American Union decided that a conference to draft this treaty should convene at Rio de Janeiro on the following 20 October. On 5 October, however, the United States requested a postponement.[67] Although her representative on the Board gave no reason for this request, Acting Secretary of State Acheson made no secret at a press conference that the cause was, in fact, the resurgence of the 'Argentine problem'. Acheson accused the Argentine government of ignoring and repudiating its international obligations, and declared that the United States would not associate with the 'present Argentine régime' in the treaty of military assistance to be negotiated at Rio.

This move by the United States administration was criticized at home as well as in Latin America. The United States obviously feared she would not get the support of the other American republics if she took up the Argentine question at the conference. Hence she proposed the treaty should be negotiated through diplomatic channels, which would have meant a series of bilateral consultations between the United States and each of the Latin American countries. There were understandably strong objections to this. In addition to Acheson's own assertion and the fear of a serious division over the Argentine question at the conference, it has been suggested that an extra-hemispheric factor was involved: that the failure of the meeting of the Council of Foreign Ministers of the great powers in London (11 September–2 October 1945), and the consequent uncertainty this failure caused, may have made the United States less willing to enter into a firm defence commitment. If this was an important consideration in the United States request for a postponement of the Rio Conference it would illustrate how her new position in world affairs was already affecting her role in the inter-American system.[68]

Of one thing there was no doubt. United States relations with Argentina were deteriorating badly, with all the repercussions this quarrel would have on the inter-American system. United States Ambassador Spruille Braden in Buenos Aires, who had been extremely vocal in denouncing the Argentine government, was appointed Assistant Secretary of State in August 1945. Secretary of State Byrnes (who had succeeded Stettinius the previous month) declared of this appointment:

---

[67] PAU, *Minutes of Special Meeting of Governing Board . . . October 5, 1945*, pp. 2–4.
[68] Whitaker, *Inter-American Affairs, 1945*, pp. 29–30.

It is particularly a recognition of his accurate interpretation of the policies of this Government in its relations with the present Government of the Argentine. As Assistant Secretary in charge of Latin American affairs, it will be his duty to see that the policies which he has so courageously sponsored in the Argentine are continued with unremitting vigor.[69]

Therefore the United States was fully—even ostentatiously—endorsing the speeches and other activities of Braden in Argentina which could only be interpreted as advocating a change of government there.

Such was the background[70] against which Dr Eduardo Rodríguez Larreta, Foreign Minister of Uruguay, proposed to the other American governments a policy of collective intervention against any member of the inter-American system repeatedly violating the essential rights of man and failing to fulfil its international obligations. Rodríguez Larreta argued that peace and democracy were parallel and, in effect, the very existence of an anti-democratic government in the western hemisphere was a danger to the other members of the inter-American system. Such a government must not be allowed to shelter behind the principle of non-intervention: ' "Non-intervention" cannot be converted into a right to invoke one principle in order to be able to violate all other principles with immunity.' Therefore, 'in view of notorious events', Rodríguez Larreta concluded, 'there is a need for a collective multilateral pronouncement, using for that purpose some of the means already counseled; either by means of an advisory committee (*Comisión dictaminante*) or by an express consultation, or by including the subject in the proposed Conference of Rio de Janeiro'.[71]

Before considering the reaction of the other American republics to Rodríguez Larreta's proposal for collective intervention it should be recalled that the Additional Protocol Relative to Non-Intervention declared inadmissible the intervention of any *one* of the American republics, directly or indirectly, and for whatever reason, in the internal or external affairs of any other of them. This wording, it has been noted, differed from Article 8 of the Montevideo Convention on the Rights and Duties of States, which said merely 'No state has the right to intervene in the internal or external affairs of another.' Therefore, collective intervention was not specifically prohibited by these

[69] *DSB*, xiii/322 (1945), p. 291.
[70] In the view of Cuevas Cancino, *Del Congreso de Panamá a la Conferencia de Caracas 1826–1954* (1955), ii. 202, Rodríguez Larreta's proposal was in the 'Bolivarian' tradition, but its chances of acceptance were spoiled by the fears aroused by Braden's policy against Perón.   [71] *DSB*, xiii/335 (1945), pp. 864–6.

inter-American agreements. The Roosevelt administration undoubt-edly thought that 'collective responsibility' had replaced unilateral intervention.

Force was given to Rodríguez Larreta's argument by the fact that, since 1936, democracy had been proclaimed an attribute of the inter-American system. First so declared at the Buenos Aires Conference of that year, this had been reiterated on numerous occasions since. Moreover, Rodríguez Larreta pointed out in his Note:

> In Panama, in 1939, it was said that—
> "On more than one occasion the American Republics have affirmed their adherence to the democratic ideal which prevails in this Hemisphere;
> "This ideal may be endangered by the action of foreign ideologies inspired in diametrically opposite principles; and
> "It is advisable, consequently, to protect the integrity of this ideal through the adoption of appropriate measures."
> In Habana, in 1940, resolution VII refers to the "Diffusion of Doctrines Tending to Place in Jeopardy the Common Inter-American Democratic Ideal or To Threaten the Security and Neutrality of the American Republics", and recommends a series of measures against propaganda originating abroad or carried out by foreign elements within the republics of the continent.
> In Rio de Janeiro, 1942, measures intended to "prevent or punish as crimes, acts against democratic institutions" were confirmed and strengthened.

We have seen that the Mexico City Conference, in addition to adopting resolutions concerned with the rights of man and social guarantees, referred to the Inter-American Juridical Committee a Guatemalan project on the 'Defense and Preservation of Democracy in America Against the Possible Establishment of Anti-Democratic Regimes in the Continent'. The safeguarding of democracy (or, in more cases, establishing it) and the protection of human rights would, in practice, involve a very great deal of intervention indeed. Was it conceivable that many American republics would accept such intervention even if it were 'collective'?

Uruguay had more reason than most to fear the Argentine govern-ment against which Rodríguez Larreta's Note was directed, and, as one of the most democratic countries in the western hemisphere, little reason to fear such collective intervention against herself. Even so, Sumner Welles asserted that the initiative had not come from Uruguay at all, but that the United States had prompted it—which was denied.

Certainly, however, Secretary of State Byrnes was quick to give his government's 'unqualified adherence to the principles enunciated by the distinguished Uruguayan Foreign Minister'.[72] Braden subsequently declared in a radio broadcast that the United States did not 'intend to stand idly by while the Nazi-Fascist ideology against which we fought a war endeavors to entrench itself in this hemisphere'. 'But our policy', he said, 'is one of *joint* action with the other republics'. Mr Ellis O. Briggs, Director of the Office of American Republics Affairs, also participating in the broadcast, thought the agreement of a substantial majority of the American nations should suffice for action to be taken, rather than a possibly unattainable unanimity.[73] The Truman administration, like that of Roosevelt earlier, thought in terms of collective action as correlative to abandoning unilateral intervention.

The Latin American countries soon showed they thought otherwise. Collective intervention could only too easily mean United States intervention with such Latin American support as she could muster given all the means of exerting pressure she commanded. They had not struggled so long to make non-intervention the cornerstone of the inter-American system, and the system itself an instrument of restraint upon their powerful neighbour, to jeopardize these achievements just when the United States was blatantly interfering in Argentina's domestic affairs. It is significant that some of the most anti-fascist and democratic governments in Latin America were among those strongly opposed to the Rodríguez Larreta proposal. The warm reception given to the Uruguayan Foreign Minister's note by the United States administration (even without the suspicion that the latter had inspired it) increased the general Latin American coolness towards it. The Latin Americans felt, not without justification, that United States policy towards Argentina was due not to any special regard for democracy, but to the fact that her government was un-cooperative. Moreover, there was the persistent feeling that the issue was between the United States and Argentina, not an hemispheric one; and the natural reaction, in spite of distrust for the Argentine government, was to sympathize with the fellow Latin American country. The United States enhanced this feeling by publishing the 'Blue Book'.

The State Department's *Consultation among the American Republics with Respect to the Argentine Situation*, published in February 1946,

---

[72] *DSB*, xiii/336 (1945), p. 892.　　　[73] Ibid. xiv/341 (1946), pp. 26–32.

contained an indictment of the Farrell-Perón government which was in large part justified. But its publication, about two weeks before a presidential election was due to take place in Argentina, proved a major blunder. To begin with, the title was an irritant to the Latin Americans, who resented the form the 'consultation' had taken.[74] Apparently publication was timed to influence the Argentine election; it probably did so, but not in the way the United States administration hoped,[75] for Perón was able to assert that the voters' choice was between him and Braden. In what was judged by impartial observers to be a fair election, Perón won the presidency and the United States suffered a humiliating moral defeat. The other Latin American countries, when approached once more, made it clear that they did not share the United States view of the Argentine problem and were anxious to make peace with Perón.[76]

The United States position was untenable; there was no other course but to retreat from it. The implementation of the Mexico City recommendations was being held up, and inter-American relations had for some time been deteriorating for reasons already mentioned. At the beginning of 1947 there had been no conference to conclude a mutual-defence pact; no Ninth International Conference of American States at Bogotá to reorganize, consolidate, and strengthen the inter-American system; and no special economic conference to consider the increasingly urgent economic problems of Latin America. Already the pattern of the post-war world was emerging: a world in which there would be new problems for the inter-American system to add to those still unsolved from the earlier period. Before we turn to the establishment of the Organization of American States and its role in the post-war world, let us examine briefly the hemispheric environment within which it operated: that is to say, inter-American relations since the end of the Second World War.

[74] Sumner Welles, *Where Are We Heading?*, p. 230, says that the 'consultation' took the form of the State Department's summoning Latin American ambassadors in Washington to hand them copies of the 'Blue Book' twelve hours before it was published.
[75] That the US administration should have entertained such hopes indicates an inability to appreciate the realities of inter-American relations at this point.
[76] This is apparent in the 'U.S. Memorandum to American Republics on Argentine Situation', *DSB*, xiv/355 (1946), pp. 666–7.

5 Inter-American Relations since the End of the Second World War

In the preceding chapter we looked at inter-American relations during the Second World War. We noted their much greater intimacy; their extension in the social and cultural fields as well as in those directly concerned with the war effort. We saw also the establishment of many new inter-American institutions, and the plans laid at the Mexico City Conference on Problems of War and Peace to reorganize and strengthen the inter-American system. The determination of the American republics to maintain their distinctive regional association after the United Nations had come into being was likewise shown—at Mexico City and San Francisco. However, we also noted significant limitations upon the degree of inter-American co-operation achieved and the period over which it lasted. Before the Second World War ended, hemispheric solidarity was weakening to an extent which threatened the fulfilment of the Mexico City recommendations and subsequently caused the postponement of the conferences at which they were to be given treaty form.

The Good Neighbour Policy: a Casualty of the War

The co-operation of Latin America with the United States during the Second World War is generally regarded as the ultimate justification of Franklin Roosevelt's Good Neighbour policy; which is one reason why there has been a tendency to exaggerate its extent and cordiality. Yet, in a very real sense, the Good Neighbour policy was a casualty of the war. For its essence was United States abstention from certain activities in Latin America; her acceptance of non-intervention as the cornerstone of the inter-American system. But during the Second World War the neighbours became partners in the struggle, with one partner very senior indeed. The United States was extremely active in Latin America, and a great deal of her activity could certainly be described as intervention. Latin American concern over this trend grew, and found expression over such matters as Argentina, the Rodríguez Larreta proposal, and the United States desire to retain certain military bases.

Perhaps, then, the end of the Good Neighbour policy was inherent in the intimacy of the wartime partnership. On the other hand, inter-American relations certainly deteriorated as the end of the war approached. We have already recognized the role of external threats in fostering hemispheric solidarity. As the danger from the Axis powers receded it was therefore understandable that this solidarity should weaken; that the Latin Americans should revert to their 'normal' feeling of distrust towards the United States. This distrust arose, as we have seen, from the great disparity of power between Latin America and the United States, and fears of how this power would be used. At the end of the Second World War the United States was much stronger even than before; the imbalance of power in the hemisphere correspondingly more marked. The policies of the United States—both positive and negative—could be decisive for the fortunes of the countries of Latin America.

The divergence of interests between the United States as a great power and the Latin American countries as small powers was accentuated by the post-war world situation. We have noted this in relation to the world organization, with which the inter-American system would have to be harmonized. Within the United Nations the United States was one of the 'Big Five', possessing the power of veto and a permanent seat in the Security Council; the Latin American countries were among the small nations hoping to influence events through the General Assembly. The United States was already involved with post-war commitments and responsibilities in other regions before hostilities ended, and the Latin American countries would be drawn more intimately into world affairs through their membership of the United Nations. These wider interests and commitments would call into question one of the basic tenets of the 'Western Hemisphere Idea': separation from the rest of the world. But not only would the western hemisphere become more intimately involved with other regions. The general international situation would have important effects upon developments within the hemisphere.

In the event, since the end of the Second World War both the world and hemispheric environments, generally speaking, have been unfavourable to strengthening the inter-American system, and relations between the United States and Latin America have been mutually unsatisfactory. First, the United States concentrated upon her wider interests—especially in Europe and the Far East—while the countries of Latin America were concerned above all with their own grave economic problems, and anxious for aid from their northern neighbour in solving them. Then, when the Cold War developed, and Latin America was remote from it, United States preoccupation with other regions increased. As for her neighbours' economic problems, in the United States view they could best be tackled by private enterprise, which the Latin American countries would do well to encourage. When the Cold War eventually came to the western hemisphere, inter-American relations deteriorated still further. Latin Americans accepted neither the United States assessment of the seriousness of the threat from international communism nor her policy to meet it. Many of them feared United States intervention more than the communist challenge, and were also afraid of being involved in her extra-continental commitments. Their attitude was something akin to neutralism, in spite of their ties with the United States in the inter-American system; but, if a serious threat existed, they argued, it could best be met by raising living standards in Latin America and by other action in the economic and social fields. This divergence of views was shown clearly at the Tenth Inter-American Conference, where the United States had to employ great pressure in order to obtain Latin American support for her anti-communist resolution. Fear of losing economic aid was the most powerful factor in securing it.

Thus, the intrusion of the Cold War into the western hemisphere furthered not hemispheric solidarity, but the concept of reciprocity: economic assistance for Latin America as a reward for supporting United States policies to meet the threat from international communism.[1] The United States found herself having to make concessions in the economic field in response to political crises; such, for example, were her agreement to establish the Inter-American Development Bank and proposal of the Alliance for Progress itself. Inter-American relations were made more difficult not only by Latin America's 'revolution of rising expectations', which was encouraged by similar 'revolutions' elsewhere in the world, but by changes south of the Rio Grande with which the United States was slow to come to terms. This last was understandable. Far-reaching economic and social changes in Latin America were bound, in many cases, to hurt United States interests and provoke the charge of 'communism' against those advocating them. Moreover, the groups in Latin America

---

[1] Cf. Louis J. Halle's assertion that 'the inter-American system is degenerating into a mere market place in which our neighbors, no longer conscious of making common cause with us, trade with us for such bounty as they can get in exchange for their votes' (Lieuwen, *Arms & Politics*, p. 241).

whose future was threatened by social revolution were, naturally, the firmest supporters of strong action against international communism. And, if the United States was prepared to assist peaceful social change, where were the middle groups—political and social—with whom ideally she might hope to co-operate?[2]

Against this background of post-war inter-American relations occurred the Cuban revolution; the events leading up to the break between Dr Fidel Castro and the United States; and the alignment of Cuba with the Soviet Union. Here was the biggest threat ever faced by the inter-American system, and the greatest challenge. To meet the challenge and combat the threat there was formulated the Alliance for Progress, the first serious step towards tackling the economic and social problems of Latin America. Whether it would form a new basis for relations between the United States and Latin America, and reverse the unhappy post-war trend, only time would reveal. In order to essay a provisional judgement on the prospects for the Alliance and the inter-American system itself, the history of inter-American relations during the period since the end of the Second World War must be looked at in greater detail.

In the preceding chapter we saw how tension between the United States and Argentina had delayed the implementation of the major recommendations of the Mexico City Conference. In particular, the conference to conclude an inter-American security pact was twice postponed before finally meeting on 15 August 1947. The Governing Board of the Pan American Union had originally fixed the date for 20 October 1945, but first the United States and then Uruguay requested postponement. During the early part of 1946 a number of American governments submitted projects for a defence treaty, which were then examined by a special committee of the Governing Board. Consultation subsequently took place with the governments on the principal points to be incorporated in the treaty.

By 1947, when the problem of Argentina was no longer an obstacle, the world international situation was deteriorating. This was the year the Cold War really got under way: the year of the Truman Doctrine, the Marshall speech adumbrating the European Recovery Programme, and the establishment of the Cominform.[3] In Professor Whitaker's view, the Cold War 'converted the United States from mere acquiescence in the strengthening of the American regional system to

---

[2] See above, p. 25.
[3] G. Connell-Smith, *Pattern of the Post-War World* (London, 1957), pp. 65 ff.

enthusiastic support of that effort'.[4] Certainly, the Inter-American Treaty of Reciprocal Assistance was the first of the 'Cold War pacts' and the forerunner of the Atlantic Alliance and others. It is described in the following chapter.

Post-War Economic Problems

Although the adoption of the treaty was the only item on the agenda of the special Inter-American Conference for the Maintenance of Continental Peace and Security, it was not the only subject discussed. In the words of the first Secretary General of the Organization of American States, 'it was noteworthy that with very few exceptions the speeches in the general discussions gave unusual emphasis to the necessity of establishing a balance in inter-American cooperation by accentuating its economic character'.[5] This is not surprising. We have already seen how, as the war drew to a close, the Latin American countries became increasingly anxious to obtain from the United States some guarantee of assistance in the difficult period of transition to peace-time economic conditions. We noted the expression of this anxiety at Mexico City, and Latin American disappointment with the United States response. The Inter-American Technical Economic Conference, due to meet in Washington in June 1945, had not taken place when the Rio Conference met.

In the meantime many Latin American fears had proved only too well founded. The lifting of wartime price controls in the United States meant that Latin Americans, who had sold in a controlled market, now had to buy in a free one. The value of Latin America's accumulated foreign exchange was, therefore, considerably diminished. But, as well as being more expensive, the machinery and other industrial equipment needed by Latin American countries was still difficult to obtain, even though the United States greatly increased her shipments between 1945 and 1947. This situation grew worse for Latin America as the United States concentrated mainly upon meeting Europe's needs. At the same time, United States imports from Latin America declined, especially of those goods produced by Latin American industries developed during the war period. Nor, in view of their depressed economic condition, could Latin America do much, for the moment, to revive its pre-war markets in other regions.

[4] 'The Organisation of American States', *YB of World Affairs, 1959* (1959), p. 118.

[5] A. Lleras Camargo, 'Report on the Ninth International Conference of American States', *Ann. OAS*, i/1 (1949), p. 53.

Economic dependence upon the United States was greater than ever before.

Mexico took the lead in stressing Latin America's economic problems. Two months before the Rio Conference, at a meeting of the Governing Board of the Pan American Union, her representative had declared:

the Government of Mexico considers that the first line of hemispheric defense is in the economic fortification of a large number of our countries, and that therefore, for inescapable reasons of defense, the Rio conference should immediately take the necessary measures to assure that the economic cooperation of the American republics be accomplished in the very near future.[6]

Nor was Mexico alone. Argentina, Chile, and Cuba joined her at Rio in demanding, in spite of United States opposition, that the question of economic co-operation be discussed.[7] Cuba went so far as to ask— in vain—for provisions in the Rio Treaty prohibiting 'threats and aggressions of an economic character'.[8] Cuba's demand arose from resentment at the use made by the United States of her sugar quota to exert pressure in seeking a settlement of private claims against the Cuban government.[9] The Mexican Foreign Minister, Jaime Torres Bodet, received enthusiastic applause when he warned delegations that economically weak countries could not take effective action against aggressors, and called for similar unity in tackling poverty and hunger as was proposed against political enemies. The Foreign Minister of Ecuador expressed the desire of Latin Americans for a Marshall Plan. Argentina requested the conference to call immediately a special economic meeting, and was supported by Bolivia, Ecuador, and Paraguay.[10]

Secretary of State Marshall, addressing the conference as head of the United States delegation, endeavoured to show both the greater plight of Europe and that the latter's rehabilitation was vital to the economy of the western hemisphere. Moreover, he asserted that long-term economic development in Latin America required 'a type of collaboration in which a much greater role falls to private citizens and

---

[6] PAU, *Minutes of Special Meeting of Governing Board, . . . July 9, 1947*, p. 5.
[7] Kunz, 'The Inter-American Treaty of Reciprocal Assistance', *AJIL*, xlii/1 (1948), p. 113. [8] Ibid. p. 114.
[9] Whitaker, 'Rio and Bogotá: Pan American Perspective', *IAEA*, i/3 (1947) p. 27.
[10] A. R. Willner, 'Case Study in Frustration: Latin America and Economic Issues at Post-War Inter-American Conferences', *IAEA*, ii/4 (1949), pp. 39–40.

groups than is the case in a program designed to aid European countries to recover from the destruction of war'.[11] Mr Truman likewise stressed the urgent needs of Europe when he addressed the Rio Conference himself just before it closed, though he promised his administration would tackle vigorously the economic problems of Latin America.[12] But nothing was done at Rio; Resolution IX of the Final Act merely deferred matters until a later date. The Inter-American Economic and Social Council was charged with preparing a basic draft agreement on inter-American economic co-operation for submission to the Ninth International Conference at Bogotá which would then fix a date for a special economic conference during the last half of 1948.

Latin America's dissatisfaction with United States policy towards its economic problems was underlined, during the interval between the Rio and Bogotá Conferences, by the establishment of the United Nations Economic Commission for Latin America (ECLA). In August 1947, at the Fifth Session of the United Nations Economic and Social Council, Chile had proposed that such a commission should be appointed. All the other Latin American countries expressed support for this proposal, but the United States did not favour it. The Inter-American Economic and Social Council had been functioning provisionally since the Mexico City Conference created it in 1945, and the United States considered there would be duplication of effort between this organ of the inter-American system and the proposed commission. Moreover, the United States representative thought the question should be considered first by the Ninth International Conference of American States. However, the Latin Americans, who were to be in frequent opposition to the United States on economic matters in the United Nations, had their way. Membership of ECLA, which came into being in February 1948, consisted of the United States, Great Britain, France, and the Netherlands, in addition to the twenty Latin American republics.[13]

The main achievements of the Ninth International Conference of

[11] Dozer, p. 242.
[12] RIIA, *Survey, 1947–8* (1952), p. 471. On the eve of the Rio Conference, President Truman had rejected the notion of a Marshall Plan for Latin America, saying there had been one in the western hemisphere for over a century: the Monroe Doctrine (!) (Willner, p. 40). This statement is of some significance in interpreting Truman's policy towards Europe at that time and also reveals little regard for Latin American feelings.
[13] See *YBUN, 1947–8* (1949), pp. 537–43; also Houston, pp. 223–32. For the resolution at Bogotá calling for a division of functions between ECLA and the Inter-American Economic and Social Council, see below, p. 218.

American States are appraised in the next chapter. At this stage two matters may be reiterated which were to dominate relations between the United States and Latin America—and therefore to determine the fortunes of the inter-American system—throughout the whole period after the end of the Second World War: Latin America's concern with its economic problems, and the growing preoccupation of the United States with the challenge from international communism. Both were given ominous point by the rioting which broke out in Bogotá during the conference, variously attributed to communist intrigue and economic misery. No satisfactory measures were taken at Bogotá to deal with either.

Resolution XXXII of the Final Act of the Ninth International Conference, 'The Preservation and Defense of Democracy in America', is generally considered the first inter-American 'anti-communist' resolution. Mecham (p. 429) calls it 'a resounding anti-Communist hemisphere resolution'. But, in fact, it was softened, as such, by the condemnation—to meet Latin American wishes—of 'any other totalitarian doctrine'. There was a similar outcome to subsequent attempts by the United States to obtain support for stronger measures against what she denounced as communist intervention than many Latin Americans were prepared to accept.

Most Latin Americans undoubtedly placed economic questions very high in their priorities at Bogotá. 'As had been the case at Rio de Janeiro, the Chairmen of the Delegations almost without exception put the main emphasis upon the economic problem in the speeches they gave during the course of the general discussion.'[14] But in his opening speech to the conference,[15] Secretary of State Marshall dispelled any illusions the Latin American delegates may have entertained of an important modification of United States policy on economic co-operation with Latin America. Marshall once more stressed his country's global commitments and especially the importance of European recovery to the whole hemisphere. Perhaps spurred on by domestic interests which had voiced fears (based on their interpretation of the draft economic agreement prepared by the Inter-American Economic and Social Council) that the rights of private investment would not be adequately safeguarded,[16] the Secretary of State emphasized the role of foreign capital in the economic

---

[14] Lleras Camargo, *Ann. OAS*, i/1 (1949), p. 55.
[15] *DSB*, xviii/458 (1948), pp. 469–73.
[16] Willner, *IAEA*, ii/4 (1949), pp. 41–42.

development of the United States, and strongly recommended it to Latin Americans.[17] He made it clear there would be little assistance from the United States Government: 'the capital required through the years must come from private sources, both domestic and foreign'. It was up to the Latin Americans to attract United States capital by according it fair and equitable treatment. A subsequent, much publicized announcement that President Truman had requested from Congress an increase of $500 millions in the lending authority of the Export-Import Bank was received with no enthusiasm by the Latin American delegates. Nor, incidentally, was this authority granted by the 80th Congress.[18]

It is hardly surprising that economic problems proved the most controversial at the Ninth Conference. The great disparity of economic strength between the United States and the countries of Latin America, their different economic philosophies and conflicting objectives ensured that any agreement would be a compromise, and an unsatisfactory one. For the Latin Americans, to whom economic co-operation meant primarily United States inter-governmental aid, it would be particularly disappointing. As we have seen, they had already shown their lack of confidence in the outcome by insisting upon the establishment of ECLA. The content and the fate of the Economic Agreement of Bogotá[19] underlined the basic differences between the 'two' parties to it.

Although the Charter of the OAS proclaims as one of its principles that 'economic cooperation is essential to the common welfare and prosperity of the peoples of the continent', and the Inter-American Economic and Social Council became one of the organs of the OAS Council, the Ninth International Conference of American States did not substantially increase inter-American economic co-operation. Another long held aspiration of the Latin Americans, the creation of an inter-American bank to facilitate their economic development, was shelved for study by the Economic and Social Council and consideration by the projected economic conference.[20]

Therefore, in spite of achievements in other fields, the Bogotá Conference emphasized trends in United States relations with Latin

---

[17] Latin Americans do not, of course, accept the argument that what has been or is good for the US is necessarily good for them.
[18] J. E. Lockwood, 'The Economic Agreement of Bogotá', *AJIL*, xlii/3 (1948), p. 617.
[19] See below, pp. 267–8.
[20] Res. XV of Final Act.

America which did not augur well for the future of the inter-American system. Laurence Duggan wrote of the conference, with some prescience:

[It] represents both the most important milestone in the development of the inter-American system and an ominous demonstration of the weaknesses which may undermine that system. . . . Bogotá showed dramatically [i.e. through the rioting] the necessity for combining with measures for inter-American solidarity on the official level, measures which will solve the deep-rooted problems of Latin America—low productivity and its corollaries: ignorance, disease, hunger, and political instability.[21]

Of the rioting in Bogotá a veteran correspondent in Latin American affairs wrote that 'whatever individual or group was immediately responsible, the ugly, undeniable fact was that overwhelming fascist influences and lack of interest shown by the Pan American Conference in relieving the poverty and suffering of exploited people were the real reasons'.[22]

Latin American discontent with United States economic aid continued throughout the years of the Truman administration. A speech by Secretary of State Dean Acheson in September 1949,[23] further illustrates the widely differing order of priorities in hemispheric objectives between the United States and her southern neighbours. In stating the basic principles guiding United States policy in the western hemisphere at the outset of his address Acheson placed last 'the promotion of the economic, social, and political welfare of the American Republics'. Among his concluding remarks, Acheson said: 'These then are our three major objectives—the security of our nation and of the hemisphere; the encouragement of democratic representative institutions; and positive cooperation in the economic field to help in the attainment of our first two objectives.' In the Latin American view, economic co-operation was a major objective in itself and not a means of furthering other, more important aims. Time was to confirm that such co-operation (at least in the sense of United States assistance in tackling their economic problems) had greater priority among Latin Americans than the other two objectives stated by Acheson.

Moreover, Acheson emphasized 'the stimulation of private effort

---

[21] *The Americas*, pp. 1–2.
[22] Inman, 'The Rise and Fall of the Good Neighbor Policy', *Current History*, xxxii/188 (1957), p. 196.
[23] *DSB*, xxi/534 (1949), pp. 462–6. Address delivered before the Pan American Soc. of the US in New York, 19 Sept. 1949.

as the most important factor in political, economic, and social purposes'. Indeed, he said—and this underlines the difficulty of reconciling the two viewpoints: 'In providing assistance for economic development, it would be contrary to our traditions to place our government's public funds in direct and wasteful competition with private funds.' For United States acceptance of the Latin American position on this issue would have involved a repudiation of some of the fundamental concepts upon which, in the judgement of the great majority of her citizens at least, her prosperity and power were founded. It is also worth noting that 'nonintervention in the internal or external affairs of any American Republic', for Latin Americans —as this study emphasizes—the cornerstone of the inter-American system and its most important principle, was placed by Acheson after 'the observance by all governments of ethical standards based on justice and respect for freely accepted international obligations', and 'protection of the legitimate interests of our people and government, together with respect for the legitimate interests of all other peoples and governments'.

In Professor Dozer's words, 'the Truman administration . . . began forthwith to push with increased aggressiveness a program to foster private United States capital investment in Latin America'.[24] The President's 'Point IV' was generally regarded in Latin America as part of such a programme. Of course Latin Americans did not regard such investment as 'economic aid', and in any case it was not on a sufficient scale in spite of the administration's efforts. Moreover, as Lloyd Mecham observed, 'a somewhat disproportionate amount of the total direct private investment was in the extractive industries, particularly petroleum'.[25]

Another important aspect of the problem of economic co-operation was pinpointed when Edward G. Miller, Jr, Assistant Secretary for Inter-American Affairs, declared it to be a 'misconception' that 'the United States because of its size and prosperity is responsible for solving the problems of the other American Republics and that when they have difficulties the United States is to blame'.[26] The context of these remarks shows clearly that Miller was talking of the obligation to furnish financial assistance. Whether such an obligation exists and, if so, to what extent, are debatable questions. It can be argued that, by pursuing a policy of limiting extra-continental influence in

---

[24] Dozer, p. 244.
[25] Mecham, p. 358.
[26] *DSB*, xxii/561 (1950), p. 521.

the hemisphere in her own interests, the United States has indeed incurred considerable responsibilities for those over whom she has established her hegemony. The role of United States economic enterprises in Latin America is likewise debatable. But, more specifically, Latin Americans claimed that their powerful neighbour had incurred responsibilities arising from their wartime co-operation in the economic field. As has already been noted, a major grievance was that the Latin Americans sold their primary products to the United States at controlled prices and later had to use the dollars they received in exchange to buy manufactured goods at uncontrolled, inflated prices.

Less than three weeks after making that speech, Miller addressed an extraordinary meeting of the Inter-American Economic and Social Council. He endeavoured to meet criticism of United States reluctance to hold the much delayed inter-American economic conference:

There has been some tendency to attribute many of the economic ills of the hemisphere to the delay in holding that Conference. There has been a tendency also to blame the United States because the Conference has not yet been held. I would like to make my Government's position perfectly clear. We would be delighted to attend any conference, anywhere, anytime, provided only that we knew what we were going to talk about once we got there. It is basic to the success of a conference that its substantive objectives be clear and that there be substantial agreement as to the desirability of these objectives as well as a reasonable prospect of attaining them. It is an incontrovertible fact that the huge, complicated problem of economic development does not lend itself to solution through the mere holding of conferences nor the passing of resolutions.[27]

In the light of the incompatible views of the United States and Latin America on basic economic problems, Miller was unquestionably right in implying that a conference would not achieve anything substantial; as later such conferences were to confirm. But it was an 'incontrovertible fact' of considerable significance in inter-American relations that the Latin Americans were eager for the promised conference and the United States was opposed to it.[28]

The United States and Latin America in the Early 1950s

Two months later (25 June 1950) hostilities broke out in Korea. The OAS Council, meeting on 28 June 1950, declared its 'firm

[27] *DSB*, xxii/564 (1950), p. 650.
[28] For a Latin American view, see J. Mejía-Palacio, 'Why an Economic Conference?', *Américas*, ix/7 (1957), pp. 2–6; Dávila, *We of the Americas*, pp. 42–43, calls it 'The Lost Conference'.

M

adherence to the decisions of the competent organs of the United Nations' and solemnly reaffirmed 'the pledges of continental solidarity which unite the American States'.[29] But only the Colombian government sent troops (an infantry battalion) to Korea. In connection with the Korean War the Fourth Meeting of Consultation of American Foreign Ministers was held in Washington from 26 March until 7 April 1951.[30] Called at the request of the United States 'to consider problems of an urgent nature and of common interest to the American States', the Meeting revealed once more the divergence of objectives between Latin America and herself. Even on the question of hemispheric security, as Richard P. Stebbins observed, 'the fact that all the American republics recognized a theoretical danger from international Communism did not mean that they agreed on the best ways of combating it, or even on the necessity of actively combating it at all'.[31] The Brazilian delegate was reported to have said bluntly that the only nation in the hemisphere actually threatened by external aggression was the United States;[32] several others urged that the best way to prevent the spread of communism in Latin America would be to raise the living standards of the masses—for which United States financial assistance was necessary.

On the question of economic co-operation, appearing on the programme of the Meeting as 'emergency economic cooperation', the United States was concerned primarily with 'production and distribution for defensive purposes'; the Latin Americans with 'measures to facilitate in so far as possible the carrying out of programs of economic development'. The Latin Americans were also anxious to avoid a repetition of their financial experience of the Second World War. In the course of replying to President Truman's address of welcome to the Meeting, the Brazilian Foreign Minister declared:

We all are ready, on our part, to bear our share of sacrifices, but we could not repeat past practices without ruining ourselves, with no benefit accruing to the world therefrom. Consequently we must work out here a formula for mutual economic cooperation which could last beyond the emergency and provide for future reconstruction. By stimulation of industrial development through technical and financial assistance, the standard of living of the inhabitants of the various parts of the Western Hemisphere

---

[29] *Ann. OAS*, ii/3 (1950), p. 222.
[30] The Meeting is referred to again below, p. 221.
[31] Stebbins, *US in World Affairs, 1951* (1952), p. 300.
[32] *The Times*, 4 Apr. 1951.

could be elevated, creating an atmosphere favorable for work and for the welfare of all.[33]

No such formula was worked out; instead, after much intensive work by the delegations, there emerged a number of general recommendations of policy embodying recognition of different interests without specific commitments to action. Such was the 'General Statement' contained in Resolution XVI of the Final Act of the Meeting (Allocations and Priorities):

That, in order to meet the emergency situation and the subsequent period of adjustment, the American States shall do all in their power to provide one another with the products and services necessary to sustain the common defense effort, and declare that the maintaining of essential civilian activities and public services and the economic development of underdeveloped countries are considered as an essential element in the total concept of defense of the American Hemisphere, without disregarding the fact that the strengthening of their defenses is the principal duty of the American States in the present emergency.[34]

Even before the conference met, the Latin Americans had reason to fear that the favourable terms of trade resulting from the Korean War were coming to be reversed 'as the United States moved to limit the prices it paid for raw materials but failed, meanwhile, to halt the advancing price of its own manufactures'.[35] In the months following the Meeting their fears were realized. Their production of raw materials was maintained at a high level, and their trade with the United States reached record figures. But inflation increased and their terms of trade deteriorated. By the end of the year a favourable balance of payments had given way to a deficit on current account for the year as a whole amounting to nearly $400 millions.[36]

Relations between the United States and Latin America did not improve during the remaining period of the Truman administration and were, indeed, at a low ebb when President Eisenhower took office in January 1953. In the same month, Secretary of State John Foster Dulles declared he saw a parallel between existing conditions in Latin America and those in China in the 1930s, when the communist movement was just beginning. And, he went on, 'the time to deal with this rising menace in South America is now'.[37] This was a

[33] Fourth Meeting of Consultation, *Proceedings* (1951), p. 136.
[34] Ibid. p. 253.
[35] Stebbins, *US in World Affairs, 1951*, p. 314.   [36] Ibid. p. 316.
[37] George Pendle, 'Latin America', in RIIA, *Survey, 1953* (1956), p. 366. Dulles's use of 'South America' for Latin America illustrates the superficial know-

good indication of Dulles's approach to Latin America. As evidence of his concern for inter-American relations, the new president, early in April 1953, sent his brother, Dr Milton Eisenhower, as his special representative to the countries of South America to consider what changes in United States Latin American policy might improve them.

Dr Eisenhower, after a five weeks' tour, submitted a report to the President in November 1953.[38] In it he stated that 'economic cooperation is without question the key to better relations between the United States and the nations to the South'. In his opinion, the United States should pursue stable trade policies with Latin America, with a minimum of mechanisms permitting the imposition of increased tariffs or quotas, and a long-range policy on basic materials providing for stockpiling certain of their (i.e. Latin American) imperishable materials when prices were declining. There should be substantial public loans (mainly by the International Bank for Reconstruction and Development) for sound economic development projects for which private financing was not available; and the United States programme of technical co-operation in Latin America should be expanded. Dr Eisenhower believed the Latin Americans misunderstood the United States position and policies. Moreover, they would have to realize 'the value to the community of private competitive enterprise and private profit'. Latin American governments would have to adopt sound budgetary, fiscal, and credit policies; bring about conditions of political and economic stability; and give assurances of fair and equitable treatment in order to attract United States capital. In spite of some new suggestions, the basic recommendations of the report differed little from the policy of the Truman administration. It was, of course, unlikely the Eisenhower administration would place less emphasis on the role of private capital than its predecessor. In his Message to Congress on 7 January 1954, President Eisenhower declared that: 'Military assistance must be continued. Technical assistance must be maintained. Economic assistance can be reduced.' There were to be exceptions (notably Korea), but Latin America was not mentioned.[39]

---

ledge of the region only too often shown by United States administrations. It is ironical that Guatemala, in Central America, was the country uppermost in Dulles's mind when he spoke of the rising menace of communism in 'South America'.

[38] M. S. Eisenhower, 'United States–Latin American Relations: Report to the President', *DSB*, xxix/752 (1953), pp. 695–717.

[39] *DSB*, xxx/760 (1954), p. 76.

The Tenth Conference (Caracas, 1954)

The United States was much more preoccupied with the problem of communism and measures to eliminate what the administration denounced as the communist-dominated government in Guatemala. This was Dulles's objective at the Tenth Inter-American Conference, held at Caracas, Venezuela (1–28 March 1954). While the United States had expressed growing disquiet over links between the Guatemalan government and the communist countries, her denunciation of Arbenz was stimulated by the latter's expropriation of lands belonging to the (United States owned) United Fruit Company. And, although the State Department denied the expropriation had anything to do with United States concern over communist influence in Guatemala, this was hardly convincing. Sr Guillermo Toriello, Foreign Minister in the Arbenz government, subsequently asserted that the latter was doomed because of Dulles's close connections with the United Fruit Company.[40] As early as April 1953 Guatemala complained to the Secretary General of the United Nations of 'open hostility and a threat of intervention in the internal affairs of the Republic of Guatemala'. The communication was brought to the attention of the Security Council, but it was not discussed.[41]

It was indeed ironical that the conference at which Dulles strove to rally the Latin American republics against the challenge of international communism should have been held in the capital of one of the most notorious dictatorships in the continent.[42] In fact, Costa Rica declined to attend in protest against the Venezuelan government. Dulles's conduct at Caracas aroused great concern amongst most Latin American delegations. In Professor Robert J. Alexander's judgement it:

shocked many seasoned observers of Latin American developments. Not only did Dulles use the full weight of the United States Government to induce the Conference to take a position uncongenial to the majority of the Latin American countries, he did it in a manner likely to lose friends and alienate the peoples of the southern part of the hemisphere.

---

[40] *La Batalla de Guatemala* (1955), pp. 65–69. See also Martínez, pp. 178 ff.
[41] *YBUN, 1953* (1954), p. 284.
[42] At the Fifth Meeting of Consultation the Venezuelan Foreign Minister described the Caracas Conference as a blot on the history of the OAS, *Actas y documentos*, (OEA/Ser. F/III. 5 (español), (1961), p. 208). He was also reported as saying that his government would oppose any resolution that invoked the agreements made at the Tenth Inter-American Conference (Ronning, *Punta del Este: the Limits of Collective Security in a Troubled Hemisphere* (1963), p. 30).

Concerned with almost nothing but the "Anti-Communist Resolution" aimed at Guatemala, Dulles seemed to the Latin Americans indifferent to their feelings, their fears of "Yankee Intervention", and the concentration of their interest on entirely different problems. He stayed at the Conference only long enough to see adoption of the Resolution. Then he took a plane home the very day the Resolution was passed, leaving his subordinates to deal with the economic and social questions which were the primary concern of the Latin American delegations.[43]

Several Latin American delegations, notably the Mexican, attempted to weaken Dulles's anti-communist resolution, but the Secretary of State rejected most of the proposed amendments.[44] He resisted attempts to extend the scope of his resolution to include such matters as promoting human rights, condemning racial discrimination, and the development of economic and social well-being. These became the subjects of weaker resolutions.

The Latin American delegations, generally speaking, accepted the premise that the extension of international communism to the hemisphere would constitute a threat. But, as the United States delegation subsequently reported, 'there was expressed a genuine concern that the declaration contained in the U.S. draft resolution might in some way be interpreted as intervention, or justifying intervention, in the genuinely domestic affairs of an American state'.[45] The truth was the Latin Americans were aware of the United States determination to overthrow the Arbenz government.

The Guatemalan Foreign Minister denounced the United States resolution as

merely a pretext for intervening in our internal affairs. By accepting this proposal, Pan Americanism would become an instrument exclusively in the service of monopolistic interests and a weapon of coercion to strangle any attempt at political and economic liberation of the oppressed peoples of Latin America. They wanted to find a ready expedient to maintain the economic dependence of the American Republics and suppress the legitimate desires of their peoples, cataloguing as "Communism" every manifestation of nationalism or economic independence, any desire for social progress, any intellectual curiosity, and any interest in progressive or liberal reforms.

He emphasized the nebulous character of the term 'international

---

[43] *Communism in Latin America* (1957), p. 400.
[44] Dulles's draft and the resolution finally adopted at Caracas are described below, pp. 230–1.
[45] *Report of Delegation of USA*, p. 9.

communism' and stated that Guatemala considered null and void the 'anti-communist' resolutions of Bogotá and Washington:

For, according to the interpretation that has been given to them and the broader scope it is desired to give them, any Latin American Government that exerts itself to bring about a truly national program which affects the interests of the powerful foreign companies, in whose hands the wealth and the basic resources in large part repose in Latin America, will be pointed out as Communist; it will be accused of being a threat to continental security and making a breach in continental solidarity, and so will be threatened with foreign intervention.[46]

Toriello was voicing the thoughts of many of his (Latin American) listeners, and he was given an ovation. But when it came to the vote, only Mexico and Argentina abstained. Clearly, hopes of receiving economic aid were a major factor in discouraging more open support for Guatemala, whose delegation naturally voted against the resolution.[47] Uruguay appended a statement to the Final Act which said that she could not have supported the resolution had not the Declaration of Caracas been adopted.[48] It said also that Uruguay understood the resolution 'has as its objective the defense of the Continent against any aggression by Soviet imperialism and is not directed against the present regime of any American State'. One of her chief delegates, Dr Justino Jiménez de Aréchaga, declared that the Uruguayans had acquiesced 'without enthusiasm, without optimism, without joy and without the feeling that we were contributing to the adoption of a constructive measure'.[49] Having secured the passage of the resolution, Mr Dulles reportedly said on leaving Caracas, 'Now of course, we shall have the task of assuring that the enemies of freedom do not move into the breach which has been disclosed within our ranks.'[50]

Subsequent events in the Guatemala affair confirmed Latin American

---

[46] Tenth Inter-American Conference, *Plenary Sessions*, Doc. 95 (English), SP-23, 5 Mar. 1954, Original: Spanish, pp. 7–9.

[47] Cf. *Hispanic American Report*, vii/3 (1954), p. 1. 'Guatemalan Foreign Minister Toriello was lionized at Caracas by the very Latin American delegations which refused to support Guatemala against the United States. While rather sordid calculations impelled some Latin American countries to support Dulles in the hope of receiving a *quid pro quo* on economic issues, they applauded the dull speeches of Toriello and compared him with a David fighting a Goliath.'

[48] This included *inter alia* a reiteration of the principle of non-intervention (mentioning specifically 'the intrusion of any form of totalitarianism'), and referred to 'an effective policy of economic well-being and social justice to raise the standard of living of their peoples'.

[49] *Hispanic American Report*, vii/3 (1954), p. 39.

[50] Pendle, in RIIA, *Survey, 1953*, p. 374.

fears.[51] The United States expressed great concern in May 1954, when the Arbenz government received a shipment of arms originating in Czechoslovakia, and she tried unsuccessfully to obtain the consent of other members of the North Atlantic Treaty Organization to search their merchant ships on the high seas for further arms shipments to Guatemala. She concluded Mutual Security Treaties with Guatemala's neighbours, Nicaragua (in April) and Honduras (in May), and sent war materials to them; but she did not request a Meeting of Consultation to consider the situation. On 19 June Guatemala was invaded from Honduras by troops led by an exiled officer, Colonel Castillo Armas. The story of Arbenz's futile efforts to have both the United Nations and the inter-American peace machinery assist him in halting the invasion is told in a later chapter.[52] The United States succeeded in preventing either of these bodies from saving him. Her ambassador, John E. Peurifoy, played a leading— indeed a flamboyant—part in arranging a new government for Guatemala. In Latin America and beyond the western hemisphere it was widely believed at the time that the United States was responsible for the overthrow of the Arbenz government. The responsibility of the Central Intelligence Agency for engineering the invasion can no longer be denied. One United States writer has described his country's action as intervention *'against foreign intervention'*.[53] This is the substance of the Roosevelt Corollary to the Monroe Doctrine. Mr Dulles claimed in a broadcast to the people of the United States: 'The events of recent months and days add a new and glorious chapter to the already great tradition of the American States.'[54] For Latin Americans, however, these events represented another chapter in the tradition of United States intervention in their internal and external affairs which had been broken temporarily by the period of the Good Neighbour policy.

To Latin American dismay over what had happened in Guatemala was soon added further disappointment to their hopes of increased United States economic assistance. They had received little encouragement at Caracas, but looked forward to their economic problems being considered when the American finance ministers met at Rio de

[51] See P. B. Taylor, Jr, 'The Guatemalan Affair: a Critique of United States Foreign Policy', *Amer. Pol. Sci. R.*, 1/3 (1956), pp. 787–806.
[52] See below, pp. 231–7.
[53] D. James, *Red Design for the Americas: Guatemalan Prelude* (1954), p. 316.
[54] US Dept of State, *Intervention of International Communism in Guatemala* (1954), p. 33.

Janeiro from 22 November until 2 December 1954. At Rio, however, the United States promised little beyond more substantial and speedier loans, with increased lending authority for the Export–Import Bank. What the Latin Americans wanted were higher and more stable prices for their raw materials; larger credits for the industrialization of their countries; United States participation in a new international bank concerned exclusively with their economic development; and encouragement in their plans for establishing a Latin American common market. These wishes were not met at the Rio Conference; nor did a special committee established after a Meeting of the Chiefs of State of the American Republics had been held in Panama City in July 1956 accomplish anything important. No less disappointing was the economic conference held at Buenos Aires in 1957. The Economic Declaration of Buenos Aires was nothing more than a statement of general principles.[55] The United States maintained that existing institutions were adequate to finance 'sound' projects.

It is true that the Buenos Aires conference accepted in principle the economic integration of Latin America and recommended co-operation with ECLA in studying it. But the United States remained at best lukewarm towards it. According to one writer:

Official United States documents and the writings of leading United States experts in Hemispheric affairs abound in circumstantial evidence that until the middle of 1960 the United States looked upon integration efforts with a mixture of ideological disapproval and deep distrust. These attitudes were closely related to a general distrust of ECLA. Over a decade, many influential people in the United States—both in the government and in the private sector—considered ECLA an intruder in Hemispheric economic relations, a defender of dangerous statist and "socialistic" tendencies, and a competitor of the OAS. Any proposals coming from or sponsored by ECLA were viewed as a continuous incitement to Latin American countries to "gang up" against the United States in order to force economic and other concessions. These attitudes were further strengthened by the thinly disguised fear of some United States foreign trade interests that expansion of intra-regional trade in Latin America—the United States' second largest market—would be detrimental to United States exporters.[56]

Certainly, the impetus towards economic integration in Latin America came from ECLA and not the OAS.

[55] See below, p. 269, n. 7.
[56] M. S. Wionczek, 'Latin American Free Trade Association', *Int. Concil.* (Jan. 1965), pp. 24–25.

The Position of the United States after 1955

In the meantime, from 1955 onwards, there had been changes in the world situation which generally were unfavourable to the position of the United States even within the western hemisphere. It was the year Mr Khrushchev emerged as leader of the Soviet Union with his proclaimed policy of 'peaceful coexistence'. In December 1955 the 'package deal' over the admission of new members began the process of enlarging the United Nations and increasing the influence of the Afro-Asian group of countries within it. The General Assembly could no longer be counted upon to provide the necessary majority for anti-communist measures; it became progressively more neutralist and, above all, anti-colonial in sentiment. In this last respect the Latin American countries were generally sympathetic towards the Afro-Asian nations. For all these countries, the problems of economic development were (and are) vastly more important than any threat from international communism, and the division of the world into rich and poor nations more meaningful than one between 'Free' and 'Communist'.

Within the western hemisphere, the situation became more difficult for the United States in the later 1950s. The Latin American countries were increasingly dissatisfied with her response to their economic difficulties and apparent predilection for dictators who co-operated with her. The fact that these years witnessed the downfall of a number of such dictators added to United States embarrassment rather than otherwise. As Richard Stebbins pointed out: 'This progressive restriction of the area of authoritarian government in Latin America had been accomplished by the people of the countries concerned with no particular encouragement, still less any active help, from the United States.'[57] And although the United States maintained that her policy towards dictators was based on the principle of non-intervention, her sincerity was questionable after her intervention to overthrow a government of which she did not approve in the case of Guatemala.[58] In 1958 the United States was made forcibly aware of Latin American resentment by the treatment meted out to Vice-President Nixon during his 'good-will' tour.

Not long before Mr Nixon set out on his eventful journey, Mr

---

[57] *US in World Affairs, 1958* (1959), p. 353.
[58] The extent to which the Arbenz government was under communist influence is debatable. There is no doubt about United States disapproval and determination to overthrow it.

Dulles had given expression to the complacency prevailing in Washington over inter-American relations when he declared on Pan American Day:

Words can scarcely express how fortunate we are in this hemisphere, how greatly blessed, to have this kind of association, which has no counterpart in all the world, and indeed in all history. . . . Indeed, never before in history has a group of nations of comparable number enjoyed, in organized form, so high a measure of fellowship and harmony. Thus we set an example from which others can profitably learn.[59]

Less than a month later this complacency was shaken by violent demonstrations against the Vice-President. For, although his visit provoked disorders in only two countries, Peru and Venezuela,[60] the United States came to realize that they were symptomatic of much wider discontent. There were particular economic grievances as well as the general ones already mentioned. These included United States restrictions and tariffs on certain basic agricultural commodities exported by Peru; restrictions on imports of Venezuelan oil; and the knowledge that the United States was contemplating quota restrictions on imports of zinc and lead—a blow to Mexico and Peru. There was also widespread criticism of United States friendship with dictators, several of whom, including Pérez Jiménez of Venezuela (overthrown the previous January) had received high decorations from the United States government. It was unfortunate President Eisenhower felt it necessary to despatch troops to the Caribbean region in case they were needed to ensure the safety of Mr and Mrs Nixon. For this action reawakened old fears of armed intervention.

While the Eisenhower administration was slow to accept the need to re-think its Latin American policy in the light of Nixon's experience, President Kubitschek of Brazil took the initiative. The Brazilian president wrote a letter to Eisenhower proposing an 'Operation Pan America' designed to revitalize the inter-American system through new measures of political and economic co-operation. President Eisenhower's reply was non-committal, and contained the following revealing sentence: 'There is a wide range of subjects to be discussed and explored, including, for example, the problem of implementing more fully the Declaration of Solidarity of the Tenth Inter-American

[59] Stebbins, ibid. p. 361.
[60] His tour took him to Uruguay, Argentina, Paraguay, Bolivia, Peru, Colombia, and Venezuela.

Conference held at Caracas in 1954.'[61] However, in August 1958 the United States government announced that it was now 'prepared to consider the establishment of an inter-American regional development institution which would receive support from all its member countries'.[62] After a visit by Mr Dulles to Brazil, an Informal Meeting of American Foreign Ministers was held in Washington from 23 to 24 September, at which the Latin Americans pressed their economic problems. The foreign ministers requested the OAS Council to set up a 'Special Committee to Study the Formulation of New Measures for Economic Cooperation', which subsequently came to be called the 'Committee of Twenty-One'. However, President Kubitschek's 'Operation Pan America' was accepted only in principle; nor did the first meeting of the Committee of Twenty-One, held in Washington from 17 November until 12 December 1958, bring any concrete proposals beyond the establishment of an inter-American development bank.[63] In the following month, Dr Milton Eisenhower made a second report (after a visit, this time, to Central America), confirming his earlier one and describing the situation as even more serious than in 1953.[64]

When the second meeting of the Committee of Twenty-One was held in Buenos Aires from 27 April until 8 May 1959 it received a visit from Dr Fidel Castro, Prime Minister of Cuba, who proposed a $30,000 million Marshall Plan for Latin America over a ten-year period. Castro declared that 'what we need can be obtained only from the United States, and only by means of public financing'.[65] Castro's overthrow of the Batista dictatorship at the end of 1958 was the most far-reaching event in Latin America since the end of the Second World War. Something of its implications for the inter-American system were noted in the first chapter of this study.[66] Above all, the emergence of Castro was a challenge to the United States and therefore bound to produce a crisis in inter-American relations. This

---

[61] *DSB*, xxxviii/992 (1958), p. 1090. The Declaration of Solidarity was, of course, the Caracas 'anti-communist' resolution.

[62] Mecham, p. 381.

[63] See below, p. 271.

[64] M. S. Eisenhower, 'United States–Latin American Relations, 1953–1958: Report to the President', *DSB*, xl/1021 (1959), pp. 89–105.

[65] OAS Council, *Special Committee to Study the Formulation of New Measures for Economic Cooperation, Second Meeting, Buenos Aires, Argentina, Apr. 1959*, Doc. CECE/II-40 (English), 2 May 1959, Original: Spanish, p. 14. See comments on Dr Castro's proposal by A. Lleras Camargo, 'The Alliance for Progress: Aims, Distortions, Obstacles', *For. Aff.*, xlii/1 (1963), p. 28.

[66] See above, pp. 33–35.

is true whether one believes Castro was a communist from the outset
or that the United States was inevitably hostile towards a genuine
social revolution—or both. The United States was subsequently to
accuse Castro of having 'betrayed the revolution', but it cannot
seriously be believed that she would have looked kindly upon revolutionary changes in Cuba. For such changes must adversely have
affected her interests. Latin Americans noted that, as in the case of
Guatemala, the expropriation of United States property preceded the
denunciation of a government as communist.

Growing antagonism between Castro and Trujillo, the right-wing
dictator of the Dominican Republic, leading to increased tension in
the generally turbulent Caribbean region, underlined the difficulties
of the United States position. Trujillo was the main target of those
Latin Americans now urging that the inter-American system should
take steps to promote democratic government and respect for human
rights among its members. With his outspoken admirers in the United
States Congress,[67] Trujillo was just the type of Latin American
dictator Washington was accused of favouring.[68] Castro, on the other
hand, represented something new in Latin America, and his very
hostility towards the United States was bound to win him supporters.
The denunciation of Castro by the United States seemed to many
Latin Americans in striking contrast to her complacency towards (if
not encouragement of) Trujillo. While the United States infinitely
preferred Trujillo to Castro the feelings of many Latin Americans
were exactly the opposite. When the Fifth Meeting of Consultation
was held at Santiago de Chile in August 1959 to consider the
Caribbean situation, the United States found herself the champion
of non-intervention in the face of strong demands for measures to
bring about the downfall of the Dominican dictator.[69]

Tension between Castro and Trujillo was much less significant,
however, than the steady deterioration in relations between the Cuban
government and the United States. Whatever Castro's sympathies
towards communism at this stage, it was abundantly clear that the

---

[67] See J. F. Rippy, *Globe and Hemisphere: Latin America's Place in the Postwar
Foreign Relations of the United States* (1958), pp. 212–19.

[68] See J. Bosch, 'Trujillo: Problema de América', *Combate*, i/5 (1959), pp. 9–13.
Bosch, who calls Trujillo 'a heritage of the United States Marine Corps', says that
the ordinary Latin American finds it strange that the US, who was so determined
to bring down Arbenz, should have no inclination to halt Trujillo's career of
abductions, murders, and aggressions against his own people and other American
peoples.

[69] The Fifth Meeting of Consultation is discussed below, pp. 241–3.

Cuban leader was determined to bring about a revolution the character of which was bound to arouse United States hostility. It is arguable that the Eisenhower administration, which recognized the new Cuban government in January 1959, could have done more to win Castro's friendship than it subsequently did. But, given the Cuban government's intention to implement a policy aimed at ending the privileged position hitherto enjoyed by the United States in the island's affairs, this was to ask a very great deal indeed. While the United States government's handling of Castro was by no means as irreproachable as it subsequently claimed,[70] it is difficult to see what course, politically possible to any United States administration, could have avoided the clash which ensued. If the clash was inevitable, so were the growing links between Cuba and international communism. For only with Soviet support could Castro hope to survive a struggle with the United States.

Mr Khrushchev and the Monroe Doctrine

As the Cuban government moved to expropriate United States properties and to conclude trade agreements with the Soviet Union and other communist countries, relations with its powerful neighbour grew dangerously worse. After showing considerable restraint in the face of provocation, the Eisenhower administration virtually ended Cuba's sugar quota in July 1960. This was denounced by Castro as 'economic aggression' in a complaint to the Security Council.[71] In the same month Khrushchev, in a speech strongly supporting the Cuban leader, was quoted as saying: 'Figuratively speaking, Soviet artillerists, in the event of necessity, can with their rocket firepower support the Cuban people if the aggressive forces in the Pentagon dare begin intervention against Cuba.' On the same day, President Eisenhower, citing Khrushchev's speech as showing a 'clear intention to establish Cuba in a role serving Soviet purposes in this hemisphere', warned that the United States would not 'in conformity with its treaty obligations, permit the establishment of a regime dominated by international communism in the Western Hemisphere'.[72] Commenting on the President's statement at a news conference three days

[70] e.g. 88th Congress, 1st Sess., *Events in United States–Cuban Relations. A Chronology, 1957–1963* (1963).
[71] See below, p. 245.
[72] US Dept of State, *Inter-American Efforts to Relieve International Tensions in the Western Hemisphere, 1959–1960* (1962), p. 217.

later, Khrushchev contended that the Monroe Doctrine had lost its validity; it was dead and should be buried.[73]

The Russian leader's assertion caused the State Department to affirm that 'the principles of the Monroe Doctrine are as valid today as they were in 1823 when the Doctrine was proclaimed'. It described the Doctrine as 'supported by the inter-American security system through the Organization of American States'.[74] This statement is a useful reminder that the Monroe Doctrine has not been 'Pan-Americanized'; it has been supplemented, but not replaced, by the inter-American system. But did the Doctrine itself, in fact, enjoy the support of the Organization of American States? On the contrary, the Caracas Conference revealed the Monroe Doctrine to be no more acceptable than it had ever been to Latin Americans. Nevertheless, the Eisenhower administration was anxious to obtain OAS support in its quarrel with Castro, and for this purpose it decided to co-operate in adopting sanctions against Trujillo. Moreover, on the eve of the Sixth and Seventh Meetings of Consultation, President Eisenhower asked Congress to authorize an additional sum of $600 millions for economic aid to Latin America.

The Sixth and Seventh Meetings of Consultation, held at San José, Costa Rica in August 1960, dealt respectively with Venezuelan charges against the government of the Dominican Republic and the question of communist intervention in the western hemisphere. The outcome of these conferences gave little satisfaction to the Eisenhower administration. For, although sanctions were voted against Trujillo at the Sixth Meeting, the declaration against Sino-Soviet intervention in the hemisphere which emerged from the Seventh did not mention Cuba by name and provided no basis for action to bring about Castro's downfall. Ronning has observed that:

> To some Latin Americans the results of the Seventh Meeting must have carried an element of retributive justice. At Caracas the Latin Americans had gone along with Dulles, only to be let down when economic problems and problems of dictatorship came up for discussion. At San José the United States had committed itself on economic assistance and on Trujillo, only to find that a very mild and uncertain resolution against Castro was the best that it could obtain.[75]

A comparison between Caracas and San José well illustrates the way

[73] *NYT*, internat. ed., 14 July 1960.
[74] *DSB*, xliii/1101 (1960), p. 170.
[75] *Law & Politics*, p. 78.

in which the hemispheric and world climates changed to the disadvantage of the United States during the six years between them.
A week after the Seventh Meeting of Consultation had ended a
third and final meeting of the Committee of Twenty-One was held
at Bogotá. At this conference the United States agreed to make
available to Latin America the additional $600 millions of economic
aid now authorized by Congress. One-sixth of this sum was for earth-
quake rehabilitation in Chile, while the balance was for 'projects
designed to contribute to opportunities for a better way of life for the
individual citizens of the countries of Latin America'. The meeting
finally adopted the 'Act of Bogotá, Measures for Social Improvement
and Economic Development within the Framework of Operation Pan
America'. United States support for the measures proposed in the
Act of Bogotá (which is discussed in some detail in Chapter VIII of
this study)[76] represented a further shift in the position of the Eisenhower administration under the pressure of events in Latin America.
It was a considerable retreat from the traditional United States view
that the economic development of Latin America could, in the main,
be left to private enterprise and that social change would automatically follow such economic development. The measures taken during
the last months of the Eisenhower administration paved the way for
Kennedy's 'Alliance for Progress' much as President Hoover's initiation of the policy of non-intervention had done for Franklin Roosevelt's Good Neighbour policy: 'a curious parallel', in the opinion of
Dr Alberto Lleras Camargo.[77]

The Invasion of Cuba

But the beginnings of a new approach towards Latin America's
economic and social problems were only part of President Kennedy's
legacy from his predecessor. The new administration inherited the
Cuban problem which had been instrumental in inducing the new
approach. During the presidential election campaign Mr Kennedy,
who previously had described Castro as 'part of the legacy of Bolívar'
and 'of the frustration of that earlier revolution which won its war
against Spain but left largely untouched the indigenous feudal
order',[78] had severely criticized the Eisenhower administration's
failure to deal adequately with the Cuban leader and called for more

[76] See below, pp. 274–6.
[77] *For. Aff.*, xlii/1 (1963), p. 31.
[78] John F. Kennedy, *The Strategy of Peace* (1960), pp. 132–3.

positive action to secure his removal.[79] In fact, for some months the Central Intelligence Agency had been planning an invasion of the island by Cuban exiles, and this project was also taken over by the new president. The urge to do something drastic was very strong. In the United States view Cuba had become a Soviet satellite in the western hemisphere: a flouting of the Monroe Doctrine that could not be tolerated. The United States objective could only be Castro's overthrow; she declared again and again that 'communism is not negotiable in this hemisphere'. Yet the United States shrank from using armed force or even the threat of it to bring about a change of government in Cuba; such action could not have been justified by any inter-American pact or the United Nations Charter. It would have done enormous damage to the inter-American system and to the position of the United States as leader of the non-communist world. The only other course open to her (apart from the unacceptable one of coexisting with Castro) seemed to be to sponsor an invasion of Cuba by Cuban exiles which would give the signal for a popular rising within the island.

So there occurred in April 1961 the ill-fated Bay of Pigs adventure.[80] It is appropriate that Guatemala should have figured so prominently as one of the places from which the invasion was planned and launched. For this operation represented an attempt by the Central Intelligence Agency to repeat the success it achieved in Guatemala in 1954. Apart, however, from all the other factors which caused failure in 1961, Guatemala was an unfortunate precedent. The Cuban situation was quite different in so many ways, and, in any case, the United States had been successful in 1954 only in the narrow sense of ridding herself of Arbenz. Cuba, in fact, was part of the price she paid for the setback to inter-American relations her intervention in Guatemala had caused, and events in the latter country since 1954 had done nothing to render more convincing the United States claim to be the upholder of freedom in the western hemisphere. Moreover, although her leaders spoke so frequently of Castro's 'having betrayed the revolution', those planning the invasion showed a distinct suspicion of Cuban exiles who had at first supported Castro but later defected from him. Former supporters of Batista were prominent in a plan whose only hope of success lay in sparking off

[79] See 'Government Documents: Senator John F. Kennedy on the Cuban Situation, Presidential Campaign of 1960', *IAEA*, xv/3 (1961), pp. 79-95.
[80] See T. Szulc and K. E. Meyer, *The Cuban Invasion: the Chronicle of a Disaster* (1962).

N

a popular uprising in the island. The Cuban fiasco revealed the continuing inability of the United States to get beyond her self-image and face reality—in this case that her sponsorship of an invasion would be more likely to rally the Cuban people to Castro than otherwise.

At first the United States denied she was involved in the Cuban invasion, but President Kennedy subsequently assumed complete responsibility for the affair. The situation has been well summarized as follows:

> As the result of this military failure, the United States was left with all the disadvantages and none of the potential advantages of the course it had adopted. No one took seriously the technical pretense that the initiative had been left to the exiles and that the United States had not been directly involved. U.S. responsibility for the whole adventure was too glaringly apparent. At home, there were some who took the view that the attempt to get rid of Castro was not unjustified under the circumstances, and that the administration's only fault lay in not pressing it to a conclusion with whatever forces were necessary. But virtually no one in Latin America or the outside world appeared to share this opinion. Not since the "Suez war" of 1956 had there been such an international outcry against "imperialist aggression". For the first time in postwar experience, the United States found itself the target of almost universal condemnation not only in Communist and neutral states but even in allied countries.[81]

Only her powerful influence prevented condemnation in the United Nations, where Cuba had for some time been protesting that the United States was planning such an invasion. The OAS was spared the embarrassment of a debate on the Bay of Pigs fiasco by Castro's understandable preference for the world body. In the immediate aftermath of the Cuban invasion—and in the face of a warning from Khrushchev that Russia reserved the right 'if armed intervention in the affairs of the Cuban people is not cut short, to take, together with other countries, all steps to render the necessary aid to the Republic of Cuba'[82]—President Kennedy asserted that, under certain circumstances, the United States would act unilaterally to safeguard her security.[83]

The Alliance for Progress

Whatever unilateral action the United States might take in some future contingency, her next step was to launch the Alliance for

[81] Stebbins, *US in World Affairs, 1961* (1962), p. 316.
[82] *NYT*, internat. ed., 19 Apr. 1961.　　　　[83] See above, p. 24.

Progress. The President had spoken of such an alliance in his in-augural address and in his first State of the Union Message to Congress. A month before the Cuban invasion he had given more details in an address to Latin American diplomats at the White House.[84] He proposed 'a vast new 10-year plan for the Americas—a plan to transform the 1960s into an historic decade of democratic progress'. It would be a co-operative effort, involving social objectives as well as economic development, and also the furtherance of demo-cracy. President Kennedy said he would shortly request a ministerial meeting of the Inter-American Economic and Social Council 'at which we can begin the massive planning effort which will be the heart of the Alliance for Progress'.

A Special Meeting of the Inter-American Economic and Social Council at the Ministerial Level was held in Punta del Este, Uruguay (5–17 August 1961).[85] This meeting adopted 'The Charter of Punta del Este, Establishing an Alliance for Progress within the Framework of Operation Pan America'. In subscribing to this charter the United States was undertaking to provide the major share of 'a supply of capital from all external sources during the coming ten years of at least 20 billion dollars', the greater part of which sum 'should be in public funds'. For their part, the Latin American governments pledged themselves to carry out *inter alia*, 'the social reforms neces-sary to permit a fair distribution of the fruits of economic and social progress'. Each country was to formulate its own national develop-ment programme for which external assistance would be forthcoming. Economic integration in Latin America, steps towards which had already been taken in spite of United States lukewarmness in the past,[86] was recognized in the Charter of Punta del Este as necessary to accelerate the process of economic development in the hemisphere. Cuba, although represented at Punta del Este, did not sign the charter and the United States made it clear in any case that she would provide no funds for the island as long as its government retained its ties with the Soviet Union.

With President Kennedy pressing on with the Alliance for Pro-gress, demands in the United States for further action against Castro received a strong fillip from events in the Dominican Republic in November 1961. Trujillo's assassination in the previous May and the

---

[84] 'Alianza para Progreso: Address by President Kennedy and Text of Message to Congress', *DSB*, xliv/1136 (1961), pp. 471–8.
[85] Official documents published in OEA/Ser. H/XII. 1 (English). The Charter of Punta del Este is described below, pp. 276–9. [86] See above, p. 165.

subsequent overthrow of his heirs did more than remove an embarrassment to the United States. A threat of further upheaval provided the occasion for a show of force, avowedly to discourage an attempt by the Trujillo family to seize power again. Without preliminary reference to the OAS, the United States despatched eight naval vessels with 1,800 marines on board to cruise 3 miles off the Dominican coast.[87] The United States government clearly was encouraged by the general absence of Latin American criticism of this move (due, doubtless, to feeling against the Trujillo dictatorship). It was applauded at home as at last taking a firm line in the Caribbean region; the loudest acclaim came from those hoping it would prove a preliminary to strong measures against Castro. Sensing the danger to himself, the Cuban leader accused the United States of intervention in the Dominican Republic in both the Security Council[88] and the OAS Council,[89] but without success.

The Emergence of 'the Six'

By the autumn of 1961 the Cuban government was the subject of charges in the OAS Council of violating human rights and conducting subversive activities against its neighbours. The outcome of the ensuing debate to decide whether a Meeting of Consultation should be convoked to consider the matter was ominous.[90] In addition to Cuba, six countries—Mexico (who opposed), Argentina, Bolivia, Brazil, Chile, and Ecuador (who abstained)—refused to support the resolution calling for the Meeting. The six included the most important nations of Latin America as well as much more than half its total population. Mexico's position was traditional, but that of Brazil, particularly, was of considerable significance. The foreign policy of President Quadros, who took office in January 1961, had already caused uneasiness in Washington. For the new Brazilian President's views, it has been nicely observed,

appeared to depart rather widely from those the United States had come to regard as normal in a Latin American chief executive. Instead of insisting on Brazil's devotion to the inter-American system and the "free world", the new President had announced an"independent" and "sovereign"

---

[87] Stebbins, *US in World Affairs, 1961*, p. 339.
[88] *SCOR*, 16th yr, 980th, 981st, & 983rd mtgs.
[89] *Acta de la Sesión Extraordinaria celebrada el 22 de noviembre de 1961*, OEA/Ser. G/II, C-a-426 (Aprobada), 22 Nov. 1961.
[90] The debate is considered in more detail below, pp. 250–2.

foreign policy which, in Washington's eyes, seemed not unlike the "positive neutrality" proclaimed by some of the Asian and African states.[91]

And, although President Quadros resigned in August 1961, his successor clearly was following the same independent line, especially on the Cuban issue. Mexico and Brazil were to be the key countries in setting limits to the support the United States was to obtain from the OAS in her policy towards Castro.

In the circumstances, the decision to hold the Meeting on 10 January 1962 (it was later postponed to 22 January) was perhaps surprising. Clearly, the Kennedy administration was prompted more by domestic political considerations than the hemispheric situation in seeking an early meeting. It was under considerable pressure to do something about Cuba. Nevertheless, some observers believed the United States should have waited until more time could be devoted to trying to win over at least one of the biggest states. A number of meetings between President Frondizi of Argentina and leading members of the Kennedy administration, including the President himself, suggest that a special effort actually was made to win over that country. Whatever transpired at those meetings, the United States seemed to entertain the hope of Argentina's support at Punta del Este —perhaps because of President Frondizi's precarious internal position and the strong anti-Castro sentiments of the Argentine military leaders. United States prestige was at stake, for the conference was seen as a contest between the United States and Cuba; the Alliance for Progress versus Castroism. The Kennedy administration was known to be pressing for economic and diplomatic sanctions.

It was soon evident at the Eighth Meeting of Consultation[92] that the United States had not won over the six (who had not voted for holding the conference in the first place) to supporting sanctions against Cuba. Brazil and Mexico had stated publicly they would not do so; they challenged the legal competence of the meeting even to consider them. So the United States delegation had to lower its sights and work instead for the expulsion of Cuba from the OAS. This course itself ran into difficulties, since no machinery existed for the suspension or expulsion of members; nor was there in any case full support for such a move. Indeed, the necessary majority for Cuba's

[91] Stebbins, *US in World Affairs, 1961*, p. 305.
[92] For further details of the Eighth Meeting, see Ronning, *Punta del Este*; Connell-Smith, 'The Future of the Organization of American States: Significance of the Punta del Este Conference', *World Today*, xviii/3 (1962), pp. 112–20; and below, pp. 252–4.

'exclusion' was obtained only after some unedifying bargaining to secure Haiti's vote. The connection between Latin American support for the United States on the Cuban issue and the approval by Congress of funds for the Alliance for Progress was only too evident without the case of Haiti to underline it. The fact that these deliberations were taking place at Punta del Este, where a few months earlier the Alliance had been launched, seemed to reflect the reciprocal character of the two meetings. Not surprisingly, Brazil's suggestion that a basis be found for coexistence with the Castro government[93] was quite unacceptable—even offensive—to the United States. The latter was able to obtain the agreement of all members of the OAS except Cuba to a declaration that the principles of Marxism-Leninism were incompatible with those of the inter-American system. But only sixteen delegations supported a resolution suspending immediately trade with Cuba in arms and implements of war, and instructing the OAS Council to study the feasibility and desirability of extending the suspension to other items; and only fourteen the exclusion of 'the present Government of Cuba' from participation in the inter-American system. The 'six' abstained on this last resolution.

President Kennedy nevertheless declared himself well pleased with the results achieved at Punta del Este, and warmly congratulated Secretary of State Rusk on his return. As the President pointed out, for the first time all the American states (except Cuba) had denounced the concept of Marxism-Leninism as being incompatible with the inter-American system. Cuba had been condemned by name and in far stronger terms than at previous conferences. In Adolf Berle's view: 'Given the circumstances, the United States and the inter-American system with it came out as well as the political facts permitted.'[94] It was even possible to argue that the very limitation of her success at Punta del Este redounded to the credit of the United States. In the words of an unofficial observer at the Meeting: 'The fact that a super power did not issue ultimatums to its weak neighbors may do far more to improve United States-Latin American relations than a force (*sic*) unanimity would have done to weaken the position of Castro within Cuba or within the hemisphere.'[95] Nor did Secretary Rusk fail to point out that the Punta del Este Conference was not

[93] Eighth Meeting of Consultation, *Actas y documentos*, OEA/Ser. F/III. 8, pp. 110–17.
[94] A. A. Berle, *Latin America—Diplomacy and Reality* (1962), p. 103.
[95] Ronning, *Punta del Este*, p. 27.

a meeting of the Warsaw Pact.[96] But, of course, the United States did exert enormous pressure at the Eighth Meeting.

The limitations of the Meeting's achievements were very real. The resolutions adopted at Punta del Este did not endorse the United States position that the very existence of Castro's government was a threat to the sovereignty and political independence of the American states. Isolating Cuba within the hemisphere would help to curb Castro's subversive activities, but would do little towards bringing about his overthrow as long as he could obtain support from extra-continental sources. Moreover, Castro's exclusion from the OAS strengthened his case for appealing to the United Nations in his quarrel with the United States. The Cuban leader, for obvious reasons, had always preferred to use the world forum, and there was now no convincing case for preventing him from doing so. Although his specific charges against the United States of 'new plans of aggression and acts of intervention' were never upheld, there was widespread sympathy among United Nations members for his contention that the United States had no right to interfere in Cuba's internal affairs. Nor did removing from the Cuban government the protection of the inter-American system's agreements on non-intervention make measures to overthrow it any more acceptable to the OAS or to the rest of the world.

In the United States it was claimed that the six governments abstaining on the 'exclusion' issue had done so not because they really disagreed with her on this, but because of internal difficulties. It cannot be doubted that domestic considerations affected the votes of the six, as they did those of the other members of the OAS. There were, however, genuine and profound misgivings on the juridical issues involved in holding the Eighth Meeting and some of the resolutions adopted there.[97] The Mexican jurist and diplomatist, Antonio Gómez Robledo, declared that only the six (whom he calls 'hard' rather than 'soft' as they were called in the United States[98]) redeemed the meeting by their firmness in adhering to their principles.[99] Gómez Robledo and other Latin Americans totally rejected

---

[96] 87th Congress, 2nd Sess., Committee Print, *Punta del Este Conference, January 1962: Report of Senators Wayne Morse and Bourke B. Hickenlooper to the Committee on Foreign Relations United States Senate, March 1962*, (1962), p. 1.
[97] e.g. A. Gómez Robledo, 'La crisis actual del sistema interamericano', *For. Int.*, iii/1 & 2 (1962), pp. 25–61, 176–208; E. Bernstein Carabantes, 'Punta del Este y las erróneas interpretaciones de un tratado', ibid. ii/4 (1962), pp. 518–34.
[98] e.g. Berle, p. 104.
[99] Gómez Robledo, *For. Int.*, iii/1 (1962), p. 31.

Senator Morse's thesis that the OAS Charter (like the United States Constitution) contained implied powers, and that therefore the exclusion of Cuba was juridically sound. Nor was the United States argument that excluding her 'present government' was not the same thing as expelling Cuba tenable since the OAS is an association of governments. In Milton Eisenhower's view the 'series of actions' taken against Cuba at Punta del Este 'was a tremendous endorsement of the theory of collective intervention'.[100] In fact, Punta del Este confirmed that an important body of Latin American opinion, even though uneasy about Cuba's ties with international communism, was even more unhappy about 'collective intervention'. To such opinion (especially influential, as we have noted, in Mexico), the surest safeguard against the latter eventuality was a strict interpretation of the Rio Treaty and the OAS Charter.

The OAS Council put the exclusion of Cuba into effect on 14 February 1962. Already the United States had imposed an almost total embargo on her trade with the island, which she said would reduce Castro's capacity to engage in acts of aggression, subversion, or other acts endangering the security of the hemisphere. Although implemented under her own laws, the United States claimed that the embargo was imposed in accordance with the decisions taken at Punta del Este. However, the latter did not authorize a general trade embargo, only a suspension of arms shipments. The OAS Council, as we have seen, was to study the feasibility and desirability of an extension of the arms embargo to other items.

The United States remained adamant in refusing to coexist with Castro, and the Kennedy administration was under constant pressure to bring about his elimination; pressure which mounted as Castro's links with Russia grew closer and reports of a Soviet military build-up on the island gained credence.[101] The United States major allies outside the hemisphere were unwilling to stop their trade with Cuba, and this stimulated demands for some unilateral action under the Monroe Doctrine. In September 1962, following a statement by the President, the United States Congress passed a joint resolution citing the Doctrine and expressing the determination:

(*a*) To prevent by whatever means may be necessary, including the use

---

[100] M. S. Eisenhower, *The Wine is Bitter: the United States and Latin America* (1963), p. 325.
[101] There was also considerable concern over the announcement in September 1962 that Russia was going to construct a fishing port in Cuba. It was feared that this would in reality be a Soviet naval base.

of arms, the Marxist-Leninist regime in Cuba from extending, by force or the threat of force, its aggressive or subversive activities to any part of this hemisphere;

(*b*) to prevent in Cuba the creation or use of an externally supported military capability endangering the security of the United States; and

(*c*) to work with the Organization of American States and with freedom-loving Cubans to support the aspirations of the Cuban people for self-determination.[102]

However, this resolution—as its critics pointed out—called for no positive action to get rid of the Castro government, whose very presence in the hemisphere must be considered a violation of the Monroe Doctrine.

At the beginning of October the Kennedy administration made a further effort to obtain more support from the Latin American countries with an informal meeting of foreign ministers in Washington.[103] In the General Assembly of the United Nations President Dorticos of Cuba denounced the United States, but expressed his country's willingness to negotiate its differences with her. Mr Adlai Stevenson, chief United States delegate, said afterwards of this speech:

The President of Cuba professes that Cuba has always been willing to hold discussions with the United States to improve relations and to reduce tensions. But what he really wishes us to do is to place the seal of approval on the existence of a Communist regime in the Western Hemisphere. The maintenance of Communism in the Americas is not negotiable.

If the Cuban regime is sincere in its request for negotiations, and wishes to lay its grievances before the appropriate forum—the Organization of American States—I would suggest the Cuban Government might start by some action calculated to awaken the confidence of the inter-American system. The obvious place to begin would be the severing of its multiple ties to the Soviet bloc.[104]

In effect the United States was inviting Cuba (as she had Guatemala in 1954) to exchange the role of plaintiff in the United Nations for that of defendant in the OAS; and Castro to deprive himself of the main source of support in his struggle against her. Meanwhile, the Soviet arms build-up in Cuba was mounting and so were demands in the United States for action to halt it.

---

[102] *Docs Am. For. Rel., 1962* (1963), pp. 372–3. The resolution was approved as Public Law 87–733 on 3 October 1962.

[103] See below, p. 255. [104] *NYT*, internat. ed., 9 Oct. 1962.

Finally in possession of proof that Soviet missiles were being installed in Cuba, President Kennedy took the action described in Chapter VII of this study.[105] Confronted by the grave crisis—and knowing the United States was determined to act unilaterally in any case—the OAS gave her a larger measure of support than on any previous such occasion. Even so, the limitations of this support must be recognized. Mexico, Bolivia, and Brazil made it clear they did not support armed invasion of Cuba to remove the missiles. And, although a number of Latin American countries offered active help to the United States in maintaining the quarantine of Cuba, only Argentina was of importance. Nor can the outcome of the Cuban crisis of October 1962 seriously be considered a vindication of the Monroe Doctrine, as some United States writers asserted.[106] The United States still lacked the necessary Latin American support for the premise that the very existence in the western hemisphere of a government under the domination of an extra-continental system was a threat to the Americas as a whole. Brazil and Mexico (representing a more widely held feeling) believed that the United States should coexist with Castro. While many observers considered the Cuban leader's influence in Latin America much diminished because the crisis had revealed him to be 'a puppet of the Soviet Union', this was offset to no small extent by Castro's refusal to allow United Nations inspection teams to verify the withdrawal of the Russian missiles.[107] Moreover, although the United States maintained that her pledge not to invade Cuba was contingent upon on-site inspection, it would now be much more difficult for her to launch an invasion of the island than it had been before the October crisis. In the meantime Castro remained in power, strengthened rather than weakened by these events, in defiance of the Monroe Doctrine and the acknowledged desire—and apparent impotence—of his great enemy to overthrow him.

Events during the year following the crisis confirmed the limited character of the United States success. The Kennedy administration was unable to secure the removal of all Soviet forces from Cuba, let alone Castro's downfall. It proved difficult to obtain support for further measures to curb the latter's subversive activities,[108] and even

---

[105] See below, pp. 256–8.

[106] See e.g., A. Van W. Thomas and A. J. Thomas, *The Organization of American States* (1963), p. 361; Stebbins, *US in World Affairs, 1962* (1963), pp. 268–9.

[107] Later on, Castro refused to sign the Soviet-supported partial nuclear test-ban treaty.　　　　　　　　　　　　　　　　[108] See below, p. 259.

harder to persuade the remaining Latin American countries who had not done so to sever their diplomatic relations with Cuba. In the meantime, inter-American relations remained generally far from satisfactory. Disappointment with the achievements of the Alliance for Progress was widespread.[109] Latin Americans resented United States control of the disbursement of Alliance funds, while in the United States it was felt the Latin Americans should do very much more to help themselves. The connection between the Alliance for Progress and United States policy towards Castro was a recurring source of frustration and resentment.

Another factor in inter-American relations, closely linked with the Alliance for Progress, was a series of military coups d'état during the period following the adoption of the Charter of Punta del Este. This was of considerable significance, since one of the major proclaimed objectives of the Alliance was to strengthen democratic institutions. President Frondizi was deposed by an army revolt in March 1962, and President Prado of Peru in the following July. During 1963 there were military coups in Guatemala, Ecuador, the Dominican Republic, and Honduras. The overthrow of Juan D. Bosch, the first legally elected president of the Dominican Republic for thirty-eight years, was particularly embarrassing for the United States since, following Trujillo's assassination, she had endeavoured to encourage democracy there as something of an antidote to Castroism. But the military coups as a whole were of great concern to her, posing awkward questions of continuing or withholding aid under the Alliance for Progress, as well as the matter of diplomatic relations.[110] Yet United States policy of strengthening the Latin American military as the strongest force against communism[111] was encouraging these coups. In each case the United States eventually accorded recognition and resumed aid (where it had been suspended). Within the OAS the military coups raised the questions of representative democracy as a requirement of membership, and what collective action (if any) could be taken in the face of them.[112] The Foreign Minister of Venezuela, who had pressed for such action by the OAS, declared in the General Assembly of the United Nations that the

---

[109] See below, pp. 279 ff.

[110] If the US continued such aid it made a mockery of the Alliance as an instrument for fostering democracy; if she withheld it the Alliance was shown to be an instrument of her foreign policy.

[111] See Lieuwen, 'Neo-Militarism in Latin America: the Kennedy Administration's Inadequate Response'. *IAEA*, xvi/4 (1963), pp. 11–19.

[112] See below, pp. 255, 289.

former would become a farce if a majority of its members were represented by dictatorships.[113] In November 1963 the OAS Council
decided (with only Guatemala opposing) to convoke a Meeting of
Consultation 'to consider the problem of strengthening democracy
in the hemisphere'.[114] But no details were fixed, and the matter was
shelved in the face of Venezuela's charges against Cuba.

The Johnson Administration

An event whose significance for inter-American relations cannot
yet be assessed was the assassination of President Kennedy on
22 November 1963. Although President Johnson promised to continue his predecessor's policy with respect to the Alliance for Progress
it was soon evident there would be a review of United States Latin
American policy. In the middle of December it was announced that
Thomas C. Mann, the United States ambassador to Mexico, would
return to the post of Assistant Secretary of State for Inter-American
Affairs which he had held under the Eisenhower administration.
Mann became also special presidential assistant with the task of
co-ordinating all aspects of United States policy towards Latin
America. His recall and new appointment were regarded with mis-
giving in Latin America where they were interpreted as a retrogressive
step.

The Johnson administration was soon faced with a new crisis over
the Panama Canal Zone,[115] and while this was in progress tension
with Cuba increased, following the arrest of Cuban fishermen off the
Florida coast and Castro's reprisal against water supplies to Guantánamo. Both these crises subsided, though their fundamental causes
remained; in both cases critics of the administration inevitably called
for 'a firmer line'. President Johnson finally brought to an end the
long-standing Chamizal dispute with Mexico,[116] though not the issue
over the salinity of the water the Mexicans received from the Colo-
rado river. The United States continued to cultivate good relations
with Mexico in spite of the Mexican position on Cuba.[117] Mexico,

[113] UN Information Centre, London, *Release* 34/63.
[114] *Acta de la Sesión Extraordinaria celebrada el 12 de noviembre de 1963*,
OEA/Ser. G/II, C-a-520 (Aprobada), 12 Nov. 1963.
[115] This crisis is described below, pp. 260–2.
[116] Stebbins, *US in World Affairs, 1963*, p. 297.
[117] President López Mateos of Mexico told a news conference at the conclusion
of a two-day meeting with President Johnson in February 1964 that he thought
the United States should seek a solution of her problems with Cuba in the United
Nations (*NYT*, internat. ed., 24 Feb. 1964). For comment on this, see Whitaker,
Orbis, viii/3 (1964), pp. 516–17.

incidentally, was the scene of General de Gaulle's first personal attempt to assert French influence in Latin America in March 1964.[118] The military coup in Brazil the following month gave that country a more strongly anti-communist government which soon severed relations with Cuba. The Johnson administration's warm welcome of what was—regardless of the shortcomings of President Goulart—the overthrow of a constitutional government in the most important Latin American country was not calculated to improve inter-American relations in the long-term.

In the short-term, however, Goulart's overthrow strengthened the United States position within the inter-American system. In the previous December, Venezuela appealed to the OAS Council against what she described as Cuban intervention and aggression: the supply of arms to Venezuelan terrorists. The Council, acting as Provisional Organ of Consultation, approved the appointment of a fact-finding committee. Mexico did not favour this step, while Brazil, 'following the co-existence-with-Cuba line', asked the committee to make its investigation 'in Venezuela as well as in Cuba, facilitating to the latter an opportunity to defend itself'.[119] Of course the Cuban government declined to co-operate with the committee (composed of members from Argentina, Colombia, Costa Rica, the United States, and Uruguay). In its report, published in February 1964, the committee declared Cuba guilty of sending arms, training guerrillas, and seeking to overthrow the Venezuelan government.[120]

Not until five months later, however, was it deemed advisable to hold a meeting of the Organ of Consultation; the change of government in Brazil in the meantime greatly enhanced the prospects of strong resolutions against Castro. It is noteworthy that while Mexico did not send her foreign minister to the Ninth Meeting of Consultation of American Foreign Ministers (which met at the Pan American Union from 21 until 26 July 1964) the Brazilian foreign minister was elected its chairman. The circumstances were more propitious for the adoption of strong measures also because Castro was now accused of specific acts of intervention and aggression against another American state; it was—at least formally—a question of Latin American support

---

[118] See below, p. 326.
[119] *NYT*, internat. ed., 4 Dec. 1963; *Acta de la Sesión Extraordinaria celebrada el 3 de diciembre de 1963*, OEA/Ser. G/II, C-a-525 (provisional), 3 Dec. 1963.
[120] *Report of the Investigating Committee appointed by the Council of the Organization of American States, acting provisionally as Organ of Consultation*, OEA/Ser. G/IV, C-i-658 (English), 18 Feb. 1964, Original: Spanish.

for Venezuela, and not for the United States. The Ninth Meeting of Consultation[121] called for the severance of diplomatic relations with Cuba, and a cessation of trade and shipping to the island. However, these measures were not supported by Bolivia, Chile, Mexico, and Uruguay, the only countries which, in fact, maintained such relations with Cuba. If implemented, these sanctions would isolate still further the Castro government from the rest of the hemisphere, but a resolution asking for the support of friendly non-American states underlined their limited effectiveness in promoting its downfall. Castro, of course, denounced the decisions taken by the Meeting, pointing out—with justification—that the acts of aggression for which he had been condemned had for long been committed on a much larger scale by the United States against himself.[122]

Some two weeks after the Meeting Chile severed her relations with Cuba, and Bolivia and Uruguay subsequently followed suit. Undoubtedly considerable pressure had been exerted upon their governments to take this action. But the Mexican government announced that it would not cut its ties with Cuba. It maintained (as it had done all along) that there was no juridical basis for invoking the Rio treaty to deal with Venezuela's charges against Cuba. It is of interest that Mexico offered to abide by any decision of the International Court of Justice on this issue.[123] Whether Mexico could hold out as the sole survivor of the original 'six' who had not supported the United States position at the Eighth Meeting of Consultation remained to be seen.

In the meantime, the United States administration appeared less concerned over inter-American relations than it had been for some time. Certainly it was not under the considerable domestic pressure to take stronger action against Castro which had determined its predecessor's policy at Punta del Este in January 1962. In comparison with the background to the Eighth Meeting of Consultation, there was little domestic interest in the outcome of the Ninth.[124] The Johnson administration was soon to be heartened by the outcome of the Chilean elections at the beginning of September 1964 which resulted in victory for the Christian Democratic presidential candidate over a rival who had communist support. The new Chilean adminis-

---

[121] It is discussed more fully below, pp. 262–4.
[122] *Washington Post*, 27 July 1964.
[123] *NYT*, 4 Aug. 1964. Dr Castro had attempted, without success, to have the International Court of Justice give judgment on the validity of the sanctions against Cuba adopted by the Eighth Meeting of Consultation. See below, p. 254.
[124] By this time Cuba as a crisis point had become overshadowed by Vietnam.

tration might prove to be just the type of 'left of centre' government upon which the success of the Alliance for Progress theoretically depended.

Yet in the spring of 1965 inter-American relations remained uneasy. The political, economic, and social situations in much of Latin America were potentially explosive, and the Alliance for Progress had yet to produce an evolutionary rather than a revolutionary answer to the region's problems. After more than a decade of comparative neglect by the United States Latin America had become, in President Kennedy's words, 'the most critical area', though it rarely was treated as such. It had produced in October 1962 perhaps the most serious international crisis of the entire post-war period. But one of the most significant aspects of the Cuban confrontation had been that it was a global and not a purely hemispheric one. There remained a special relationship between the United States and Latin America, but now it was importantly affected by the wider international situation.

The Cuban revolution and Castro's alignment with international communism meant that the western hemisphere was now a part of the international balance of power system: a situation which it had always been the principal objective of United States Latin American policy to avert. What happened in Cuba had to be considered in the light of other areas of international crisis such as Berlin and South Vietnam. The future of the Castro government was intimately connected with the overall problem of coexistence between the United States and the Soviet Union. Moreover, the United States was driven to seek the support of her European allies in implementing her policy towards Cuba; her limited success was indicative of the changed world situation which had given these countries a greater degree of independence. At the same time, under the impact of the Cold War in the western hemisphere, leading Latin American countries such as Mexico and Brazil[125] were moving away from alignment with the United States towards neutralism. The United States was still not prepared to coexist with Castro,[126] and continued to seek ways of bringing about his overthrow. She was determined to prevent the establishment of another Soviet satellite in the Americas. But just

---

[125] How far the military coup in Brazil would permanently affect this trend remained to be seen.

[126] Overtures by Castro (see, for example, *Washington Post*, 17 and 22 July 1964) were rejected by Rusk at the Ninth Meeting of Consultation (OEA/Ser. F/II. 9 (English). Doc 24, 22 July 1964, pp. 6–7).

as she was being impelled towards acceptance of a rapprochement with the Soviet Union in the Cold War, so she would have to adjust herself to the new limitations on the exercise of her power and influence in the western hemisphere which events in recent years had revealed.

6   The Organization of American States

THE plans laid at the Inter-American Conference on Problems of War and Peace for reorganizing and strengthening the inter-American system after the end of the Second World War have already been noted. There were to be a collective-security treaty; an organic pact for the system; and an instrument consolidating the existing machinery for settling inter-American disputes. These plans were affected by the necessity to harmonize the regional with the world system of the post-war era. One factor shaping the latter was the establishment of the United Nations; others would be the development of the Cold War, the growing force of nationalism in the colonial dependencies, and the 'revolution of rising expectations' among the peoples of the underdeveloped countries. With this world system the inter-American system would become increasingly involved.

In the preceding chapter a short examination was made of the hemispheric environment, showing how this was affected by the role in the world not only of the United States, but also—even if to a much less extent—by the countries of Latin America. Generally speaking, relations between the United States and Latin America deteriorated after the end of the Second World War. It proved increasingly difficult to harmonize the policies of the super-power of the hemisphere, with her global commitments and vast economic interests, and those of the other twenty republics in the inter-American system—small, relatively powerless, more concerned with their economic and social problems than with the global struggle of their great neighbour. When the western hemisphere became a battleground in this struggle, the situation, as we have seen, became critical.

Whether the inter-American system has served to mitigate these difficulties will be considered later in this study. First, however, it will be necessary to examine the instruments forged after the Second World War to fulfil the tasks of the inter-American system: the Inter-American Treaty of Reciprocal Assistance, signed at the Inter-American Conference for the Maintenance of Continental Peace and Security; and the Charter of the Organization of American States and the American Treaty on Pacific Settlement, both signed at the Ninth International Conference of American States. This chapter

o

will also include a brief account of the relationship between the OAS and the United Nations as it was established in these three documents and certain resolutions contained in the Final Act of the Ninth International Conference.

The Inter-American Conference for the Maintenance of Continental Peace and Security met from 15 August to 2 September 1947, at the Hotel Quitandinha, Petropolis, some 40 miles from Rio de Janeiro. Twenty American states were represented, most of them, including the United States, by delegations led by their foreign ministers. The Secretary General of the United Nations received a special invitation to attend as an observer, and was present for the opening of the conference. The Governing Board of the Pan American Union decided against inviting Nicaragua, whose *de facto* government had not been recognized by a majority of the other American states. This decision, taken when the host country, Brazil, referred the question to the Governing Board, was of very doubtful legality.[1] Furthermore, towards the end of the conference, the government of Ecuador was overthrown by coup d'état and the Ecuadoran delegation was not allowed to sign the Final Act or the treaty.[2]

The Inter-American Treaty of Reciprocal Assistance, 1947

The only item on the agenda was the treaty, although economic questions were raised at the conference.[3] Before the detailed provisions of the proposed defence treaty were agreed upon, two general issues were considered: first, whether the obligations to be undertaken and procedures to be followed in the event of an armed attack should be different from those in the case of other acts or threats of aggression; and, secondly, whether a similar distinction should be made between aggression committed by a non-American state against an American state and aggression by one American state against another.

The question of distinguishing between armed attack and other forms of aggression was particularly important because of the provisions in the United Nations Charter dealing with regional arrangements. For, as has already been noted, while Article 51 of the Charter recognizes 'the inherent right of individual or collective self-defence if an armed attack occurs', Chapter VIII states that 'no enforcement

---

[1] See e.g. Kunz, *AJIL*, xlii/1 (1948), p. 113.
[2] Texts of Final Act and treaty in *Int. Conf. Am. States*, 2nd Suppl.
[3] See above, pp. 150–2.

action[4] shall be taken under regional arrangements . . . without the authorization of the Security Council'. Thus members of a regional grouping may take immediate action in self-defence against armed attack, but may act only with the authorization of the Security Council in the case of any other act or threat of aggression. In view of this distinction, the Rio Treaty has a dual character. It is an instrument providing for collective defence against armed attack in harmony with Article 51 of the United Nations Charter and a regional arrangement under Chapter VIII (Arts, 52–54) in the event of any other act or threat of aggression. Nevertheless, Article 51 is the juridical basis of the treaty which, indeed, contains no reference to Chapter VIII nor to its being a regional arrangement.[5] This omission was significant in view of the fact that the threat of 'indirect aggression' was to be the western hemisphere's main security problem in the post-war world.

The question of differentiating between aggression originating within the continent and aggression from outside, the second major problem at the outset, aroused much discussion. A number of states favoured immediate defence measures to meet aggression from outside the hemisphere and a formula stressing peaceful settlement in the case of aggression by an American state.[6] But a majority, led by the United States, stood out for a single procedure, so that the measures to be taken depended *in principle* on whether or not armed aggression had taken place (and where), and not upon the source of the aggression. Nevertheless, special pacifying action would be taken should conflict arise between American states.

The Inter-American Treaty of Reciprocal Assistance consists of a preamble and twenty-six articles. In Article 1, the signatories formally condemn war and undertake, in their international relations, not to use force or the threat of force contrary to the provisions of the United Nations Charter or of the treaty. They agree in Article 2, to settle peacefully all controversies between them and to use procedures in force in the inter-American system before referring their disputes to the General Assembly or the Security Council of the United Nations.

[4] The UN Charter does not define 'enforcement action'. This became a practical issue for the OAS when sanctions were recommended against the Dominican Republic by the Sixth Meeting of Consultation in 1960. See below, pp. 247–8.

[5] See below, p. 193.

[6] Venezuela proposed two separate treaties or at least different sets of procedures; Argentina one treaty covering extra-continental aggression only (*Report of Delegation of USA*, pp. 16–17).

Article 3 enunciates the principle that an armed attack against an American state shall be considered an armed attack upon all, and each signatory undertakes to assist in meeting it by exercising the inherent right of individual or collective self-defence recognized by Article 51 of the United Nations Charter. Should such an armed attack occur within a region defined in the following article, or within the territory of an American state, each of the signatories, on the request of the state or states directly attacked 'and until the decision of the Organ of Consultation of the Inter-American System', may determine what immediate measures it may[7] take to fulfil its obligations. The Organ of Consultation shall meet as soon as possible to examine these measures and agree upon collective ones.

Article 4 defines the limits of the region or security zone.[8] This extends from the North to the South Poles, and includes not only the continental territories of the twenty-one American republics, but also Canada, the European colonies in the western hemisphere, and Greenland, though not Iceland. It includes an extensive area of the Atlantic and Pacific Oceans, but not the Hawaiian islands, which are included as part of the territory of the United States. In 'Statements'[9] regarding this region, Guatemala reaffirmed her claims to Belice—which caused Mexico to assert her interest in the same territory; Argentina hers to the Falkland, South Georgia, and South Sandwich Islands; and both Chile and Argentina restated their claims to sovereignty over portions of Antarctica. The United States, with reference to these statements, declared her view that 'the Treaty of Rio de Janeiro has no effect upon the sovereignty, national or international status of any of the territories included in the region defined in Article 4 of the Treaty'.

Measures of self-defence provided for under Article 3 are permissible until the Security Council of the United Nations has taken the necessary action to maintain international peace and security

---

[7] The word 'may' raises the question of whether the signatories need take any action at all pending the meeting of the Organ of Consultation. On this point, see e.g. Gómez Robledo, 'El Tratado de Río', *For. Int.*, i/i (1960), pp. 55–56.

[8] A map showing the security zone is contained in *Report of Delegation of USA*, p. 58. Mexico took the lead in proposing that the region be defined in the treaty (ibid. p. 19), but the Latin Americans generally were anxious not to become involved in possible conflicts outside the hemisphere arising from US extra-continental commitments.

[9] These were included in the Final Act of the conference. Honduras and Nicaragua entered reservations to the Rio Treaty concerning their boundary dispute. See below, pp. 239–40.

(Art. 3 para. 4),[10] and the signatories agree immediately to furnish the Security Council (through the Governing Board of the Pan American Union), in conformity with Articles 51 and 54 of the United Nations Charter, with 'complete information concerning the activities undertaken or in contemplation in the exercise of the right of self-defense or for the purpose of maintaining inter-American peace and security' (Art. 5). The rights and obligations of the signatories under the United Nations Charter are reaffirmed in Article 10.

Should an armed attack upon an American state occur outside the region and outside the territory of that state, or should the inviolability, territorial integrity, sovereignty, or political independence of any American state be affected by an aggression which is not an armed attack, or by any conflict within or outside the continent, or by any other fact or situation that might endanger the peace of America, 'the Organ of Consultation shall meet immediately in order to agree on the measures which must be taken in case of aggression to assist the victim of the aggression or, in any case, the measures which should be taken for the common defense and for the maintenance of the peace and security of the Continent' (Arts. 3 and 6). The phrase 'any other fact or situation that might endanger the peace of America' is very broad. The Guatemalan delegation wished to add to it the words 'or the democratic structure of the American governments', but, although warmly supported by Uruguay, who had submitted a proposal of her own providing for consultation in the event of a 'serious attempt' against the basic rights and freedom of the individual, it was opposed (like the Uruguayan) by nearly all the others. The Cuban delegation tried unsuccessfully to have a reference inserted in the treaty to 'economic aggression'.[11] Article 6, dealing with measures in the event of an aggression which is not an armed attack, does not refer to the Security Council, although any 'enforcement action' clearly would require authorization by that body. Mexico had wanted the Rio Treaty to specify that previous authorization of the Security Council was necessary in such cases, but it was generally agreed that this was implicit in Article 10.[12]

In the case of conflict between American states, without prejudice to the right of self-defence under Article 51 of the United Nations

---

[10] The treaty does not state whether the Security Council or the members of the inter-American system will decide when the 'necessary action' has been taken. On this point see Gómez Robledo, *For. Int.*, i/1 (1960), pp. 56–59. Clearly, the signatories of the Rio Treaty understood that they would make the decision.
[11] *Report of US Delegation*, p. 25.   [12] Ibid. pp. 35–36, 180–1.

Charter, the signatories, meeting in consultation, shall call upon the contending states to suspend hostilities and restore the *status quo ante bellum*,[13] and take, in addition, 'all other necessary measures to reestablish or maintain inter-American peace and security and for the solution of the conflict by peaceful means'. Rejection of this pacifying action will be considered in determining the aggressor and in the application of measures by the consultative meeting (Art. 7).

Article 8 lists measures, ranging from the recall of diplomatic missions to the use of armed force, which may be agreed by the Organ of Consultation, and Article 9 gives some examples of acts which shall be considered as aggression in addition to those which the Organ of Consultation shall characterize as such. They are:

a. Unprovoked armed attack by a State against the territory, the people, or the land, sea or air forces of another State;
b. Invasion, by the armed forces of a State, of the territory of an American State, through the trespassing of boundaries demarcated in accordance with a treaty, judicial decision, or arbitral award, or, in the absence of frontiers thus demarcated, invasion affecting a region which is under the effective jurisdiction of another State.

The Organ of Consultation referred to in the previous articles will normally be the Meeting of Foreign Ministers of the American Republics ratifying the treaty (Art. 11), but the Governing Board of the Pan American Union may act provisionally as an organ of consultation until a Meeting can take place (Art. 12). Any ratifying state may initiate a Meeting of Consultation through the Governing Board (Art. 13), which decides by an absolute majority whether to call one (Art. 16). The Organ of Consultation takes its decisions by a vote of two-thirds of the ratifying states, less the parties involved in the case of a dispute between American states (Arts. 17 and 18).[14] All ratifying signatories are bound by decisions to apply measures to meet aggression 'with the sole exception that no State shall be required to use armed force without its consent' (Art. 20).

The treaty is to come into effect (between the states which ratify) with the deposit of two-thirds of the ratifications and will then be registered with the Secretariat of the United Nations. It will remain in force indefinitely, but may be denounced by any signatory on

---

[13] For some observations on the role of the OAS in restoring the *status quo* rather than resolving underlying conflicts in the western hemisphere see below, pp. 303–4.
[14] This applies also to Art. 16.

giving two years' notice. It actually came into effect on 3 December 1948, when the fourteenth signatory (Costa Rica) deposited its ratification. It was eventually ratified by all the signatories.

Thus was responsibility for the defence of the western hemisphere placed formally upon all the members of the inter-American system. In practice, of course, the United States would still provide an overwhelmingly large proportion of the military power which would make the Rio Treaty effective. And her influence in the system would give her by far the biggest, if not the decisive voice in determining when there occurred 'an aggression which is not an armed attack'. Moreover, there remained in the background the Monroe Doctrine embodying the 'inherent right' of individual self-defence as well as the claim of the United States to determine for herself when her security was threatened in the hemisphere.

The Rio Treaty differs from all previous inter-American agreements in one very important respect: it is a regional treaty within a broader international organization. Its juridical basis is the exercise of the right of individual and collective self-defence recognized by Article 51 of the United Nations Charter.[15] We have already seen how the American states pressed for the inclusion of this right in the Charter at San Francisco, specifically to make possible the implementation of the Act of Chapultepec. As noted, too, there are numerous references to the United Nations Charter in the Rio Treaty and to the rights and obligations of the American states under it.

Senator Vandenberg, later Chairman of the United States Senate Foreign Relations Committee, described the Rio Pact as 'not a substitute for the United Nations. It is a supplement to the United Nations and part of its machinery'.[16] But clearly the major role of the pact was envisaged as lying in the field of action not requiring prior authorization by the Security Council, where already the veto was being used to the disadvantage of the United States and her friends. Later on, the question of forms of aggression not constituting armed attack—to which Article 51 is not applicable—was to prove much more important and raise difficult issues within the inter-American system.

---

[15] In the light of subsequent developments it is of interest to note the observation of Kunz, *AJIL*, xlii/1 (1948), p. 120: 'The Rio Treaty is built entirely upon Art. 51 of the Charter and on the conception of "armed attack". It can, therefore, only be a system of self-defense, not a system of sanctions.'

[16] E. S. Furniss, Jr, 'The United States, the Inter-American System and the United Nations', *Pol. Sci. Q.*, lxv/3 (1950), p. 424.

In the meantime the Rio Treaty was not complete in itself and looked forward at various points to the Ninth International Conference of American States which was to fulfil other tasks laid down at Mexico City. At Bogotá, for instance, a treaty was to be concluded improving the inter-American peace machinery; also, the matter of a permanent military council was to be discussed. But above all, the Ninth Conference was to adopt an organic pact which would at last give a treaty basis to the inter-American system.

The Ninth Conference (*Bogotá, 1948*)

The Ninth International Conference of American States met at Bogotá from 30 March to 2 May 1948. All twenty-one republics were represented, though there had been some doubt about inviting Nicaragua, whose government had not been recognized by a number of the others. Ten, including the United States, sent their ministers of foreign affairs. Secretary of State George Marshall, who remained for four of the five weeks of the conference, headed a strong delegation which also included the Secretaries of Commerce and the Treasury. The United Nations was represented by an observer with advisers.

The programme of the conference and its regulations had been carefully prepared by the Governing Board of the Pan American Union. The programme was divided at the opening session among six working committees, upon each of which all the participating countries were represented. Two of these committees were given the task of drafting a charter for the reorganized inter-American system; the First being concerned mainly with the nature and purposes of the system and the Second with problems of organization. They had before them the 'Project of Organic Pact of the Inter-American System' drafted by the Governing Board in accordance with Resolution IX of the Mexico City Conference.[17] The task of the Third Committee was to prepare an inter-American treaty on the pacific settlement of disputes which would co-ordinate and improve existing inter-American peace instruments. The Fourth Committee was concerned with economic questions, and the Inter-American Economic and Social Council had prepared a draft agreement in accordance with a resolution adopted at Rio de Janeiro the previous year.[18]

---

[17] PAU, *Project of Organic Pact of the Inter-American System, Submitted to the Ninth International Conference of American States by resolution of the Governing Board of the Pan American Union at the meeting of February 4, 1948*, Document CB-10-E. (1948).   [18] See above, p. 152.

The Fifth dealt with social and cultural matters, including two proposed conventions on the rights of women. The Sixth Committee handled political and juridical issues, notably the problem of European colonies in the western hemisphere;[19] the recognition of *de facto* governments; the defence and preservation of democracy; and a declaration on the rights and duties of man.

Because of the riots of 9 April,[20] these arrangements were changed. The Steering Committee, composed of the heads of the delegations, assumed a dominant role. On the basis of its decisions, the six working committees drafted the conclusions of the conference, which consisted of five treaties or formal agreements and a Final Act containing forty-six recommendations and resolutions. The five treaties or agreements were: the Charter of the Organization of American States; the American Treaty on Pacific Settlement or 'Pact of Bogotá'; the Economic Agreement of Bogotá; the Inter-American Convention on the Granting of Political Rights to Women; and the Inter-American Convention on the Granting of Civil Rights to Women. This chapter will be concerned with the first two of these agreements: the OAS Charter and the Pact of Bogotá.

The Charter of the Organization of American States, 1948

In drafting the Charter of the Organization of American States the question arose of how comprehensive the document should be. The United States favoured limiting the Charter's scope and including such matters as the rights and duties of states and of men, for example, in separate agreements. Mexico, on the other hand, was the strongest advocate of the Charter's being an 'all-embracing, self-contained document which would incorporate the standards of conduct of states and individuals and the principles of inter-American economic, social, and cultural cooperation, as well as provisions on security matters and on the pacific settlement of disputes'.[21] In the event, the Charter does contain chapters on principles and on the rights and duties of states; short chapters on economic, social, and cultural co-operation; and chapters on the pacific settlement of disputes and collective security. But no declaration of the rights and

---

[19] On the insistence of the Latin American delegations (excluding that of Brazil) a resolution (XXXIII) was adopted at Bogotá to create an 'American Committee on Dependent Territories'. [20] See above, pp. 153, 155.
[21] *Report of Delegation of USA*, p. 13. For claims by Mexicans regarding the leading role of Mexico in determining the scope of the OAS Charter, see Gómez Robledo, *Idea y experiencia de América*, p. 203, and L. Quintanilla, 'La convivencia americana', *Cuadernos Americanos*, cxxi/2 (1962), p. 79.

duties of man is included; the Rio Treaty is only referred to and not incorporated; and there was a separate treaty on pacific settlement.

Not until the conference itself did the twenty-one republics finally decide that the document establishing the treaty basis of their system should be called 'The Charter of the Organization of American States'. Moreover, they reached this decision only with difficulty and after sharp debate.[22] A number of delegates supported retaining the existing name, Union of the American Republics, which, as we have seen, was adopted at the Fourth (Buenos Aires) Conference in 1910. But the Argentine delegation strongly opposed this suggestion and any other term which might imply some kind of 'super-state'. Certain Latin American countries (notably Mexico) favoured applying the name 'Pan American Union' to the organization as a whole, but this was opposed on several grounds.[23] The title 'Inter-American System', used in the resolutions contained in the Act of Chapultepec, had virtually no support. 'Organization' having eventually been preferred to any other name descriptive of the system, 'States' was adopted, rather than 'Republics' or 'Nations', to designate the members. This last decision looked forward to the possibility of Canada or some new American state subsequently joining the OAS.

The OAS Charter contains 112 Articles grouped into 18 chapters and divided into 3 parts. The first part deals with the nature, purposes, and principles of the Organization of American States; the fundamental rights and duties of states; pacific settlement of disputes; collective security; and economic, social, and cultural standards. The second part describes the organs through which the organization accomplishes its purposes. The third part contains miscellaneous provisions, deals with ratification and entry into force of the Charter, and affirms that none of its provisions shall be construed as impairing the rights and obligations of the member states under the Charter of the United Nations.

The first chapter, entitled 'Nature and Purposes', describes the organization as being 'within the United Nations . . . a regional agency' and refers to its 'regional obligations under the Charter of the United Nations'. Five essential purposes are proclaimed: to strengthen the peace and security of the continent; to prevent possible

[22] Ninth International Conference of American States, *Actas y documentos* (1953–4), iii. 141–5, 500–4, &c.

[23] e.g. the US felt it might lead to some' confusion, while Argentina objected to the word 'union'. Incidentally, confusion of the PAU with the organization as a whole has nevertheless persisted.

causes of difficulties and to ensure the pacific settlement of disputes that may arise among the member states; to provide for common action on the part of those states in the event of aggression; to seek the solution of political, juridical, and economic problems that may arise among them; and to promote, by co-operative action, their economic, social, and cultural development. All American states ratifying the Charter are members of the organization,[24] and any new political entity arising from the union of several member states shall become a member after itself doing so. In the latter event the states constituting the new political entity would lose their individual membership. Recurrent attempts to form a Central American grouping inspired this article.[25]

The question of membership is also referred to in Article 108, which declares 'The present Charter shall remain open for signature by the American States and shall be ratified in accordance with their respective constitutional procedures'. Thus no qualifications other than being an American state and having ratified the Charter were required for membership of the OAS.[26] The draft organic pact submitted by the Governing Board of the Pan American Union to the Bogotá Conference had provided that 'The American States are, as of right, members of the Inter-American System' (Art. 2). It also declared that 'The American States, in order to enjoy the rights and benefits of the Inter-American System, shall fulfill in good faith the obligations inherent in their membership in the System' (Art. 3). During the debates on this question the Brazilian delegation proposed that membership should be conditional not only upon ratification of the Charter, but also upon possessing a democratic form of government.[27] This restriction on the long-established concept of 'inherent right' to participation in the inter-American system was not accepted by the conference. Nor was Article 3 of the draft organic pact included

[24] Ecuador wanted a special article dealing with the admission of new states coming into being within the hemisphere (i.e. as the result of European dependencies being granted independence), but the US and Mexico argued that this question was already covered by existing articles (*Actas y documentos*, iii. 289–90).

[25] In October 1951 the foreign ministers of Costa Rica, Guatemala, Honduras, Nicaragua, and El Salvador, meeting in San Salvador, signed a treaty establishing the Organization of Central American States. For an unofficial translation of the 'Charter of San Salvador' and comment by C. G. Fenwick, see *Ann. OAS*, iv/3 (1952), pp. 351–5.

[26] The OAS Charter lays down no procedure for the admission of new members. This was not, in fact, established until December 1964, when the First Special Inter-American Conference resolved that it should be by a two-thirds majority vote in the OAS Council (see below, pp. 297–8.)

[27] *Actas y documentos*, iii. 64, 92.

in the Charter. Indeed, the Charter contains no provision for either expulsion from the OAS or suspension of the rights of membership for violations of its provisions. A suggestion for the inclusion of such an article had been rejected at an early stage in the preparatory work by the Governing Board.[28] Withdrawal from the organization is provided for, however (Art. 112).

The second chapter is, in the main, a reaffirmation of principles already proclaimed as ideals of the inter-American system; but greater emphasis is now laid upon democracy. Article 5(*d*) asserts that 'the solidarity of the American States and the high aims which are sought through it require the political organization of those States on the basis of the effective exercise of representative democracy'. An attempt to include a definition of democracy, made at the suggestion of the Brazilian and Uruguayan delegations, was, however, abandoned in the face of the difficulties involved. Although it was agreed that a statement of the rights and duties of man should not be included in the Charter, but rather form the subject of a separate declaration without contractual force, in Article 5(*j*) 'the American States proclaim the fundamental rights of the individual without distinction as to race, nationality, creed or sex'.

Of some interest is paragraph (*e*) of Article 5: 'The American States condemn war of aggression: victory does not give rights.' The Argentine delegation vigorously proposed that the phrase 'victory does not give rights' should be included. But the United States opposed this on the grounds that it was properly applicable only to a victorious aggressor. As a result, the Argentine proposal was linked to the condemnation of war of aggression.[29] This argument recalls the debate on 'the right of conquest' at the First International Conference of American States and the stand then taken by the United States.[30]

Chapter III, 'Fundamental Rights and Duties of States', was included in the Charter on the unanimous vote of the Latin American delegations, but with the United States abstaining. In the latter's view such a chapter, unless couched in very general terms, would involve highly technical and even controversial issues. The Latin Americans, however, pointed out that agreement had already been reached on a comprehensive statement of the basic rights and duties of states at Montevideo in 1933. The Montevideo Convention on the

---

[28] *Report of Delegation of USA*, p. 16.
[29] *Actas y documentos*, iii. 84, 174–81, 300, &c.
[30] See above, p. 43.

Rights and Duties of States did, in the event, form the basis of Chapter III of the OAS Charter. But there were several significant differences.

Article 12, affirming that 'the jurisdiction of States within the limits of their national territory is exercised equally over all the inhabitants, whether nationals or aliens', concerns the important question of diplomatic intervention. Article 9 of the Montevideo Convention (which the United States had accepted with reservation) read as follows:

The jurisdiction of states within the limits of national territory applies to all the inhabitants.

Nationals and foreigners are under the same protection of the law and the national authorities and the foreigners may not claim rights other or more extensive than those of the nationals.

In committee at Bogotá this had been modified to read:

The jurisdiction of states within the limits of their national territory is exercised equally over all the inhabitants. Nationals or foreigners are under the same protection and owe the same obedience to the laws and the authorities of the country.

The United States objected, of course, to the phrase 'under the same protection' in the second sentence of the committee draft, and insisted on the right of making diplomatic representations should the treatment accorded to her citizens fall below 'recognized standards'. So the offending sentence was deleted and the phrase 'whether nationals or aliens' added to the first. Even so, there were three contrary votes, and the delegations of Mexico and Ecuador made statements to the effect that 'the approval of article 12 does not modify or reduce the scope of article 9 of the Montevideo convention on the rights and duties of states with respect to those countries that have signed and ratified that convention'.[31]

The principle of non-intervention is reaffirmed in Articles 15:

No State or group of States has the right to intervene, directly or indirectly, for any reason whatever, in the internal or external affairs of any other State. The foregoing principle prohibits not only armed force but also any other form of interference or attempted threat against the personality of the State or against its political, economic and cultural elements.

and 17:

The territory of a State is inviolable; it may not be the object, even

---

[31] *Report of Delegation of USA*, pp. 36–37.

temporarily, of military occupation or of other measures of force taken by another State, directly or indirectly, on any grounds whatever. No territorial acquisitions or special advantages obtained either by force or by other means of coercion shall be recognized.

Article 15 represents an expansion of the provisions of the Additional Protocol of Buenos Aires. For while the latter spoke only of intervention by any one state, Article 15 applies also to any group of states. This expansion reflects Latin American fear of 'collective intervention', which had been stimulated by the Rodríguez Larreta proposal in 1945.[32]

Whether the term 'group of states' in this context could be applied to the OAS itself would give cause for much future debate.[33] In the meantime the principle of non-intervention had to be reconciled with that of collective security, especially since the American states had signed the Rio Treaty and the United Nations Charter. Article 19, therefore, declares that 'Measures adopted for the maintenance of peace and security in accordance with existing treaties do not constitute a violation of the principles set forth in Articles 15 and 17.'

A further extension to the principle of non-intervention is contained in Article 16, which affirms that no state may use or encourage the use of coercive measures of an *economic* (author's italics) or political character in order to force the sovereign will of another state and obtain from it advantages of any kind. The Cuban delegation, which had raised this matter unsuccessfully at the Rio de Janeiro Conference the previous year, was the foremost supporter of a move to condemn 'economic aggression'. After some debate, Cuba accepted Article 16, and a similar one was inserted in the Economic Agreement. Cuba had been much put out by the United States Sugar Act of 1947; over a decade later 'economic aggression' was to be of much greater significance in relations between the two countries.

Chapters IV and V, dealing respectively with the important questions of pacific settlement of disputes and collective security, are short and general, for separate treaties cover them: the Pact of Bogotá and the Rio Treaty of Reciprocal Assistance. Article 20 (in Chapter IV) reiterates the obligation of the signatories contained in Article 2 of the Rio Treaty to submit inter-American disputes to the peaceful procedures in force in the inter-American system before submitting them to the Security Council of the United Nations.[34]

[32] See above, pp. 142–4.
[33] See below, pp. 294–5.
[34] See below, p. 216.

The three remaining chapters of Part One are devoted to economic,[35] social,[36] and cultural standards,[37] which are described briefly and in very general terms. They are condensations of longer drafts proposed by the Mexican delegation, and were included in response 'to an approach to the charter persistently urged by Mexico, based on the concept that the document should embrace all aspects of inter-American cooperation'.[38]

Part Two of the Charter describes the organs through which the Organization of American States accomplishes its purposes. They are six: the Inter-American Conference; the Meeting of Consultation of Ministers of Foreign Affairs; the Council; the Pan American Union; the Specialized Conferences; and the Specialized Organizations.

The Inter-American Conference and the Meeting of Consultation

The Inter-American Conference, the new, abbreviated name for the International Conference of American States, is described (Art. 33) as 'the supreme organ' of the OAS. As such, 'it decides the general action and policy of the Organization and determines the structure and functions of its Organs, and has the authority to consider any matter relating to friendly relations among the American States'. But, Article 33 goes on, 'these functions shall be carried out in accordance with the provisions of this Charter and of other inter-American treaties'. For the existence of the Charter itself has limited the powers of the Inter-American Conference. Moreover, the Charter can only be amended at an Inter-American Conference convened for that purpose and any such amendment must then be ratified by two-thirds of the member states. Previous conferences, because of the absence of a charter or constitution, had not been so restricted.

All member states have the right to be represented at the Inter-American Conference, which shall convene every five years at the time fixed by the Council of the organization, after consultation with the government of the country where it is to be held. Each state is entitled to one vote. The programme and regulations of the Conference are to be prepared by the Council and submitted to the member states for consideration. No provision is made for a 'special' as opposed to a 'regular' conference, but a 'special Inter-American

---

[35] See below, p. 266.
[36] See below, p. 273.
[37] See below, pp. 283–4.
[38] *Report of Delegation of USA*, pp. 38–39.

Conference' may be held 'in special circumstances and with the approval of two-thirds of the American Governments' (Art. 36).[39]

The Meeting of Consultation of Ministers of Foreign Affairs is to be held 'in order to consider problems of an urgent nature and of common interest to the American States, and to serve as the Organ of Consultation' (Art. 39). It does not meet annually, as provided for at Mexico City, but whenever necessary. Any member state may request the Council to call a Meeting of Consultation, and the Council decides, by an absolute majority, whether a meeting shall be held (Art. 40). As in the case of the Inter-American Conference, the programme and regulations of the Meeting of Consultation are prepared by the Council and submitted to the member states for consideration. 'In case of an armed attack within the territory of an American State or within the region of security delimited by treaties in force, a Meeting of Consultation shall be held without delay.' The calling of such a meeting shall be the responsibility of the Chairman of the Council, who shall at the same time call a meeting of the Council itself (Art. 43).

The Organ of Consultation will be advised by an Advisory Defense Committee, composed of the highest military authorities of the American states participating in the Meeting of Consultation. The United States had wanted an Inter-American Defense Council as a dependent organ of the Council, and this had been provided for in the Governing Board's organic pact. In the face of opposition at the conference, however, the plan was dropped, but the existing Inter-American Defense Board was continued by a resolution included in the Final Act.

The OAS Council

Under the Charter, the Governing Board is separated from the Pan American Union and becomes the Council of the Organization of American States. This reflects the widening scope of the Governing Board's activities. Yet there was considerable opposition at the Ninth International Conference to the Council being granted political powers, and the resolution at Mexico City under which it was agreed that the Board

shall take action, within the limitations imposed upon it by the International

---

[39] The First Special Inter-American Conference was held at the Pan American Union, 16–18 Dec. 1964 (see below, pp. 297–8).

Conferences of American States or pursuant to the specific direction of the Meetings of Ministers of Foreign Affairs, on every matter that affects the effective functioning of the inter-American system and the solidarity and general welfare of the American Republics . . .

was changed as Article 50 of the OAS charter to read:

The Council takes cognizance, within the limits of the present Charter and of inter-American treaties and agreements, of any matter referred to it by the Inter-American Conference or the Meeting of Consultation of Ministers of Foreign Affairs.

Nevertheless, the Council's authority was enhanced by the power it was given by Article 40 to decide whether or not to convoke a Meeting of Consultation in cases arising under Article 39; and even more by its role as Provisional Organ of Consultation.[40]

The Council is composed of one especially appointed representative of each member state, having the rank of ambassador. The appointment may be given to the diplomatic representative accredited to the government of the country in which the Council has its seat. As we have seen, the composition of the Council—or, rather, of the Governing Board as it was—like the discussion of political questions, had been a controversial issue of long standing in the development of the inter-American system. At Bogotá, Mexico strongly pleaded the case for special representatives devoting their full time to their OAS responsibilities, but some of the smaller countries regarded this as unnecessary and too expensive.[41] Apparently, only some six governments had conformed to the Mexico City resolution that the Board should be composed of delegates who were not representatives accredited to the United States government, 'and upon the insistence of a number of the other republics, the Governing Board, prior to the Ninth Conference, had in effect set the resolution aside pending final decision at Bogotá'.[42] Thus the OAS Charter reversed the Mexico City resolution and reverted to a formula similar to the one agreed upon at Havana in 1928.[43]

The Council is responsible for the proper discharge by the Pan American Union of the duties assigned to it. It has increased responsibilities in respect of the specialized organizations and will establish the bases for fixing the quota each government is to contribute to

---

[40] See below, p. 301.
[41] *Actas y documentos*, ii, 147–80, &c.; *México en la IX Conferencia Internacional Americana* (1948), pp. 70–72.
[42] *Report of Delegation of USA*, p. 20. [43] See above, p. 67.

the maintenance of the Pan American Union. It also has the duty to promote and facilitate collaboration between the Organization of American States and the United Nations as well as between the inter-American specialized organizations and similar international agencies. Functioning at the seat of the Pan American Union, the Council formulates its own regulations.

The OAS Council has three organs of its own: the Inter-American Economic and Social Council; the Inter-American Council of Jurists; and the Inter-American Cultural Council. These organs have technical autonomy within the limits of the Charter under statutes drawn up by the Council after consultation with the governments. All three are composed of representatives of all member states; in the case of the Economic and Social Council it is specified that these will be 'technical delegates'. In agreement with the Council, they are to establish co-operative relations with the corresponding organs of the United Nations and with national or international agencies that function within their respective spheres of action.

The Inter-American Economic and Social Council is to function at the seat of the Pan American Union, meeting on its own initiative or that of the Council of the organization. The seats of the other two councils are not specified, and they are to meet only when convened by the Council; but each has a small permanent body to undertake preparatory studies between meetings. The Inter-American Juridical Committee of Rio de Janeiro, composed of jurists from nine countries selected by the Inter-American Conference, will perform this function for the Council of Jurists. A Committee for Cultural Action,[44] composed of members of five states also chosen at each Inter-American Conference, will act in that capacity for the Cultural Council. The Economic and Social Council, meeting more frequently, is not provided with a corresponding committee and is given the additional function of acting as 'coordinating agency for all official inter-American activities of an economic and social nature'.

The question of creating a permanent military agency arose at both the Mexico City and Rio Conferences, and the Governing Board's draft organic pact included an Inter-American Defense Council as a fourth organ of the Council. But there was strong opposition to this project from two quarters. Argentina, whose delegation had wanted the Council itself to have only administrative powers, thought the military body should be independent of the latter's control and

[44] It has its seat in Mexico City.

established, not by the Charter, but by a separate protocol to the Rio Treaty.[45] Mexico took the lead in opposing the inclusion of such a permanent military body within an essentially pacific inter-American system.[46] The Advisory Defense Committee was agreed upon as a compromise. As Dreier has observed:

> The nonmilitary character of the O.A.S. is indicated by the fact that the only reference to military affairs appearing in the Charter concerns the creation of an Advisory Defense Committee which is to meet only on special convocation, notably to give advice in connection with the consideration of military measures to be taken under the Treaty of Rio de Janeiro. This committee has in fact never been organized.[47]

Other Organs of the OAS

The Pan American Union retains under the Charter much the same functions as previously. It is 'the central and permanent organ of the Organization of American States and the General Secretariat of the Organization'. The former Director General of the Union becomes the Secretary General of the Organization[48] and the former Assistant Director General the Assistant Secretary General. The holders of the two former offices (Dr Alberto Lleras Camargo and Dr William Manger) were, in fact, recommended by resolution of the Bogotá Conference for appointment to the new ones. The Secretary General is to participate with voice, but without vote, in the deliberations of the Inter-American Conference, the Meeting of Consultation, the Specialized Conferences, and the Council and its organs. The heads of the respective departments of the Pan American Union, appointed by the Secretary General, shall be executive secretaries of the Inter-American Economic and Social Council, the Council of Jurists, and the Cultural Council.

The Specialized Conferences, previously known as technical inter-American conferences, are to meet to deal with special technical matters or to develop specific aspects of inter-American co-operation.[49] The Specialized Organizations are 'the intergovernmental organizations established by multilateral agreements and having

---

[45] *La República Argentina en la IX Conferencia Internacional Americana* (1949), pp. 177–8.

[46] *México en la IX Conferencia*, pp. 126–30; Dreier, *Hemisphere Crisis*, pp. 46–47.

[47] Dreier, *Hemisphere Crisis*, pp. 45–46.

[48] The Secretary General is elected by the Council for a ten-year term. He may not be re-elected or succeeded by a person of the same nationality.

[49] For a list of Specialized Conferences, 1902–63, see *PAU, Conferencias Especializadas Interamericanas: compilación de datos* (1964?).

specific functions with respect to technical matters of common interest to the American States'.[50] They are to establish co-operative relations with world agencies of the same character in order to coordinate their activities. But, in concluding agreements with international agencies of a world-wide character, the Inter-American Specialized Organizations shall preserve their identity and their status as integral parts of the Organization of American States, even when they perform regional functions for such international agencies.

Under Article 53 of the Charter the Council of the Organization has the duty of submitting to the member governments and the Inter-American Conference proposals for the creation of new Specialized Organizations, or for the combination, adaptation, or elimination of existing ones. The Council is given further tasks in rationalizing the Specialized Organizations, including the setting up of a register of these bodies, in a separate resolution of the Conference (III). The relationship between the Specialized Organizations and the OAS is to be determined by agreements concluded between them and the Council.

Miscellaneous Provisions of the Charter

Part Three contains, first, a chapter headed 'The United Nations', stating that 'none of the provisions of this Charter shall be construed as impairing the rights and obligations of the Member States under the Charter of the United Nations'. The following chapter on miscellaneous provisions deals mainly with the privileges and immunities to be enjoyed by the Organization and its component parts. The final chapter concerns ratification and entry into force. The Charter is to enter into force among the ratifying states when two-thirds of the signatories have deposited their ratifications;[51] it shall remain in force indefinitely. Amendments to the Charter may be adopted only at an Inter-American Conference convened for that purpose. The final

[50] At this point there were 6 inter-American bodies which were to be designated as Specialized Organizations: the Pan American Sanitary Bureau (establ. 1902); the American International Institute for the Protection of Childhood (1927); the Inter-American Commission of Women (1928); the Pan American Institute of Geography and History (1929); the Inter-American Indian Institute (1940); and the Inter-American Institute of Agricultural Sciences (1944). The OAS Charter also refers to 'other American organizations of recognized international standing' which number many more, and which the Council was to rationalize.

[51] The OAS Charter entered into effect on 13 Dec. 1951, when the fourteenth ratification was deposited by Colombia. It was registered with the General Secretariat of the UN on 16 Jan. 1952. Argentina was the last to deposit her ratification (10 Apr. 1956). The Charter had been effective on an interim basis under Resolution XL of the Final Act of the Ninth International Conference.

article contains the denunciation clause: 'After two years from the date on which the Pan American Union receives a notice of denunciation, the present Charter shall cease to be in force with respect to the denouncing State, which shall cease to belong to the Organization after it has fulfilled the obligations arising from the present Charter.'

The American Treaty on Pacific Settlement (1948)[52]

After the Charter of the OAS, the most important document signed at the Ninth Conference was the 'American Treaty on Pacific Settlement', or the 'Pact of Bogotá'. Its object was to coordinate the hemispheric instruments for the prevention and peaceful solution of controversies. The Pact of Bogotá was to replace the existing agreements which hitherto had made up the inter-American peace system: Treaty to Avoid or Prevent Conflicts between the American States, of 3 May 1923; General Convention of Inter-American Conciliation, of 5 January 1929; General Treaty of Inter-American Arbitration and Additional Protocol of Progressive Arbitration, of 5 January 1929; Additional Protocol to the General Convention of Inter-American Conciliation, of 26 December 1933; Anti-War Treaty of Non-Aggression and Conciliation, of 10 October 1933; Convention to Coordinate, Extend and Assure the Fulfillment of the Existing Treaties between the American States, of 23 December 1936; Inter-American Treaty on Good Offices and Mediation, of 23 December 1936; Treaty on the Prevention of Controversies, of 23 December 1936.

The pacific settlement of disputes between American states, as this study has noted, has been a basic principle of the inter-American system from the outset. The subject has appeared on the agenda of every International Conference of American States and has been discussed at several 'special' conferences. But although the principle that all inter-American disputes should be settled by peaceful means has long been accepted, its embodiment in acceptable treaty form has proved elusive. At the beginning of 1948, none of the agreements noted above had been ratified by all the American states.

Plans for reorganizing and strengthening the inter-American system naturally included the coordination and improvement of its peace machinery. As we noted, the Mexico City Conference recommended that the Inter-American Juridical Committee should prepare immediately a draft inter-American peace system which would

[52] Text in *Int. Conf. Am. States*, 2nd Suppl., pp. 200–13.

'coordinate the continental agreements for the prevention and pacific solution of controversies'. Two drafts, in fact, were prepared and the second (revised and more rigid in its requirements) submitted to the Ninth Conference. On this basis the Third Committee of the conference drew up the treaty which, in the words of Article 23 of the OAS Charter, was to 'establish adequate procedures for the pacific settlement of disputes, and . . . determine the appropriate means for their application, so that no dispute between American States shall fail of definitive settlement within a reasonable period'.[53]

The Pact of Bogotá provides for procedures of Good Offices and Mediation (Chapter 2); Investigation and Conciliation (Chapter 3); Judicial Procedure (Chapter 4); and Arbitration (Chapter 5). The order in which they are listed does not affect the choice of the parties to have recourse to whichever procedure they think most appropriate in each case. Negotiation is not included, since the treaty is concerned with the settlement of controversies that cannot, in the opinion of the contending parties, be settled through normal diplomatic channels.

Chapter 1 contains a general obligation to settle disputes between the signatories by pacific means and to use regional peace machinery before referring them to the Security Council of the United Nations (Article II).[54] Any of the pacific procedures described in the following chapters may be used, according to the preferences of the parties concerned. Matters exempted from the application of these procedures are listed in Articles V–VII: first, those within the domestic jurisdiction of one of the parties, the International Court of Justice deciding, if necessary, whether a controversy comes within this category; secondly, 'matters already settled by arrangement between the parties, or by arbitral award or by decision of an international court, or which are governed by agreements or treaties in force on the date of the conclusion of the present Treaty'; thirdly, those matters involving diplomatic representation.

Under this last Article (VII), the signatories 'bind themselves not to make diplomatic representations in order to protect their nationals,

---

[53] According to W. Sanders, 'The Organization of American States: Summary of the Conclusions of the Ninth International Conference of American States', *Int. Concil.*, (June 1948), p. 401, the Pact of Bogotá was drafted 'in the extraordinarily brief period of about four working days. The committee which dealt with this matter was unable to get under way until toward the end of the Conference and in fact completed its work under the great pressure of the impending closing date of the Conference.'
[54] See below, p. 216.

or to refer a controversy to a court of international jurisdiction for that purpose, when the said nationals have had available the means to place their case before competent domestic courts of the respective state'. This study has referred on numerous occasions to the traditional conflict between the interests and standpoint of the United States and those of the Latin American countries on this subject, and it is not surprising that the United States entered a reservation against Article VII.

The procedures of good offices and mediation are concerned with bringing the parties to a dispute together so that they may reach a solution themselves. In the case of good offices the initiative comes from the third party or parties, whereas the mediator or mediators are chosen by mutual agreement between the disputants. In the event of failure to reach agreement through these procedures the latter shall have recourse without delay to any of the other procedures of peaceful settlement.

The procedure of investigation and conciliation involves submitting the controversy to a Commission of Investigation and Conciliation established in accordance with detailed provisions contained in Chapter 3 of the treaty. The Commission, consisting of five members, may be either one set up on an *ad hoc* basis from a permanent panel of 'American conciliators' drawn up by the Pan American Union from persons appointed by each of the signatories of the Bogotá Pact, or one having been previously agreed upon on a bilateral basis by the parties concerned in the dispute. The Council of the OAS will convoke the Commission of Investigation and Conciliation on the request of the party initiating this procedure. The Commission will report on the dispute and make recommendations to the parties, but these will not be binding upon them.

The chapter on Judicial Procedure is concerned with the role of the International Court of Justice, to whose Statute all American states are parties. Each signatory of the Bogotá Pact recognizes, in relation to any other American state, the jurisdiction of the Court as compulsory *ipso facto* in all disputes of a juridical nature arising between them, in conformity with Article 36(2), of the Statute. Any disputant is entitled to have recourse to the International Court in the event of failure of conciliation or agreement upon arbitral procedure. In the event of the Court declaring itself to be without jurisdiction to hear the case (for reasons other than those listed in Articles V–VII of the Pact of Bogotá), there will be compulsory arbitration.

Chapter 5, on Arbitration, declares that the signatories may submit to arbitration differences of any kind arising between them, whether juridical or not. But, in the event of compulsory arbitration as mentioned above, an Arbitration Tribunal shall be set up within three months by the Council of the Organization with the co-operation of both parties or, if necessary—after a further fifteen days—without the co-operation of one of them.

Chapter 6, 'Fulfillment of Decisions' states that should one of the signatories

fail to carry out the obligations imposed upon it by a decision of the International Court of Justice or by an arbitral award, the other party or parties concerned shall, before resorting to the Security Council of the United Nations, propose a Meeting of Consultation of Ministers of Foreign Affairs to agree upon appropriate measures to ensure the fulfillment of the judicial decision or arbitral award.

The disputants may, by agreement, petition the General Assembly or the Security Council of the United Nations, through the Council of the OAS, to request an advisory opinion of the International Court of Justice on any juridical question (Chapter 7).

The treaty is to come into effect for the signatories in the order in which they deposit their ratifications and, as it does so, the treaties, conventions, and protocols which it replaces shall cease to be in force for the ratifying states.

Reservations were made to the Pact of Bogotá by Argentina, Bolivia, Ecuador, the United States, Paraguay, Peru, and Nicaragua. Unfortunately, those of the United States, in particular, are such as to render practically inoperative the principles of compulsory arbitration and compulsory jurisdiction of the International Court, which are the main strength of the Pact. The latter therefore shares the basic weakness of other efforts to ensure the pacific settlement of international disputes. The Secretary General of the OAS in his report on the Ninth Conference was excessively optimistic in describing it as 'certain to go down in the history of international law as part of the foundation for the era of institutional peace that is approaching'.[55]

The OAS and the United Nations

It is beyond the scope of this study to make a detailed comparison between the OAS and the world organization,[56] but three points are

[55] *Ann. OAS*, i/1 (1949), p. 44.
[56] See Canyes, *The Organization of American States and the United Nations* (1963).

perhaps worth making. They concern principles, membership, and organs. As we have already noted, the juridical equality of states is one of the basic principles of the inter-American system, and non-intervention its cornerstone. The United Nations is based on the principle of the sovereign equality of all its members, and 'nothing contained in the present Charter shall authorize the United Nations to intervene in matters which are essentially within the domestic jurisdiction of any state'. The term 'sovereign equality' is weaker than 'juridical equality' which is, of course, incompatible with the favoured position enjoyed by the permanent members of the Security Council. The United Nations 'domestic jurisdiction' clause is not comparable with the articles in the OAS Charter dealing with non-intervention. Its Charter makes it clear that the United Nations has no authority to intervene in the domestic affairs of its members, but says nothing about intervention as between the members themselves. On the other hand, the OAS Charter, while containing several clauses on the subject of intervention by one state or group of states, does not declare that the OAS itself has no authority to intervene except under certain circumstances.[57] Reference has already been made to the question of whether the phrase 'group of states' is applicable to the OAS.[58]

Membership of the OAS is restricted to American states, but not by any other qualification,[59] while membership of the world body 'is open to all . . . peace-loving states which accept the obligations contained in the present Charter and, in the judgment of the Organization, are able and willing to carry out these obligations'. But, while the OAS Charter provides only that American states which ratify the document are members of the organization, the United Nations Charter lays it down that admission is 'effected by a decision of the General Assembly upon the recommendation of the Security Council'. The OAS Charter contains no provision on suspension or expulsion of its members, whereas both are provided for in the United Nations Charter and effected in the same way as admission.

As regards the principal organs, comparison is difficult. The OAS has no Trusteeship Council (although its Latin American members have been much concerned about the future of dependent territories in the western hemisphere, and insisted at Bogotá on the creation of a committee to consider the question); nor an American International

---

[57] Mexico subsequently attempted to have the OAS make such a declaration. See below, p. 295.

[58] See above, p. 202.　　　　　　　　　[59] But see below, pp. 297–8.

Court of Justice (although there have been numerous projects to establish one). The nearest approach to the Security Council in the OAS is the Meeting of Consultation which, although not in permanent session, is the principal regional body for dealing with security questions. The OAS contains no organ equivalent to the General Assembly, in which any issue of common interest may be raised; the Inter-American Conference meets normally only once in five years, and its agenda is necessarily limited. The United Nations possesses no organ comparable with the OAS Council. The Secretary General of the OAS does not possess the authority given to his counterpart in the world body, who may bring to the attention of the Security Council 'any matter which in his opinion may threaten the maintenance of international peace and security'.

Much more important is the relationship between the OAS and the United Nations. Some indication of this has been given already. Obviously the very existence of the world organization would impose limitations upon the activities of the regional system— as was acknowledged at Mexico City and written into the Act of Chapultepec. Article 51 of the United Nations Charter is the juridical basis of the Inter-American Treaty of Reciprocal Assistance. The establishment of the United Nations with all the American republics among its members made it necessary for the inter-American system itself to have a constitution defining its relations with the world body. We have already noted the many references to the United Nations in the OAS Charter and the Rio Treaty, and those in the Pact of Bogotá.

The description of the OAS as being 'within the United Nations . . . a regional agency' (Art. 1 of the OAS Charter) and the reference to its 'regional obligations under the Charter of the United Nations' (Art. 4) are significant. For they underline the separate identity of the OAS (understandably, since the inter-American system was over fifty years old when the United Nations Charter was signed) and the fact that the relationship with the United Nations is only one aspect of its 'nature'. The OAS is not just a regional agency 'of' or even 'within' the United Nations; it is only in so far as its activities come 'within the United Nations' that it is a regional agency with regional obligations.

On the other hand, the fields in which the United Nations is concerned include the vital one of international peace and security. Here the United Nations has priority, and both the Rio Treaty and the OAS Charter contain articles declaring that none of their provisions shall be construed as impairing the rights and obligations of the signatories under the Charter of the United Nations. The latter contains an article (103) stating that 'in the event of a conflict between the obligations of the Members of the United Nations under the present Charter and their obligations under any other international agreement, their obligations under the present Charter shall prevail'. Unfortunately, this does not resolve the matter.

In Chapter VI of the United Nations Charter (Pacific Settlement of Disputes) the Security Council is authorized to 'investigate any dispute, or any situation which might lead to international friction or give rise to a dispute, in order to determine whether the continuance of the dispute or situation is likely to endanger the maintenance of international peace and security' (Art. 34). Any member of the United Nations may bring any dispute, or any situation of the nature referred to in Article 34, to the attention of the Security Council or of the General Assembly (Art. 35(1)). At the same time Article 33 in this chapter states:

1. The parties to any dispute, the continuance of which is likely to endanger the maintenance of international peace and security, shall, first of all, seek a solution by negotiation, enquiry, mediation, conciliation, arbitration, judicial settlement, resort to regional agencies or arrangements, or other peaceful means of their own choice.

2. The Security Council shall, when it deems necessary, call upon the parties to settle their dispute by such means.

Regional arrangements are the subject of Chapter VIII of the United Nations Charter, Article 52 of which declares:

1. Nothing in the present Charter precludes the existence of regional arrangements or agencies for dealing with such matters relating to the maintenance of international peace and security as are appropriate for regional action, provided that such arrangements or agencies and their activities are consistent with the Purposes and Principles of the United Nations.

2. The Members of the United Nations entering into such arrangements or constituting such agencies shall make every effort to achieve pacific settlement of local disputes through such regional arrangements or by such regional agencies before referring them to the Security Council.

3. The Security Council shall encourage the development of pacific settlement of local disputes through such regional arrangements or by such regional agencies either on the initiative of the states concerned or by reference from the Security Council.

4. This Article in no way impairs the application of Articles 34 and 35.

As we have seen, the obligations placed upon members of the United Nations to make use of regional arrangements or agencies to settle their disputes are reinforced by specific undertakings by the members of the OAS to use the procedures of the inter-American system to resolve their controversies before referring them to the world body. In this connection it is worth noting that, while in Article 2 of the Rio Treaty the parties 'undertake to submit every controversy which may arise between them to methods of peaceful settlement and to endeavor to settle any such controversy among themselves by means of the procedures in force in the Inter-American System before referring it to the General Assembly or the Security Council of the United Nations' the comparable articles of the OAS Charter[60] and Pact of Bogotá[61] (20 and II respectively) do not mention the General Assembly. This omission, suggested by the chairman of the delegation of Ecuador at the Ninth Conference, ostensibly was intended to preserve for the General Assembly the free discussion of any question likely to threaten peace and security.[62] But it cannot be doubted that Ecuador was influenced by her dissatisfaction with the settlement, concluded under the auspices of the inter-American system, of her long-standing boundary dispute with Peru.[63] Other Latin American countries might find themselves in a similar position.

Action that may be taken under regional arrangements is, however, limited. For while Article 53 states that 'the Security Council shall, where appropriate, utilize such regional arrangements or agencies for enforcement action under its authority', it goes on to say that 'no enforcement action shall be taken under regional arrangements or by regional agencies without the authorization of the Security Council . . .'. Moreover, 'the Security Council shall at all times be kept fully informed of activities undertaken or in contemplation under regional arrangements or by regional agencies for the maintenance of international peace and security' (Art. 54).

It has already been noted that the Rio Treaty contains no reference to Chapter VIII of the United Nations Charter or to its being a regional arrangement or agency, although, in fact, some of its provisions are subject to its signatories' rights and obligations under the articles quoted above. The Inter-American Treaty of Reciprocal

---

[60] See above, p. 202.
[61] See above, p. 210.
[62] See *Ann. OAS*, i/1 (1949), pp. 29–30; and F. Fernández-Shaw, *La Organización de los Estados Americanos (O.E.A.): una nueva visión de América* (1963), pp. 316 ff.
[63] See above, p. 122.

Assistance declares itself to be based on Article 51 of the United Nations Charter which comes in Chapter VII: 'Action with respect to threats to the peace, breaches of the peace, and acts of aggression'. Article 51 reads:

Nothing in the present Charter shall impair the inherent right of individual or collective self-defense if an armed attack occurs against a Member of the United Nations, until the Security Council has taken the measures necessary to maintain international peace and security. Measures taken by Members in the exercise of this right of self-defense shall be immediately reported to the Security Council and shall not in any way affect the authority and responsibility of the Security Council under the present Charter to take at any time such action as it deems necessary in order to maintain or restore international peace and security.

A number of problems are evident from this short examination of the relationship between the OAS and the United Nations—according to their constituent documents—in the field of maintaining international peace and security. The distinction between 'pacific settlement of disputes' and 'action with respect to threats to the peace, breaches of the peace, and acts of aggression' is not clear-cut. What one party might call a dispute—and therefore to be dealt with by the regional peace procedures—the opposing party might denounce as aggression and appeal to the Security Council. Then there is the question of aggression other than by armed attack, which is not covered by Article 51 so that action to meet it is subject to the limitations imposed in Chapter VIII. One of the most important of these limitations, as we have just noted, is that no 'enforcement action' may be taken under regional arrangements without the authorization of the Security Council. Like the term 'aggression', 'enforcement action' is open to interpretation. On the other hand, a limitation on the Security Council's role in dealing with inter-American disputes is inherent in the possession by the United States of a veto (as well as greater influence than any other power) in that United Nations organ. This is particularly important since any Latin American country having United States support in a dispute would be unlikely to wish to appeal to the United Nations rather than to the OAS. Which brings us to the broader question of how far and in what ways membership of the regional body qualifies the rights of its members in the United Nations. This, and the particular points mentioned above, were to raise important issues in the coming years.

Regional arrangements under Chapter VIII of the United Nations

Charter are concerned only with the maintenance of peace and security, reflecting the decision at San Francisco to limit the regional approach to this field. Nevertheless provision is made in the OAS Charter for relations between the latter and the United Nations in other fields. As we have seen, the Specialized Organizations of the OAS were to establish co-operative relations with world agencies of the same character in order to co-ordinate their activities. But, in so doing, they would preserve their identity and status as integral parts of the OAS, even when performing regional functions of such agencies.[64] This re-emphasizes the separate identity and status of the inter-American system as a whole, to which reference has already been made.

A further link in the economic and social fields was made necessary by the establishment in February 1948 (in accordance with Art. 68 of the United Nations Charter), of the United Nations Economic Commission for Latin America (ECLA). Resolution X of the Final Act of the Bogotá Conference called for a division of functions between ECLA and the Inter-American Economic and Social Council. It provided for a committee to be appointed by the latter to work out a formula with ECLA in Santiago, Chile, where the United Nations body had its headquarters.

Among other aspects of the relationship between the OAS and the United Nations several are worth noting or reiterating. Action taken in the field of peace and security is to be reported to the Security Council. Inter-American treaties are to be registered with the Secretariat of the United Nations. Representation of the United Nations at inter-American conferences is provided for in Resolution XXXIX of the Final Act of the Bogotá Conference. The Secretary General of the United Nations, or his representative, is to be invited to attend Inter-American Conferences and Meetings of Consultation of Ministers of Foreign Affairs 'in order that the Members of the world organization may be kept informed as to the work and the conclusions of those conferences'. In fact, Mr Trygve Lie, Secretary General of the United Nations, attended the Inter-American Conference for the Maintenance of Continental Peace and Security, and his representative, Mr Byron Price, the Ninth International Conference of American States. We have already noted the important role of the International Court of Justice—one of the principal organs

---

[64] The Pan American Health Organization serves as regional office of the World Health Organization.

of the United Nations—in the American Treaty on Pacific Settlement.

Conclusion

Such then briefly are the three basic documents of the reorganized inter-American system and the relationship—on paper—between the OAS and the United Nations. The OAS maintains its separate identity, but its status and role have been importantly affected by the simple fact of the world body's existence. In the crucial field of maintaining international peace and security there are real, though disputable, limitations upon the freedom of action of the OAS. How far would the inter-American system work in harmony with the United Nations, where, even before the Ninth International Conference of American States took place, the wartime alliance between the Western powers and the Soviet Union (on which the United Nations was based) was breaking down? Would the OAS be strengthened should the United Nations prove ineffective in the field of peace and security? And what about activities in the economic and social fields, of increasing importance in the post-war world? Would the OAS and the United Nations be partners or rivals?

We have already examined the world and hemispheric environments in which the inter-American system would be operating in the post-war period. We have noted how unfavourable in many ways both have been to the strengthening of the regional association embracing the United States and the countries of Latin America. Let us now see how, under these difficult circumstances, the Organization of American States has fulfilled its tasks, beginning, in the following chapter, with the security of the western hemisphere and the pacific settlement of inter-American disputes.

7 The OAS and the Peace and Security of the Hemisphere

THE role of the inter-American system in safeguarding international peace and security in the western hemisphere since the adoption of the OAS Charter has been complicated by a number of factors. First, as was noted in Chapter VI, the Organization of American States has been operating within the framework of the United Nations. Secondly, the external threat to the peace and security of the Americas has been primarily one of 'indirect aggression' or subversion. Thirdly, and especially since the Cuban revolution, it has sometimes been difficult to distinguish between inter-American disputes and extra-continental intervention. Fourthly—and, again, this has become more the case since the Cuban revolution—the question of peace and security has been linked increasingly with such matters as representative democracy, human rights, and economic and social development, OAS concern with which, incidentally, will be the subject of more detailed examination in the following chapter.

This study has shown how the maintenance of international peace within the hemisphere has been a major purpose of the inter-American system from the outset, although only limited success had been achieved either in establishing effective peace machinery or in solving inter-American disputes up to the outbreak of the Second World War. It has shown also how, from the Inter-American Conference for the Maintenance of Peace (Buenos Aires, 1936) onwards, the inter-American system took steps to meet threats to peace from outside the continent. Wartime co-operation has been described in some detail in Chapter IV, where the dominant role of the United States in providing for the defence of the hemisphere was stressed. It was also pointed out how, although the Act of Chapultepec looked forward to the conclusion of an inter-American collective-security pact after the war was over, the Latin American countries were not willing to allow the United States the continued use of the military base facilities she had acquired during the war period.

Chapter VI described the Inter-American Treaty of Reciprocal Assistance and the Charter of the Organization of American States, showing their provisions for meeting threats to the peace and security of the hemisphere as well as their relationship with the United Nations in this field. It was noted that no permanent military agency was created by the OAS Charter, but that the Inter-American Defense Board was continued by a resolution of the Ninth International Conference.[1] In the period between the end of the Second World War and the Bogotá Conference, however, the United States Congress had shown itself unwilling to approve a programme of inter-American military co-operation proposed by the Truman administration.[2] By 1948 the United States was much more concerned with the Cold War in other regions of the world.

The Defence of the Hemisphere

After the outbreak of the Korean War, however, the United States sought the co-operation of Latin America in strengthening the defence of the hemisphere. The Fourth Meeting of Consultation of American Foreign Ministers resolved not only to support the United Nations action in Korea, but:

To recommend to the American Republics that they orient their military preparation in such a way that, through self-help and mutual aid, and in accordance with their capabilities and with their constitutional precepts, and in conformity with the Inter-American Treaty of Reciprocal Assistance, they can, without prejudice to their individual self-defense and their internal security: (*a*) increase those of their resources and strengthen those of their armed forces best adapted to the collective defense, and maintain those armed forces in such status that they can be promptly available for the defense of the Continent; and (*b*) cooperate with each other, in military matters, in order to develop the collective strength of the Continent necessary to combat aggression against any of them.[3]

Later in 1951 the United States Congress passed the Mutual Security Act and under its provisions Mutual Defense Assistance Agreements were eventually signed with twelve Latin American countries, beginning with Ecuador in January 1952. Under the terms of this first pact the United States government agreed to 'make available . . . equipment, materials, services, and other military assistance designed to promote the defense and maintain the peace

---

[1] The Emergency Advisory Committee for Political Defense was dissolved, however, on the recommendation of the Committee on Inter-American Organizations. See *Ann. OAS*, ii/1 (1950), pp. 42–43.

[2] Lieuwen, *Arms & Politics*, p. 197.

[3] Final Act, Res. III. *Proceedings*, p. 239.

Q

of the Western Hemisphere'. In return, Ecuador promised to make effective and exclusive use of this assistance for implementing defence plans, to build up and maintain her own defensive capacities, 'to facilitate the production and transfer . . . of . . . strategic materials required by the United States', and to co-operate with the United States in limiting her trade with the Soviet bloc.[4] The United States was able to obtain missile tracking stations in the Dominican Republic and on Fernando de Noronha Island through agreements with Trujillo and the government of Brazil.

Thus as during the Second World War, and for the same fundamental reason, defence arrangements since 1947 have been on a bilateral basis. The Inter-American Defense Board, in the words of Professor Edwin Lieuwen, has 'inevitably become primarily a piece of window dressing'. And he goes on:

After sixteen years of semimonthly meetings it is still trying to come up with a comprehensive hemisphere defense plan. The Board achieves little because its members do not choose to give it real authority. No Latin American nation is anxious to give up any sizable measure of control over its armed forces. Besides, genuine military planning is hampered by the secrecy surrounding the classified clauses of the bilateral MDA Pacts. Since no nation except the United States really knows exactly what contribution twelve of the twenty countries are expected to make toward hemisphere defense, the Board can plan only in very general terms. Understandably, the United States, with its ultramodern weapons and its defense commitments elsewhere, is reluctant to reveal fully its own plans for hemisphere defense.[5]

For, as from the very beginning of the inter-American system, the defence of the western hemisphere has been virtually the exclusive concern of the United States, with the countries of Latin America neither able nor willing to make a substantial contribution to it. As this study has tried to indicate, United States motives for associating the Latin American countries with the defence of the continent against external military threats have always been primarily political.[6]

---

[4] Lieuwen, *Arms & Politics*, p. 201.   [5] Ibid. pp. 214–15.

[6] In 1962 there was established by the Inter-American Defense Board an 'Inter-American Defense College' the purpose of which is to 'conduct courses of study on the inter-American System and the military, economic, political, and social factors that constitute essential components of inter-American defense, in order to enhance the preparation of selected personnel of the armed forces of the American Republics for undertakings of international cooperation'. The establishment of this new organ was opposed by Brazil, Mexico, and Venezuela, formally on the juridical grounds that the Inter-American Defense Board had not the competence

The United States has been much more anxious to obtain Latin American co-operation in meeting the threat of subversion, especially since the possibility of a 'communist bridgehead' being established in the hemisphere first arose in the early 1950s. Combating the intervention of international communism has been a much more significant matter for the inter-American system in recent years than co-operation to meet possible armed aggression. This has led the United States to emphasize the training of Latin American officers in 'counter-insurgency' and generally to strengthen the military as the strongest anti-communist group in Latin America.

Inter-American Disputes, 1948–54

For some years before the problem of communist intervention in the western hemisphere came to overshadow the work of the OAS, the inter-American system had to deal with a number of disputes arising between member states. Most of these occurred in the Caribbean and Central American region, traditionally a turbulent part of the hemisphere, where the Convention on the Duties and Rights of States in the Event of Civil Strife (signed at the Sixth International Conference of American States in 1928) has been most frequently violated. All the countries in the region had pledged themselves to prevent the organization in their territory of armed rebellion against the recognized governments of their neighbours, and to disarm and intern rebel forces crossing national frontiers. Unfortunately, these pledges were often broken, and governments encouraged (and even instigated) plots to overthrow other régimes of which they disapproved for one reason or another. Linked with this form of intervention has been the question of diplomatic asylum.[7]

As we have seen, the main instrument devised at the Bogotá Conference to ensure the peaceful settlement of inter-American disputes was the American Treaty on Pacific Settlement or Pact of Bogotá. But we also saw the inadequacies of this instrument and noted its limited ratification. It is unlikely ever to be fully ratified in its present form, and the possibility of revising it was discussed at

---

to create it and thus extend its own activities (see *Acta de la Sesión Extraordinaria celebrada el 11 de abril de 1962*, OEA/Ser. G/II, C-a-439 (Aprobada), 11 Apr. 1962, pp. 45–52.

[7] This has been a Latin American rather than an inter-American question. See, for example, Ronning, *Law & Politics*, ch. v; and J. J. Caicedo Castilla, *El panamericanismo* (1961), ch. xiv.

the Tenth Inter-American Conference.[8] In these circumstances, inter-American disputes have been dealt with under the terms of the Inter-American Treaty of Reciprocal Assistance or by recourse to the Inter-American Peace Committee. Although primarily concerned with defence against armed aggression, the Rio Treaty does provide for collective measures not only 'if the inviolability or the integrity of the territory or the sovereignty or political independence of any American State should be affected by an aggression which is not an armed attack or by an extra-continental or intra-continental conflict', but also if they are affected 'by any other fact or situation that might endanger the peace of America'.

The Inter-American Peace Committee, which is not mentioned in the OAS Charter, was provided for at the Second Meeting of Consultation.[9] Although subsequently established in Washington, however, it was not utilized during the war, and apparently was overlooked at the Ninth International Conference. Then in September 1947 the Dominican Republic requested the Director General of the Pan American Union to take the necessary steps to install it. This was done in July 1948, by the Chairman of the OAS Council. At first called 'The Inter-American Committee on Methods for the Peaceful Solution of Conflicts', it was renamed in July 1949 'The Inter-American Peace Committee'. Its statutes were approved in May 1950, and sent to the governments of the American republics; before that time the committee had been governed by temporary regulations. Any American state could call the committee's attention to any inter-American dispute, and the committee could proceed to study it and give an opinion. The Peace Committee could offer its good services to facilitate a solution, but possessed no power to enforce any decision.

Hardly had the Peace Committee been installed when the Dominican Republic requested its services in a dispute with Cuba, alleging that revolutionary activities were being developed on Cuban territory against her government. There was obvious antipathy between the Cuban President Grau San Martín and the Dominican dictator, Rafael L. Trujillo. Having investigated the situation, the committee

[8] See Res. XCIX of the Final Act.
[9] See above, p. 115. The statutes of the Inter-American Peace Committee (both original and revised), and a brief account of all disputes brought before it, up to and including the Guatemala crisis of 1054, are contained in the Committee's *Report to the Fifth Meeting of Consultation of Ministers of Foreign Affairs*, OEA/Ser. F/II. 5, Doc. 5 (English) 1959.

recommended direct negotiations between the parties, which both accepted. Before the Peace Committee received its second request, the Rio Treaty was invoked for the first time.

Just as the Dominican Republic had brought the Peace Committee into active existence in time to hear her complaint against Cuba, so did Costa Rica cause the Rio Treaty to enter into full effect among the ratifying states (by depositing the fourteenth instrument of ratification on 3 December 1948) in time to invoke it against Nicaragua.[10] Costa Rica charged that her territory had been invaded by an armed force proceeding from Nicaragua. The Nicaraguan government, while denying any part in the events taking place in Costa Rica, counter-charged that the Costa Rican (and Guatemalan) government had fostered the 'Caribbean Legion' ('Composed entirely of outlaws, fugitives, and mercenaries of various nationalities, of unemployed rogues'),[11] which threatened the peace of the region. The enmity between the liberal Costa Rican government of José Figueres and the Somoza dictatorship was behind this dispute.

The OAS Council called a Meeting of Consultation of American Foreign Ministers—but without fixing a place or date for it—and was then able to set itself up as Provisional Organ of Consultation. This 'juridical stratagem'[12] was to be employed on numerous subsequent occasions. In such a capacity the Council appointed a committee, consisting of representatives of Brazil, Colombia, Mexico, and the United States, to study the situation in both Costa Rica and Nicaragua. Established on 15 December, this committee made its report nine days later. It found that the revolutionary movement in Costa Rica undoubtedly had been organized mainly in Nicaraguan territory and that the Nicaraguan government had failed to prevent this. Only after the most important group of revolutionaries had already crossed the Costa Rican border did the Nicaraguan government take measures to prevent aid being given to the rebels from its territory. The Nicaraguan armed forces took no part in the revolutionary movement on Costa Rican territory, but the committee did

---

[10] Costa Rica also informed the President of the Security Council that her territory had been invaded by armed forces coming from Nicaragua. The matter was not put on the Security Council's agenda, however, since the Chairman of the OAS Council told the president that the OAS had been seized of the question and had established an investigating commission in accordance with the Rio Treaty (*YBUN, 1948–49* (1950), p. 431).

[11] PAU, *Inter-American Treaty of Reciprocal Assistance, Applications* (1964), i. 29. Unless otherwise indicated, quotations concerned with disputes dealt with under the Rio treaty are from this document.

[12] Dreier, *Hemisphere Crisis*, p. 61.

'have the impression that some members of the Nicaraguan military forces might perhaps, on their own initiative, have given technical aid to the groups that later crossed the border'.

While thus condemning Nicaragua at least for negligence, the committee added:

On the other hand, it cannot be denied that for many months before the invasion the so-called Legion of the Caribbean, or Caribbean Legion, with material and moral help from the Costa Rican Government, enjoyed official sympathy and facilities for carrying out its programs and activities, both of which, according to general opinion in the Caribbean area, were designed to overthrow certain governments, among them the present regime in Nicaragua.

The two parties were called upon to abstain from hostile acts against each other and subsequently signed a treaty of amity containing a pledge to fulfil their obligations under the Convention on the Duties and Rights of States in the Event of Civil Strife. It also included an agreement by both governments 'to apply the American Treaty on Pacific Settlement, known as the Pact of Bogotá, recognizing that Treaty as having full validity as to disputes between them, even before it is formally ratified and enters in consequence into effect between all the American Republics'. When the amity pact was signed (21 February 1949) the OAS Council declared the reasons for convoking the Meeting of Consultation of American Foreign Ministers no longer existed, and terminated its own role as Provisional Organ of Consultation. In Dreier's view 'the O.A.S. came through its first test with flying colors', even though 'the failure of the two countries to make these agreements effective produced a more serious repetition of the aggression five years later'.[13]

The next inter-American dispute is of interest as involving both the Rio Treaty and the Inter-American Peace Committee. On 16 February 1949 the government of Haiti requested the OAS Council to convoke a Meeting of Consultation to consider 'certain acts that constituted a moral aggression susceptible of creating a situation between that country and the Dominican Republic capable of endangering the peace'. These acts were allegedly in support of a conspiracy to overthrow the government of Haiti. The Council decided not to convoke the Organ of Consultation when the two parties agreed to reach a settlement through peaceful procedures,

[13] *Hemisphere Crisis*, p. 60.

and the matter passed to the Peace Committee. A delegation was sent to Haiti and the Dominican Republic, and on 9 June 1949 a declaration was signed in Washington by representatives of the two countries and the members of the committee, promising:

That they do not and will not tolerate in their respective territories the activities of any individuals, groups, or parties, national or foreign, that have as their object the disturbance of the domestic peace of either of the two neighboring Republics or of any other friendly Nation.

and:

that they will resort to direct negotiation; and whenever necessary, to the procedures of peaceful settlement for the solution of any difference in the future between the Dominican Republic and the Republic of Haiti.

On 3 August 1949 Cuba requested the good offices of the Inter-American Peace Committee in solving a dispute between herself and Peru over her embassy in Lima having granted asylum to two Peruvian citizens. She withdrew her request a fortnight later, however, after the asylees had left the embassy. On the day Cuba made her request the United States asked the committee to consider the generally disturbed situation within the Caribbean region. Although the representatives of Argentina and Mexico doubted its juridical competence to deal with situations of a general nature, the committee requested information from all member governments. Only a minority responded, however, and the sole outcome was a reiteration of 'the lofty and indispensable postulates of our international relationships'. For:

The Committee believes that its duty in this matter is limited to the solemn reaffirmation of certain standards and principles that are basic for American peace and solidarity, principles and standards whose proper observance would, in the opinion of the Committee, not only keep such a situation as the one under consideration from arising, but avoid even the slightest symptom of disturbed relations among the American States.[14]

In Mecham's view, 'The United States should have known when it requested the meeting that effective measures which did not compromise the nonintervention principle were non-existent.'[15]

In January 1950 the Rio Treaty was invoked for the third time. Haiti requested a meeting of the Organ of Consultation to consider a situation threatening the peace of the continent arising from the

[14] Quoted from *Ann. OAS*, ii/1 (1950), p. 25.   [15] Mecham, p. 399.

Dominican Republic's violation of the Joint Declaration of 9 June 1949 (ending their previous controversy), and 'in addition . . . frequent violations of Haitian territory by planes and by Dominican soldiers'. The Dominican Republic denied the charges, and herself requested the convocation of the Organ of Consultation to consider the situation in the Caribbean region arising from the conspiracies against her by the governments of Cuba and Guatemala as well as Haiti. Following the procedure adopted over the Costa Rica–Nicaragua dispute, the OAS Council constituted itself Provisional Organ of Consultation and sent an investigating committee to the four countries involved (who all agreed to receive it) and to Mexico—at her specific invitation. This committee found the charges made by Haiti to be substantiated, but that Cuba and Guatemala had harboured and, in some cases, aided subversive armed groups which openly aimed at overthrowing the Dominican government.

The OAS Council finally adopted a series of resolutions. The government of the Dominican Republic was requested to take immediate and effective measures to prevent its officials from tolerating or instigating subversive or seditious movements against other governments. The Dominican Republic and Haiti were both called upon to comply with the Joint Declaration of 9 June 1949 and to avoid the continuation of hostile propaganda against each other. The governments of Cuba and Guatemala were requested to adopt adequate measures to prevent the use of their territories for the organizing of conspiracies against the security of other countries and to prevent illegal traffic in arms. A committee of five members was appointed 'which, always respecting the principle of non-intervention, will acquaint itself with the manner in which Resolutions I and II are being carried out and place itself at the service of the interested Parties to facilitate compliance with the said Resolutions, in a thoroughly conciliatory spirit'. Another resolution reaffirmed the principles of representative democracy, but declared that these principles in no way:

authorize any Government or group of Governments to violate inter-American commitments relative to the principle of non-intervention or to give the appearance of legitimacy to violations of the rules contained in Article 1 of the Havana Convention of 1928, on Duties and Rights of States in the Event of Civil Strife, the Protocol Relative to Non-Intervention (Buenos Aires, 1936), and Article 15 of the Charter of the Organization of American States.

The OAS Council was recommended to study the possibilities of furthering, with due respect to the sovereignty of states, the effective exercise of representative democracy; the strengthening and perfecting of the Convention on the Duties and Rights of States in the Event of Civil Strife; and the regimen of political asylees, exiles, and refugees.

'Given the obstacle of nonintervention', declared Mecham, 'the recommendations of the Provisional Organ of Consultation were about as much as could be expected, that is, very little. Once more, we wearily note, the guilty parties were admonished to observe their solemn commitments. Apparently, sanctions were unthinkable.'[16] The Special Committee for the Caribbean (set up by the OAS Council) functioned until May 1951. During this period there were no further disputes requiring the utilization of the inter-American peace machinery. Later (November) in 1951 Cuba requested the services of the Inter-American Peace Committee when the Dominican authorities seized five Cuban sailors. This dispute ended with a joint declaration of peacefulness and non-intervention. Two years later the government of Colombia brought the Peace Committee's attention to a dispute with Peru over the granting of asylum to Sr Haya de la Torre in the Colombian embassy in Lima. Since Peru declined its good offices, the committee recommended bilateral negotiations to resolve the problem.

The Case of Guatemala

In 1954 there occurred the Guatemala crisis, the political significance of which was discussed earlier.[17] This crisis involved both a dispute between American states and the question of extra-continental intervention in the western hemisphere. It also raised the question of competence between the United Nations and the OAS in the field of international peace and security, and the rights and obligations of states as members of these two bodies. Several months before hostilities broke out in Guatemala the Tenth Inter-American Conference had been held at Caracas. At this conference, incidentally, the Inter-American Peace Committee (which had submitted a report of its work from the time of its organization in 1948 to 31 July 1953) was commended (Resolution CI), and a new statute proposed for it (CII).[18] But the most important subject at the Tenth Inter-American

---

[16] Mecham, pp. 401–2.
[17] See above, pp. 161–4.　　　　　　　　　[18] See below, p. 243.

Conference was the intervention of international communism in the Americas.

We have already noted how the Ninth International Conference of American States adopted a resolution on 'The Preservation and Defense of Democracy in America' against intervention by international communism 'or any other totalitarian doctrine'.[19] By the time the Tenth Conference met the United States was accusing the Guatemalan government of being so far under communist control as to constitute a Soviet bridgehead in the hemisphere and a threat to American peace and security. Secretary of State Dulles introduced at Caracas a resolution the core of which was contained in the passage declaring:

That the domination or control of the political institutions of any American State by the international communist movement, extending to this Hemisphere the political system of an extra-continental power, would constitute a threat to the sovereignty and political independence of the American States, endangering the peace of America, and would call for appropriate action in accordance with existing treaties.[20]

This was, in effect, an endorsement of the Monroe Doctrine,[21] which would be challenged by the mere existence of a communist government in the western hemisphere.[22] The Latin Americans were not prepared to support this, for it would reopen the door to intervention against any government the United States might denounce as being under the control of international communism. They knew that, specifically, the United States wanted their approval in overthrowing the Arbenz government of Guatemala, regarding whose communist character many of them had serious reservations.

In view of Latin American objections, the key passage was amended so that the last phrase read: 'and would call for a Meeting of Consultation to consider the adoption of appropriate action in accordance with existing treaties'.[23] And to allay Latin American fears of inter-

---

[19] See above, p. 153.   [20] *Report of Delegation of USA*, p. 8.
[21] At a news conference after his return from Caracas Dulles gave the impression that he regarded the anti-communist resolution eventually adopted as such an endorsement: US Dept. of State, *Intervention of International Communism in Guatemala*, pp. 10–11.
[22] In a radio and television address given on 30 June 1964, Dulles declared of the Guatemalan crisis: 'This intrusion of Soviet despotism was, of course, a direct challenge to our Monroe Doctrine, the first and most fundamental of our foreign policies' (Ibid. p. 30).
[23] Although Dulles maintained that this resolution did not affect 'existing treaties' (*Report of Delegation of USA*, p. 59), Gómez Robledo has termed it the 'Caracas Corollary' to the Rio Treaty (*For. Int.*, i/1 (1960), p. 47).

vention in their internal affairs, the following paragraph was added to the resolution:

This declaration of foreign policy made by the American republics in relation to dangers originating outside this Hemisphere is designed to protect and not to impair the inalienable right of each American State freely to choose its own form of government and economic system and to live its own social and cultural life.

Even so, Mexico and Argentina abstained in the vote on this resolution and, of course, Guatemala, against whom it was directed, opposed it. Among those delegations which supported Dulles's resolution only certain dictatorships did so without misgivings.[24] John C. Dreier, who was United States Ambassador to the OAS at the time, wrote some years later:

. . . the Resolution, duly approved by more than a sufficient majority of governments, has turned out to be largely ineffectual because, in the last analysis, the Latin American countries have generally been more concerned with its potential danger as a basis for intervention led by the United States than with the danger of Communist intervention in their own affairs.[25]

This has been the key problem and the major obstacle to effective measures by the inter-American system to meet the challenge from international communism.

On 19 June 1954 the Guatemalan government requested the Inter-American Peace Committee to meet on an emergency basis to 'adopt the necessary measures' in view of acts instigated by Honduras and Nicaragua which violated both the principle of non-intervention and the sovereignty of Guatemala.[26] The Guatemalan government had also complained to the Security Council of the 'open aggression . . . perpetrated by the Governments of Honduras and Nicaragua at the instigation of certain foreign monopolies'. It requested an urgent meeting of the Council to consider its complaint in accordance with Articles 34, 35, and 39 of the United Nations Charter. The Inter-American Peace Committee met within three hours of receiving the Guatemalan complaint, but before it could despatch a special sub-

---

[24] e.g. Nicaragua and the Dominican Republic (Tenth Inter-American Conference, *Documents of the Plenary Sessions*, Doc. 129 (English), SP-29, 8 Mar. 1964, Original: Spanish, p. 6; Doc. 146 (English), SP-31, 9 Mar. 1954, Original: Spanish. p. 4).
[25] *Hemisphere Crisis*, p. 53.
[26] This and other passages quoted are taken from Inter-American Peace Committee, *Report on the Controversy between Guatemala, Honduras, and Nicaragua*, CIP-131/54.

committee to investigate the situation, the Guatemalan government asked for a suspension of the mission. This request was made 'in view of the fact that the case had been submitted to the Security Council of the United Nations on the same date as to the Committee and that the Security Council, in a meeting on *Sunday, June 20*, had already taken cognizance of the Guatemalan complaint of aggression'. The Guatemalan government subsequently withdrew its original request 'for the purpose of having its attitude wholly in conformity with the scope of the resolution approved yesterday by the Security Council, which, according to the official text issued, makes no reference to regional organizations'.

The Security Council, of which the United States representative, Mr Henry Cabot Lodge, was president at the time, met on 20 June to hear the Guatemalan case; Honduras and Nicaragua were also represented at the meeting. Guatemala charged that she was the victim of aggression and requested the Security Council to call upon Honduras and Nicaragua to intern the insurgent forces operating from their territory. She also asked the Council to send an observation commission to Guatemala. The two accused countries denied the charges, which they said should be dealt with by the OAS. This last was also the strongly expressed contention of the United States. Cabot Lodge vigorously denounced the Soviet Union's support of Guatemala's request as interference in the affairs of the western hemisphere. Brazil and Colombia (the Latin American members of the Security Council) proposed a resolution referring the matter to the OAS, which, slightly amended, was supported by ten members of the Council but vetoed by the Soviet Union. Finally, an ineffective resolution proposed by France was adopted under which the Council called for 'the immediate termination of any action likely to cause bloodshed and [requested] all Members of the United Nations to abstain, in the spirit of the Charter, from giving assistance to any such action'.

Following this debate, Honduras and Nicaragua requested the Inter-American Peace Committee to designate a special subcommittee to visit them and Guatemala to investigate the situation. When Guatemala was approached for her co-operation she replied that she 'cannot consent to having this matter brought before that body before the decision of the Security Council is fully carried out' and that 'any referral to an organization distinct from the Security Council at this time might serve as a pretext for escaping from the obligation of complying with the aforesaid decision of the Council'. In a further communication, Guatemala informed the committee that:

First, the Government of Guatemala does not accept, and is opposed to, the Inter-American Peace Committee's intervening in a matter like the case of the foreign interventionist aggression from which Guatemala suffers and which it has denounced, because a matter of this kind comes under the jurisdiction of the Security Council of the United Nations and must remain there pursuant to the provisions of the Charter of the United Nations; and, furthermore, because the nature of such a matter—aggression—excludes it from the sphere of action of the Inter-American Peace Committee. . . .

Second, the Government of Guatemala is greatly displeased to see a body as high and useful as the Inter-American Peace Committee shown disrespect to the extent of taking advantage of its exalted mission and its generous concern with continental peace and solidarity to cover a maneuver of aggressors endeavoring to neutralize the action brought by the Government of Guatemala before the Security Council of the United Nations and the Government of Guatemala could not under any circumstances lend itself to a maneuver of this kind.

On 25 June the Security Council met again, at the request of Guatemala and the Soviet Union. The United States strongly opposed the adoption of a provisional agenda containing the Guatemalan complaint. Cabot Lodge declared that the issue involved was nothing less than the future of the whole system of international peace and security created by the United Nations Charter. With some exaggeration—to say the least—he asserted that:

When the charter was being drafted, the most critical single issue was that of the relationship of the United Nations as a universal organization to regional organizations, notably the already existing Organization of American States. There were a good many days in San Francisco when it seemed that the whole concept of the United Nations might fail of realization because of the difficulty of reconciling these two concepts of universality and regionalism.[27]

Cabot Lodge contended that the Guatemalan crisis was a local dispute which the United Nations Charter itself declared (Art. 52 (2)) should be dealt with through regional arrangements where these existed. The OAS was such an arrangement 'which through its regularly constituted agencies is dealing actively with the problem

[27] Quoted from US Dept of State, *Intervention of International Communism in Guatemala*, pp. 18–19.

now'. He rejected Guatemala's claim that, not having ratified the OAS Charter, she was not a member of that organization, on the reasonable grounds that she had 'claimed and . . . exercised all the privileges of membership for a number of years'. The Soviet representative (Guatemala was not invited to attend pending the adoption of the agenda) maintained that the Security Council had the duty to consider the Guatemalan complaint, both because it had already dealt with it and because of its primary responsibility to maintain peace. The provisional agenda was not adopted, however. Four nations voted in favour, five (including the three American republics) against, and two (France and Great Britain) abstained. The Council would take no action until it should have an opportunity of receiving a report from the Inter-American Peace Committee.

Under these circumstances, the Guatemalan government decided to co-operate with the Peace Committee, which then made arrangements for a team to visit the three countries involved on 28 June. On 26 June ten members of the OAS, including the United States, called for a Meeting of Consultation in view of 'the demonstrated intervention of the international communist movement in the Republic of Guatemala and the danger which this involves for the peace and security of the Continent'.[28] A special meeting of the OAS Council met on 28 June and convoked a meeting of the Organ of Consultation for 7 July at Rio de Janeiro. It is ominous that the Council did not at once constitute itself Provisional Organ of Consultation as it had done on previous occasions. By the time the OAS Council took this decision the overthrow of the Arbenz government was virtually assured. Once a new government took office the 'dispute' ceased to exist. The Peace Committee's investigating team got no farther on its journey than Mexico City.

On 2 July the OAS Council, meeting in special session, adopted a resolution, presented by Honduras and seconded by the United States, postponing *sine die* the Meeting of Consultation set for 7 July. Argentina, however, believed the affair should be investigated and implied that the countries accused by Guatemala would welcome the opportunity to have the truth of their denials of complicity confirmed;[29] but the matter was not pursued further. The documents concerning the OAS action in the matter were sent to the United Nations.

[28] PAU, *Inter-American Treaty of Reciprocal Assistance. Applications*, i. 159.
[29] *Acta de la Sesión Extraordinària celebrada el 2 de julio de 1954.* OEA C-a-155, pp. 920–2.

As an international issue, the Guatemalan crisis was, *inter alia*, a conflict of jurisdiction: a question of competence between the world organization and the regional body. This conflict was not resolved by the outcome,[30] and it certainly was *not* established that: 'Without a doubt, the justifications Guatemala gave for seeking Security Council intervention in the matter in preference to OAS intervention were illegal, both under the Charter of the United Nations and under the treaties governing the Inter-American system.'[31] The Guatemalan case merely underlined the difficulty of distinguishing between a dispute and an act of aggression, as well as that of reconciling the rights and obligations of members under the United Nations and OAS Charters in the field of peace and security. Guatemala maintained that she was the victim of aggression, and therefore entitled to have her case dealt with by the Security Council, although on two occasions the Arbenz government appealed to the Inter-American Peace Committee. The United States was likewise inconsistent in declaring in the Security Council that this was a local dispute—while maintaining in the OAS that it was a question of extra-continental intervention.

Of course the United States was referring to two distinct matters. In the Security Council she argued that Guatemala's complaint was a local dispute which should be dealt with by the regional body. In the OAS, however, she was planning, not to hear Guatemala's complaint, but to rally support against the Guatemalan government. This is shown by the terms of the request for a Meeting of Consultation. Thus, it has been well observed:

it appears that the transfer of the case from the Security Council to the OAS was not simply a matter of having the latter substitute for the former as a peaceful settlement mechanism, but a device for reversing the terms of the case. The OAS was prepared to treat Guatemala as the defendant, not the plaintiff. Whereas the Security Council had appealed for the cessation of the attack, the OAS declared its intent to consider means for expediting the demise of the government of Guatemala. In insisting that the government of Guatemala should resort to the OAS, the United States was recommending what it hoped and intended would prove a suicidal act.[32]

But United States delay in calling for a Meeting of Consultation

[30] It is further considered below, pp. 313–14.
[31] Thomas & Thomas, *Non-Intervention*, p. 166.
[32] I. L. Claude, Jr, 'The OAS, the UN, and the United States', *Int. Concil.*, (Mar. 1964), p. 30.

suggests that this was a mere smoke-screen. As the instigator of the invasion which was the subject of Guatemala's complaint to the Security Council, the United States used the 'regional' argument in order to prevent any action by the United Nations which might prejudice the success of her operations against Arbenz.

Fundamentally, the Guatemalan crisis was a conflict between the United States and Russia. The former was determined to prevent the Soviet Union from using the United Nations to save the Arbenz government which she herself was engaged in overthrowing. It is noteworthy that: 'In this instance, the Soviet veto was a device not for paralyzing the Security Council, but for preventing the United States from reducing that body to inactivity by invoking the pretext of regional jurisdiction.'[33] The United States was successful in achieving her immediate objective, but at a price that was evident long before the role of her Central Intelligence Agency in the affair became common knowledge.

There were considerable misgivings on all sides over what had occurred. It was generally felt that Guatemala should have been given a hearing by the Security Council; and it is significant that two major allies of the United States, France and Great Britain, abstained in the vote to have the Guatemalan situation put on the Security Council's agenda the second time it was raised, thereby not supporting the United States in opposing its inclusion. In his first report to the General Assembly following the affair, the Secretary General of the United Nations said rather pointedly: ' . . . a policy giving full scope to the proper role of regional agencies can and should at the same time fully preserve the right of a Member nation to a hearing under the Charter'.[34] The implications of the Guatemalan crisis for the countries of Latin America were serious. The Uruguayan delegate put the matter as follows in the General Assembly:

[Uruguay] combines membership in the United Nations with membership in the Organization of American States, in the belief that the principles of the regional system and the safeguards which it offers cannot be invoked in order to prevent States from having direct and immediate access to the jurisdiction of the United Nations or to deprive them, no matter how temporarily, of the protection of the agencies of the world community. The legal protection offered by both systems should be combined, never substituted for one another.

---

[33] Claude, *Int. Concil* (Mar. 1964), p. 33.
[34] *GAOR*, 9th sess. Suppl. 1 (A/2663), p. xi.

Applying this to the Guatemalan crisis, he said:

> The negative decision adopted by the Security Council constitutes a very serious precedent for the countries of America since its result must be to diminish or delay, so far as they are concerned, the respective application of the juridical safeguards against aggression established in the Charter of the United Nations and in subsequent resolutions, such as the 1950 resolution on "Uniting for Peace".

The Uruguayan delegation felt strongly that 'any protest to the United Nations against aggression is entitled at least to a hearing'.[35] In the same General Assembly debate, several other Latin American countries denied that membership in the OAS restricted their right to have immediate recourse to the United Nations. Even Brazil, who had supported the United States in the Security Council, disavowed the implications that the latter could not deal with the question.[36]

Nor did the OAS come out well from the affair. Dreier records, in something of an understatement, that 'the case of Guatemala had somewhat stained the shining armor of the O.A.S.'.[37] Of course the Guatemalan government's vacillation between the Inter-American Peace Committee and the Security Council weakened its case. But in view of what was declared to be a dangerous situation the OAS was ominously dilatory. For this, as has already been affirmed, the United States must bear the major responsibility. If the Arbenz government had indeed represented a serious threat to the western hemisphere, the credit for defending the American states against it cannot go to the OAS. It is true its existence enabled the United States to make a case in the Security Council for delaying United Nations action which might have enabled Arbenz (and so the threat to hemispheric security) to survive. But it is doubtful whether many Latin Americans (at all events) would regard such a role as creditable.

Inter-American Disputes, 1955–9

Significantly, the next international crisis in the western hemisphere was the occasion of perhaps the most successful action taken by the OAS to date. In Dreier's view, 'It brought the prestige of the O.A.S. to a high point not only in the hemisphere but in the world at large'.[38] When the government of Costa Rica complained to the

---

[35] *GAOR*, 9th sess. 481st mtg., p. 98.
[36] Ibid. 479th, 485th, 486th, and 488th mtgs, pp. 85, 147–8, 150, 174.
[37] *Hemisphere Crisis*, p. 62. [38] Ibid.

R

OAS Council in January 1955 that its territory had been invaded from Nicaragua, the regional body took prompt measures. Acting (according to precedents) as Provisional Organ of Consultation, the OAS Council set up an investigating committee and sent it to Costa Rica and Nicaragua; a number of countries made aircraft available to this committee. When Costa Rica appealed for military assistance, the United States, at the request of the OAS Council,[39] supplied her with four combat planes. The Nicaraguan government, which must have felt the United States action a poor return for its strong support in the Guatemalan affair, asserted its innocence of the Costa Rican accusation and expressed willingness to co-operate with the OAS. This meant the end of its attempt to overthrow President Figueres and the conclusion of a new pact of friendship between the two countries. But there was no condemnation of the Nicaraguan government, even though the committee was fully convinced of its guilt in the matter.[40] The United Nations was not involved, although, in accordance with Article 54 of its Charter, the Security Council (as on previous occasions) was kept informed of developments in the dispute and action being taken to settle it.[41] In this case the OAS was operating under the most favourable circumstances. The United States wanted to utilize its machinery and did so with the support of most of the other members.

In the autumn of 1955 the boundary dispute between Ecuador and Peru flared up again. We noted earlier how the two countries had agreed on a Protocol of Peace, Friendship and Boundaries at Rio de Janeiro in 1942.[42] On 8 September 1955 Ecuador requested the OAS Council to convoke a Meeting of Foreign Ministers to consider her charge that Peru was endangering her territorial integrity, sovereignty, and independence by a heavy concentration of forces on the boundary between the two countries and the stationing of vessels of the Peruvian navy 'in the vicinity of the Ecuadorian

---

[39] But, according to Dreier (*Hemisphere Crisis*, p. 64): 'in a masterpiece of veiled language and only after long and bitter debate'.

[40] Ibid. p. 65. The Ecuadoran member of the investigating committee entered a reservation to its report stating that, although in general agreement with it, he considered that the evidence identifying the author or authors should have been included. Moreover, he asserted that there should be an early Meeting of Foreign Ministers to consider the possibility of establishing an Inter-American Police Force and the improvement of the system for controlling the traffic in arms and ammunition, and for limiting armaments within the requirements of hemispheric defence.

[41] *YBUN, 1955* (1956), pp. 78–79. For OAS action in the dispute, see PAU, *Inter-American Treaty of Reciprocal Assistance. Applications*, i. 167–228.

[42] See above, p. 122.

coastline'.[43] She was convinced 'that any moment, Peru intends to launch an invasion of Ecuador, and thereby violate her national sovereignty and integrity'. Since, however, Ecuador had also submitted her complaint to the four guarantor states of the Rio Protocol, the Council decided not to apply the Rio Treaty to the case and Ecuador withdrew her request. An investigating committee of military observers from the guarantor states reported no unusual activity after making aerial and land reconnaissance. The guarantor states nevertheless proposed steps to reduce tension between Ecuador and Peru. But that was not the end of the boundary problem, and in September 1960 Ecuador unilaterally abrogated the Rio Protocol.[44] Her action was not recognized by the guarantor nations.

Another long-standing boundary dispute erupted in 1957: that between Honduras and Nicaragua. It had been the subject of an arbitral award by the King of Spain in 1906 which, supporting the claims of Honduras, was not accepted by Nicaragua.[45] Since then the two countries had each controlled parts of the disputed region. On 1 May 1957 Honduras invoked the Rio Treaty alleging Nicaragua had 'invaded Honduran territory with military forces by crossing the boundary line of the Coco or Segovia River, established by the King of Spain in his arbitral award of December 23, 1906'.[46] The following day, Nicaragua counter-charged Honduras with aggression and also invoked the Rio Treaty. Acting as Provisional Organ of Consultation, the OAS Council sent an investigating committee to the two countries, which brought about a cease-fire agreement. The Council then created an *ad hoc* committee to continue discussions with Honduras and Nicaragua over the resolution of their dispute. Finally, both parties agreed to have recourse to the International Court of Justice and to abide by its decision. The Court handed down its judgment in November 1960, confirming the validity of the King of Spain's award and Nicaragua's obligation to give effect to it. In February 1961 Nicaragua requested the Inter-American Peace Committee's good offices in resolving questions arising from the execution of the International Court's judgment. The committee visited both Honduras and Nicaragua (and the disputed region), and a Honduran-

---

[43] For an account of this dispute, see *Applications*, i. 231–41.

[44] The boundary dispute was one of the reasons for the postponement of the Inter-American Conference due to have been held at Quito in 1959.

[45] Both Honduras and Nicaragua entered reservations to the Rio Treaty on this issue. See above, p. 192, n. 9.

[46] *Ann OAS*, ix/3 (1957), p. 264. For the documents of this dispute see PAU, *Inter-American Treaty of Reciprocal Assistance, Applications*, i. 245–321.

Nicaraguan Mixed Commission was set up under the chairmanship of the committee's chairman. The Peace Committee was able to report to the Eighth Meeting of Consultation of Foreign Ministers that this dispute was virtually settled.[47]

The Cuban Challenge

In the meantime, Castro's victory in Cuba had added greatly to the turbulence in the Caribbean region[48] and heightened the ideological conflict between the right-wing dictatorships and those who sought to overthrow them. Castro, who held up his own revolution as an example for other Latin American countries to follow, took the lead in promoting activities aimed at the elimination of the Dominican and other neighbouring governments. President Betancourt of Venezuela, where the Pérez Jiménez dictatorship had been overthrown a year earlier, was at first associated with Cuba in these activities, though he behaved with more circumspection towards the United States and later became a major target of Castro's hostility.

On 27 April 1959 Panama complained to the OAS Council that her territory had been invaded by forces (about eighty armed men) sailing from Cuba, and requested the convocation of a Meeting of Consultation. This request was granted and an investigating committee appointed by the Provisional Organ of Consultation. Although the committee found that the invasion had come from Cuba, it made no formal complaint against her government. The latter admitted no responsibility for the invasion and co-operated with the investigating committee. The OAS Council closed the matter on 18 June by recommending member states to strengthen measures to prevent similar situations from occurring and, where appropriate, to adhere to the 1928 Convention on Duties and Rights of States in the Event of Civil Strife or the Protocol to it adopted in 1957.[49]

On 2 June 1959 Nicaragua informed the OAS Council that she had been invaded by forces entering her territory from Costa Rica and had also received intelligence that they were to be reinforced by sea. There was opposition to convoking the Organ of Consultation from Cuba and Venezuela, whose representatives declared the

---

[47] Inter-American Peace Committee, *Report to the Eighth Meeting of Consultation of Ministers of Foreign Affairs*. OEA/Ser. L/III, CIP/1/62 (English) (1962), pp. 3–17.

[48] For an account, with some documentation, of the tensions in the Caribbean region in the years 1959–60 see US Dept of State, *Inter-American Efforts to Relieve International Tensions in the Western Hemisphere, 1959–1960*, (1962).

[49] PAU, *Inter-American Treaty of Reciprocal Assistance, Applications*, i. 325–65.

problem an internal one, since the forces were Nicaraguan exiles who had taken up arms against an anti-democratic government. Nevertheless a Meeting of Consultation was convoked (as usual without setting a place or date) and an investigating committee established. The committee found that Nicaragua had been invaded by armed revolutionaries proceeding from Costa Rica, and the OAS Council recommended member states to 'strengthen the measures designed to maintain peace, observing the principle of nonintervention'. During the debate on the committee's report, Cuba declared her sympathy with the efforts of peoples suffering from oppression to liberate themselves from tyranny, although she observed faithfully the principle of non-intervention. Her delegate said that his government had taken strong and effective measures to prevent the departure of armed expeditions from its territory and to restrain Nicaraguan revolutionaries in Cuba.

At the beginning of July 1959 the Dominican Republic drew the attention of the OAS Council to 'the serious situation that has arisen in the Caribbean area as a result of two invasions of Dominican territory by armed groups, organized, trained, and equipped in territory of the Republic of Cuba'. She also accused Venezuela of participation in these activities. The representatives of Cuba and Venezuela strongly denied the charges and accused the Dominican government of being responsible for the mounting tension in the Caribbean region. During the discussion on the Dominican complaint it was proposed (initially on the suggestion of Haiti, but with the support of, among others, the United States) that a Meeting of American Foreign Ministers should be held to consider 'the general situation in the Caribbean area as a problem of an urgent nature and of common interest to the American States'. The Dominican Republic withdrew her note asking for the convocation of the Organ of Consultation, and Cuba and Venezuela were assured that the proposed Meeting of Consultation was not linked with the Dominican request. The United States Ambassador declared that the purpose of such a meeting would not be:

to air or judge charges by one country against another; rather it would be to review all the information available to the OAS on tensions existing in the area, to examine the causes thereof, and to suggest courses of action that would revitalize the basic principles of the OAS, which had been jeopardized by the existing situation. These principles he listed as those of nonintervention, collective security, and the desire of the people of this Hemisphere for an increasingly effective exercise of representative democracy.[50]

The Fifth Meeting of Foreign Ministers of the American Republics, convened under Articles 39 and 40 of the OAS Charter, met at Santiago, Chile from 12 to 18 August 1959.[51] Its main task in dealing with the causes of tension in the Caribbean region was how to reconcile the principle of non-intervention with growing Latin American demands for action to promote the effective exercise of representative democracy and observation of human rights—in addition to economic development and social change. The standard-bearer for the cause of revolutionary change in all these fields was, of course, Cuba, while the Dominican Republic was the main target of those Latin Americans seeking measures to eliminate right-wing dictators. There were angry exchanges between the Cuban and Dominican representatives at Santiago, and it is of interest that the Cuban Foreign Minister roundly condemned an interpretation of non-intervention which shielded dictatorships from international action to safeguard human rights. The United States came out strongly for the principle of non-intervention and against attempts to overthrow governments by force in the hope of establishing democracy. The Final Act of the Fifth Meeting, including the 'Declaration of Santiago, Chile', endeavoured to harmonize non-intervention with concern for human rights and the effective exercise of representative democracy, and to further economic development in order to enhance the prospects of political stability and democracy. These matters will be discussed in the following chapter.

The Inter-American Peace Committee, which was recognized as 'a permanent entity', was given the task of examining 'methods and procedures to prevent any activities from abroad designed to overthrow established governments or provoke instances of intervention or aggression . . .'; the relationship between violations of human rights or the absence of representative democracy, on the one hand, and the political tensions affecting the peace of the hemisphere, on the other; and the relationship between economic underdevelopment and political instability. The committee was immediately to initiate broad studies on these subjects and prepare a preliminary report on

[50] US Dept of State, *Inter-American Efforts to Relieve International Tensions*, p. 20. Other references on this page are from ibid. pp. 16–18.
[51] Fifth Meeting of Consultation, *Actas y documentos*, OEA/Ser. F/III. 5 (español) (1961).

which the American governments might make their observations. Later, it would submit a definitive report to the Eleventh Inter-American Conference, or, if such action should be indicated, to a Meeting of Consultation of Ministers of Foreign Affairs for pertinent decisions. The committee was authorized to act on its own initiative or at the request of governments, but in either case investigations within the territory of any state required the latter's express consent. The powers granted by this resolution (IV) were to be effective until the Eleventh Inter-American Conference decided whether or not to include them in the Peace Committee's statutes.

The delegation of Ecuador had proposed that the statutes of the Peace Committee should be revised and the OAS Council prepare a report on this for the Eleventh Inter-American Conference. The original statutes were amended by the OAS Council in May 1956 in accordance with Resolution CII of the Tenth Inter-American Conference. Under the amended statutes, only a state directly concerned in a dispute or controversy with another American state might request action by the committee, and the latter could act only with the consent of the other party or parties. Ecuador believed these changes had hampered the committee's work. The Fifth Meeting of Consultation referred the Ecuadoran resolution for study and report to the Inter-American Juridical Committee at Rio.

Even while the Santiago Meeting was in progress, Haiti complained she had been invaded by an armed expedition which had set out from a port in Cuba, where the authorities had declared themselves unable to prevent its departure. The Inter-American Peace Committee investigated the situation, but Haiti made no formal accusation against the Cuban government, merely requesting OAS support and co-operation in preventing further such acts of aggression.

The next three complaints heard by the Peace Committee were made against the Dominican Republic, two by Venezuela, and one by Ecuador. The first Venezuelan accusation was of an attempt to drop subversive leaflets on her territory by an aircraft flying from Ciudad Trujillo (they were actually dropped, by error, over the Dutch island of Curaçao). The committee concluded that this flight could not have taken place without the connivance of the Dominican government. Ecuador's complaint, in February 1960, was of the Dominican government's refusal to allow a number of its citizens who had taken asylum in the Ecuadoran embassy to leave the country, and of certain measures adversely affecting the status and personnel of the embassy. The committee's efforts to resolve this controversy failed because the Dominican government refused to co-operate.

Much more significant for the inter-American system was the second Venezuelan charge. On 17 February 1960 Venezuela requested the committee to investigate 'the flagrant violations of human rights by the Government of the Dominican Republic, which are aggravating the tensions in the Caribbean'. The OAS Council, to whom the complaint was originally addressed, had decided that the Peace Committee was the appropriate organ to consider it. Although refused permission to visit the Dominican Republic, the committee gathered a considerable amount of evidence and concluded in a report submitted to the OAS Council on 6 June 1960 that:

> On the basis of the evidence which it has been able to gather, the Committee has reached the conclusion that international tensions in the Caribbean region have been aggravated by flagrant and widespread violations of human rights which have been committed and continue to be committed in the Dominican Republic. . . . These acts constitute the denial of fundamental rights set forth in the American Declaration of the Rights and Duties of Man, as well as of principles of the Charter of the Organization of American States.

And, in its final words:

> . . . the Committee stresses the fact that international tensions in the Caribbean area, far from diminishing, have been increased and that, in its view, these tensions will continue to increase so long as the flagrant violations of human rights in the Dominican Republic persist.

In the meantime, the committee had submitted (14 April 1960) its special report to the OAS Council on the 'Relationship Between Violations of Human Rights or the Nonexercise of Representative Democracy and the Political Tensions That Affect the Peace of the Hemisphere'.[52]

Before the Dominican Republic was again the subject of a charge in the OAS Council, the Peace Committee received complaints against Cuba. On 9 May 1960 Guatemala charged the Castro government with a 'defamatory campaign', 'illegal and interventionist acts', and, later, with planning a seaborne invasion of her territory. On 21 June the United States presented the Peace Committee with a memorandum entitled 'Provocative Actions of the Government of

---

[52] See below, pp. 292 ff.

Cuba Against the United States Which Have Served To Increase Tensions in the Caribbean Area'. The deteriorating relations between the United States and Cuba at this time have already been described.[53] On 4 July 1960 Venezuela called for an immediate convocation of the Organ of Consultation, under Article 6 of the Rio Treaty, to

consider the acts of intervention and aggression of the Government of the Dominican Republic against the Government of Venezuela that culminated in the attempt upon the life of the Venezuelan Chief of State on June 24 last, and so that it may take appropriate measures to defend the sovereignty of Venezuela and maintain the peace and security of the Americas.

Before setting a date for a meeting of the Organ of Consultation, the OAS Council appointed a committee to investigate the Venezuelan charges. This committee concluded that the Dominican government was indeed implicated in the plot to overthrow the Venezuelan government and in the assassination attempt. The Sixth Meeting of Consultation was subsequently scheduled to convene on 16 August 1960 at San José, Costa Rica, to consider this report.

Meanwhile, during those exchanges between the United States and the Soviet Union which have already been noted,[54] Castro complained to the Security Council (11 July 1960) of United States intervention and economic aggression against Cuba. The United States denied these charges and pointed out that both her relations with Cuba and the situation arising from the attempt of the Soviet Union to intervene (through Cuba) in the western hemisphere had been referred to the OAS for consideration. Her representative therefore argued that the Security Council should take no action on the Cuban complaint, at least until the regional body had had an opportunity 'to deal with the problem through the application of established inter-American procedures'. The Security Council decided, by nine votes to none (with Russia and Poland abstaining), not to consider the question pending a report from the OAS. On 13 July Peru had requested a prompt Meeting of Consultation to consider 'the exigencies of hemisphere solidarity, the defense of the regional system, and the defense of American democratic principles in the face of threats that might affect them'. The purpose of the Meeting would, in fact, be to discuss Cuba and Soviet intervention in the hemisphere.[55] During

---

[53] See above, pp. 169 ff.   [54] See above, pp. 170–1.
[55] Some Latin American observers remarked that Peru's request for the Meeting of Consultation coincided suspiciously with a substantial loan from the US and an increase in the Peruvian sugar import quota. President Eisenhower stated that this was merely part of the US programme of co-operation with friendly Latin

the discussion in the OAS Council of the Peruvian request, the United States declared Cuba's action in taking the charges against her to the Security Council a challenge to the inter-American system, disregarding Article 2 of the Rio Treaty and Article 20 of the OAS Charter, 'which obligated member states to seek solutions through the regional organization'. Cuba's representative replied that she was fully within her rights to have recourse to the Security Council since the 'serious situation resulting from the reiterated threats, harassments, maneuvers, reprisals, and aggressions which my country is suffering from the United States Government' was a threat to international peace and security.[56] It was decided to hold a Seventh Meeting of Consultation at San José immediately following the Sixth. Before these Meetings took place, the United States and Cuba each submitted a memorandum to the Inter-American Peace Committee accusing the other of responsibility for the increased international tensions in the hemisphere, while the committee itself prepared a report on the tensions in the Caribbean region for submission to the Seventh Meeting.

The San José Meetings (August 1960)

The Sixth Meeting of Consultation of American Foreign Ministers took place at San José, Costa Rica (16–21 August 1960.)[57] It is an important landmark in the history of the inter-American system because, for the first time, sanctions were adopted (under the Rio Treaty) against a member state. There was considerable Latin American support for sanctions against the Dominican Republic but the United States did not favour them. Secretary of State Herter doubted their value as a means of bringing democracy to the Dominican Republic (which was regarded as the way to end her aggression), and proposed instead the establishment of an OAS commission to supervise elections in that country. This was opposed, notably by Mexico, as intervention, and the United States decided to vote with the Latin Americans in what proved to be the vain hope of their support for strong measures against Castro (in whose case the United States was subsequently to favour sanctions). At San José the Dominican Republic was condemned for 'acts of aggression and

---

American nations (J. F. Rippy and A. Tischendorf, 'The San José Conference of American Foreign Ministers', *IAEA*, xiv/3 (1960), p. 61).

[56] *Inter-American Efforts to Relieve International Tensions*, p. 55.

[57] Sixth Meeting of Consultation, *Actas y documentos*, OEA/Ser. F/III.6 (español) (1961).

intervention against the State of Venezuela', and the Sixth Meeting agreed:

1. To apply the following measures:
   a. Breaking of diplomatic relations of all the member states with the Dominican Republic;
   b. Partial interruption of economic relations of all the member states with the Dominican Republic, beginning with the immediate suspension of trade in arms and implements of war of every kind. The Council of the Organization of American States, in accordance with the circumstances and with due consideration for the constitutional or legal limitations of each and every one of the member states, shall study the feasibility and desirability of extending the suspension of trade with the Dominican Republic to other articles.[58]
2. To authorize the Council of the Organization of American States to discontinue, by a two-thirds affirmative vote of its members, the measures adopted in this resolution, at such time as the Government of the Dominican Republic should cease to constitute a danger to the peace and security of the hemisphere.[59]
3. To authorize the Secretary General of the Organization of American States to transmit to the Security Council of the United Nations full information concerning the measures agreed upon in this resolution.[60]

The Sixth Meeting was also significant for the question of the competence of regional agencies within the United Nations. When the text of the Final Act was transmitted to the Security Council, the Soviet Union requested that the Council should consider and endorse the resolution applying sanctions. The United States, supported by the two Latin American members of the Council (Argentina and Ecuador), proposed that the Security Council should 'take note of' and not 'approve' the OAS action. In the Soviet view (shared by Poland), the Council had to approve the OAS resolution because of its primary responsibility for the maintenance of international peace and security and because, under Article 53 of the United Nations Charter, no 'enforcement action' could be taken by regional agencies without its authorization. Russia and Poland maintained that the measures agreed upon in the OAS resolution fell within the meaning of the term 'enforcement action' referred to in Article 53.

---

[58] See below, p. 250.
[59] The OAS Council took action to discontinue these measures on 4 Jan. 1962: *Acta de la Sesión Ordinaria celebrada el 4 de enero de 1962*, OEA/Ser. G/II, C-a-431 (Aprobada), 4 Jan. 1962.
[60] Sixth Meeting of Consultation, *Final Act*, OEA/Ser. C/II. 6 (English) (1960), pp. 5–6.

The United States rejected the Soviet interpretation, pointing out that none of the members of the OAS had sought authorization from the Security Council to implement the San José resolution; they had merely remitted the latter in accordance with Article 54 of the United Nations Charter. Other members of the Council stressed that the measures agreed upon by the OAS did not involve the use of armed force, which needed authorization by the Council. In other words, they were interpreting 'enforcement action' to mean only 'use of armed force'. Finally, the Soviet Union did not press her resolution to a vote, and the Security Council adopted the American text by nine votes to none, with two (communist) abstentions.[61]

As has already been indicated,[62] the Seventh Meeting of Consultation (22–29 August 1960) achieved far less in dealing with the problem of Cuba's relations with the United States and communist intervention in the hemisphere than the Sixth Meeting had done in respect of the Venezuelan charges against the Dominican Republic— for reasons already discussed. Just as the words of the resolution convoking the meeting had been studiously vague, so did the resulting Declaration of San José[63] not mention Cuba by name. In this declaration, the Seventh Meeting condemned intervention by an extra-continental power in the affairs of the American republics and denounced acceptance of the threat of such intervention by an American state as endangering American solidarity and security; rejected the attempt of the Sino-Soviet powers to make use of the political, economic, or social situation of any American state; reaffirmed the principle of non-intervention; reiterated the incompatibility of the inter-American system with any form of totalitarianism, and recommended all American states to act in accordance with the principles contained in the Declaration of Santiago, Chile;[64] proclaimed that

all member states of the regional organization are under obligation to submit to the discipline of the inter-American system, voluntarily and freely agreed upon, and that the soundest guarantee of their sovereignty and their political independence stems from compliance with the provisions of the Charter of the Organization of American States;

declared that all controversies between member states should be re-

---

[61] *YBUN, 1960* (1961), pp. 164–5. The question of competence is discussed further below, pp. 313–15.   [62] See above, pp. 171–2.
[63] Seventh Meeting of Consultation, *Final Act*, OEA/Ser. C/II. 7 (English) (1960), pp. 4–5.   [64] See below, pp. 291–2.

solved through inter-American peace procedures; and reaffirmed 'its faith in the regional system and its confidence in the Organization of American States, created to achieve an order of peace and justice. . . .'

Although United States Secretary of State Herter described the Declaration as a 'clear indictment' of the Castro government, this was far from being so. The Mexican delegation made a statement for inclusion in the Final Act affirming its conviction: 'that this is a resolution of a general character for all the member states of the Organization, and that in no way is it a condemnation or a threat against Cuba, whose aspirations for economic improvement and social justice have the fullest support of the Government and the people of Mexico.'[65] The OAS had certainly not supported the United States view that the mere existence of the Castro government was a threat to the hemisphere calling for strong action against it.

The abortive United States attempt to overthrow Castro by sponsoring an invasion by Cuban exiles[66] strengthened Cuba's case for appealing to the United Nations, where for some time she had been protesting that the United States was planning such an invasion, rather than to the OAS in her conflict with the United States. Cuba's case was being considered in the General Assembly when the landings took place. The United States, whose delegate denied she was involved in the invasion, was able to prevent the passage of any resolution implying that she was. Nevertheless, she was unable to secure the adoption of a resolution which would have referred the question to the OAS. In the view of one writer:

The net effect of the whole debate, apart from the embarrassment it inflicted on the United States, was to weaken the force of the historic U.S. contention that inter-American difficulties were essentially the business of the inter-American organization rather than of the United Nations as a whole. This was a principle for which the United States had stood up vigorously as recently as 1960. In 1961, it was no longer able to make its

---

[65] It is of interest that Guatemala appended a statement to the Final Act declaring her view 'that the American states would have been justified in assuming a stronger attitude' (i.e. towards Cuba, whom she named). For Guatemala was involved in the plans for invading Cuba. Moreover, the Guatemalan government subsequently accused Mexico of permitting communist forces to be trained on her soil for an invasion of Guatemalan territory. It was unable to substantiate these charges, the formulation of which was probably an attempt to embitter Mexico's relations with the US (Inter-American Peace Committee, *Report to Eighth Meeting of Consultation*, OEA/Ser. L/III, CIP/I/62 (1962), pp. 18–21.

[66] See above, pp. 172–4.

view prevail against the contrary opinion of a large part of the U.N. membership.[67]

In the General Assembly, the Mexican delegation submitted (unsuccessfully) 'what might be called a renegade Latin American draft,[68] implicitly condemning United States intervention in Cuba and calling for peaceful settlement without reference to the OAS'.[69] Mexico continued to maintain that the Cuban question should be dealt with by the United Nations.[70]

Meanwhile, the United States had come to regard Trujillo as a liability in her relations with Latin America, and she was even more anxious to lay the ground for severe measures against Castro. Therefore, shortly after the San José Meetings, the Eisenhower administration took steps to deprive the Dominican Republic of the favourable terms upon which she sold sugar to the United States. In January 1961, the OAS Council recommended extending the suspension of trade with the Dominican Republic to include the export of oil, oil products, trucks and spare parts. But six Latin American countries abstained in this vote. Brazil took the view that new acts of intervention in the affairs of other states must be proved against the Trujillo government to justify new sanctions.[71] In the light of this opposition it is clear the United States was determined to bring about changes in the Dominican government, if not the overthrow of Trujillo. Since the United States was the only significant source of the items named in the OAS Council's recommendation the new sanctions were, in practice, unilateral.[72]

The Punta del Este Meeting (*January 1962*)

Following the assassination of Trujillo and its immediate aftermath in the Dominican Republic,[73] the Cuban problem came once more before the OAS. On 16 October 1961 Peru requested the convocation of the Organ of Consultation (under Article 6 of the Rio

[67] Stebbins, *US in World Affairs, 1961*, p. 317.

[68] Five Latin American countries (Bolivia, Brazil, Chile, Ecuador, and Mexico) joined Cuba in supporting this draft and one (the Dominican Republic) abstained (*YBUN*, 1960, p. 163).

[69] Claude, *Int. Concil.* (Mar. 1964), pp. 40–41.

[70] See above, p. 184, n. 117.

[71] *NYT*, internat. ed., 5 Jan. 1961. The minutes of the OAS Council's meeting are contained in *Acta de la Sesión Ordinaria celebrada el 4 de enero de 1961*, OEA/Ser. G/II, C-a-397 (Aprobada), 4 Jan. 1961, pp. 5–92.

[72] See J. Slater, 'The United States, the Organization of American States, and the Dominican Republic, 1961–1963', *Int. Org.*, xviii/2 (1964), pp. 273–4.

[73] See above, pp. 175–6.

Treaty) to consider what she denounced as the Cuban government's violations of human rights and its subversive activities in other American republics.[74] The OAS Council decided on 22 November 1961 that the Inter-American Peace Committee should investigate these charges. In the meantime (14 November) Colombia (strongly supported by the United States) called for a Meeting of Consultation, also under Article 6 of the Rio Treaty,

to consider the threats to the peace and to the political independence of the American states that might arise from the intervention of extracontinental powers directed toward breaking American solidarity, and particularly to:

    a. Point out the various types of threats to the peace or certain acts that, if they occur, justify the application of measures for the maintenance of the peace and security, pursuant to Chapter V of the Charter of the Organization of American States and the provisions of the Inter-American Treaty of Reciprocal Assistance;

    b. Determine the measures that it is advisable to take for the maintenance of the peace and security of the Hemisphere.[75]

In fact, the object was to consider measures to be taken against Cuba. When the Colombian request was discussed in the OAS Council it brought out an important difference of opinion among members of the inter-American system regarding its validity—and wisdom.[76] The Mexican delegate, in particular, expressed deep concern over its juridical basis. He argued that, according to the Rio Treaty, there must be not merely a threat to the peace, but a threat that affects 'the inviolability or the integrity of the territory or the sovereignty or political independence of any American State'. He declared there was no urgency in the situation, and the Chilean delegate observed that the Colombian resolution referred to threats that 'might arise'. But in spite of the wording of Colombia's request, those supporting it—and, above all, the United States—claimed that the alignment of the Cuban government with international communism represented a present threat. Under the terms of the anti-communist resolution adopted at the Tenth Inter-American Conference this 'would call for a Meeting of Consultation to consider the adoption of appropriate action in accordance with existing treaties'. It is significant that the

---

[74] Inter-American Peace Committee, *Report to Eighth Meeting*, pt. III, App. 1-A.
[75] OEA/Ser. F/II. 8 (English), Doc. 3 (English), 7 Jan. 1962, Original Spanish.
[76] *Acta de la Sesión Extraordinaria celebrada el 14 de noviembre de 1961*, OEA/Ser. G/II, C-a-422 (Aprobada), 14 Nov. 1961; *Acta de la Sesión Extraordinaria celebrada el 4 de diciembre de 1961*, ibid. C-a-427 (Aprobada), 4 Dec. 1961.

United States did not invoke the resolution which Mr Dulles had secured at Caracas at the cost of so much Latin American resentment.[77] As we have seen, six countries (in addition to Cuba) did not support the convocation of the Eighth Meeting of Consultation.[78]

The opposition of these nations—were it maintained—would set very definite limits to the action the Meeting of Consultation would take against Castro. A week before the Meeting convened the Inter-American Peace Committee published its report on Peru's charges against Cuba. The committee had not received the co-operation of the Cuban government in making its investigation. The report confirmed the latter's alignment with communist countries and its denial of certain fundamental human rights to its citizens, but it produced little substantial evidence of subversive activities against its neighbours.

Nevertheless, the Eighth Meeting of Consultation (Punta del Este, Uruguay, 22–31 January 1962) achieved more to meet the challenge of international communism than any previous conference had done, though its results fell short of what the United States would have liked.[79] With the exception of Cuba herself, all the American republics agreed 'that adherence by any member of the Organization of American States to Marxism-Leninism is incompatible with the inter-American system and the alignment of such a government with the communist bloc breaks the unity and solidarity of the hemisphere'; and 'that the present Government of Cuba, which has officially identified itself as a Marxist-Leninist government, is incompatible with the principles and objectives of the inter-American system'. But only fourteen delegations voted for those parts of the same Resolution (VI) which stated 'that this incompatibility excludes the present Government of Cuba from participation in the inter-American system' and 'that the Council of the Organization of American States and the other organs and organizations of the inter-American system adopt without delay the measures necessary to comply with this resolution'.[80] Seventeen agreed that 'the present

---

[77] It was cited, however, in a memorandum prepared by the Department of Legal Affairs of the PAU before the Eighth Meeting took place (presumably to justify its convocation in juridical terms): Eighth Meeting of Consultation, *Background Memorandum on the Convocation of the Meeting*. OEA/Ser. F/II. 8, Doc. 2 (English) Corr., 2 Jan. 1962, Original: Spanish, pp. 30–31.

[78] See above, p. 176.

[79] See above, pp. 177 ff., and Eighth Meeting of Consultation, *Final Act*, OEA/Ser. C/II. 8 (English) (1962).

[80] The OAS Council complied with this resolution on 14 Feb. 1962, *Acta de la Sesión Ordinaria celebrada el 14 de febrero de 1962* (OEA/Ser. G/II, C-a-433

Government of Cuba has voluntarily placed itself outside the inter-American system'.

Resolution II of the Final Act adopted at Punta del Este established a 'Special Consultative Committee on Security against the Subversive Action of International Communism'. Composed of experts on security matters, selected by the OAS Council from a list of candidates submitted by the governments, the committee would advise member states requesting assistance. It is of interest that Bolivia (alone) abstained from approving this measure, because of her experience with the Emergency Advisory Committee for Political Defense during the Second World War.[81] Resolution VII excluded immediately the present Government of Cuba from the Inter-American Defense Board. Sixteen states (Brazil, Chile, Ecuador, and Mexico abstaining) supported Resolution VIII calling for an immediate suspension of trade in arms with Cuba, and asking the OAS Council to study the question of its extension to other items. Other resolutions of the Meeting dealt with non-intervention and self-determination, the holding of free elections, the Alliance for Progress, and the revision of the Statute of the Inter-American Commission on Human Rights. The Punta del Este decisions went a long way towards isolating Cuba within the hemisphere, but of course did nothing to prevent the Castro government obtaining support outside it.

In February 1962 Cuba renewed her charges in the General Assembly that the United States was intervening in her affairs and planning aggression against her, and protested against the Punta del Este resolutions.[82] The United States defended the actions of the Eighth Meeting of Consultation and accused the Cuban government of subversive activities against other Latin American countries. She was supported by all the other Latin American countries in opposing a communist-sponsored resolution in the General Assembly which would have called in question OAS competence to take the Punta del Este decisions. The Venezuelan representative pointed out that while the United Nations Charter presupposed the peaceful coexistence of states with different political systems, membership in the OAS involved a pledge to observe the principle of representative democracy, as well as other principles and practices based on its Charter and the

---

Aprobada), 14 Feb. 1962. Actually, the Cuban delegate walked out of the meeting (*NYT*, 15 Feb. 1962).

[81] See above, pp. 125–6.   [82] *YBUN, 1961* (1963), pp. 120–3.

s

relevant treaties and conventions. Any American state which renounced these principles, as Cuba had done, automatically placed itself outside the inter-American system. Nor, in Venezuela's view, did the resolutions adopted at Punta del Este constitute interference in Cuba's internal affairs, since collective action under the OAS Charter could not be regarded as a violation of the principle of non-intervention. Not all the Latin American countries accepted the validity of these last two Venezuelan assertions. But Cuba obtained no satisfaction from her complaints to the General Assembly. She then accused the United States in the Security Council of forcing the OAS to adopt 'illegal enforcement measures' against her at Punta del Este. Here the United States contended successfully that the Dominican case in 1960 had established a precedent that non-military sanctions did not require Security Council approval, and Cuba's request that the International Court of Justice should give an opinion on this question was rejected.[83]

During the next months the OAS faced other problems. A dispute between Bolivia and Chile over the use of the waters of the Lauca River (which flows from Chile into Bolivia) came before the OAS Council in April 1962. The Bolivian government requested the convocation of the Organ of Consultation to consider what she described as Chilean aggression.[84] When the Council appealed to both parties to adopt one of the available inter-American peace procedures, Chile declared it was a legal issue which should be dealt with by arbitration or the International Court of Justice.[85] On 3 September, Bolivia withdrew temporarily from participation in the activities of the OAS, although she returned the following month in the interests of hemispheric solidarity to meet the crisis over Soviet missiles in Cuba. This was the first time any member of the OAS had withdrawn, even temporarily. On 17 June 1963, after an OAS commission had been studying her dispute with Chile for nearly a year, Bolivia announced she was withdrawing permanently from the OAS Council because of the latter's failure to solve the Lauca waters dispute.[86] In July 1962 the overthrow by military coup d'état of civilian government in Peru following the limited electoral success of Sr Haya de la Torre brought

---

[83] *YBUN, 1962* (1964), pp. 101–4.
[84] *Acta de la Sesión Extraordinaria celebrada el 20 de abril de 1962*, OEA/Ser. G/II, C-a-441 (Aprobada), 20 Apr. 1962.
[85] *Acta de la Sesión Extraordinaria celebrada el 24 de mayo de 1962*, ibid. C-a-448 (Aprobada), 24 May 1962.
[86] *NYT*, 18 June 1963. At the end of 1964 Bolivia announced that she would resume her seat on the OAS Council.

a new crisis to the OAS. A group of member states (Venezuela, Costa Rica, Honduras, and the Dominican Republic) requested the convocation of a Meeting of Consultation to consider what policy should be followed in the face of military coups. The core of this group's argument was that the overthrow of a democratic government was itself a threat to the peace of the hemisphere and a violation of the OAS Charter.[87] After several meetings on this subject, the OAS Council accepted a compromise, supported by the United States, that there should be a general study of the problem of military coups rather than some action to deal specifically with the situation in Peru.[88]

The Crisis of October 1962

But everything else was overshadowed in the autumn of 1962 by the Cuban crisis. At an informal meeting of American foreign ministers and special representatives held in Washington on 2 and 3 October, Secretary of State Rusk endeavoured to obtain greater Latin American support for United States policy towards Castro. The meeting made no concrete decisions or formal recommendations, but the communiqué, in which, on the insistence of Brazil and Mexico, the principle of non-intervention was inserted, did call for special measures:

The meeting observed that it is desirable to intensify individual and collective surveillance of the delivery of arms and implements of war and all other items of strategic importance to the communist regime of Cuba, in order to prevent the secret accumulation in the island of arms that can be used for offensive purposes against the Hemisphere.[89]

This meeting has been described as providing 'something of a springboard for future American action'.[90] Certainly, the United States at once announced unilateral measures aimed at preventing the use of American, allied, and neutral shipping for transporting supplies to Cuba from communist countries. Whether these unilateral measures came 'within a collective framework regarding the Cuban situation' is debatable.[91]

---

[87] This was in line with the Rodríguez Larreta Doctrine (see above, pp. 142–4 and E. Rodríguez Larreta, 'El derecho a la intervención colectiva', *Combate*, ii/7 (1959), pp. 23–26; G. J. Facio, 'Impulso democrático al sistema interamericano', *Combate*, ii/10 (1960), pp. 48–56).

[88] OEA/Ser. G/II, C-a-456, 458–60.   [89] *Docs Am. For. Rel.*, 1962, p. 372.

[90] R. St J. Macdonald, 'The Organization of American States in Action', *Univ. Toronto Law J.*, xv/2 (1964), p. 400.

[91] Thomas & Thomas, *The OAS*: 'By implication this communiqué gave the

On 22 October 1962, in the knowledge that Soviet missiles were being installed in Cuba, President Kennedy declared his intention of instituting a naval quarantine and increased aerial surveillance of the island, and made simultaneous appeals to the Security Council and the OAS Council. This last action was unprecedented in the history of the inter-American system. Mr Rusk, who personally presented the United States resolution to the OAS Council on 23 October 1962, explained:

> Mr. Chairman, I want to say a word about the action being taken simultaneously in the Security Council of the United Nations. The threat is to our Hemisphere and we have the primary responsibility and duty to act as we are now doing, as a Hemisphere. But the threat originates from outside the Hemisphere and it is appropriate that the extracontinental power which challenges our inter-American commitments and our deliberations must also be dealt with in the forum in which that power participates. It is therefore fitting in this case that the Security Council of the United Nations be requested to call upon this member to refrain from his aggressive actions against us and to seek to enforce upon him its decisions.[92]

In the Security Council, the United States representative, Adlai Stevenson, presented a resolution which:

1. *Calls* as a provisional measure under Article 40 for the immediate dismantling and withdrawal from Cuba of all missiles and other offensive weapons;
2. *Authorizes and requests* the Acting Secretary-General to dispatch to Cuba a United Nations observer corps to assure and report on compliance with this resolution;
3. *Calls for* termination of the measures of quarantine directed against military shipments to Cuba upon United Nations certification of compliance with Paragraph 1;
4. *Urgently recommends* that the United States of America and the Union of Soviet Socialist Republics confer promptly on measures to remove the existing threat to the security of the Western Hemisphere and the peace of the world, and report thereon to the Security Council.[93]

The Security Council also received a letter from Cuba and a resolution from the Soviet Union, both condemning the United States quarantine.

United States government a greater degree of flexibility in taking unilateral measures within a collective framework regarding the Cuban situation' (p. 329).

[92] OEA/Ser. G/II, C-a-462 (Aprobada), 23 Oct. 1962, pp. 8–9.
[93] See Draft Res. *SCOR*, 17th Yr, 1022nd mtg, 23 Oct. 1962.

In the OAS Council, the United States requested the formal convocation of a Meeting of Foreign Ministers and action by the Council
as Provisional Organ of Consultation. In consequence, a resolution
was adopted sanctioning for the first time the use of armed force
under the terms of the Rio Treaty. The Council resolved:

1. To call for the immediate dismantling and withdrawal from Cuba of all
   missiles and other weapons with any offensive capability;
2. To recommend that the member states, in accordance with Articles 6
   and 8 of the Inter-American Treaty of Reciprocal Assistance, take all
   measures, individually and collectively, including the use of armed force,
   which they may deem necessary to ensure that the Government of Cuba
   cannot continue to receive from the Sino-Soviet powers military material
   and related supplies which may threaten the peace and security of the
   Continent and to prevent the missiles in Cuba with offensive capability
   from ever becoming an active threat to the peace and security of the
   Continent;
3. To inform the Security Council of the United Nations of this resolution
   in accordance with Article 54 of the Charter of the United Nations and
   to express the hope that the Security Council will, in accordance with
   the draft resolution introduced by the United States, dispatch United
   Nations observers to Cuba at the earliest moment;
4. To continue to serve provisionally as Organ of Consultation and to
   request the Member States to keep the Organ of Consultation duly informed of measures taken by them in accordance with paragraph two
   of this resolution.[94]

This resolution meant, in fact, support for the United States quarantine (which was not officially proclaimed until after the OAS
Council had met; President Kennedy cited the OAS resolution in his
proclamation),[95] and any further measures she might take to remove
the missiles. All members except Uruguay, whose delegation had not
received instructions,[96] supported the first part of the resolution.

---

[94] *Docs Am. For. Rel.*, *1962*, pp. 382–3.
[95] It is noteworthy that, to quote Q. Wright, 'The Cuban Quarantine', *AJIL*,
lvii/3 (1963), p. 557: 'The main argument put forward by the United States to
justify the quarantine was that it was permitted by Articles 6 and 8 of the Rio
Treaty of 1947, implemented by the Consultative Organ of the Organization of
American States in its resolution at Washington on October 23, 1962.' But, as
Wright points out: 'The resolution could not, however, in law affect the rights of
the Soviet Union, against which the quarantine was primarily directed. A state's
rights, under international law, cannot be reduced by a treaty to which it is not a
party' (p. 558). In his view: 'The episode has not improved the reputation of the
United States as a champion of international law' (p. 563). For a justification of
the quarantine in juridical terms, based on the authority of the Rio Treaty, see
A. Chayes, 'Law and the Quarantine of Cuba', *For. Aff.*, xli/3 (1963), pp. 550–7.
[96] Uruguay subsequently supported the resolution.

But Brazil, Mexico, and Bolivia abstained on the second part, indicating that they did not support armed invasion of Cuba.[97]

The crisis of October 1962 was ended by direct exchanges between the United States President and the Soviet leader. In the United Nations, a 'large number' of countries prevailed upon U Thant to secure a suspension of the arms shipments and the quarantine, thus averting a clash between the two sides. No vote was taken in the Security Council, for U Thant's intervention had the effect of leaving the United States and the Soviet Union free to negotiate the withdrawal of the offending weapons between themselves. The Acting Secretary General visited Cuba, but was unable to persuade Dr Castro to agree to United Nations inspection of the sites as the United States had demanded. The latter did not press this matter, however, realizing that were it referred to the General Assembly (following a presumed Soviet Union veto), the result would almost certainly have been unsatisfactory to her. Instead, she continued her aerial surveillance of the island—an action which certainly would not have been endorsed by the Assembly.[98] When the United States and Russian leaders finally informed U Thant (in January 1963) that their negotiations had been completed, the Security Council dropped the question.[99]

As far as the OAS was concerned, its role in the Cuban crisis of October 1962 cannot truly be described as a positive one. Although, formally, the United States acted in conformity with the OAS Council's resolution of 23 October, the latter had been passed in the face of a *fait accompli*: the proclaimed determination of the United States to take certain measures and the knowledge that she had already initiated them. The other members of the inter-American system 'had no significant voice in the formulation or execution of the policy at all';[100] they accepted United States policy, and the OAS acted, on this occasion, as the 'rubber stamp' its critics have always

---

[97] OEA/Ser. G/II, C-a-463 (Aprobada), 23 Oct. 1962; Thomas & Thomas, *The OAS*, p. 331.

[98] A justification of this aerial surveillance—in violation of Cuba's air space—can only be made in terms of necessary defence. It is impossible to take seriously the argument of Thomas & Thomas, *The OAS*, p. 336: 'Cuba, of course, could hardly claim that these flights, whether taken individually or collectively, were illegal intervention, for Cuba by its own conduct had excluded itself from the inter-American community, and probably from the international community of civilized states.'

[99] For an account of the role of the UN in the Cuban crisis (with documentary references), see *YBUN, 1962*, pp. 104–12. It must be noted that this role was one of mediation; the world organization did not support the US position.

[100] Macdonald, *Univ. Toronto Law J.*, xv/2 (1964), p. 406.

described it as being. Perhaps the most significant aspect of the matter was that Brazil, Mexico, and Bolivia felt impelled—and able—to make their reservations. Moreover, the degree of support the United States obtained was to meet the immediate crisis, not for her general policy towards the Cuban government. This became apparent when attempts were made to strengthen inter-American machinery for combating communist subversion.

In April 1963, when the OAS Council met to formulate a statute for the Special Consultative Committee on Security established by decision of the Eighth Meeting of Consultation, there was deep disagreement over the powers to be given it. All members accepted that a government's consent was necessary before the committee could be sent into its territory, but only thirteen supported a proposal to give the Council the right to initiate security investigations by a majority vote even if the country concerned in them objected. Brazil voted against this, and Bolivia, Chile, the Dominican Republic, Haiti, Mexico, and Venezuela abstained.[101] When, in the following July, the Council adopted a report by the Special Committee containing the suggestion that member countries accept 'a little sacrifice' of civic and political freedom and human rights in order to enforce measures against subversion, Chile voted against adoption, while Brazil, Haiti, Mexico, and Venezuela abstained. It is noteworthy that Venezuela, a main target of Castro's propaganda and his strong opponent, took a leading part in opposing these measures.[102] The United States decided to abandon plans for asking the OAS to declare an economic embargo against Cuba.[103]

Other Troubles in the Caribbean Region

In the meantime, the Caribbean region continued to be turbulent, and not only because of the activities of Castro and his opponents. Twice during 1963 disputes between the Dominican Republic and Haiti were investigated by special commissions appointed by the OAS Council acting as Provisional Organ of Consultation.[104] A crisis

---

[101] *Acta de la Sesión Extraordinaria celebrada el 23 de abril de 1963*, OEA/Ser. G/II, C-a-487 (Aprobada), 23 Apr. 1963, pp. 35–56, 67–79; *Macdonald*, p. 412.

[102] *Acta de la Sesión Extraordinaria celebrada el 3 de julio de 1963*, OEA/Ser. G/II, C-a-500 (Aprobada), 3 July 1963; *NYT*, internat, ed., 4 July 1963.

[103] *NYT*, internat. ed., 5 July 1963.

[104] In April the Dominican Republic complained of Haitian provocations; in August Haiti charged that the Dominican Republic had supported a small invading force of Haitian exiles. Both cases are described briefly in Macdonald, *Univ. Toronto Law J.*, xv/2 (1964), pp. 414–26; see also Stebbins, *US in World Affairs*, *1963*, pp. 293–5. The PAU has issued a list of its published documents relating

had developed between these neighbouring republics when, after its embassy in Port-au-Prince had been violated by Haitian troops, the Dominican government mobilized and demanded reparations. The origins of the dispute lay, however, in the character of the two governments. In Haiti, François Duvalier's unconstitutional extension of his power provoked the internal situation in which the Dominican embassy was entered by troops searching for his opponents. In the Dominican Republic, the democratically elected President Juan Bosch accused Dr Duvalier of denying human rights to his own people and of plotting against the Dominican government. Bosch's antipathy towards Duvalier was fully shared by the United States, and it seems probable that the Dominican President believed he would have the latter's support for his belligerent policy.

These disputes between the Dominican Republic and Haiti have several important features. They illustrate once again the link between the violation of human rights and international tensions in the Caribbean region. They confirmed that although the Duvalier government was unpopular in Latin America generally, most members of the OAS were not prepared to violate the principle of non-intervention to bring about its downfall. Therefore, although she exerted considerable pressure upon Duvalier (cutting off economic aid, recalling her ambassador, and stationing amphibious forces off Haiti's coast), the United States did not send her forces into Haiti. It is noteworthy that, on both occasions, Haiti appealed to the Security Council, although agreeing subsequently that the disputes should be dealt with by the OAS.[105] Ironically, Duvalier survived, while Bosch was overthrown by a right-wing military junta.[106] Indeed, Bosch's downfall, rather than any action by the OAS, eventually brought about a relaxation of tension between the two countries. The OAS seems, however, to have exercised a restraining influence on all the main parties concerned: the Dominican Republic, Haiti, and the United States.

At the beginning of 1964 the OAS was faced with a crisis involving the United States and Panama: its strongest member and one of the weakest. Sparked off by an incident over the unauthorized flying of their national flag by United States students in the grounds of their school in the Panama Canal Zone, the dispute was an old one.

---

to the situation between the Dominican Republic and Haiti (OEA/Ser. G/VI, C/INF-246, Rev. 2, 15 Oct. 1964).

[105] See below, pp. 313–14.   [106] See above, p. 183.

Panama had long criticized the annual payment she received for the zone as inadequate (it was raised to $1·9 millions in 1955), and complained of racial discrimination against her citizens. More recently, she had been concerned to establish, in principle, her sovereignty over the zone (which, of course, she did not exercise) through flying her flag there; and the right to do so—alongside that of the United States—was conceded in 1963. However, Panamanian nationalism is affronted by the United States presence, and a desire to 'nationalize' the Canal is inherent in the situation.

Following riots and loss of life in the incident of January 1964, Panama charged the United States in both the Security Council and the OAS with aggression. The United States did not oppose consideration of Panama's charges by the United Nations body, but both countries agreed to mediation by the Inter-American Peace Committee.[107] Although peace was soon restored in the Canal Zone, it proved very difficult to settle the differences between the disputants, since the Panamanian government insisted that the United States should negotiate a revision of the 1903 treaty between the two countries, while the United States government would agree only to 'discuss differences' between them. The truth was that, in an election year, and already on the defensive against domestic criticism of its failure to take more positive action against Castro, the Johnson administration could not afford to appear too conciliatory towards Panama. On 4 February the OAS Council acceded to a Panamanian request for a convocation of the Organ of Consultation, and constituted itself Provisional Organ of Consultation.[108] An investigating committee was sent to Panama. It reported that, although United States troops had used a 'disproportionate' amount of fire-power to repel mob incursions into the zone, Panama's charge of aggression was not justified.[109] Eventually, after an impasse had been reached at one stage over the United States refusal to enter into 'negotiations' with Panama, the OAS Council was able to announce (3 April 1964) that the two countries had agreed to resume diplomatic relations and 'to seek the prompt elimination of the causes of conflict between the two countries, without limitations or preconditions of any kind'.[110]

---

[107] The question remained, however, on the Security Council's agenda. See below, p. 314.
[108] *Acta de la Sesión Extraordinaria celebrada el 4 de febrero de 1964*, OEA/Ser. G/II, C-a-533 (Aprobada), 4 Feb. 1964.
[109] *NYT*, internat. ed., 17 Feb. 1964.
[110] *Américas*, xvi/5 (1964), p. 42.

Thus the Panama crisis ceased, at least for the time being, to be a problem for the OAS.[111]

The Ninth Meeting of Consultation (Washington, 1964)

In the meantime, as we have seen, Venezuela had charged Cuba with aggression and intervention, and an OAS investigating committee had found her charges substantiated.[112] The Ninth Meeting of Consultation of American Foreign Ministers met from 21 to 26 July 1964 at the Pan American Union[113] 'to consider measures that must be taken to deal with the acts of intervention and aggression on the part of the Cuban Government affecting the territorial integrity and the sovereignty of Venezuela, as well as the operation of its democratic institutions'.[114] All but four members of the OAS—Bolivia, Chile, Mexico, and Uruguay—agreed in Resolution I of the Final Act (paragraph 3):

a. That the governments of the American states not maintain diplomatic or consular relations with the Government of Cuba;
b. That the governments of the American states suspend all their trade, whether direct or indirect, with Cuba, except in foodstuffs, medicines, and medical equipment that may be sent to Cuba for humanitarian reasons; and
c. That the governments of the American states suspend all sea transportation between their countries and Cuba, except for such transportation as may be necessary for reasons of a humanitarian nature.

The Government of Cuba was warned (in paragraph 5):

that if it should persist in carrying out acts that possess characteristics of aggression and intervention against one or more of the member states of the Organization, the member states shall preserve their essential rights as sovereign states by the use of self-defense in either individual or collective form, which could go so far as resort to armed force, until such time as the Organ of Consultation takes measures to guarantee the peace and security of the hemisphere.

Also, as part of the same resolution (paragraph 6), the American

[111] On 18 Dec. 1964 President Johnson announced that the US had decided to proceed with the building of a sea-level canal to replace the existing Panama route, and to negotiate a new canal treaty with the Panamanian government (*NYT*, internat. ed., 23–24 Jan. 1965).
[112] See above, p. 185.
[113] Ninth Meeting of Consultation, *Documentos de la Reunión*, OEA/Ser. F/II. 9 (español) (1964).
[114] Ninth Meeting of Consultation, *Final Act*, OEA/Ser. C/II. 9 (English) (1964), p. 1.

foreign ministers urged 'those states not members of the Organization of American States that are animated by the same ideals as the inter-American system to examine the possibility of effectively demonstrating their solidarity in achieving the purposes of this resolution'. Other resolutions of the Ninth Meeting of Consultation included a 'Declaration to the People of Cuba' and one on 'Regional and International Economic Coordination'.

In a 'Statement' included in the Final Act of the Meeting, the delegation of Chile declared that it had abstained from voting on the operative part of Resolution I because it doubted whether the term 'aggression' could legally be used to describe the acts committed by the Cuban government. It voted against paragraph 3 of that resolution because it was 'firmly convinced that the measures agreed to are not appropriate to the particular case that has brought about the application of the Inter-American Treaty of Reciprocal Assistance'; and against paragraph 5 because it believed 'that there are discrepancies between the provisions of that paragraph and those of Article 51 of the Charter of the United Nations and of Article 3 of the Rio Treaty'. Its abstention on paragraph 6 was consistent with its attitude towards paragraph 3. Nor could it give positive support to the 'Declaration to the People of Cuba' since, while agreeing with its basic content, it maintained relations with the Cuban government and believed 'precisely' in the principle of non-intervention.

The Mexican delegation also made a 'Statement' for inclusion in the Final Act. It declared its conviction 'that the measures provided for in the third paragraph of the operative part of Resolution I, which the Delegation of Mexico voted against, lack foundation, inasmuch as the Inter-American Treaty of Reciprocal Assistance does not envisage, in any part, the application of such measures in situations of the kind and nature dealt with by this Meeting of Consultation'; and made 'a specific reservation to the fifth paragraph of the operative part of the same resolution since it endeavors to extend, in such a way as to be incompatible with the provisions of Articles 3 and 10 of the Inter-American Treaty of Reciprocal Assistance, the right to individual or collective self-defense'.

How far had the Ninth Meeting of Consultation furthered the peace and security of the Americas? It had taken more steps to isolate Cuba within the hemisphere which—if implemented by those countries not already having done so—would lessen somewhat Castro's opportunities for subversion. Notice had been served on the

Cuban leader that any future intervention such as that for which he had just been condemned might provoke much stronger action against him. Resolution I(5), as we have seen, contained the ominous reference to 'armed force' by individual members of the OAS, which possibly could be used to furnish an inter-American basis for some subsequent action by the United States against Castro. When Bolivia, Chile, and Uruguay subsequently agreed to implement the Meeting's decisions only Mexico's refusal to do so prevented the achievement of full solidarity on the question of applying sanctions to the Cuban government. Thus, 'the six' of Punta del Este had been reduced to one.

But if the mere existence of the Castro government, linked with international communism, threatened the western hemisphere—as the United States maintained—then the threat remained. However, there was not hemispheric solidarity on this point. Since Latin American trade with Cuba was already insignificant, the measures taken by the Ninth Meeting of Consultation would not appreciably weaken the Cuban government or make supporting it more expensive to the Soviet Union. This last could only be achieved if other non-communist powers outside the inter-American system ceased trading with Cuba, as Resolution I(6) called upon them to do. There was no sign that they would heed this request. Therefore, for the time being at least, the OAS was concerned only with preventing what almost all its members now condemned as Cuban aggression and intervention against the peace and security of the hemisphere.

At the same time, while most members of the inter-American system regarded the Castro government as a threat to hemispheric security, there were important differences among them about the best means of countering it. Apart from opposition to intervention against Castro, it was widely felt that the best way of preventing the extension of communist influence in the hemisphere was through positive measures in non-military fields: economic and social development, the promotion of representative democracy, and concern for human rights. Co-operation in these fields had been the proclaimed objective of the inter-American system long before the Cuban revolution. It is to the work and achievements of the OAS in pursuing this objective that we must now turn.

8 The OAS and Other Fields of Inter-American Co-operation

UNDOUBTEDLY, the peace and security of the western hemisphere have been the main preoccupation of the Organization of American States. As we have seen, however, only comparatively recently has the inter-American system become a system of collective security, and in the early phases of its existence it was concerned primarily with non-political questions. The exchange of commercial information and of university professors, for example, long antedates the establishment of the Inter-American Defense College. Since the end of the Second World War much greater attention than ever before has been given to inter-American co-operation in non-political fields. This has been due largely to a growing awareness of the links between peace and security on the one hand and economic development, social justice, and the exercise of representative democracy on the other. It has been due also to increasing demands of the Latin Americans for action in these fields (as compared with United States overriding concern with security against communist penetration of the hemisphere), without which the inter-American system has little positive meaning for them.

The purpose of this chapter is to consider the role of the OAS in fields other than those of international peace and security under three main headings: economic and social co-operation; cultural co-operation; and juridical co-operation. Under the latter heading concern with human rights and the exercise of representative democracy will be considered. This chapter also describes developments in the institutions of the inter-American system since the adoption of the OAS Charter.

Economic and Social Co-operation

This study has noted how the promotion of commerce was a principal motive for the United States initiating the Pan American movement, and the prompt collection and distribution of commercial information was the purpose of the institutions established by the First International Conference of American States. However, we have also seen that fundamental economic problems were not dealt with by the international conferences until the seventh of the series, although Argentina attempted, unsuccessfully, to have them discussed at the sixth.[1] Developments during the Second World War have been specified, including the establishment of the Inter-American Financial and Economic Advisory Committee, which later (at Mexico City in 1945) was replaced by the Inter-American Economic and Social Council. The preoccupation of the Latin American countries with their economic problems at the Mexico City and Rio Conferences was likewise observed.

Economic problems were also prominent—and controversial—at the Ninth International Conference of American States. The OAS Charter proclaims one of its purposes to be the solution of economic problems that may arise among the member states, and another to promote, by co-operative action, their economic development. Among the principles of the OAS, the Charter declares economic co-operation to be 'essential to the common welfare and prosperity of the peoples of the continent'. In Chapter VI of the Charter, 'Economic Standards':

> The Member States agree to cooperate with one another, as far as their resources may permit and their laws may provide, in the broadest spirit of good neighborliness, in order to strengthen their economic structure, develop their agriculture and mining, promote their industry and increase their trade (Art. 26).
>
> If the economy of an American State is affected by serious conditions that cannot be satisfactorily remedied by its own unaided effort, such State may place its economic problems before the Inter-American Economic and Social Council to seek through consultation the most appropriate solution for such problems (Art. 27).

The Charter establishes the Inter-American Economic and Social Council as one of the organs of the OAS Council, having 'for its principal purpose the promotion of the economic and social welfare of the American nations through effective cooperation for the better utilization of their natural resources, the development of their agriculture and industry and the raising of the standards of living of their peoples'. To accomplish this purpose the Council would:

a) Propose the means by which the American nations may give each other

---

[1] See above, p. 66.

technical assistance in making studies and formulating and executing plans to carry out the purposes referred to in Article 26 and to develop and improve their social services;

b) Act as coordinating agency for all official inter-American activities of an economic and social nature;

c) Undertake studies on its own initiative or at the request of any Member State;

d) Assemble and prepare reports on economic and social matters for the use of the Member States;

e) Suggest to the Council of the Organization the advisability of holding specialized conferences on economic and social matters;

f) Carry on such other activities as may be assigned to it by the Inter-American Conference, the Meeting of Consultation of Ministers of Foreign Affairs, or the Council of the Organization.

Composed of 'technical delegates', the Inter-American Economic and Social Council was to meet on its own initiative or on that of the OAS Council.

The enormous difficulty of furthering inter-American economic co-operation in practice, however, was underlined by the content and fate of the Economic Agreement of Bogotá, one of the three major documents of the conference.[2] After heated discussion, this agreement was signed with so many reservations as to have made it virtually useless even had it been ratified. It proved impossible to reconcile the economic philosophy and interests of the world's most advanced industrial power with those of twenty other countries most of which were relatively little industrialized and over-dependent upon the sale of raw materials to the first country. Two points in the agreement may suffice to illustrate the basic differences between the United States and Latin America[3] and the obstacles to a satisfactory agreement on economic co-operation. Over raw materials, the Latin Americans were understandably concerned with the fall in prices which they had so recently experienced. On their insistence, therefore, the second paragraph of Article 3 of the Economic Agreement contained a reaffirmation by the American States of 'their resolution that, as a general policy, there should be taken into account the need to compensate for the disparity that is frequently noted between the prices of raw materials and the prices of manufactured products, by

---

[2] For fuller comment on this document see Lockwood, *AJIL*, xlii/3 (1948), pp. 611–20.

[3] Within the context of inter-American economic co-operation the OAS is certainly divided into the 'one' and the 'twenty'. See above, pp. 24–25.

establishing the necessary balance between them'. Moreover, Article 30 reads:

> The States agree to cooperate among themselves and with other producing and consumer nations, for the purpose of concluding inter-governmental agreements to prevent or correct dislocations in international trade in regard to raw materials that are basic and essential for the economies of the producing countries of the Hemisphere, such as tendencies and situations of persistent disequilibrium between production and consumption, of accumulation of substantial surpluses, or of sharp fluctuations in prices, without prejudice to the provisions of the second paragraph of Article 3.

The United States delegation entered a formal reservation against both the second paragraph of Article 3 and Article 30.

On the other hand, Article 25, included on United States insistence, read:

> The States shall take no discriminatory action against investments by virtue of which foreign enterprises or capital may be deprived of legally acquired property rights, for reasons or under conditions different from those that the Constitution or laws of each country provide for the expropriation of national property. Any expropriation shall be accompanied by payment of fair compensation in a prompt, adequate and effective manner.

A number of Latin American countries, including Argentina and Mexico, made reservations to Article 25, reaffirming the primacy of their national constitutions and laws, and demonstrating once more that the Calvo Doctrine and the old problem of diplomatic intervention were still alive. But all these reservations proved superfluous, since the Economic Agreement of Bogotá was not ratified. Thus, in spite of what was written in the OAS Charter, the Ninth Conference produced little that was substantial in the way of inter-American economic co-operation.

Under the circumstances it was impossible for the Inter-American Economic and Social Council (IA-ECOSOC) to achieve very much. The United States favoured bilateral arrangements through her own lending agencies, while the Latin American countries found the United Nations Economic Commission for Latin America (ECLA) more helpful than IA-ECOSOC. Not surprisingly, therefore, the latter came to have little prestige, and when new efforts were made to further inter-American economic co-operation in the late 1950s, *ad hoc* groups (such as the Committee of Twenty-One)[4] were formed for the purpose.[5] Meanwhile, the most valuable work of IA-ECOSOC was in the field of technical co-operation, which is described briefly below.[6]

Latin American disappointment with the outcome of the economic conferences held at Rio de Janeiro (1954) and Buenos Aires (1957) has already been noted.[7] However, the latter, the long-awaited Economic Conference of the Organization of American States, did declare 'the advisability of establishing gradually and progressively, in multilateral and competitive form, a Latin American regional market' and recommend IA-ECOSOC to co-operate with ECLA in 'studies and activities leading to [its] creation'.[8] The United Nations body, concerned with the subject since the previous year, had submitted a study entitled 'ECLA Activities Relating to Payments and a Regional Market in Latin America', to the Buenos Aires Economic Conference. It is significant that the move towards regional markets in Latin America received impetus from ECLA, and not from within the OAS. Of course, this move was an expression of Pan Latin Americanism rather than Pan Americanism. Regional economic integration in Latin America was encouraged by developments in Western Europe; and the presence of observers from a large number of extra-continental nations at Buenos Aires reflected an awareness that Latin America's economic problems could not be solved within a purely hemispheric framework.

In 1958, following Vice-President Nixon's unhappy experience, two important steps were taken in the field of inter-American economic co-operation: President Kubitschek put forward his proposals for 'Operation Pan America', and the United States government finally agreed to the establishment of an Inter-American Development Bank. In an *aide mémoire* on 'Operation Pan America', the Brazilian government declared that the aim was to enhance the role of Latin America in the defence of the West through its economic development and the concomitant promotion of democracy. Operation Pan America was described as being 'conceived as involving the

---

[4] See above, p. 168.
[5] For further comments on IA-ECOSOC's inadequacies see Northwestern Univ., 'The Organization of American States', in 86th Congress, 2nd Session, Senate, Doc. No. 125, pp. 210 ff.   [6] See below, pp. 273–4.
[7] See above, p. 165. For the resolutions adopted at the Rio Conference, see *Ann. OAS*, vi/4 (1954), pp. 258–89. The Final Act of the Buenos Aires Conference appears in ibid. ix/3 (1957), pp. 213–35.
[8] Res. XL of Final Act (ibid. p. 232). But see above, p. 165.

joint action of the twenty-one republics of the Western Hemisphere, the preservation of its strictly multilateral nature being indispensable'. The basic objectives of the Operation were tentatively listed as:

1. Reaffirmation of the principles of hemispheric solidarity;
2. Recognition of underdevelopment as a problem of common interest;
3. Adaptation of inter-American organs and agencies, if necessary, to the requirements of more dynamic action to carry on the struggle against underdevelopment;
4. Technical assistance for increased productivity;
5. Measures to stabilize the market for basic commodities;
6. Adaptation to present needs and expansion of the resources of international financial institutions;
7. Reaffirmation of private initiative in the struggle against underdevelopment; and
8. Revision by each country, where necessary, of its fiscal and economic policy, for the purpose of assuring means to promote economic development.

The Brazilian government proposed certain topics 'that might be analysed during the preparatory inquiries, consultations, and meetings':

1. Study and adoption of measures favoring the use of private capital of the industrialized countries in under or semi-developed areas; more effective mobilization and utilization of available private capital for underdeveloped economies;
2. Increase in the volume and an easing of the terms of loans made by international public credit agencies, or the creation of inter-American financing institutions organized with the same objective in mind;
3. Study and adoption of other measures to strengthen the domestic economies, principally to fight inflation and to encourage savings and the investment of savings;
4. Study and adoption of measures for the equitable regulation of the market in basic commodities;
5. Study of joint measures to be adopted to meet the problems arising from the formation of large economic blocs, such as the so-called "European Common Market"; studies and measures leading to the establishment of regional markets in the Hemisphere; and
6. Expansion and diversification of technical assistance programs, using all available resources in the field.[9]

---

[9] *"Operation Pan America" and the Work of the Committee of 21: Basic documents and reports, August 1958–August 1960*, OEA/Ser. X/3.1.1 (English), 15 Aug. 1960, Original: English, pp. 1–4.

Operation Pan America was discussed at an Informal Meeting of American Foreign Ministers in September 1958 and by the first meeting of the Committee of Twenty-One.[10] However, the Brazilian government did not receive warm support for its proposals. The United States had considerable reservations regarding the idea of an overall plan for Latin American development, and the political aspects of the proposals appeared to give concern to some of the other delegations. To allay such concern, the Brazilian government affirmed that 'Latin America's integration in Western efforts to guarantee peace was not to be interpreted as an identification with Anglo-American foreign policy or with NATO'.[11]

Following the United States decision to support the establishment of an inter-American development bank, and a resolution of the Informal Meeting of American Foreign Ministers, the first meeting of the Committee of Twenty-One set up a group of experts to draw up its statutes. The Inter-American Development Bank came into existence at the end of 1959, when eighteen countries, pledged to furnish 87 per cent of the capital, had ratified its charter. The declared purpose of the new institution was 'to contribute to the acceleration of the process of economic development of the member countries, individually and collectively'. The bank was to have a provided capitalization of $1,000 millions, of which the United States would put up $450 millions, Argentina and Brazil $113 millions each, Mexico $72 millions, Venezuela $60 millions, with smaller amounts from the remaining American republics. The Inter-American Development Bank was designed to assist the Latin American countries on a sound financial basis, but with the advantage, from their point of view, over the United States lending agencies that the borrower was not required to purchase within the hemisphere. The greatest part of the bank's funds was to finance hard loans, but its charter provided for a Special Operations Fund of $150 millions to finance projects not necessarily self-liquidating. The bank was to be located in Washington (to the great disappointment of Venezuela, who had hoped its location would be Caracas[12]) and have a board of directors, national governors, and a secretary general. It would assist the member states in planning development, assigning

---

[10] See above, p. 168.

[11] V. L. Urquidi, *The Challenge of Development in Latin America* (1964), p. 146.

[12] For criticism of US insistence that the bank be located in Washington rather than Caracas, see Manger, *Pan America in Crisis*, p. 85.

priorities, and preparing loan projects. The bank, although a part of the inter-American system, was to be a completely autonomous agency.

In the meantime the Committee of Twenty-One had held two further meetings. At the second (Buenos Aires, April–May 1959), it was agreed that an American state experiencing a severe economic crisis might call for a meeting of foreign ministers since 'the principles of solidarity that inspire Pan American cooperation in the political field and in that of mutual security necessarily include the economic field'. The OAS Council subsequently approved this resolution. The second meeting of the Committee of Twenty-One established a subcommittee that would submit its studies of Operation Pan America to the Eleventh Inter-American Conference. The latter was postponed, however, and the Brazilian initiative, as such, was lost. The third and final meeting of the Committee of Twenty-One, however, was the most significant. For, stimulated by the Cuban revolution and the possibility of Castroism spreading to other parts of Latin America, the United States government had announced its intention to ask Congress to authorize an appropriation of $500 millions for a special inter-American social-development fund. President Eisenhower promised his country would co-operate in promoting a programme of social progress and economic growth in the Americas to improve the condition of the people. Before considering the Act of Bogotá, which emerged from the third meeting of the Committee of Twenty-One, let us assess briefly inter-American social co-operation up to that point.

Like economic co-operation—from which, of course, it is not always easily separated—effective social co-operation within the inter-American system has been a comparatively recent development. Yet the longest established of the specialized organizations of the OAS is the Pan American Health Organization. As the Pan American Sanitary Bureau it was founded in 1902, implementing a resolution adopted at the Second International Conference of American States. The rights of women were discussed at the Fifth International Conference in 1923, where it was decided to include social questions on the agenda of future conferences. Three of the remaining specialized organizations were in the field of social co-operation: the American International Institute for the Protection of Childhood (1927); the Inter-American Commission of Women (1928); and the Inter-American Indian Institute (1940). A large number of what came to be known as the 'specialized conferences' held before the outbreak of the Second World War dealt with social questions.[13]

The OAS Charter proclaims the promotion of social development to be one of the organization's 'essential purposes', and, as one of its principles, that 'social justice and social security are bases of lasting peace'. Chapter VII, 'Social Standards', declares:

The Member States agree to cooperate with one another to achieve just and decent living conditions for their entire populations. (Art. 28.)

The Member States agree upon the desirability of developing their social legislation on the following bases:

a) All human beings, without distinction as to race, nationality, sex, creed or social condition, have the right to attain material well-being and spiritual growth under circumstances of liberty, dignity, equality of opportunity, and economic security;

b) Work is a right and a social duty; it shall not be considered as an article of commerce; it demands respect for freedom of association and for the dignity of the worker; and it is to be performed under conditions that ensure life, health and a decent standard of living, both during the working years and during old age, or when any circumstance deprives the individual of the possibility of working. (Art. 29.)

We have already noted the establishment and functions of the Inter-American Economic and Social Council. The Ninth International Conference of American States adopted two conventions in the field of social co-operation: the Inter-American Convention on the Granting of Political Rights to Women, and the Inter-American Convention on the Granting of Civil Rights to Women. Among other resolutions on social matters it also adopted the Inter-American Charter of Social Guarantees, to which, because of her federal system of government, the United States did not subscribe.

The inadequacies of IA-ECOSOC have been referred to and the view advanced that its most valuable work was in the field of technical co-operation. The bases for the OAS Program of Technical Assistance were laid in a resolution adopted at the First Extraordinary Meeting of IA-ECOSOC on 10 April 1950. A Coordinating Committee on Technical Assistance (CCTA) was established, comprising the Secretary General of the OAS, and representatives of the Pan American Union and the six inter-American Specialized Organizations. The technical programme was to consist basically of technical

---

[13] For a list of Special Pan American Conferences up to Sept. 1940, see *Int. Conf. Am. States*, 1st Suppl., App. A, pp. 381–452.

education projects. These projects were to be carried out, as far as possible, through regional technical training centres located in various member countries. The programme would be supported by annual voluntary contributions made by the member states. CCTA was to maintain close liaison with the United Nations Technical Assistance Programme as well as with the United States bilateral technical co-operation programmes. Within the OAS Program of Technical Assistance regional centres were subsequently established to provide such things as technical education for improving agriculture and rural life, and training in house construction, economic and financial statistics, and the evaluation of natural resources.

Valuable though this was, inter-American economic and social co-operation were required on a far larger scale. The beginning of a new effort was envisaged in the Act of Bogotá. This document,[14] adopted at the third meeting of the Committee of Twenty-One on 13 September 1960, recommended to the OAS Council 'measures for social improvement and economic development within the framework of Operation Pan America'. In a preamble it recognized that 'the preservation and strengthening of free and democratic institutions in the American republics requires the acceleration of social and economic progress in Latin America' and 'a new and vigorous program of inter-American cooperation'. The Act of Bogotá contains four chapters. The first, 'Measures for Social Improvements', lists measures for improving conditions of rural living and land use (including a review of land-tenure legislation), housing and community facilities, educational systems and training facilities, and public health. It also lists measures for mobilizing domestic resources (including the improvement of fiscal and financial practices) in order to support the programme.

The second chapter, 'Creation of a Special Fund for Social Development', reads as follows:

1. The delegations of the governments of the Latin American republics welcome the decision of the Government of the United States to establish a special inter-American fund for social development, with the Inter-American Development Bank to become the primary mechanism for the administration of the fund.
2. It is understood that the purpose of the special fund would be to contribute capital resources and technical assistance on flexible terms and conditions, including repayment in local currency and the relending of

---

[14] PAU, *Act of Bogotá* (1961).

repaid funds, in accordance with appropriate and selective criteria in the light of the resources available, to support the efforts of the Latin American countries that are prepared to initiate or expand effective institutional improvements and to adopt measures to employ efficiently their own resources with a view to achieving greater social progress and more balanced economic growth.

The third chapter, 'Measures for Economic Development' recommended that special attention should be given to an expansion of long-term lending, 'particularly in view of the instability of exchange earnings of countries exporting primary products and of the unfavorable effect of the excessive accumulation of short- and medium-term debt on continuing and orderly economic development'. It also recommended 'that urgent attention be given to the search for effective and practical ways, appropriate to each commodity, to deal with the problem of the instability of exchange earnings of countries heavily dependent upon the exportation of primary products'.

The fourth chapter, 'Multilateral Cooperation for Social and Economic Progress', was concerned with strengthening IA-ECOSOC. The OAS Council was asked to convene within sixty days a special meeting of senior government representatives which would:

a. Examine the existing structure of the Inter-American Economic and Social Council, and of the units of the Secretariat of the Organization of American States working in the economic and social fields, with a view to strengthening and improving the Inter-American Economic and Social Council;

b. Determine the means of strengthening inter-American economic and social cooperation by an administrative reform of the Secretariat, which should be given sufficient technical, administrative and financial flexibility for the adequate fulfillment of its tasks;

c. Formulate recommendations designed to assure effective coordination between the Inter-American Economic and Social Council, the Economic Commission for Latin America, the Inter-American Development Bank, the United Nations and its Specialized Agencies, and other agencies offering technical advice and services in the Western Hemisphere;

d. Propose procedures designed to establish effective liaison of the Inter-American Economic and Social Council and other regional American organizations with other international organizations for the purpose of study, discussion and consultation in the fields of international trade and financial and technical assistance;

e. And formulate appropriate recommendations to the Council of the Organization of American States.

In the event, this special meeting recommended that, except when called upon to meet an emergency situation under the terms of Article 27 of the OAS Charter, IA-ECOSOC should hold only two short and consecutive meetings each year. The first, attended by technical representatives, would carry out preparatory work on the topics to be submitted to the second. The second meeting, held at ministerial level, would review the social and economic progress of the member states; examine the achievements and problems of each country; exchange views on measures that might be adopted to promote economic and social progress; and prepare reports on future prospects. These and other recommendations for improving IA-ECOSOC were incorporated in its revised statutes and regulations approved by the OAS Council in November 1961.

The Alliance for Progress

It was a Special Meeting of the Inter-American Economic and Social Council at the Ministerial Level, held in Punta del Este, Uruguay (5–17 August 1961), that officially inaugurated the Alliance for Progress. From this special meeting emanated the 'Declaration to the Peoples of America' and 'The Charter of Punta del Este'. Some reference has already been made to the objectives of the Alliance.[15] How far, in fact, did it involve multilateral inter-American economic and social co-operation?

The first basic requirement for the economic and social development of the American republics stated in the Charter of Punta del Este is: 'That comprehensive and well-conceived national programs of economic and social development, aimed at the achievement of self-sustaining growth, be carried out in accordance with democratic principles.' The scope of these national development programmes is outlined in Chapter II of the section of the Charter (Title II) headed 'Economic and Social Development'. The need for immediate and 'short-term action' measures while the national plans were being formulated is recognized in Chapter III, and the United States promised that she would:

assist in carrying out these short-term measures with a view to achieving concrete results from the Alliance for Progress at the earliest possible moment . . . the United States will provide assistance under the Alliance, including assistance for the financing of short-term measures, totalling more than one billion dollars in the year ending March 1962.

---

[15] See above, p. 175.

The following chapter was concerned with external assistance in support of national development programmes. Again, the United States promised to assist 'those participating countries whose development programs establish self-help measures and economic and social policies and programs consistent with the goals and principles of this Charter'. But the participating countries were also to 'request the support of other capital-exporting countries and appropriate institutions so that they may provide assistance for the attainment of these objectives'. In the field of technical assistance projects, which the United States promised to help finance and in which the OAS General Secretariat, ECLA, and the Inter-American Development Bank had already agreed to co-operate, the member governments and these organizations were, when appropriate, to seek the co-operation of the United Nations and its specialized agencies.

In order to provide technical assistance in planning development programmes, the three organizations mentioned above would have available 'a group of programming experts whose service can be used to facilitate the implementation of this Charter'. This group is described in the second paragraph of Chapter V (Organization and Procedures):

2. The Inter-American Economic and Social Council, on the joint nomination of the Secretary General of the Organization of American States, the President of the Inter-American Development Bank, and the Executive Secretary of the United Nations Economic Commission for Latin America, will appoint a panel of nine high-level experts, exclusively on the basis of their experience, technical ability, and competence in the various aspects of economic and social development. . . . They will be attached to the Inter-American Economic and Social Council, but will nevertheless enjoy complete autonomy in the performance of their duties. . . .

The following paragraphs continue:

3. Each government, if it so wishes, may present its program for economic and social development for consideration by an ad hoc committee, composed of no more than three members drawn from the panel of experts referred to in the preceding paragraph together with an equal number of experts not on the panel. The experts who compose the ad hoc committee will be appointed by the Secretary General of the Organization of American States at the request of the interested government and with its consent.

4. The committee will study the development program, exchange opinions with the interested government as to possible modifications and, with the consent of the government, report its conclusions to the Inter-American

Development Bank and to other governments and institutions that may be prepared to extend external financial and technical assistance in connection with the execution of the program.

Although 'the ad hoc committee shall not interfere with the right of each government to formulate its own goals, priorities, and reforms in its national development programs', its recommendations 'will be of great importance in determining the distribution of public funds under the Alliance for Progress which contribute to the external financing of such programs'.

The final paragraph of Title II of the Charter of Punta del Este states that 'the Inter-American Economic and Social Council will review annually the progress achieved in the formulation, national implementation, and international financing of development programs; and will submit to the Council of the Organization of American States such recommendations as it deems pertinent'.

Title III of the Charter contains proposals for furthering the economic integration of Latin America, including the establishment of 'effective relationships' between the Latin American Free Trade Association and the group of countries adhering to the Central American Economic Integration Treaty,[16] 'as well as between either of these groups and other Latin American countries'. Title IV, 'Basic Export Commodities', contains agreements on national and international measures to lessen 'cyclical or seasonal fluctuations in the incomes of those countries that still depend heavily on the export of raw materials', and for correcting 'the secular deterioration in their terms of trade'.

Appended to the Charter of Punta del Este were a number of resolutions on economic and social development; economic integration; and basic export commodities. Those under the first-named title concerned a 'Ten-Year Education Program of the Alliance for Progress'; a 'Ten-Year Public Health Program of the Alliance for Progress'; a 'Taxation Program'; and the establishment by the OAS Secretary General of 'Task Forces for Programming'. Resolution D

---

[16] The Treaty establishing a Free-Trade Area and instituting the Latin American Free-Trade Association was signed at Montevideo on 18 Feb. 1960 by representatives of Argentina, Brazil, Chile, Mexico, Paraguay, Peru, and Uruguay, with provision for Bolivia's adherence. Colombia and Ecuador subsequently adhered to the Montevideo Treaty. In December 1960 El Salvador, Guatemala, Honduras, and Nicaragua signed the General Treaty of Central American Integration and agreement to establish a Central American Bank for Economic Integration. For an account of these developments, see Urquidi, *Free Trade and Economic Integration in Latin America* (1962).

provided for an 'Annual Review of Economic and Social Progress and Annual Meetings of the Inter-American Economic and Social Council at the Ministerial Level'; while Resolution E, entitled 'Public Opinion and the Alliance for Progress', was concerned with measures to stimulate 'understanding and active cooperation from all the peoples of America'.

Only to a small extent, then, did the Alliance for Progress involve multilateral, inter-American economic and social co-operation, and the role of the OAS was a limited one. The Latin American governments would prepare their own national development plans, though they could receive assistance from members of the OAS panel of nine experts. However, as far as external financing was concerned, responsibility lay in the main with agencies of the United States government, such as the Agency for International Development (AID) and the Export-Import Bank, working directly with the individual Latin American governments. As Dr Lleras Camargo observed:

> Inter-American organs were set up to study and prepare plans for national development, but it was left entirely to the United States' initiative not only to find the way in which its contribution should be made available, but also to arrive at some standard of judgment as to how and when and to whom support should be apportioned for carrying out Alliance plans. The result was to create a pattern of bilateral operation . . .[17]

This was to be a major complaint of the Latin American delegates when IA-ECOSOC met at the ministerial level in Mexico City from 22 to 27 October 1962 for the first annual review of the Alliance's progress.

By the end of its first year the Alliance for Progress had only modest achievements to its credit.[18] Few countries had submitted national development plans, and the average per capita income in Latin America increased much less than the 2·5 per cent minimum annual target set in the Punta del Este Charter. It is significant that the Mexico City Meeting appealed to developed countries outside the hemisphere for support:

> The IA-ECOSOC calls upon all of the industrialized countries of the Free World to assist in achieving the objectives of the Alliance for Progress. The IA-ECOSOC declares that the various instrumentalities of the inter-American system are prepared at all times to cooperate fully with other

---

[17] Lleras Camargo, *For. Aff.*, xlii/1 (1963), p. 35.
[18] See IA-ECOSOC, *The Alliance for Progress: its First Year 1961–1962* (1963).

international institutions to this end, including in particular the Organization for Economic Cooperation and Development and the Development Assistance Committee.[19]

At the same time, in order to improve the machinery of the Alliance, it was resolved:

> That two outstanding Latin Americans shall be charged with studying the structure and activities of those organizations and agencies of the inter-American system that have responsibilities in regard to the Alliance for Progress, and with making, if necessary, recommendations regarding those structural and procedural changes that are required in the system and in its various organs in order that the Alliance for Progress may take on the efficiency and the dynamic qualities called for by the Charter of Punta del Este.[20]

These two outstanding Latin Americans were former President Juscelino Kubitschek of Brazil and former President[21] Alberto Lleras Camargo of Colombia.

The two senior statesmen made their recommendations for revitalizing the Alliance for Progress to a meeting of the OAS Council on 15 June, 1963.[22] Although their reports differed somewhat in interpreting the causes of the Alliance's shortcomings, both were agreed on the need to establish a new coordinating agency within the framework of the OAS. This would be composed of five Latin American representatives (one from each of five geographical areas) and one representative from the United States. The Kubitschek and Lleras reports were subsequently studied by the member governments and presented to the second annual review of the Alliance which took place at the ministerial level at São Paulo, Brazil from 11 to 16 November 1963.[23]

At the end of the second year the picture was still unsatisfactory. Largely because of the poor performances of Argentina and Brazil, the overall per capita income fell again below the target. The continued economic stagnation of Latin America, and increasing

---

[19] *DSB*, xlvii/1224 (1962), p. 900.

[20] IA-ECOSOC, *First Annual Meeting at the Ministerial Level, Held in Mexico, D.F., from October 22 to 27 1962: Final Report*, OEA/Ser. H/XII. 4 (English), p. 24.　　　[21] And, of course, OAS Secretary General.

[22] OAS Council, *Report on the Alliance for Progress, Presented by Senator Juscelino Kubitschek, Former President of Brazil*, OEA/Ser. G/V, C-d-1102 (English), 15 June 1963 (Original: Portuguese); *Report on the Alliance for Progress, Presented by Dr Alberto Lleras, Former President of Colombia*, ibid. C-d-1103 (English), 15 June 1963 (Original: Spanish).

[23] This meeting at ministerial level was preceded, like the previous one at Mexico City, by a meeting at 'expert level'.

dissatisfaction with the achievements of the Alliance for Progress, made a revision of its machinery more urgent. The São Paulo Meeting therefore agreed to set up an Inter-American Committee on the Alliance for Progress under a Latin American chairman.[24] This new body would be given the main responsibility for reviewing programmes and projects under the Alliance, and recommending allocations of resources. But the United States, not surprisingly, refused to give the new committee control over the disbursement of Alliance funds as proposed by several Latin American delegations. A proposal by Brazil, the main critic of the Alliance at São Paulo, for a $20 billions development fund to be administered multilaterally was shelved for further study. The new committee (CIAP) was inaugurated in March 1964 under the chairmanship of Carlos Sanz de Santamaría, former finance minister of Colombia.[25]

In the meantime, meeting at Alta Gracia, Argentina, in February–March 1964, the Latin American countries (with the United States represented only by an observer) discussed formulating a common policy for the United Nations Trade and Development Conference due to open at Geneva on 23 March. The Alta Gracia conference expressed the view that Latin America's economic problems were caused mainly by the policies pursued by the major industrialized powers, and emphasized the need to co-operate with other under-developed nations in Asia, Africa, and Europe in order to achieve better terms of trade. In the event, the division between the developed and developing countries was most marked at the Geneva Conference of which, incidentally, the Argentine economist Raúl Prebisch was Secretary General.

The third annual review of the Alliance for Progress showed that the per capita income for Latin America had at last increased beyond the target of 2·5 per cent, due principally to the economic recovery of Brazil. But the meeting of IA-ECOSOC at ministerial level, held at Lima, 5–11 December 1964, revealed continuing Latin American dissatisfaction with the Alliance. The Latin American delegates were critical of United States trade policies, including the failure of Congress to implement the world coffee price stabilization agreement, a lapse in her sugar import legislation, and Congressional endorsement

---

[24] IA-ECOSOC, *Final Report of the Second Annual Meeting at the Ministerial Level, Held in São Paulo, Brazil, November 11–16, 1963* (provisional version), OEA/Ser. H/X. 4, CIES/580 (English), 16 Nov. 1963, Original: Spanish, pp. 13–19.
[25] M. I. Anderson, 'New Era for the Alliance: the Inter-American Committee on the Alliance for Progress', *Américas*, xvi/6 (1964), pp. 1–7.

of meat import quotas. They repeated the views they had expressed at Geneva earlier in the year. The gap between promise and performance in the Alliance for Progress remained wide. The Lima Meeting recognized that results were poor in such key areas as agrarian reform, education, public health, inflation control, and investment for growth.[26] The fourth annual report of the Social Progress Trust Fund,[27] reflected the same picture of general improvement, but weakness in crucial fields, especially agricultural production.

As the Alliance for Progress moved towards the end of its fourth year it had numerous achievements to its credit; inter-American economic and social co-operation was now taking place on a far larger scale than ever before. It was, of course, too early to speak of success or failure. But it was evident the Alliance had not captured the imaginations of the people of the western hemisphere as a 'New Deal' for Latin America.[28] There was a notable lack of a political mystique so necessary for the success of the ten-year plan launched by President Kennedy as the beginning of a new era in inter-American relations. Also lacking was firm support for the movement towards economic integration in Latin America, even though this was called for in the Punta del Este Charter. The United States and most international lending agencies were less than helpful, with the important exception of the Inter-American Development Bank.[29] In spite of the new impetus given by the Inter-American Committee on the Alliance for Progress, the latter still seemed to be substantially an instrument of United States policy rather than a truly inter-American effort in the field of economic and social co-operation. Until there were greater political and social changes both north and south of the Rio Grande it was difficult to see how it could be otherwise.

Cultural Co-operation

Although not as urgent for inter-American relations as co-operation in the economic and social fields, cultural co-operation is clearly of fundamental importance in building up hemispheric solidarity; for eventually transforming an association of American states into a real inter-American community. This has been especially the case since the United States and the countries of Latin America have not shared

[26] *NYT*, 6, 7, 9, and 14 Dec. 1964; IA-ECOSOC, *Third Annual Meeting at the Ministerial Level, Held in Lima, Peru, from December 5–11, 1964, Final Report*, OEA/Ser. H/XII. 9 (English) (1964). [27] See above, pp. 274–5.
[28] Cf. L. Gordon, *A New Deal for Latin America: the Alliance for Progress* (Cambridge, Mass., Harvard UP, 1963).
[29] Wionczek, *Int. Concil.* (Jan. 1965), pp. 25–27, 39.

a common culture, even disregarding the increasingly significant factor of the continent's traditionally forgotten man: the Indian.

From the Second onwards, resolutions concerned with furthering intellectual co-operation were adopted at the International Conferences of American States. These included:

the exchange of professors and students, the establishment of scholarships and fellowships, the standardization of university curricula, the recognition of professional degrees, the protection of historical and archaeological records and monuments, the establishment of a geographical institute, the publication of maps, duties and postal rates on books and periodicals, the establishment of special chairs for language and literature study, American bibliography, journalism, and other topics.[30]

Moreover, numerous special conferences were held to discuss common problems and further mutual understanding among members of the inter-American system in the intellectual and cultural fields. Among such were the Pan American Scientific Congresses; the Inter-American Conferences on Education; the Pan American Congresses of Architects; and the General Assemblies of the Pan American Institute of Geography and History. At the Pan American Union a Division of Intellectual Cooperation had the task of promoting intellectual exchanges of all kinds. Also situated in the Pan American Union building, the Columbus Memorial Library, founded as a result of resolutions adopted at the First and Second International Conferences, has played an important role in the field of intellectual co-operation.

At the Ninth International Conference new measures were adopted for furthering inter-American cultural co-operation. The OAS Charter proclaimed among its principles that 'the spiritual unity of the continent is based on respect for the cultural values of the American countries and requires their close cooperation for the high purposes of civilization' and that 'the education of peoples should be directed toward justice, freedom and peace'. Chapter VIII, 'Cultural Standards', contains two articles:

Article 30

The Member States agree to promote, in accordance with their constitutional provisions and their material resources, the exercise of the right to education, on the following bases:

a) Elementary education shall be compulsory and, when provided by the State, shall be without cost;

---

[30] Ball, *Problem of Inter-American Organization*, p. 40.

b) Higher education shall be available to all, without distinction as to race, nationality, sex, language, creed or social condition.

Article 31

With due consideration for the national character of each State, the Member States undertake to facilitate free cultural interchange by every medium of expression.

Moreover, one of the three organs of the OAS Council was to be the Inter-American Cultural Council, whose purpose 'is to promote friendly relations and mutual understanding among the American peoples, in order to strengthen the peaceful sentiments that have characterized the evolution of America, through the promotion of educational, scientific and cultural exchange'.

The principal functions of the Cultural Council were to be:

a) To sponsor inter-American cultural activities;
b) To collect and supply information on cultural activities carried on in and among the American States by private and official agencies both national and international in character;
c) To promote the adoption of basic educational programs adapted to the needs of all population groups in the American countries;
d) To promote, in addition, the adoption of special programs of training, education and culture for the indigenous groups of the American countries;
e) To cooperate in the protection, preservation and increase of the cultural heritage of the continent;
f) To promote cooperation among the American nations in the fields of education, science and culture, by means of the exchange of materials for research and study, as well as the exchange of teachers, students, specialists and, in general, such other persons and materials as are useful for the realization of these ends;
g) To encourage the education of the peoples for harmonious international relations;
h) To carry on such other activities as may be assigned to it by the Inter-American Conference, the Meeting of Consultation of Ministers of Foreign Affairs, or the Council of the Organization.

Thus the Inter-American Cultural Council was concerned not only with cultural exchange among the American states, but also with the promotion of education and cultural advancement (including special programmes for the Indians) in individual countries. Both objectives were related to peace and harmonious international relations. The Council, meeting only occasionally, was to have a permanent subcommittee, sitting in Mexico City and named the Committee for Cultural Action. This committee, consisting of specialists in education or cultural fields from five member states of the OAS, would prepare any studies the Cultural Council assigned to it. At the First Meeting of the Inter-American Cultural Council, held in Mexico City in September 1951, the Pan American Union[31] was requested to prepare a preliminary draft of a 'Cultural Charter of America' for presentation to the Tenth Inter-American Conference. This treaty would bring all inter-American cultural agreements into a single instrument.[32]

Since the draft treaty was not ready in time, however, the Tenth Inter-American Conference instructed the Pan American Union to continue its work. The completed document would be submitted to the Second Meeting of the Inter-American Cultural Council for consideration, after it had been studied and approved by the Committee for Cultural Action (Resolution IV). The Caracas conference also adopted a 'Declaration on Cultural Cooperation' (Resolution II), and a 'Convention for the Promotion of Inter-American Cultural Relations'. The draft cultural charter was eventually approved at the Second Meeting of the Inter-American Cultural Council, held at Lima in May 1956, and transmitted to the OAS Council for inclusion on the agenda of the Eleventh Inter-American Conference.[33] A Third Meeting of the Inter-American Cultural Council was held at San Juan, Puerto Rico, in November–December 1959.[34] In the meantime, inter-American cultural co-operation was furthered by agencies already mentioned: the Columbus Memorial Library; the Pan American Institute of Geography and History; the Committee for Cultural Action; and the (renamed) Department of Cultural Affairs at the Pan American Union.

It has been noted that the Inter-American Cultural Council was not concerned solely with cultural exchange among the American states, but also with the promotion of education and cultural advancement. Indeed, the most pressing problem in the development of inter-American cultural relations was that of education. The Second

[31] The Dept of Cultural Affairs in collaboration with the Dept of International Law.

[32] *Ann. OAS*, iv/2 (1952), p. 151. For the resolutions and recommendations approved by the First Meeting of the Inter-American Cultural Council, see pp. 149–75.

[33] Ibid. viii/3 (1956), pp. 222–3. For the resolutions and recommendations approved by the Second Meeting of the Inter-American Cultural Council, see pp. 205–33.

[34] For the Final Act of the Third Meeting, see OEA/Ser. C/V. 3 (English).

Inter-American Meeting of Ministers of Education, held at Lima in May 1956 and attended by observers from UNESCO (and Canada), called for intensified and co-ordinated efforts to tackle illiteracy in Latin America.[35] The Alliance for Progress, as we have noted, included a ten-year education programme for each of the Latin American republics. Under this programme each country was recommended to adopt 'an over-all education plan for the attainment of precisely defined goals within the next ten years, for the purpose of raising the cultural level of the peoples of Latin America and fitting them to participate constructively in economic and social development'. In order to supplement available domestic resources to carry out the over-all plans for education, the Inter-American Fund for Social Development, the Inter-American Development Bank, and other sources of credit would grant loans for 'well-conceived national and regional educational development projects, particularly those for school buildings and equipment'. The OAS, in co-operation with the specialized agencies of the United Nations concerned and 'other interested institutions', would provide technical assistance to countries requesting it 'for the preparation, financing and execution of national plans and specific projects for the development of education'. A Special Task Force was to be established by the OAS Secretary General to assist the member states in preparing their national development programmes.[36] There was subsequently held at Santiago, Chile in 1962, a Conference on Education and Economic and Social Development in Latin America sponsored jointly by UNESCO, the OAS, and ECLA. This conference adopted recommendations on standards and principles for guidance in planning and executing educational programmes.[37]

Juridical Co-operation

Since the establishment of the inter-American system was itself an act of juridical co-operation, this has been fundamental. Moreover, at the outset, the overwhelming power of the United States caused the Latin American countries to seek juridical safeguards against its abuse. This has been an important factor behind most efforts— already noted—to codify public and private international law in the Americas; to establish agreements on intervention and diplomatic

[35] *Ann. OAS*, ix/2 (1957), pp. 138–57.
[36] OAS/Ser. H/XII. 1 (English), pp. 27–29, 34.
[37] C. G. Fenwick, *The Organization of American States: the Inter-American Regional System*, (1963), p. 485.

representation; and to adopt a common policy on such matters as the recognition of governments. It has also been important in the failure to set up an Inter-American Court of Justice. Since the adoption of the OAS Charter juridical questions of particular significance have been the recognition of *de facto* governments; respect for human rights and the effective exercise of representative democracy; and the definition of intervention.

The Charter designates the Inter-American Council of Jurists as one of the organs of the OAS Council. Under Article 67, it was 'to serve as an advisory body on juridical matters; to promote the development and codification of public and private international law; and to study the possibility of attaining uniformity in the legislation of the various American countries, insofar as it may appear desirable'. Its permanent committee, the Inter-American Juridical Committee of Rio de Janeiro, composed of jurists from nine countries, was to 'undertake such studies and preparatory work as are assigned to it by the Inter-American Council of Jurists, the Inter-American Conference, the Meeting of Consultation of Ministers of Foreign Affairs, or the Council of the Organization'. It could also undertake studies and projects of its own. As we have seen, this body, until 1942 the Inter-American Neutrality Committee, had played an important part in the reorganization of the inter-American system recommended at Chapultepec. The Juridical Committee met annually, while the Council of Jurists held meetings less frequently.[38] The Department of International Law of the Pan American Union formed the Secretariat of the Council of Jurists.

Even before the OAS Charter was adopted, the Inter-American Juridical Committee was concerned with the recognition question. We have already seen how United States recognition policies had long been criticized by Latin Americans as a form of intervention. But the Latin American countries themselves were divided on this issue. At Mexico City in 1945, for example, while Ecuador insisted that a change of government was an internal matter which should not affect the continuance of diplomatic relations (and therefore proposed abolishing the recognition of *de facto* governments), Guatemala recommended that recognition should be withheld from anti-democratic governments arising in the hemisphere, especially those originating from a coup d'etat against 'Governments of a legally established

---

[38] The Fifth Meeting of the Council of Jurists took place in San Salvador, El Salvador, from 25 Jan. until 5 Feb. 1965.

democratic structure'. Both these proposals were referred to the Inter-American Juridical Committee for a report to the Ninth International Conference of American States.[39]

But the Juridical Committee was unable to complete its report on this problem before the Ninth Conference because of conflicting opinions in evidence again at Bogotá. The main difference was between those who favoured the Ecuadoran standpoint (approximately that of the Estrada Doctrine[40]), and those believing that 'recognition, or the maintenance of diplomatic relations, should be made contingent upon the observance of certain important inter-American principles'.[41] So there emerged, not a common recognition policy, but a statement of principle representing a compromise. The Ninth Conference declared (Resolution XXXV) that the continuity of diplomatic relations was desirable; the practice of recognition should not be used as a means of individually obtaining unjustified advantages under international law (this had been proposed by Mexico as an addition to the other two proposals which were introduced by the United States);[42] and recognition did not imply any judgement upon the domestic policy of the government in question. The Inter-American Council of Jurists was assigned the task of preparing a project and a report on the recognition of *de facto* governments for study by the Tenth Inter-American Conference (Resolution XXXVI).

The Council of Jurists failed in its task, however. At its first meeting (Rio de Janeiro, 22 May–15 June 1950) it declared that 'divergent opinions of doctrine were expressed on essential points, excluding the possibility of reaching at this meeting a formula acceptable to an absolute majority of the representatives of the member states'.[43] According to Charles G. Fenwick:

> The United States delegation took the position that recognition was not a 'right', that the tests governing recognition were not juridical in nature, and that it could not subscribe to the effort of certain of the delegations to give them that character. The same position was taken when an attempt was made to prescribe the observance of fundamental rights as a condition of recognition.[44]

---

[39] *Report of Delegation of USA to Inter-American Conference on Problems of War and Peace*, pp. 349–51, 354–5. Final Act of the Conference, Res. XXXIV & XXXVIII.   [40] See above, p. 31.

[41] *Report of Delegation of USA to Ninth International Conference of American States*, p. 82.

[42] Ibid. p. 83.   [43] Quoted in Ronning, *Law & Politics*, p. 25.

[44] Matthews, *The United States and Latin America*, p. 203.

At its second meeting (Buenos Aires, 20 April–9 May 1953) the Council of Jurists noted that 'an almost unanimous opinion has been expressed to the effect that it is as yet premature to conclude a convention on the subject'.[45] Under the circumstances, it was decided not to include the subject of recognition of *de facto* governments on the agenda of the Tenth Inter-American Conference.

In the early 1960s the recognition question became prominent again following a number of military coups d'état, to which reference has already been made.[46] Following the military take-over in Peru in July 1962, the governments of Venezuela, Costa Rica, the Dominican Republic, and Honduras requested a Meeting of Consultation of Foreign Ministers 'to consider the attitude which the Governments of the Member States should adopt with regard to regimes arising from coups d'état'. These governments argued that a coup d'état violated obligations of a juridical character and therefore the members of the OAS had the right under the Charter to call a Meeting of Consultation to decide upon their attitude towards the new régime. The Peruvian delegate, however, declared that to hold such a meeting would violate the principle of non-intervention. When a vote was taken, only seven countries favoured convoking the meeting, while eight abstained and five opposed. The United States, who had at first refused recognition to the Peruvian military junta, granted it a week after the vote was taken.[47] In Ronning's view, 'the United States seems to have settled on a formula of extending recognition after a number of Latin American states have done so'.[48] At all events, in the spring of 1965 the inter-American system possessed no collective policy on the question of recognizing *de facto* governments.

In the field of human rights, which became a matter of increasing world-wide concern during the post-Second World War period, the Ninth International Conference of American States adopted the American Declaration of the Rights and Duties of Man (Resolution XXX),[49] and asked the Inter-American Juridical Committee to prepare a draft statute providing for the creation and functioning of an Inter-American Court to guarantee the rights of man. After examination by the American governments the statute would be transmitted to the Tenth Inter-American Conference for study (Resolution

[45] Inter-American Council of Jurists, *Second Meeting, Final Act*, Res. III.
[46] See above, pp. 183–4, 254–5.   [47] Fenwick, p. 301.
[48] *Law & Politics*, p. 26.
[49] This was some months before the UN Universal Declaration of Human Rights was adopted.

XXXI). A Cuban proposal that 'the right of resistance is recognized in case of manifest acts of oppression or tyranny' was referred to the Juridical Committee for study and report to the OAS Council (Resolution XXXVII). However, the committee did not consider it would be feasible to create the proposed court, since this would involve a radical transformation of the constitutional systems in effect in all the American countries. It also concluded that the doctrine of the right of resistance could not be accepted.[50]

The Tenth Inter-American Conference included on its agenda 'measures for promoting human rights without impairing national sovereignty and the principle of nonintervention'. Within these terms of reference action was severely limited. Resolution XXVII of the Final Act of the conference recommended that the American states:

adopt progressively measures to adjust their domestic legislation to the American Declaration of the Rights and Duties of Man and the Universal Declaration of Human Rights, and that, within the limits of their sovereignty and in accordance with their respective constitutional provisions, they take appropriate measures to ensure the faithful observance of those rights.

The question of a court to protect human rights was referred to the OAS Council for study and subsequent consideration by the Eleventh Inter-American Conference (Resolution XXIX). Uruguay had wanted to establish a commission on human rights, but a majority of the delegations opposed this as 'somewhat premature'.[51]

By the time the Fifth Meeting of Consultation of Foreign Ministers took place in 1959, however, the attitude of many governments had changed. Tension in the Caribbean region had underlined the connection between the denial of human rights and political instability. The American Foreign Ministers resolved at Santiago that the Council of Jurists should prepare for submission to the Eleventh Inter-American Conference, draft conventions on both human rights and the creation of an inter-American court to protect them. In the meantime, the OAS Council was to organize an Inter-American Commission on Human Rights, composed of seven members elected from panels presented by the governments. This body met for the first time in October 1960. Its work consisted mainly of exchanging information with governments and making proposals for measures of co-operation. Although empowered to receive complaints from

---

[50] *Ann. OAS*, iii/1 (1951), p. 35.   [51] *Report of Delegation of USA*, p. 30.

individuals of the denial of human rights, the commission was not permitted to make individual decisions on them. The scope of the commission's activities was restricted, of course, by the principle of non-intervention. Incidentally, the United States took the lead in opposing greater authority being given to the commission.[52]

Closely related to the question of respect for human rights was that of promoting democracy. We have already noted how Article 5(*d*) of the OAS Charter declares that 'the solidarity of the American States and the high aims which are sought through it require the political organization of those States on the basis of the effective exercise of representative democracy'. But this general declaration neither defines democracy nor constitutes a firm treaty obligation to practise it. The Fifth Meeting of Consultation took steps in the direction of making good these deficiencies. Having affirmed that 'the existence of anti-democratic regimes constitutes a violation of the principles on which the Organization of American States is founded, and a danger to united and peaceful relationships in the hemisphere', 'The Declaration of Santiago, Chile' went on to specify 'some of the principles and attributes of the democratic system in this hemisphere, so as to permit national and international public opinion to gauge the degree of identification of political regimes and governments with that system':

1. The principle of the rule of law should be assured by the separation of powers, and by the control of the legality of governmental acts by competent organs of the state.
2. The governments of the American republics should be the result of free elections.
3. Perpetuation in power, or the exercise of power without a fixed term and with the manifest intent of perpetuation, is incompatible with the effective exercise of democracy.
4. The governments of the American states should maintain a system of freedom for the individual and of social justice based on respect for fundamental human rights.
5. The human rights incorporated into the legislation of the American states should be protected by effective judicial procedures.
6. The systematic use of political proscription is contrary to American democratic order.
7. Freedom of the press, radio, and television, and, in general, freedom

---

[52] Dreier, *Hemisphere Crisis*, p. 104.

of information and expression, are essential conditions for the existence of a democratic regime.

8. The American states, in order to strengthen democratic institutions, should cooperate among themselves within the limits of their resources and the framework of their laws so as to strengthen and develop their economic structure, and achieve just and humane living conditions for their peoples. . . .

A resolution entrusted to the OAS Council the task of preparing a draft convention on the effective exercise of representative democracy for submission to the Eleventh Inter-American Conference.

The Fifth Meeting called upon the Inter-American Council of Jurists to study 'the possible juridical relationship between respect for human rights and the effective exercise of representative democracy, and the right to set in motion the machinery of American international law in force'. This study was in fact made by the Juridical Committee, a majority of whose members agreed that there was a direct relationship between respect for human rights and the effective exercise of representative democracy; favoured the conclusion of a convention on human rights providing for its implementation through a commission and a court; but did not accept that there existed at the present time any legal basis in its charter or elsewhere for OAS action 'in defense or for the restoration of democracy under that heading alone'. In the majority view the American states had quite properly indicated their opposition to intervention for this purpose.[53]

Nevertheless, during the ensuing years the OAS became increasingly concerned with the character of certain of its member governments, ostensibly because of the links between the absence of respect for human rights and of effective exercise of representative democracy on the one hand, and international tension within the hemisphere on the other.[54] This, as we saw in the previous chapter, had been the subject of a study made by the Inter-American Peace Committee. More specifically, the Peace Committee had concluded in June 1960 that 'international tensions in the Caribbean region have been aggravated by flagrant and widespread violations of human rights which have been committed and continue to be committed in the Dominican Republic'.

---

[53] Ball, *Int. Org.*, xv/i (1961), p. 29.

[54] The main cause of such international tension was, of course, the determination of certain members of the OAS to overthrow régimes which they accused of denying human rights and the effective exercise of representative democracy to their peoples.

Nor can it be doubted that the character of the Trujillo government was the determining factor in the application of sanctions against the Dominican Republic at the Sixth Meeting of Consultation.[55] It is significant that the United States Secretary of State tried unsuccessfully to have the OAS supervise free elections in the Dominican Republic rather than impose sanctions.[56] Incidentally, after the death of Trujillo an important precedent was set when an OAS technical assistance mission was sent to the Dominican Republic to advise the new government on the establishment of an electoral system.[57] In the meantime, charges against Castro included the denial of fundamental human rights to the Cuban people. The Inter-American Commission on Human Rights was involved particularly with complaints against the governments of the Dominican Republic and Cuba. At the Eighth Meeting of Consultation the American Foreign Ministers agreed that the Commission should be strengthened (Resolution IX); they also recommended that 'the governments of the American states whose structure or acts are incompatible with the effective exercise of representative democracy' should hold free elections (Resolution IV). The crises between the Dominican Republic and Haiti in 1963 likewise illustrate the growing concern of the OAS with the character of some of its member governments.[58]

The related questions of human rights and the effective exercise of representative democracy thus became much more important for the inter-American system during the early 1960s. New measures concerned with them were awaiting consideration by the often-postponed Eleventh Inter-American Conference. Prospects for the success of the relevant draft conventions were not good. Already the United States had made it clear she could not subscribe to them,[59] and she was not alone. The main obstacle was, of course, the fact that effective action in these fields involved intrusion into the domestic affairs of the national sovereign states of which the inter-American system is composed. As the Inter-American Peace Committee stated in its report on 'The Relationship between Violations of Human

---

[55] This seems to be confirmed by a subsequent decision of the OAS Council calling for economic sanctions against the Dominican Republic even though, as the six countries abstaining observed, there had been no further acts of aggression to justify this decision. See above, p. 250.

[56] See above, p. 246.

[57] See H. Wells, 'The OAS and the Dominican Elections', *Orbis*, vii/1 (1963), pp. 150–63.

[58] See above, pp. 259–60.

[59] In a statement appended to the Final Act of the Fifth Meeting: OEA/Ser. C/II. 5 (Eng.), pp. 18–19.

Rights or the Nonexercise of Representative Democracy and the Political Tensions That Affect the Peace of the Hemisphere': '. . . the Committee can under no circumstances suggest any formula that would violate the nonintervention principle or the solemn inter-American commitments which have as their aim the preservation of the right of each state to work out its own political destiny'.[60]

The importance of the principle of non-intervention in the inter-American system has already been emphasized. It has also been pointed out that, as the outstanding problem of inter-American relations, intervention has been concerned with United States policies although many Latin American governments (above all in the Caribbean region) have long been guilty of interfering in each other's affairs. During the period since the end of the Second World War such interference by Latin American governments became more serious when pressure for social revolution 'made the struggles for control of governments something quite different from the traditional rivalry among factions within the old oligarchy and the army, which in the past had seldom threatened the established economic and social order'.[61] This was seen very clearly in the antagonism between Castro and Trujillo and its effect upon international relations in the Caribbean region. We noted how, against this background, the United States found herself the champion of non-intervention at the Fifth Meeting of Consultation in the face of Latin American demands for action to secure the downfall of the Dominican dictator.

Yet the Latin American countries were still strongly opposed to intervention in principle and, in the post-war world, this took the form, above all, of opposition to 'collective intervention', which they feared would mean in practice, intervention by the United States. This opposition had shown itself in reaction to the Rodríguez Larreta proposal shortly after the war and in the most inclusive statement of the principle of non-intervention, which appeared as Article 15 of the OAS Charter:

No State or group of States has the right to intervene, directly or indirectly, for any reason whatever, in the internal or external affairs of any other State. The foregoing principle prohibits not only armed force but also any other form of interference or attempted threat against the personality of the State or against its political, economic and cultural elements.

Although the OAS is, of course, more than a 'group of States', it is

[60] CIP-2-60, p. 4.   [61] Ronning, *Law & Politics*, p. 70.

clear the drafters of the Charter had no intention of granting it the right of intervention forbidden to its members.[62]

Nevertheless, at the Fifth Meeting of Consultation, Mexico proposed a draft resolution on non-intervention specifically declaring that:

> The Organization of American States shall not have power to intervene in matters that are essentially within the domestic jurisdiction of its members, unless this principle contravenes the application of the measures and procedures provided in Chapter V of the Charter of the Organization, and defined in the Inter-American Treaty of Reciprocal Assistance.[63]

The Mexican view was that the OAS Charter should be brought into line with the Charter of the United Nations which, in Article 2(7), states:

> Nothing contained in the present Charter shall authorize the United Nations to intervene in matters which are essentially within the domestic jurisdiction of any state or shall require the Members to submit such matters to settlement under the present Charter; but this principle shall not prejudice the application of enforcement measures under Chapter VII.

The Mexican draft was referred by the Fifth Meeting of Consultation to the Inter-American Juridical Committee. The latter decided (with the Mexican representative dissenting) against adopting the draft, on the grounds that the provisions of the OAS Charter already safeguarded the domestic jurisdiction of member states against intervention, while any further declaration 'whether clarifying, interpretive, or of any other nature' would 'not have the legal force to amend the Charter'. In the view of all the representatives, Article 2(7) of the United Nations Charter was itself unsatisfactory.[64]

As a result of another resolution adopted by the Fifth Meeting of Consultation, the Inter-American Juridical Committee also considered the adoption of an 'Instrument Relating to Violations of the Principle of Nonintervention'. The instrument which emerged (for

---

[62] Cf. Thomas & Thomas, *The OAS*, p. 165.

[63] *Inter-American Efforts to Relieve International Tensions*, pp. 151–2. The Mexican Foreign Minister declared at the Fifth Meeting that the OAS was not and could not be a 'super state' and was as much bound as its individual members not to intervene in the internal affairs of an American state: Fifth Meeting of Consultation, *Actas y documentos*, OEA/Ser. F/III. 5 (español), pp. 84–85. The Colombian Foreign Minister also condemned collective intervention: ibid. pp. 69–70.

[64] Inter-American Juridical Committee, *Opinion on the Legal Aspects of the Draft Declaration on Nonintervention presented by the Mexican Delegation*, OEA/Ser. I/VI. 2, CIJ-58 (English), Feb. 1961.

consideration by the Eleventh Inter-American Conference) listed a number of acts which, in addition to others, should be considered as violations of the principle of non-intervention on the part of any state. The United States member of the committee entered a dissenting statement in which he emphasized the impossibility of finding a satisfactory definition of the term 'intervention'. In this he was undoubtedly right. But it is none the less significant that the Latin American members of the Juridical Committee disagreed with him.[65] More important than attempting to define intervention, however, was the problem of reconciling the principle of non-intervention with other principles and objectives of the inter-American system. We have already seen something of this problem and further reference will be made to it in the concluding chapter of this study. For Latin Americans the problem concerned especially the conflict between non-intervention and action to bring about economic and social change; for the United States it was concerned primarily with 'collective responsibility' for meeting the challenge from international communism.

Institutional Developments

Following the adoption of the OAS Charter, various organs provided for in that document had to be established and their statutes approved by the OAS Council. In the case of the Specialized Organizations, these had to be brought into relationship with the corresponding agencies of the United Nations. This was done through the conclusion of agreements.[66] Meanwhile, in fulfilment of its obligations as a regional agency within the United Nations, the OAS kept the world body informed of its activities where appropriate and the United Nations was invited to send representatives to major inter-American conferences. A number of new inter-American agencies were established during the post-war period and the Inter-American Peace Committee was activated. Among the most important of the new bodies were the Inter-American Development Bank; the Inter-American Commission on Human Rights; the Special Consultative Commission on Security; the Inter-American Committee on the Alliance for Progress; and the Inter-American Nuclear Energy Commission.

[65] Inter-American Juridical Committee, *Instrument Relating to Violations of the Principle of Nonintervention*, Doc. CIJ-51 (English), Feb. 1959 (*sic.* This date is prior to the Fifth Meeting of Consultation).
[66] See Fenwick, pp. 532–43.

In the meantime there were important developments affecting the principal organs of the OAS. It is significant that during the seventeen years between the adoption of the OAS Charter and the year 1965, the Inter-American Conference, 'the supreme organ' of the inter-American system, met only once, although the Charter stipulates that it should convene every five years. By 1965, in fact, eleven years had already elapsed since the Tenth Conference and the Eleventh had, in effect, been postponed *sine die*. Since these years were so crucial for the inter-American system this suggests that perhaps the Inter-American Conference has been virtually dropped and that its functions have passed to other bodies. In Dreier's view, the Conference is not suitable for contemporary requirements. It is:

an antiquated body that is virtually incapable of exercising its important functions. The fact that most conferences last at least one month virtually rules out the possibility that the secretary of state of the United States or foreign ministers of leading Latin American countries can attend for anything but a small part of its deliberations.[67]

The solution, maintains Dreier, 'is for the functions of the Inter-American Conference to be curtailed to those truly involving decisions concerning "the general action and policy of the Organization", and to have the Conference itself merged in all but name with the Meetings of Foreign Ministers'.[68]

In fact there was a trend in that direction. In December 1964, however, there took place at the Pan American Union the First Special Inter-American Conference.[69] Its purpose was to establish the procedure for the admission of new members which, as we have seen, was not included in the OAS Charter.[70] In the 'Act of Washington' the conference resolved:

1. That any independent American state that desires to become a member of the Organization should so indicate by means of a note addressed to the Secretary General, in which it declares that it is willing to sign and ratify the Charter of the Organization of American States and to accept all the obligations inherent in the condition of membership in the Organization, especially those relating to collective security expressly set forth in articles 24 and 25 of the Charter of the Organization.

---

[67] *Hemisphere Crisis*, p. 121.
[68] Ibid. p. 122.
[69] First Special Inter-American Conference, *Documentos de la Conferencia*, OEA/Ser. E/XII. 1 (español), Washington, Dec. 1964.
[70] See above, p. 199, n. 26.

2. That, once it is informed of the matter by the Secretary General, the Council of the Organization, in accordance with articles 108, 50, and 51 of the Charter, shall determine by the vote of two thirds of the member states whether it is appropriate that the Secretary General be authorized to permit the applicant state to sign the Charter of the Organization and to accept the deposit of the corresponding instrument of ratification.

3. That the Council of the Organization shall not take any decision with respect to a request for admission on the part of a political entity whose territory, in whole or in part, is subject, prior to the date of this resolution, to litigation or claim between an extracontinental country and one or more member states of the Organization of American States, until the dispute has been ended by some peaceful procedure.[71]

Two points regarding the Act of Washington are worth noting. First, while adherence to the Rio Treaty is not made a prior condition of OAS membership, Articles 24 and 25 of the Charter involve the obligation to carry out its provisions. In the United States judgement, expressed at the conference, 'it would be difficult to envisage an American State being an effective member of the Organization without becoming a party to the Rio Treaty'.[72] Nevertheless, Uruguay, Venezuela, and Ecuador appended statements to the Final Act expressing their view that any new member would have to adhere to the Rio Treaty. The second point concerns the claims of certain Latin American countries to territory administered by Great Britain. Although this was covered by the Act of Washington, Guatemala, Argentina, and Venezuela reiterated their claims in statements appended to the Final Act.

The First Special Inter-American Conference, at which half the members of the OAS had been represented by their foreign ministers, had thus dealt with a question that had been of growing importance since the emergence as independent nations of the former British dependencies, Jamaica and Trinidad and Tobago.[73] A second special conference was due to be held at Rio de Janeiro in May 1965 'in order to consider, among others, various matters of fundamental importance in strengthening the inter-American system that are included on the agenda of the Eleventh Inter-American Conference'. It appears likely, therefore, that the Special Inter-American Conference rather

[71] First Special Inter-American Conference, *Final Act*, OEA/Ser. C/I. 12 (English), Washington, 1964, p. 5.
[72] OEA/Ser. E/XII. 1 (English), Doc. 23, 17 Dec. 1964, p. 3.
[73] These two countries were represented by observers at the First Special Inter-American Conference.

than the Meeting of Consultation will take the place of the Inter-American Conference.

How far, in the meantime, had the Meeting of Consultation already taken over the functions of the Inter-American Conference? Since the adoption of the OAS Charter the Meeting of Consultation was convened six times, three times as the Organ of Consultation under the terms of the Rio Treaty (the Sixth, Eighth and Ninth), and three times under Articles 39 and 40 of the Charter 'to consider problems of an urgent nature and of common interest to the American States'. During the course of these meetings, as we have seen, a number of policy decisions were taken of a far-reaching character. The inter-American system became much more concerned than hitherto with the economic and social development of the hemisphere; and with human rights and the effective exercise of representative democracy. A number of important new agencies were created. On the Meeting's competence, Fenwick has asserted that:

While the Charter describes the Conference as the supreme policy-making body it is clear that the decisions of the Meeting of Consultation when held under the Rio Treaty are of equal authority with those of the Conference when confined to the circumstances giving rise to the meeting. Probably the same conclusion could be reached in respect to decisions taken in respect to "problems of an urgent nature and of common interest to the American States" under Article 39 of the Charter. This second conclusion, however, is more or less academic, inasmuch as the functions of the Conference are not so sharply defined as to give rise to a conflict of authority between the two bodies.[74]

If these decisions of the Meeting of Consultation did not impinge upon the authority of the Inter-American Conference, they did tend to render the convening of the supreme organ unnecessary. One decision of the Eighth Meeting of Consultation, however, aroused serious controversy concerning its competence: the exclusion of 'the present Government of Cuba' from participation in the inter-American system. This, in the view of the governments refusing to support it, was not juridically possible without an amendment to the OAS Charter, requiring adoption at 'an Inter-American Conference convened for that purpose'. In the event, the exclusion of Cuba was effected by the OAS Council and other inferior organs of the inter-American system.

Before turning to the OAS Council, another important development

[74] Fenwick, p. 91.

of the Meeting of Consultation should be noted: two Informal Meetings of American Foreign Ministers, both held in Washington. The first took place on 23–24 September 1958, and dealt with economic matters, establishing the Committee of Twenty-one.[75] The second, on 2–3 October 1962, concerned measures to meet the Soviet arms build-up in Cuba.[76] After the first meeting the OAS Council prepared draft rules for this type of conference. In Dreier's opinion this development saved the Meetings of Consultation 'from a fate similar to that of the Conference', since they 'had developed into full-dress conferences, complete with protocol, committees and sub-committees, and numerous technical advisers'. Following the first Informal Meeting of Foreign Ministers ('this unofficial precedent'), 'the Fifth, Sixth, Seventh, and Eighth Meetings of Consultation resumed their original character: agendas were limited to subjects requiring urgent attention, and the negotiations were carried on directly among the foreign ministers'.[77]

We noted how, at the Ninth International Conference of American States, there was considerable opposition to granting the OAS Council power to take 'political decisions'.[78] The Charter did, in fact, restrict the Council to taking 'cognizance, within the limits of the present Charter and of inter-American treaties and agreements, of any matter referred to it by the Inter-American Conference or the Meeting of Consultation of Ministers of Foreign Affairs'. Nevertheless, the powers of the Council were at once the subject of controversy. No satisfactory outcome resulted from the Council itself requesting the Council of Jurists to prepare a study of the scope of its powers, a task which was passed to the Juridical Committee. It is significant, however, that the United States argued against the majority (Latin American) view that the powers of the Council should be defined in a protocol or resolution, and stressed the matter of 'implied powers'.[79]

Basically, like the Governing Board of the Pan American Union which it replaced, the OAS Council was the central administrative and supervisory body of the inter-American system, concerned with such matters as directing the work of the Pan American Union; promoting collaboration with the United Nations; and fixing the

---

[75] See above, p. 168.   [76] See above, p. 255.
[77] *Hemisphere Crisis*, pp. 123–4.   [78] See above, pp. 204–5.
[79] Inter-American Juridical Committee, *Opinion on the Scope of the Powers of the Council of the Organization of American States*, OEA/Ser. I/VI. 2, CIJ-59, Mar. 1961.

quota each member government contributed to the OAS. Most of the Council's time was taken up with this work, which it performed through its various committees. Dreier has criticized the Council 'for its tendency to dedicate itself to relatively unimportant procedural and technical issues, and to evade its responsibility for dealing with those of major importance'.[80] But the majority of member governments were unwilling to grant the Council wider powers enabling it to take the initiative in policy making, although it received specific assignments of a political character from the Inter-American Conference and Meetings of Consultation. It was given a limited role in implementing the Alliance for Progress.

In one field the OAS Council greatly enhanced its role: as Provisional Organ of Consultation under the Rio Treaty. Yet if the Council had been entrusted with power to investigate situations threatening the peace and security of the hemisphere before calling a Meeting of Consultation this development would not have taken place. As it was, the Council was compelled under the terms of the Rio Pact to call a Meeting of Consultation and to constitute itself Provisional Organ of Consultation. Consequently, as we have seen, the Council resorted to a 'juridical stratagem', whereby it convoked a Meeting of Consultation without setting a place or date. Then, as Provisional Organ of Consultation, it was able to take the measures necessary to deal with the situation which had occasioned the invoking of the treaty and subsequently cancel the convocation of the Meeting of Foreign Ministers. In response to the Cuban crisis of October 1962 the OAS Council actually approved measures, including the use of armed force, which might be necessary to remove the threat to the peace and security of the hemisphere.[81]

Thus the OAS Council acquired greater authority within the inter-American system than was envisaged for it by the framers of the Charter.[82] It became much more than an administrative body. Whether it could be strengthened further so as to enable it to play

---

[80] *Hemisphere Crisis*, pp. 124.

[81] For further consideration of the development of the OAS Council see Dreier, 'The Council of the OAS; Performance and Potential', *JIAS*, v/3 (1963), pp. 297–312.

[82] But see Gómez Robledo, *For. Int.*, i/1 (1960), p. 78. Gómez Robledo points out that the Uruguayan delegate at Quitandinha, who (supported by 3 more delegates) had wanted the OAS Council to be the organ of consultation, forecast that in the vast majority of cases a meeting of foreign ministers would not be necessary. And, he says, it was tacitly approved by all the delegations that the provisional character of the Council as organ of consultation did not mean that its decisions were provisional, requiring ratification by the Meeting of Consultation.

the dynamic part in the inter-American system its critics have suggested, raises the broader question of whether the member states desire to give the inter-American system itself a more important role in the international relations of the hemisphere. This, in turn, involves an appraisal of the inter-American system to assess how far it has fulfilled its purposes and has served the interests of its members. Such an appraisal and a consideration of the future prospects of the inter-American system form the subject of the concluding chapter.

9   Achievements and Prospects

The Peace and Security of the Hemisphere

In appraising the inter-American system the first question to be
considered is how far it has fulfilled its proclaimed purposes. Among
these, the maintenance of peace in the hemisphere and the pacific
settlement of inter-American disputes have been prominent from the
outset. This study has described the various peace instruments drawn
up before the outbreak of the Second World War and shown their
inadequacies. In particular, it has noted their failure to resolve the
two major inter-American disputes of the period between the great
wars, the Chaco and Leticia controversies, and how the League of
Nations was involved with both. Before the Second World War, the
inter-American peace system had been outside the Pan American
Union and its Governing Board; a proposal that the latter should
act as a council of conciliation had been rejected.[1] Nor did the Pact
of Bogotá, one of the three constituent documents of the post-war
Organization of American States, receive the full ratification denied
to most of the earlier peace instruments it was meant to supersede.
(In the April of 1965 it had been ratified by only nine member states.)
As a consequence the wartime Peace Committee was brought to life
to deal with inter-American disputes, and the Rio Pact was also used
for this purpose.

How successfully has the inter-American peace machinery handled
its tasks since the adoption of the OAS Charter? Certainly, it has had
numerous successes in terminating conflicts arising between nations
of Central America and the Caribbean region. Both the Peace
Committee and the OAS Council have generally acted quickly in
response to threatening situations or actual conflict in that area. The
Guatemalan crisis of 1954 was a notable exception. But, as has been
well observed:

> It is noteworthy that the work of these groups has had the effect of re-
> establishing the status quo. In almost all cases, the activities of the OAS
> have been terminated after cessation of violence. There has been almost
> no effort to change the underlying conditions which initially fomented the

---

[1] See above, p. 71.

strife. Since such basic causes reside within the nations themselves and since the OAS in its political activities tries scrupulously to avoid intervention in the domestic affairs of its member states, it does not attempt at present to deal with more than those surface manifestations of tensions that result in inter-American disturbances.[2]

Since these words were written (1959) the situation in Central America and the Caribbean region has become much more critical. What Dreier described as 'the benefits of the O.A.S. way of dealing with some of the particularly delicate aspects of an intrafamily conflict'[3] became less obvious, and, in his view, 'the O.A.S. machine ground to a stop as it faced the fresh problems of a new revolutionary period'.[4] Another important aspect of the new revolutionary period was the direct involvement of the United States as a disputant favouring the *status quo* in the face of threats to her interests (in Cuba and Panama). The inter-American system could hardly be expected to solve such disputes, and there was a growing tendency on the part of the Latin American republics in conflict with the United States to appeal to the United Nations rather than—or as well as—to the OAS. Nor has the inter-American system an impressive record in solving disputes in which the United States has not been a party, as the continuing territorial controversy between Ecuador and Peru, and Bolivia's temporary withdrawal from the OAS over the Lauca waters question bear witness.

Linked with the peace of the hemisphere is the question of disarmament, a matter with which the inter-American system has concerned itself very little. More recently, in view of the excessive expenditure by most Latin American governments on their military establishments, limitation of armaments has been recommended (for example, in Resolution VIII of the Final Act of the Seventh Meeting of Consultation) in order to free considerable financial resources for economic and social development. Little progress has been made, however, and, as this study has shown, the position of the military has been strengthened in many Latin American countries. The proposal by a number of American states, including Brazil and Mexico, for the 'denuclearization' of Latin America was viewed with considerable reserve by the United States.

As regards common action to meet aggression, since the Act of

---

[2] Northwestern Univ., in 86th Congress, 2nd Session, Senate, Doc. No. 125, p. 217.
[3] *Hemisphere Crisis*, p. 65.   [4] Ibid. p. 73.

Chapultepec this has been a purpose of the inter-American system in the case of aggression by an American as well as by a non-American state. In all cases except two where charges of aggression have been made against an American state, however, there has been recourse to conciliation rather than the imposition of sanctions. The exceptions occurred when sanctions were applied against the Dominican Republic by the Sixth Meeting of Consultation at San José in August 1960 and against Cuba at the Ninth Meeting in 1964. Sanctions were also applied against Cuba by the Eighth Meeting of Consultation, although she had not been formally charged with aggression. It is not possible to determine to what extent the existence of the inter-American system has discouraged aggression by American states against each other. It has been suggested in this study, however, that the OAS has at times exercised a restraining influence upon its members: as, for example, upon the Dominican Republic, Haiti, and the United States in the crisis involving these three countries in 1963.[5]

How far has the inter-American system provided for the defence of the hemisphere against extra-continental aggression? This has been a purpose of the inter-American system for a much shorter period of time than the maintenance of peace within the Americas. Even after the defence of the hemisphere was made formally the responsibility of all the American states, the deterrent to extra-continental armed aggression continued to be furnished by the military power of the United States. This is confirmed by the lack of a command structure with armed forces at its disposal within the inter-American system in contrast with the situation in Western Europe and the North Atlantic. The limited role of the Inter-American Defense Board has been indicated.[6] The contribution of the inter-American system to the security of the hemisphere against external aggression has been to provide the multilateral framework within which the United States has concluded bilateral defence agreements with over half the countries of Latin America.

Inter-American military co-operation, predominantly on a bilateral basis between the United States and individual Latin American countries, has been concerned primarily with measures to meet subversion: counter-insurgency. For, apart from the missile crisis of October 1962, the American states have regarded the major threat to the security of the hemisphere as being from subversion by the forces of

[5] See above, p. 260. [6] See above, p. 222.

international communism, especially after Cuba's alignment with the
Soviet Union. Again, the main initiative in meeting the communist
challenge came from the United States, who had to overcome considerable opposition from some of the most important Latin American
countries before the OAS took strong measures to isolate the Castro
government. The work of the Special Consultative Committee on
Security has been limited by the reluctance of member governments
to allow it functions beyond providing advisory services, and then
only on request.[7]

On balance, then, the inter-American system has been active and
by no means unsuccessful in helping to maintain the peace of the
hemisphere though it has met with little success in solving disputes
between member states. It is not effectively a military alliance. We
have seen the two main reasons for this: opposition of Latin American countries to the inter-American system becoming such an alliance,
and the limited contribution they could in any case make to it. On
the other hand, the inter-American system has given the United
States political support in her task of providing the effective deterrent
to possible armed attack, and in some degree also in countering communist subversion within the hemisphere.

Political, Economic, and Juridical Problems

To what extent have the American states sought 'the solution of
political, juridical and economic problems that may arise among
them' through the inter-American system, another proclaimed
purpose of the organization? It must be reiterated that the inter-
American system represents only a fraction of inter-American relations as a whole; most international relations in the western hemisphere are conducted on a bilateral basis. Generally speaking, only
problems which have not been susceptible of solution bilaterally or
those of concern to a number of American states have been dealt with
within the inter-American system. Often they have been problems in
which the Latin American countries have taken one position and the
United States another. For this reason the consideration of political
and economic (as distinct from commercial) problems was at first very
limited, mainly on United States insistence. 'The function of these
Pan American Conferences', the United States delegates used to be

---

[7] Special Consultative Committee on Security, *Report on the Work Done during
its Third Regular Meeting, November 16 to December 11 1964*, OEA/Ser. L/X/II. 7,
11 Dec. 1964, Original: Spanish, p. 18. See also above, p. 259.

instructed, 'is to deal so far as possible with non-controversial subjects of general interest.'[8] Nevertheless, political and even economic questions could not be entirely excluded from the earlier conferences; they have been prominent since the adoption of the OAS Charter.

Attempts to solve juridical problems have been made within the inter-American system from the beginning, again with the United States and the Latin American countries very often taking opposing positions on the main issues. Some of the most important of these, of long-standing, have been the treatment of aliens and their property; intervention; the recognition of governments; and diplomatic asylum. More recently, the inter-American system has become concerned with the juridical aspects of safeguarding human rights and promoting the effective exercise of representative democracy. All these juridical problems have of course also been political ones; and closely allied with the political problems of the American states are their economic ones. We have seen how the Latin American countries have tried to use the inter-American system to resolve their economic difficulties with the United States.

A further purpose of the inter-American system is to promote by co-operative action the economic, social, and cultural development of the member states. This study has shown how, although the inter-American system has fostered to some extent economic, social, and cultural relations between the member states over a long period, co-operation to promote *development* in these fields is very recent. The financial resources of the inter-American programmes formulated for this purpose (for example, the OAS Technical Cooperation Program) have, moreover, been very limited. Not until the Act of Bogotá and the Alliance for Progress were much greater funds made available and more far-reaching plans for economic, social, and cultural development thus made possible. It is too early to assess the results of these plans, though disappointment with the achievements of the Alliance for Progress has been noted, and the latter has been criticized as being an instrument of United States policy rather than a truly co-operative effort. Nevertheless, the inter-American system has become very much more concerned with the economic, social, and cultural development of its member states in the last five years, even if the results up to now have been modest compared with the size of the task.

[8] See above, p. 64.

Has it Lived Up to its Principles?

How far has the inter-American system lived up to its principles, or, rather, to what extent have its ideals been transformed into realities? For there has always been a wide gulf between the principles upon which the inter-American system has claimed to be based on the one hand, and the actualities of international relations in the western hemisphere and the condition of the vast majority of the peoples of the Americas on the other. It has long been claimed that the inter-American system is an association of equals, in contrast with other international organizations embracing large and small nations. Nevertheless, for a long time the United States enjoyed a privileged position within the Pan American Union, as well as treaty rights enabling her to intervene in the internal affairs of several of the other members of the inter-American system. In the Convention on Rights and Duties of States adopted by the Seventh International Conference of American States the juridical equality of states was proclaimed an inter-American principle. The United States subsequently relinquished her treaty rights of intervention and her privileged position in the Pan American Union.

Since then the inter-American system has lived up to its principle of the juridical equality of states. The United States has no 'veto' within the OAS, as she and the other permanent members of the Security Council possess in the United Nations. But how important is this formal position in comparison with the actual degree of power exercised by the United States in determining the programmes and policies of the inter-American system? The United States has usually been able to marshal the necessary majorities for proposals, if she has desired their adoption strongly enough to use the pressures at her command to secure their passage. At the same time lack of United States support renders ineffectual the adoption of resolutions in most fields of inter-American co-operation. Moreover, the United States pays approximately two-thirds of the regular budget of the Pan American Union and makes special contributions and grants to OAS agencies and programmes. Without her leadership, which generally has been exercised with considerable effort at self-effacement in recent years,[9] it is doubtful whether the inter-American system would achieve anything notable.

The inter-American system could hardly be described by even its

[9] For some occasions when it was not, see Manger, *Pan America in Crisis*, p. 85.

most dedicated supporter as an association of democratic states. Yet in 1936, at Buenos Aires, the American republics declared the existence of a 'common democracy throughout America', and in the OAS Charter it was asserted that 'the solidarity of the American States and the high aims which are sought through it require the political organization of those States on the basis of the effective exercise of representative democracy', though efforts to make this a condition of membership were unsuccessful.[10] We saw in the previous chapter how the OAS has attempted to grapple with the difficult problem of furthering the effective exercise of representative democracy in the hemisphere. But we also saw earlier that since the Alliance for Progress was launched in 1961, with the strengthening of democratic institutions as one of its principal aims, there have been so many military coups d'état as to make a mockery of this particular inter-American principle.

We noted that the OAS did not hold a Meeting of Consultation to consider what action might be taken to strengthen representative democracy in the face of these coups.[11] The inter-American system has shown much greater readiness to deal with threats from the Left than with those from the Right. Yet, in spite of Castroism and the activities of Russia and China in Latin America, by far the more formidable threat to democratic institutions in the hemisphere has come from the Right, which, of course, has been strengthened by the preoccupation of the American governments with the communist challenge. United States policy, which is mainly responsible for that of the OAS on this question, seems to correspond with Mecham's view that: 'if the United States is interested in stability, order, and democratic progress, it behooves this country to continue to give support through the military-assistance program to the professional military in Latin America; they are fair insurance against Communist *coups* in any of the governments'.[12] It may be doubted that the military in Latin America are fair insurance against communist coups; it is certain they are a constant threat to democratic institutions in much of Latin America. In the field of promoting representative democracy the record of the inter-American system is dismal, with little prospect of improvement in the early future. The trend in the spring of 1965 was away from fulfilment of this principle.

The Charter of the OAS reaffirms the principle that 'international

---

[10] See above, p. 199.
[12] Mecham, p. 340.

[11] See above, pp. 183–4, 255, 289.

law is the standard of conduct of States in their reciprocal relations'. We have seen the concern of the inter-American system with the codification of international law within the hemisphere as early as the Second International Conference of American States.[13] 'In no area of the world', it has been observed, 'has there been so much discussion and serious effort directed toward the formation of a regional legal order.'[14] Yet it has not been found possible to proceed very far with the codification of either private or public international law in the Americas. Whether there exists an 'inter-American regional law' is debatable;[15] at the most (apart from the inter-American treaties) this can be said to consist only of certain principles regarded specifically as American (such as non-intervention) or Latin American (such as the rights of diplomatic asylum) and these cannot supersede general international law. It is significant that inter-American disputes of a juridical character have been referred to the International Court of Justice at The Hague and that all projects to establish an Inter-American Court of Justice have come to nothing.[16]

The most ominous aspect of the failure to establish an inter-American court has been United States opposition to such an institution. For we have already noted that from the beginning the United States has resisted Latin American efforts to formulate principles of 'American international law' limiting rights she claims under general international law. Juridical questions, as we have seen, tend to divide the United States and the countries of Latin America, because the latter feel, with reason, that the traditional rules of international law favour the United States and other great powers who developed and seek to perpetuate them. We saw this, for example, in the case of the treatment of aliens and of their property, which was the subject of dispute between the United States and the Latin American countries at the First International Conference of American States. This issue remains unresolved today, as the 'separate opinion' of the United States representative on the Inter-American Juridical Committee in the latter's report on the 'Contribution of the American Continent to the Principles of International Law that Govern the Responsibility of the State' confirms.[17] Nor has the United States sided with the

[13] See above, p. 50.
[14] Ronning, *Law & Politics*, p. 3.
[15] Cf. Fenwick, pp. 158–70.
[16] See *Report on the Results of the Second Inquiry on the Establishment of an Inter-American Court of Justice, submitted by the Committee on Juridical-Political Affairs*, OEA/Ser. G /IV, C-i-688 (English) Rev., 25 Nov. 1964, Original: Spanish.
[17] OEA/Ser. I/VI. 2, CIJ-61, English, Jan. 1962.

Latin American countries in their juridical disputes with extra-continental powers who are her allies over such questions as terri-torial waters and European colonies and 'occupied territories'.[18]

The OAS Charter reaffirms as principles of the inter-American system 'the fundamental rights of the individual without distinction as to race, nationality, creed or sex' and that 'social justice and social security are bases of lasting peace'. As with 'the effective exercise of representative democracy' efforts to transform these ideals into reali-ties are recent and their success so far very limited. We saw in the previous chapter how the United States has made clear her inability to subscribe to conventions on these subjects because of her federal constitution. The Latin American countries, too, are very reluctant to accept international action to put these principles into effect; which illustrates an inherent weakness of any international organiza-tion, whose members are concerned above all to safeguard their national sovereignty.

This brings us to the principle of non-intervention, so often described as the cornerstone of the inter-American system. A great deal—necessarily—has been said in the preceding pages about this principle: valued so highly by Latin Americans and sometimes useful to the United States (above all, in justifying her dealings with right-wing dictators). But non-intervention is impossible either to define or for the most powerful state in the hemisphere to practise in an absolute sense. The United States has lived up to the principle in the narrow interpretation of not sending her marines into the territory of her small neighbours ever since her first pledge at Montevideo in 1933.[19] But, in the wider sense, intervention is inherent in United States power. Whatever policy the United States pursues in Latin America will be intervention in some form; the question is how the objectives in furtherance of which she seeks to influence her weaker neighbours are regarded by the latter. The Bay of Pigs affair was one kind of intervention; the Alliance for Progress another. The promotion of the inter-American system and the support she gives it represent—as this study has tried to show—an attempt by the United States to shape the international relations of Latin America in her own interests. Whether this policy is to be considered intervention will depend basically upon whether it seems to have been beneficial

---

[18] See above, p. 27.
[19] Two weeks after the celebration of the seventy-fifth anniversary of the inter-American system, the US was to violate this principle by sending her marines into the Dominican Republic (see Postscript, below, p. 336).

or detrimental to the interests of the Latin Americans. For, as Ronning has well observed:

. . . it is only fair to point out that most Latin American critics of United States intervention, while speaking in terms of intervention *generally*, more often than not have in mind those cases of "intervention for the wrong reasons", that is, intervention in support of a detested dictator or in support of United States investors.[20]

In the view of another writer, 'nonintervention is not so much a juridical "doctrine" as a political tool capable of being manipulated, stretched, or even ignored'.[21]

Relations with Other International Organizations

Let us turn now to relations between the inter-American system and wider international organizations. We noted at an early stage in this study the links between the inter-American system and the conferences held at The Hague in 1899 and 1907. The United States and Mexico were the only American states represented at the First Hague Conference, but most of the other members of the inter-American system subsequently adhered to the three conventions signed there. Incidentally, the first two awards of the Hague tribunal were in cases originating in the western hemisphere.[22] All the American states were invited to the Second Hague Conference to which, as we saw, the Third International Conference of American States referred the question of the use of force for the collection of public debts (in effect, the Drago Doctrine, upon which the United States and the Latin American countries were in disagreement).[23]

While the United States was instrumental in forging links between the inter-American system and the Hague Conferences she opposed the establishment of anything more than marginal relations with the League of Nations. Nevertheless, Latin American membership of the League could not be ignored, for often it affected attitudes and policies within the inter-American system. It has been asserted that 'Latin American loyalty to the League, for example, was directly responsible for the failure of the attempt which the United States made in 1936 to impose its neutrality legislation on the Pan American system'.[24] Moreover, a number of disputes between American states

---

[20] *Law & Politics*, pp. 84–85.
[21] Slater, *Int. Org.*, xviii/2 (1964), p. 286.
[22] Humphrey, p. 53.
[23] See above, pp. 50 ff.
[24] Humphrey, p. 77.

were brought before the Council or Assembly of the League of Nations. At the Seventh and Eighth International Conferences of American States questions were raised over co-operation between inter-American and other international organizations and the admission of observers from the latter to inter-American conferences. But little action was taken. Contacts remained limited to those between Pan American agencies and such non-political bodies as the International Labour Office and the International Health Section of the League of Nations.[25]

With the United Nations, of which the United States was a founder member, the situation, of course, was different. We saw, in Chapter VI, the links between the two international organizations as established by their charters.[26] How far, in practice, have the inter-American system and the United Nations been complementary and to what extent rivals in the western hemisphere? In the field of international peace and security, most situations involving American states have been dealt with by the Inter-American Peace Committee or under the Rio Treaty, and the United Nations merely informed of the action taken. However, several hemispheric crises have raised serious questions about the relationship between the OAS and the United Nations in this field. There have been two main issues; the competence of the Security Council to deal with inter-American disputes (that is, whether these must be considered in the first place by the OAS) and the autonomy of the regional body in imposing sanctions upon its members. The first issue came into prominence in 1954 when Guatemala appealed to the Security Council against aggression by her neighbours. Although the United States succeeded in preventing the world body from dealing with Guatemala's complaint, she was unsuccessful in securing endorsement of the principle that members of the OAS are obliged to have recourse to that organization before appealing to the United Nations—in spite of undertakings to do so written into the main inter-American agreements. Cuba, Haiti, and Panama have all succeeded in obtaining a hearing in the Security Council[27] of complaints either against or

[25] As we have seen (above, p. 131), observers from the General Secretariat of the League of Nations and the International Labour Office were present at the Mexico City Conference on Problems of War and Peace (1945). By that time, of course, plans for establishing the United Nations were well advanced and the question of the relationship between the inter-American system and the new world body had become an important consideration in the former's reorganization.

[26] See above, pp. 214–19.

[27] And, in the case of Cuba, as we have seen, in the General Assembly.

involving the United States. And although Haiti and Panama agreed to their cases being heard first by the OAS, these remained on the Security Council's agenda. The increasing likelihood of a Latin American country in dispute with the United States (or opposed by her in a dispute with another Latin American country) taking its case to the United Nations rather than to the OAS represents a serious threat to the inter-American system.

On the other hand, in spite of the clear statement in Article 53 of the United Nations Charter that 'no enforcement action shall be taken under regional arrangements or by regional agencies without the authorization of the Security Council', the OAS has succeeded in practice in exercising an autonomy in the imposition of sanctions against its members. When economic sanctions were imposed against the Dominican Republic in 1960, the United States argued successfully in the Security Council that these did not constitute 'enforcement action' requiring its authorization. She confirmed and consolidated this success in 1962, when Cuba complained to the Security Council against the sanctions imposed against her at Punta del Este. A Cuban request to have the International Court of Justice give judgment on the issue was not granted. Then, in the following October, the OAS Council recommended military sanctions the validity of which was not seriously questioned at the height of such a grave crisis. In this situation, Professor Inis Claude has observed:

the United States argument rested upon the principle that the OAS must be considered an autonomous agency, entitled to protect the security of its region without hindrance from the United Nations. This episode provided the ultimate confirmation of the proposition that the real objective of the United States has not been the restrictive interpretation of Article 53, but its virtual repeal insofar as it purports to inhibit the operation of the OAS.[28]

In fact, this meant complete freedom of action for the United States, since the OAS Council merely accepted a *fait accompli*.[29]

The implications of the OAS Council's decisions in October 1962 are far-reaching for the future of both the inter-American system and the United Nations. Military sanctions were recommended in spite of the fact that there had been no armed attack on any signatory of the Rio Treaty. The argument that such measures were justified because of the 'offensive character' of the weapons installed in Cuba is invalid because no distinction is recognized in international law between

[28] Int. Concil. (Mar. 1964), p. 60.   [29] See above, p. 258.

offensive and defensive weapons. As Professor Schwarzenberger has pointed out:

it is as impossible to distinguish between offensive and defensive nuclear missiles and aircraft as between offensive and defensive walking-sticks. The offensive or defensive character never lies in the weapon, but in its use. To maintain that while, by definition, weapons under exclusive United States control in countries neighbouring on the Soviet Union or aboard United States fleets and Polaris submarines are defensive, Russian-controlled weapons in the Caribbean are offensive is a remarkable feat of special pleading.[30]

The notion of 'anticipatory self-defense'[31] extends to the point of absurdity the inherent right of individual or collective self-defence acknowledged in Article 51 of the United Nations Charter. It is an argument for preventive war. Again, at the Ninth Meeting of Consultation, the concept of aggression was strained in the condemnation of Cuba. Only the power and influence of the United States, of course, enabled the inter-American system to achieve this independence of the United Nations in the field of international peace and security.

Yet there can be no doubt the Latin American countries as a whole have seen the United Nations as something of a counterpoise to the power of the United States. Although generally supporting the latter on cold-war issues, they have often taken an independent position on economic, colonial, and racial questions. Several Latin American countries, as we have seen, supported the primacy of the United Nations in the Guatemalan crisis and strongly affirmed that the rights of members under the United Nations Charter were not diminished by their membership of the OAS. Mexico has maintained that the Cuban question should be dealt with by the United Nations. Sometimes Latin American countries have openly criticized the inter-American system in the world body, as, for example, Venezuela did over the growing number of military dictatorships included in it.[32]

At least until the implementation of the Alliance for Progress, the Latin American countries found the United Nations much more useful in assisting them to deal with their economic and social problems than

---

[30] Georg Schwarzenberger, *The Misery and Grandeur of International Law, An Inaugural Lecture Delivered at University College London, 24 October 1963* (London, 1964), p. 8.

[31] See Lyman M. Tondel, Jr, ed., *The Inter-American Security System and the Cuban Crisis* (1964), p. 52.

[32] See above, pp. 183–4.

the agencies of the inter-American system. In Dreier's words: 'Far more effective work on the economic and social problems of Latin America has, in fact, been done by United Nations agencies. . . . From the standpoint of direct economic returns, membership in the United Nations proved to be a better investment for the Latin American countries than membership in the O.A.S.'[33] The outstanding United Nations agency at work in Latin America has been ECLA, of which Albert Hirschman has written:

> The arresting feature of ECLA is that it possesses attributes not frequently encountered in large international organizations: a cohesive personality which evokes loyalty from the staff, and a set of distinctive beliefs, principles and attitudes, in brief an ideology, which is highly influential among Latin American intellectuals and policymakers. To a considerable degree, this achievement is due to ECLA's director, Dr. Raúl Prebisch, who, in 1949, while not yet heading the organization (he was appointed Executive Secretary in 1950), wrote that veritable ECLA manifesto, *The Economic Development of Latin America and Its Principal Problems* (United Nations, 1950).[34]

Reference has been made to ECLA's role in stimulating economic integration in Latin America, leading to the General Treaty of Central American Integration (and agreement to establish a Central American Bank for Economic Integration), and the Montevideo Treaty providing for a Latin American Free Trade Association.[35] The Latin American countries have also derived advantages from belonging to such world bodies as the International Bank for Reconstruction and Development and the International Monetary Fund. They have also benefited from the activities in the region of other United Nations agencies, such as UNESCO, the Food and Agriculture Organization and the Children's Emergency Fund. Co-operation between these bodies and comparable organizations of the inter-American system has increased since the inauguration of the Alliance for Progress. There can be no doubt that the economic and social problems of the western hemisphere cannot be solved except with the co-operation of extra-hemispheric countries and international organizations.[36] The Alliance for Progress acknowledges this and it was

---

[33] *Hemisphere Crisis*, p. 81.
[34] *Latin American Issues: Essays and Comments (1961)*, p. 13.
[35] See above, pp. 269; 278, n.16.
[36] New efforts have been made in this direction, e.g. the OAS was concerned with the establishment in Jan. 1964 of a non-governmental organization named the Atlantic Community Development Group for Latin America. According to

further brought out by the United Nations Trade and Development Conference at Geneva in 1964.[37]

To what extent is the future of the inter-American system linked with that of the United Nations? It can be argued that the more effective the world body the less scope there would be for regional groupings. This would certainly seem to be so in the case of military alliances, for the present regional defence organizations stemmed from a lack of confidence in the United Nations as a system of collective security. But the inter-American system basically is not a military alliance and, unlike NATO, SEATO, and the other defence organizations, it preceded the establishment of the United Nations. Its continued existence is dependent upon neither the fortunes of the United Nations nor the state of the Cold War, though it has been importantly influenced by both. The inter-American system will persist so long as it seems to offer advantages to the states composing it.

What Has So Far Been Achieved?

This brings us to a much more significant question than whether the inter-American system has fulfilled its stated purposes or lived up to its proclaimed principles: how far has it served the interests of the United States and the countries of Latin America? What advantages have they derived from it in the past and may they hope to gain from its continued existence?

Historically, as we have seen, the inter-American system was promoted by the United States in order to secure Latin American acceptance of her own national policy of restricting extra-continental influence in the western hemisphere. The limitation of such influence would ensure the United States the hegemony over the American continent which her leaders had long since regarded as rightfully hers. The Monroe Doctrine had staked a claim in 1823; by the end of the nineteenth century the United States was able to make it good. The launching of the Pan American movement in the 1880s was a facet of her emergence as a world power.

But the Pan American movement was not initiated by the United

---

Américas, xvi/2 (1964), p. 46: 'Tentatively called the ADELA Investment Company, the new organization will channel private capital from Europe, the United States, Canada, and Japan into joint ventures with Latin American businessmen. With the help of loans from the Inter-American Development Bank, ADELA hopes to mobilize an estimated $200,000,000 for investment in Latin America. Several major corporations on both sides of the Atlantic have pledged their support for the program.'

[37] See above, p. 281.

States solely as a means of furthering the establishment of her hegemony in the western hemisphere. She was concerned, at the same time, to make such hegemony acceptable to the Latin Americans; so that they would not wish to seek extra-continental support against her. For this purpose, advocates of Pan Americanism appealed for 'hemispheric solidarity'. They asserted that the American republics were bound together in a special relationship setting them apart from the rest of the world and, specifically, from the powers of Europe. The United States and Latin America, they maintained, shared a system superior to that of Europe which would be threatened by an extension of the European system to the hemisphere. Moreover, they claimed that the ideal of a united hemisphere had originated in Latin America. Pan Americanism was presented as a movement fulfilling the ideals of Simón Bolívar, the most revered of Latin American figures, though the Liberator's aims had been very different from those which now motivated the policy of the United States.

The inter-American system also served to bolster the self-image of the United States, now emerging as a world power but wanting to seem to herself as well as to others to be behaving differently from the traditional great powers with their spheres of influence and empires. She wanted to believe that her association with the smaller countries of the American continent differed fundamentally from great power–small power relationships in other regions of the world; that the Monroe Doctrine had been beneficial to the countries of Latin America and was compatible with their sovereignty and self-respect. Possessed of weak neighbours in the western hemisphere, the United States chose Pan Americanism where European powers would have chosen the path of imperialism. The self-image of the United States is extremely important in any analysis of inter-American relations, and, of course, of United States foreign policy generally. It has already been suggested that Latin America has provided something of a laboratory for the development of United States foreign policy.

During the first forty or so years following the First International Conference of American States, the United States consolidated her position of hegemony in the western hemisphere. But she failed to convince the countries of Latin America that the inter-American system was beneficial to them. The Monroe Doctrine was associated with repeated interventions by the United States in Central America and the Caribbean region. Pan Americanism was regarded in Latin America as 'a cloak for Yankee imperialism' and the Pan American

Union as, in effect, a colonial office. By 1928 the International Conference of American States had become a platform for voicing Latin American resentment instead of one for demonstrating hemispheric solidarity. Only far-reaching changes in the inter-American system could make it a useful instrument of United States foreign policy. This, we have seen, meant primarily acceptance of the principle of non-intervention.

In subscribing to the principle of non-intervention the United States considered she was giving up unilateral armed intervention, in return for which the inter-American system would ensure 'collective responsibility'. Given her enormous power and influence in the hemisphere, the renunciation of armed force, which seemed in any case to have outlived its usefulness, was not a considerable sacrifice viewed against the gain in goodwill it would bring. By the 1930s Latin American ill-will was causing the United States growing concern, which increased following the rise of the dictators in Europe and their attempts to penetrate Latin America. So the inter-American system became a symbol of the Good Neighbour policy and a means of attempting to draw the countries of the hemisphere together to meet the challenge of the extra-continental, Axis powers.

It is generally agreed that the inter-American system served the United States well during the Second World War.[38] At the Meetings of Consultation of American Foreign Ministers the United States obtained general support for her policies, and, within the framework of decisions taken at these conferences, was able to make bilateral arrangements for such purposes as the use of bases and the increased production of strategic raw materials. We noted how, at the Second Meeting of Consultation, the United States obtained hemispheric acceptance of her own no-transfer principle.[39] While not requiring any serious armed contribution from Latin America to the war effort, the United States did seek political support, especially in countering Axis subversion in the hemisphere. She was able to use the inter-American system to this end, as, for example, in establishing the Emergency Advisory Committee for Political Defense. The Second World War, as we have seen, brought a proliferation of new inter-American agencies as well as the decision to reorganize and strengthen the inter-American system.

[38] Although I have expressed the view that the degree of inter-American harmony achieved during the Second World War has been exaggerated. See above, p. 146.
[39] See above, pp. 113–14.

With the establishment of the United Nations and the growing involvement of the United States in the peace settlement, the future of the inter-American system—traditionally so closely linked with the policy of isolationism—was placed in doubt. In fact, however, the inter-American system assumed a new importance in United States foreign policy. Although determined to pursue a global policy, and opposed to the concept of 'spheres of influence' in other regions of the world, the United States had no intention of relinquishing her hegemony in the western hemisphere. Condemning both the colonial empires of certain western European powers and control of eastern Europe by the Soviet Union, the United States would not accept that these were analogous with the situation in Latin America. In the western hemisphere she was able to point to the inter-American system, an old-established association of juridically equal states, now recognized as a legitimate regional grouping within the United Nations. Moreover, the Rio Treaty, based upon Article 51 of the latter document, gave the inter-American system the right to initiate action to meet armed aggression against any of its members. The United States has therefore been able to use the inter-American system to limit United Nations concern—and that of extra-continental powers—with the affairs of the western hemisphere.

Following the development of the Cold War the United States was anxious for the political support of the other members of the inter-American system. At first, when the Cold War seemed remote from the western hemisphere, this meant, above all, support in the United Nations, where the twenty-one members of the inter-American system originally formed over 40 per cent of the total membership. This support was for United States policies in other regions of the world (for example her action in Korea was endorsed in the OAS Council as well as supported within the United Nations), and also in opposition to attempts by other nations to raise embarrassing American issues in the world body. Subsequently, when the Cold War came to the western hemisphere, the United States found the inter-American system even more useful in limiting United Nations involvement with the problems it caused. The United States used the existence of the inter-American system to mask her overthrow of the Arbenz government in Guatemala; and she has succeeded to a very large extent in isolating Cuba within the hemisphere. Castro's survival has been due to extra-continental support which, regardless of any possible action by the inter-American system, the United States has not been able to prevent. It is significant that the United States based the legality of her quarantine measures against Cuba in October 1962 upon the fact that they were taken, with the support of the inter-American system, under the terms of the Rio pact.[40] Her representative in the General Assembly said his country had received a 'mandate' from the OAS to protect the western hemisphere and would use 'all means necessary' to carry it out. Moreover, he cited the OAS resolution of 23 October as inferentially endorsing the aerial surveillance of Cuba.[41]

On balance, it may be said that the inter-American system has served the interests of the United States in helping her to maintain a position of hegemony in the western hemisphere in a form compatible with her own traditional antipathy towards what she considers the essentially 'non-American' concepts of spheres of influence and imperialism. It has helped to give her a considerable degree of success in securing Latin America's acquiescence in her own policy of limiting extra-continental influence in the hemisphere. The United States has succeeded in marshalling a majority of Latin American governments to condemn a member of the inter-American system seeking extra-continental assistance against her on the grounds that such intervention threatened hemispheric solidarity and ideals. The existence of the inter-American system has enabled the United States to claim that her own undertakings in other regions of the world give no cause for other powers to attempt to intervene in the western hemisphere. Such intervention would not be merely against the United States, but against the inter-American system as a whole, whose members share a community of interests. This premise was expressed in a communiqué issued by the Informal Meeting of American Foreign Ministers and Special Representatives in Washington, 2–3 October 1962:

> The meeting observed that the inter-American regional system has had since its beginnings characteristics of its own that are expressed in specific provisions agreed upon by a community of nations for its collective security and, therefore, that a military intervention of communist powers in Cuba cannot be justified as a situation analogous to the defensive measures adopted in other parts of the Free World in order to face Soviet imperialism.[42]

To be able to make such a claim undoubtedly has been important to

---

[40] See above, p. 257, n. 95.
[41] *NYT*, 17 Nov. 1962; see also UN, General Assembly, 17th sess., *Official Records*, 1st Committee, 1279th Mtg, p. 174.   [42] Stebbins, *Docs, 1962*, p. 371.

the United States in the Cold War, and the more genuine she can make it the more effective the inter-American system will be in safeguarding United States interests in the western hemisphere in the face of the growing challenge to them.

As for the countries of Latin America, the most obvious way in which the inter-American system has served their interests is in establishing the principle of non-intervention, imposing some restraint upon the use of United States power as a price of inter-American co-operation. Within the inter-American system, and especially at the Inter-American Conference and the Meeting of Consultation, the United States is confronted by all the Latin American countries together. It has been observed that 'the inter-American conferences have often had all the earmarks of a Latin American alliance against the United States', although the same writer points out that: 'The United States has generally been able to use its influence with enough governments to prevent the "alliance" from including all or even a majority of Latin American states'.[43] The history of the inter-American system shows, however, that when feeling on some issue has been deep and widespread among the Latin Americans at these conferences it has exerted an influence on United States policies which probably would not have been possible by individual countries through normal diplomatic exchanges.[44]

The Latin Americans have been able to use the inter-American system with greater success, so far, to restrain the United States in the use of her political and military power than to induce her to grant them economic assistance. As we have seen, not until 1958 was there a substantial modification of United States policies on inter-American economic and social co-operation, beginning with her agreement to the Inter-American Development Bank, and followed by the Act of Bogotá and the Alliance for Progress. However, while the inter-American system is associated with the Alliance, it does not control the disbursement of funds. The trend has been for this association to become closer under Latin American pressure, but it seems extremely unlikely that the United States will relinquish the control she now exercises.

The inter-American system undoubtedly has served the interests of the countries of Latin America in bringing them together in this

---

[43] Ronning, *Law & Politics*, p. 158.
[44] An outstanding example is their stand on non-intervention at Montevideo in 1933. See above, pp. 87–90.

form of multilateral diplomacy. One great source of weakness of these states has been their limited contacts with each other. Relations between the countries of Latin America have become more intimate (if not always more friendly) within the inter-American system. It would be ironical indeed if a system conceived to promote Pan Americanism should be instrumental in fostering effective Pan Latin Americanism: Latin American solidarity rather than a truly inter-American community. Such an eventuality is perhaps remote at the present time. But on certain issues such as non-intervention and their economic condition and aspirations there has already grown up a community of interests among the Latin American members of the inter-American system.

It would seem from this brief analysis that the main disadvantage to the United States of her membership of the inter-American system lies in such curbs as it has placed upon her exercise of the enormous power she possesses in the hemisphere, while for the countries of Latin America this lies in the limitations it has imposed upon the development of extra-continental relationships which might have offset the imbalance of power between themselves and the United States. It may well be asked, however, how far membership of the inter-American system has been, in fact, responsible for these restraints and to what extent they have been imposed by external factors. Would it be feasible, for example, for the United States to invade Cuba today if she had OAS acquiescence, or even support? We noted, for example, the influence of external factors upon the development of the Good Neighbour policy. Nor can it be doubted that the most effective limitation upon Latin America's extra-continental relationships has been the unwillingness and inability— until very recently—of any non-American power seriously to challenge United States hegemony in the western hemisphere.

Clearly, the inter-American system has served the interests of the United States much more than it has those of the Latin American countries. This, of course, is only a reflection of the vast disparity of power within the hemisphere. The inter-American system has helped the United States maintain her hegemony and safeguard her interests in the hemisphere with the minimum intervention from extra-continental powers and influence.

Yet the inter-American system has never been truly isolated from international society as a whole; it has always been in some degree affected by the world environment. The extent to which its fortunes have been shaped by extra-continental factors has increased considerably since the end of the Second World War. The most important of these factors have been the establishment of the United Nations (the effects of which have already been discussed in this chapter), the development of the Cold War, and the growing division of the world into developed and economically backward countries.

One most significant result of the Cold War has been the much more intimate links which have developed between the United States and Western Europe. The North Atlantic Treaty Organization is a much closer alliance than the inter-American system, some of whose members reject the idea that it is a military alliance at all. This last point was underlined, incidentally, when Dulles suggested establishing links between the OAS and NATO in December 1957 [45] We have noted how the United States has refused to support the Latin American countries in their efforts to end colonialism in the western hemisphere, which concern the future of American territories possessed by certain of her European allies. In considering whether the Atlantic Alliance is a more natural grouping than the inter-American system it is worth reiterating that Canada, with whom the United States has much more in common and is much more intimately linked than with the countries of Latin America, is not a member of the OAS. In spite of their traditional relationship with the United States—not to mention the Rio Treaty of 1947—the countries of Latin America have never fully supported her position in the Cold War. There has always been fear of involvement in the United States extra-continental commitments and of a renewal of United States intervention in meeting the communist challenge within the hemisphere.

In recent years a growing number of Latin Americans have moved nearer to the position of the Afro-Asian neutralists, rejecting the division of the world into 'Free' and 'Communist', and regarding as more relevant to their problems a division between rich and poor nations.[46] For, as Sr Carlos Sanz de Santamaría, subsequently

---

[45] Whitaker, *YB of World Affairs, 1959*, pp. 138–9. President Prado of Peru had already proposed establishing ties between the OAS and NATO, but there was considerable opposition from other Latin American governments (Dozer, pp. 385–6). On the other hand, the OAS has a Regional Office for Europe which maintains liaison with the European Economic Community, the Organization for Economic Co-operation and Development, the European Free Trade Association, the Secretariat of the General Agreement on Tariffs and Trade, and the UN Specialized Agencies.

[46] This division was very marked at the UN Conference on Trade and Development held at Geneva in the spring of 1964.

appointed chairman of the Inter-American Committee on the Alliance for Progress,[47] observed in 1960:

> Although we Ibero-Americans belong totally to the Western World, in philosophy, ethical concepts and ideals of individual freedom, our living conditions are much more like those in other areas of the world. We, unfortunately, belong to that group of countries so-called 'underdeveloped'. We are backward countries with a very low standard of living. . . .[48]

It could be added that the vast masses of Latin Americans (Indo-Americans and not Ibero-Americans) share neither the standard of living nor the 'philosophy, ethical concepts and ideals of individual freedom' of the Western world. It is doubtful whether the countries of Latin America have ever been wholeheartedly members of the 'Free World'; but there is no doubt they feel themselves today to be among the poor. Nor can the fact that most of the poorer peoples of the world are coloured be overlooked in considering the situation within the inter-American system.

The world environment has also played a part in fostering Pan Latin Americanism in recent years. We have noted the role of the United Nations Economic Commission for Latin America in encouraging economic integration in the region. The treaties establishing the Central American Common Market and the Latin American Free Trade Association were stimulated, too, by the setting up of the European Economic Community. Moreover, the world balance of power between the United States and the Soviet Union has given the Latin American countries a degree of freedom in developing extra-continental relationships which, though limited so far, is greater than they have possessed for a very long time. Certain of the larger Latin American countries, and notably Brazil and Mexico, have already indicated an intention to follow a more 'independent' foreign policy. This will involve more than the development of greater commercial and other relations with the communist countries. A renewal of closer ties with Western Europe to offset the preponderance of United States influence is also under way, as perhaps foreshadowed—albeit modestly—by General de Gaulle's Latin American tour in 1964.

Thus the world environment since the end of the Second World War has had a much greater influence upon the inter-American system than hitherto, and generally an unfavourable one. Yet the

[47] See above, p. 281.
[48] In an address delivered to the World Affairs Council, Boston, Mass., 15 Dec. 1960. Quoted in *Current History*, xl/236 (1961), p. 200.

United States and the Latin American countries have demanded much more of the inter-American system than ever before. Since the alignment of Cuba with the Soviet Union, the United States has wanted full support in meeting the challenge of international communism within the western hemisphere. Ever since the end of the Second World War the countries of Latin America have sought to use the inter-American system to secure United States economic aid on a scale and under conditions acceptable to themselves. Both parties have had disappointments. In recent years, too, under the impact of the Cuban revolution and general world situation, there have been greater demands within the inter-American system for action to promote human rights, social justice, and democracy. All these demands have come into conflict with the principle of non-intervention, with which they seem to be irreconcilable. Perhaps only a drastic reassessment of what constitutes intervention can pave the way to more fruitful inter-American co-operation. But any modification of the cornerstone of the inter-American system will be firmly opposed in varying degrees and circumstances by all its members.

Proposals for Strengthening the Inter-American System

In the meantime, feeling has grown that the achievements of the inter-American system have been altogether too modest, and numerous suggestions have been put forward for improving its performance. Some observers have stressed the need to strengthen inter-American institutions, and notably to make the OAS Council a more dynamic body able to take political initiatives. Manger, for example, believes that although 'in its over-all influence the Council is more important than the Inter-American Conference' it 'has not measured up to its possibilities'. This he feels may be due to the calibre of its membership, 'which is not as high as it might be', but more likely to the divisive effect of its concern with inter-American disputes as Provisional Organ of Consultation under the Rio Treaty, which he deplores.[49]. And Dreier, as we have seen, has criticized the Council for evading major issues and devoting its time to minor ones.[50] It has also been suggested that the Secretary General of the OAS should play a part comparable with that of his namesake in the United Nations.[51]

[49] *Pan America in Crisis*, pp. 74–75, 52–53.   [50] See above, p. 301.
[51] T. Szulc, 'The Inter-American Regional System: Present Status and Future Prospects', in Manger, ed., *The Alliance for Progress: a Critical Appraisal* (1963), p. 120. See also editorials in *Washington Post*, 12 Dec. 1961 and 5 Sept. 1962.

Doubtless the inter-American system suffers from institutional weaknesses, but they are not a fundamental cause of its limitations. It must always be borne in mind that the inter-American system is an association of national sovereign states, even if the OAS possesses in some measure a juridical personality of its own apart from that of its members.[52] The OAS Council consists of representatives of the member states acting on the instructions of their governments. The role of the OAS Secretary General, who, of course, is in a different position from the Council members, has been much more limited than that of the United Nations Secretary General because of several factors. We have noted the initiative given the latter under the United Nations Charter.[53] More importantly, the interplay of forces within the world organization (reflecting the stalemate between the great powers and the consequent growth of influence of the smaller nations) has made it convenient for all concerned to accord greater authority to the United Nations Secretary General. No comparable situation exists, at present, within the inter-American system. Manger records how:

> In the first few years following the adoption of the Bogotá Charter the Secretary General of the OAS [like the UN Secretary General] . . . sought to use his annual report as a medium for commenting on current questions. The reaction of the Council, however, was so unfavorable as almost to constitute a reprimand; so much so that the practice was discontinued and the annual reports have since been limited to a mere factual recital. No Secretary General has since had the temerity to express himself, other than in general and platitudinous terms on any issue of hemispheric importance.[54]

Nevertheless, in October 1964, the Secretary General, Dr José A. Mora, submitted to the OAS Council a nine-point programme for strengthening the inter-American system.[55] His proposals were: an annual political meeting at the ministerial level to examine the general situation of the regional community;[56] greater utilization of the OAS Council; reinforcement of the procedures of pacific settlement; the

---

[52] For some observations on the juridical personality of the OAS see Thomas & Thomas, *The OAS*, pp. 42 ff.

[53] See above, p. 214.

[54] *Pan America in Crisis*, p. 79.

[55] *Strengthening the Inter-American System: Statement by the Secretary General, Dr. José A. Mora*, OEA/Ser. G/V, C-d-1258 (English) Corr., 15 October 1964, Original: Spanish.

[56] Resolution IX of the Final Act of the Mexico City conference in 1945 had provided for regular annual Meetings of the American Foreign Ministers (see above, p. 134). This provision was not included in the OAS Charter, however.

urgent admission of new members to the organization[57]; strengthening respect for human rights and fundamental freedoms; the need for ensuring the effective exercise of representative democracy; the need for the OAS to strengthen its relations with parliaments and establish closer co-operation with non-governmental organizations in the hemisphere; study of the problem of the agricultural and industrial use of international rivers; and the promotion of Latin American integration as a fundamental objective of the OAS. It remains to be seen how much consideration will be given to Dr Mora's points.

Another proposal for improving the inter-American system has been to reduce the dominant position of the United States within it. This suggestion is linked with that of strengthening its institutions, since it is argued, with some reason, that the Latin American members will not give greater authority to an organization so concentrated in Washington. Manger poses the question:

> If the seat of the Council were to be established elsewhere than in Washington, would there be a disposition on the part of the member governments to delegate to it greater authority, perhaps even that of acting on every matter that affects the solidarity and general welfare of the American Republics? And in that event, would the governments also be inclined to raise the level of their representation, not so much in title as in quality, so that the Council could adequately undertake the responsibilities corresponding to it? If so, the transfer might be worth contemplating.[58]

A group of United States political scientists have proposed that the headquarters of the OAS should be relocated in an 'inter-American district', forming a Pan American capital somewhere in Middle America.[59] Two comments may be made on these suggestions. In the first place, moving the Pan American Union from Washington, which has been mooted over a long period of time, would not change the reality of United States power. Secondly, the psychological gain from removing the symbol of her domination might well be offset by a diminished United States interest in the organization.[60] And United States interest, in the form of political and financial support,[61] is vital

---

[57] This point was dealt with by the First Special Inter-American Conference (see above, pp. 297–8). [58] *Pan America in Crisis*, p. 76.
[59] Northwestern Univ., in 86th Congress, 2nd session, Senate, Doc. No. 125, pp. 252–3.
[60] Cf. Macdonald, *Univ. of Toronto Law J.*, xv/2 (1964), p. 429: 'one wonders if . . . less assertiveness by the United States would not vitalize the organization. It would either have that galvanizing effect or it would bring about the organization's demise'.
[61] The US not merely pays such a large share of the OAS budget, but does so

to the inter-American system. Its future, like its past, depends very largely upon the extent to which the United States uses it rather than unilateral or bilateral action in her Latin American policy.

What function do the American states want the inter-American system to perform in their international relations today? Do they want to use it to tackle the basic problems facing the western hemisphere, or as a mere façade proclaiming common ideals and goals in the most grandiloquent terms while the real business of inter-American politics is conducted bilaterally in quite different terms? In the past the inter-American system has only too often been such a façade, professing aspirations so remote from reality as to induce little but cynicism. The future of the inter-American system will depend upon how seriously the member states take its often reiterated principles in view of growing demands from the American peoples for their fulfilment.

A realistic appraisal of the situation reveals that the inter-American system is at present a form of coexistence; coexistence not only between a rich, powerful state and twenty small, weak ones sharing the same continent, but between different social systems and much else besides. Perhaps more harmonious inter-American relations can best be promoted by a franker recognition of differences between the United States and the countries of Latin America.[62] The inter-American system is not a natural grouping, but primarily the creation of United States foreign policy. It has served to mitigate what is basically a delicate relationship because of the excessive imbalance of power in the hemisphere. The United States, while safeguarding her interests and being prepared to act unilaterally in the last resort, has paid a certain price for what might be called the 'legitimacy of multilateralism' furnished by the inter-American system. The OAS label, as was suggested in the introduction to this study, has tended to make agreements with the United States more acceptable to Latin American countries.[63] For such is the

---

with a promptness uncharacteristic of the members as a whole. At the end of February 1964 more than half the total annual budget was still outstanding in quotas from this year and previous years. At that time, only three countries had completed paying both present and previous quotas: the Dominican Republic, the US, and Venezuela. Ten countries owed money from previous years as well as their current quotas. As a result, many approved programmes of the Pan American Union had to be curtailed: *Américas*, xvi/5 (1964), p. 43.

[62] See the criticism by 'Ypsilon' of the inter-American family concept and argument for 'deemphasizing the inter-American tie' in Hirschman, pp. 53–59.

[63] See above, p. xv.

strength of hostility to the United States in Latin America that Mecham could assert: 'It is fairly safe to predict that in the long run the future of the OAS will depend on the extent to which Latin-American governments can free themselves of the mass pressures of anti-United States hostility' (p. 479). Edwin Lieuwen found this judgement 'hard to take seriously',[64] but it is a reminder that the OAS is an association of governments which means very little to the people of the hemisphere and that the warmest supporters of the inter-American system in Latin America only too often have been the most unrepresentative governments. There has not yet been created a true inter-American community: something that would require far-reaching changes in both Latin America and the United States.

The need for changes in Latin America is obvious. It is among the twenty republics that the gap between ideals and realities is greatest. The Alliance for Progress is a belated programme to bring about the necessary changes in terms of economic and social development and the wide enjoyment of social justice and democratic government. The Alliance also professes support for economic integration in Latin America, which inevitably would lead eventually to some form of political federation. Perhaps an inter-American system comprising two entities of comparable size and strength would be more stable and generally more satisfactory than the present one.[65] Or perhaps a Pan Latin American grouping would no longer have comparable ties with the United States. At all events, such a prospect is remote at the moment. In the meantime, developments in the world at large have increased the pressure for changes in Latin America and emphasized the differences between the United States and her fellow members of the inter-American system.

Conclusion

Ever since she began the Pan American movement the United States has been trying to bring about change in the countries of Latin America: to make them more stable; to encourage them to elect 'good men'; to persuade them to adopt a more favourable attitude towards private, capitalistic enterprise and representative democracy—in short, to re-make them in her own image. But she has been opposed

---

[64] In his review of Mecham's book in *HAHR*, xlii/4 (1962), p. 588.
[65] See, for example, S. de Madariaga, *Latin America between the Eagle and the Bear* (1962), pp. 178–9.

to changes in Latin America which challenged her own values and threatened her interests. On the whole, the United States has been very conservative in her Latin American policies, favouring the *status quo* and opposed to revolutionary change. Her recent conversion to such things as national plans and social reform programmes in Latin America is belated and its sincerity must be open to doubt. Indeed, it is asking a very great deal of the United States to expect her to help finance programmes in Latin America so much at variance with her own firmly held philosophy and domestic policies, especially since the changes they are designed to bring about are likely to encourage the emergence of new leaders less sympathetic to her economic interests than those who have controlled the southern republics in the past. The United States government may be convinced of the necessity of supporting these programmes; it has already encountered considerable difficulty in carrying Congress and public opinion with it.[66]

A basic difficulty facing the United States in her international relations today is the degree to which her approach is out of harmony with world trends. To put it simply, she is strongly conservative in a world demanding revolutionary changes; a world most of whose people are poor and coloured, in which the Cold War does not seem to be the burning issue, and United States preoccupation with it appears something of an obsession. Latin America is naturally a part of this world. Unfortunately, the people of the United States have not faced the realities of the international situation.[67] Their leaders have encouraged them to believe that United States foreign policy objectives have been shared by other countries to a much greater extent than has been the case. This has led to disappointment and frustration when the co-operation of their allies has appeared less than whole-hearted on what seem to (North) Americans to be critical issues; and United States administrations have been under strong pressure

[66] It must always be borne in mind that the United States is not a monolithic entity. Apart from the question of pressures upon the administration from Congress and public opinion, there are the competing influences of the different government departments and agencies. While, for example, the State Department might be concerned with the Alliance for Progress and the encouragement of reformist governments in Latin America, the Defense Department would stress co-operation with the military. There have also been the activities of the Central Intelligence Agency, operating not only independently of the State Department, but even pursuing conflicting policies. All this has adversely affected United States relations with Latin America.

[67] See, for example, J. W. Fulbright, *Old Myths and New Realities: and Other Commentaries* (New York, 1964).

to undertake unilateral action. This has been true in respect of the inter-American system, as this study has shown. At the Eighth Meeting of Consultation, for example, the opposition of 'the six' to Cuba's exclusion from the OAS was generally ascribed to fear by their governments of domestic 'subversive elements' rather than genuine difference from the United States on this issue. In fact at Punta del Este the United States received her strongest support, as has been only too often the case within the inter-American system, from the least representative Latin American governments.[68]

But not only do the United States philosophy and domestic policies make it extremely difficult for her to accept the very different approach to economic and social problems of the Latin Americans. The domestic situation in the United States is itself important in convincing the Latin Americans of her sincerity. Such things as racial discrimination and seeming indifference to the considerable amount of poverty within the United States herself have made it far from easy for her to present a convincing image of a country anxious to promote progress among her neighbours. In this connection it is worth remarking that one of the most important factors in the success of the Good Neighbour policy was its being accompanied by the New Deal within the United States. Significantly, President Kennedy on several occasions protested that the United States had a revolutionary tradition and welcomed change, but his protest carried little conviction as a reflection of his country's attitude. It is difficult to see how the United States can be an effective leader of change in Latin America without undergoing considerable change herself. But, although the Johnson administration is committed to further action on both civil rights and poverty, there are few signs that the American people are prepared for anything like a really new deal for the underprivileged groups in their own midst.

Within the inter-American system the United States sees clearly the limitations imposed upon action by the principle of non-intervention which, after all, is directed primarily at her. But she certainly would not tolerate the 'collective responsibility' in her affairs which she has advocated in the case of Latin American countries. She has demanded free elections in Cuba and the Dominican Republic, for example, but would be outraged by any suggestion of OAS observers ensuring the voting rights of Negroes in elections in her own states.

[68] There were notable exceptions, among which Colombia and Venezuela may be cited.

Her federal form of government, she maintains, precludes her sub-scription to conventions on human rights and democracy.[69] Incident-ally, her political system does make significant changes in her Latin American policy extremely difficult. But basically the problem is that the United States does not see the need to change herself in order to strengthen the inter-American system; for her it is a question of the Latin American governments carrying out their responsibilities and treaty commitments. In the meantime the overriding aim of United States Latin American policy—as always, the determining factor in shaping the fortunes of the inter-American system—is to eliminate the communist challenge in the western hemisphere. This does not augur well for inter-American relations.

So the present outlook for the inter-American system is not en-couraging. The Alliance for Progress, which it was hoped would in-augurate a new era in inter-American relations comparable with the Good Neighbour policy, so far has been a disappointment to both the United States and Latin America. Moreover, the role of the inter-American system in the Alliance has been a limited one, so that the latter has been essentially an instrument of United States policy. The United States, not without reason, blames the Latin American governments for not carrying out the reforms to which they pledged themselves at Punta del Este in August 1961. But her own position and policy are equivocal. For the Alliance to be successful in achiev-ing its stated objectives far-reaching changes are needed in Latin America; in fact a relinquishment of power (economic, social, and political) by those whose policies have hitherto blocked the kind of progress the Alliance is designed to bring about. Not surprisingly, these groups have shown little readiness to give up their power through such things as land reform and equitable tax systems, and it would not in any case have been easy for the United States to bring pressure to bear upon them to do so. But the fact is that these groups have been most co-operative with the United States in the past, both over her investments in their countries and, more recently, in supporting her position on the Cuban question.

[69] It is of interest that the US refused to support a resolution (XXX) at the Tenth Inter-American Conference which paid tribute 'to the countries that have included in their legislation the right of suffrage for illiterates, thus seeking to broaden and strengthen the institutions of representative democracy'. Her delega-tion explained that its abstention had been based 'on the nature of the constitu-tional system of the United States and the undesirability for the Conference *to pass judgment on the electoral system of the respective countries*' [author's italics] (*Report of Delegation of USA*, p. 30).

z

This situation has been aggravated by the numerous military coups in Latin America since the Alliance for Progress was concluded. The Kennedy administration was placed in a dilemma by this development, which, though a setback to the Alliance as a means of furthering democracy, was encouraged by United States support of the Latin American military as a factor in combating communism. Military coups generally led to a stronger anti-Castro policy, as in the case of Argentina after the fall of Frondizi. Those responsible generally professed to be acting to remove a threat of communism. The Johnson administration made no attempt to conceal its delight at the overthrow of President Goulart of Brazil in April 1964, which clearly it anticipated would bring to an end that country's 'independent' foreign policy and secure her support for stronger measures against Castro.

In the spring of 1965 the Cuban crisis still overshadows inter-American relations and jeopardizes the future of the inter-American system. The continued existence of Castro's government, though hardly a serious threat to the United States or Latin America in military terms, does place the Monroe Doctrine virtually in abeyance —thus constituting an enormous affront to United States pride—and certainly challenges the conservative forces in Latin America. The refusal of the United States to coexist with Castro makes tension in the Caribbean region inevitable, quite apart from the Cuban government's subversive activities against its neighbours. Yet, to accept Cuba within the inter-American system while she maintains her links with the Soviet Union is impracticable, too; Castro has, in fact, placed Cuba outside the inter-American special relationship. Incidentally, the position of the Guantánamo base makes much more dangerous an already highly anomalous situation. If Cuba's alignment with the Soviet Union persists, this could eventually transform international relations within the western hemisphere, with the Latin American republics developing extra-continental links of a character and on a scale undermining the special relationship with the United States based primarily upon the absence of such links.[70]

As the inter-American system prepared to celebrate 'seventy-five years of peace and progress'[71] the outlook, then, was far from propitious. At any time the Cuban problem might erupt and present

[70] Nor should Cuba's growing economic links with non-communist countries outside the western hemisphere be overlooked. These also have important implications for the future of the inter-American system.

[71] The theme adopted by the OAS for the occasion.

the United States with a strong temptation to settle accounts with Castro. Meanwhile, the Johnson administration had made clear its determination not to allow the establishment of 'a second Cuba' in the hemisphere. The Cuban experience, it could be argued, had demonstrated that the only way to prevent such an occurrence was for the United States to take swift unilateral action should a communist take-over of another Latin American country seem likely. Her fellow members in the OAS could not be relied upon to accept United States judgement on when this situation had arisen, but her power would ensure some measure of endorsement by the inter-American system of whatever course she adopted. President Johnson had already shown himself particularly insensitive to the views of his allies generally, and would be unlikely to place the future of the inter-American system before what seemed to him the immediate interests of the United States. Yet, if the latter did violate the non-intervention clauses of the OAS Charter to deal with what she decided was a communist threat, the inter-American system would be revealed as an instrument useful for easing day-to-day relations with Latin America but not one to be entrusted with vital issues affecting the interests of its most powerful member. The threat of such an eventuality hung over the inter-American system in April 1965.

Postscript, July 1965 : The Dominican Crisis

THE crisis in the Dominican Republic provides material for a fitting postscript to this study of the inter-American system. For it underlines some of the main points that have been made, and confirms important trends which have been noted. The postscript is divided into three parts: a brief account of the development of the Dominican crisis up to July 1965; an attempt to show how certain cardinal features of the inter-American system have been highlighted by the crisis; and an assessment of the significance of the crisis for the future of the system.

The crisis began on 24 April 1965, when a revolt took place in Santo Domingo against the ruling military junta with the apparent aim of restoring to power the former President Juan Bosch who had been overthrown by a coup in September 1963.[1] On 28 April, with the outcome of the revolt still undetermined, President Johnson sent in several hundred marines because, he asserted, United States lives were in danger and the authorities in Santo Domingo were no longer able to guarantee their safety. This action, taken without reference to the Organization of American States, was a clear violation of the OAS Charter, specifically of Articles 15 (forbidding intervention 'for any reason whatever') and 17 (forbidding even temporary military occupation 'on any grounds whatever').[2] The United States government attempted to justify its precipitate action with a plea that there had been no time for consultation. But it is noteworthy that, as in the case of Nicaragua nearly forty years earlier,[3] no foreigners were killed in the Dominican Republic until after the arrival of the marines.[4] The whole affair was, in fact, painfully reminiscent of the Roosevelt Corollary and the period of intervention that lasted until the launching of the Good Neighbour policy.

Having taken, unilaterally, what it considered the first necessary step in the Dominican situation, the United States government turned to the inter-American system for its endorsement. The OAS Council

[1] See above, p. 183.
[2] For the full text of these articles, see above, pp. 201–2.
[3] See above, pp. 76 ff.
[4] This point is well made by Bryce Wood in a letter published in *NYT*, 13 June 1965.

agreed on 30 April to convoke the Tenth Meeting of Consultation, under Articles 39 and 40 of the OAS Charter, to consider the 'serious situation created by the armed strife in the Dominican Republic'. The Council also called for an immediate cease-fire and urged the establishment of an international neutral zone. The Papal Nuncio in Santo Domingo (the dean of the diplomatic corps there) was requested to use his good offices to negotiate the cease-fire. Within the OAS, as well as outside it, there was considerable criticism of the United States intervention. Some delegates argued that such intervention was unjustified under any circumstances; others that it was not justified in what was purely an internal dispute. Mexico and Chile introduced resolutions calling for the withdrawal of United States forces from the Dominican Republic, but they were not voted upon. The OAS Secretary General, Dr Mora, was authorized to go to Santo Domingo to discuss a cease-fire with the leaders of the opposing forces, the Latin American ambassadors there and the Papal Nuncio.

The Tenth Meeting of Consultation opened at the Pan American Union on 1 May. It was composed mainly of 'special delegates' representing the foreign ministers. The Meeting appointed a five-man conciliation commission (consisting of representatives of Argentina, Brazil, Colombia, Guatemala, and Panama) to visit the Dominican Republic 'to do everything possible to obtain the re-establishment of peace and normal conditions'. Dr Mora was to remain in Santo Domingo to represent the OAS presence and continue to use his good offices with the contending parties. At the Meeting the United States delegate (Ambassador Ellsworth Bunker) defended his country's unilateral action by declaring: 'This is not intervention in any sense by the United States in the affairs of the Dominican Republic. United States forces were dispatched purely and solely for humanitarian purposes for the protection of the lives not only of United States citizens but the lives of citizens of other countries as well.'[5] This bland assertion carried little conviction even then.

On the following day President Johnson announced what was by now common knowledge: the real reason for his intervention:

The revolutionary movement [in the Dominican Republic] took a tragic turn. Communist leaders, many of them trained in Cuba, seeing a chance to increase disorder, to gain a foothold, joined the revolution. They took

---

[5] *Américas*, xvii/5 (May 1965), pp. 42–43.

increasing control. And what began as a popular democratic revolution, committed to democracy and social justice, very shortly moved and was taken over and really seized and placed into the hands of a band of communist conspirators. . . . The American nations cannot, must not, and will not permit the establishment of another communist government in the Western Hemisphere.[6]

Many more United States forces were sent into the Dominican Republic, until they numbered over 20,000: a show of power designed to demonstrate the Johnson administration's determination that another communist satellite should not be established in the Americas. The United States government subsequently produced a list of over fifty 'Communist and Castroist' leaders whom it accused of seizing control of the Dominican uprising. This was greeted with considerable scepticism. Yet, although accusing the rebels of being dominated by communists, the Johnson administration continued to protest that it was not taking sides in the revolt!

Meanwhile, the United Nations had been apprised of the Dominican situation. The Security Council had been informed of both the United States action and the resolutions of the OAS. The Soviet Union called for an urgent meeting of the Security Council on 1 May; it was not convened, however, until two days later. Her delegation submitted a draft resolution condemning the United States intervention, and demanding the immediate withdrawal of United States forces from the Dominican Republic. The United States was able to prevent the adoption of this resolution, but a majority of the Security Council was unwilling to have the question virtually left to the OAS as she urged. France was critical of the intervention, and so was Uruguay, one of the two Latin American members of the Council.[7] The Uruguayan delegate declared that the OAS Charter prohibited any intervention, direct or indirect, and that his country did not regard the 'Johnson Doctrine', which was 'a corollary of the Monroe Doctrine', as compatible with that charter. He urged the Security Council to exert its authority in the situation.

At the Tenth Meeting of Consultation the United States pressed for the creation of an inter-American peace force to be sent to the

---

[6] *Américas*, xvii/5 (May 1965), p. 43.
[7] The other was Bolivia, now supporting the United States. As we have seen at the Eighth and Ninth Meetings of Consultation Bolivia had abstained on the key resolutions, and she had entered a reservation to her vote in favour of measures by the OAS in the Cuban missile crisis of October 1962. In November 1964 President Paz Estenssoro was overthrown by a military coup.

Dominican Republic. Opponents of this proposal feared it would merely give an OAS label to what was essentially a United States operation; that it would sanction 'collective intervention' and create a dangerous precedent. The United States experienced considerable difficulty in securing the necessary two-thirds majority support. Chile, Ecuador, Mexico, Peru, and Uruguay opposed the resolution, while Venezuela abstained from voting. The fourteen affirmative votes included that of the Dominican Republic, the diplomatic authority of whose delegation was, to say the very least, open to question.[8] However, an inter-American peace force was eventually set up, with a Brazilian commander;[9] Brazil furnished a contingent of men, as did Costa Rica, El Salvador, Honduras, and Nicaragua. The United States forces were to be nominally under the Brazilian commander, who had a United States 'deputy'. With the arrival of small Latin American contingents, some of the marines were withdrawn; but United States troops still constituted an overwhelming majority of the inter-American peace force.

After a secret mission sent by President Johnson to Santo Domingo in the middle of May had met with failure, the United States supported a Brazilian proposal for the creation of a three-man commission to seek a political solution of the crisis. The key figure would be the United States ambassador to the OAS; the other members were from Brazil and El Salvador. Officially the new commission was to collaborate with Dr Mora in seeking 'the establishment of peace and conciliation that would permit the functioning of democratic institutions in the Dominican Republic'. It replaced the first, five-man commission. Mexico and Uruguay opposed the creation of the new body, while Argentina, Chile, and Venezuela abstained in the vote. Argentina now had reservations to her earlier support of the United States. Meanwhile, on 15 May the Secretary General of the United Nations announced the appointment of Sr José Antonio Mayobre (a Venezuelan), Executive Secretary of ECLA, as his special representative in the Dominican Republic.

---

[8] For the Latin American governments supporting this resolution, it must have been partly a face-saving gesture. Even the most firmly anti-communist among them could have had no wish to appear as endorsing United States intervention; they were anxious to help cover it up with measures by the OAS. Others may have hoped such measures would bring the intervention to an earlier end and do something to salvage the prestige of the inter-American system.

[9] Brazil's staunch support of the United States—a reversal of her 'independent' policy, which followed the overthrow of President Goulart—has been a very important factor in recent inter-American relations. It remains to be seen how long it will last. See above, pp. 29–30.

The United States continued her efforts to secure the formation of an anti-communist government in Santo Domingo. Neither the rebel leader, Colonel Francisco Caamaño, nor former President Bosch was acceptable to her. In spite of her continued protestations that she was neutral in the struggle and wanted only that the Dominican people should have freedom to choose a new government, her very presence denied them such a choice and her actions, whether consciously or inadvertently, favoured the military junta. Rebel forces were frequently in conflict with those of the United States which were gradually encroaching upon the area controlled by Caamaño. Various efforts at mediation broke down, and it appeared that the position of the rebels was gradually weakening. Caamaño not unnaturally denounced both the United States and the OAS, and clearly would have preferred to deal with the United Nations; neither did the junta, believing its victory was now assured, look with favour upon the inter-American peace force. The latter had failed to develop into a truly representative body and remained dominated by United States forces. Only Brazil and a few of the smaller republics actively supported it. And on 20 July both factions in the Dominican struggle, separately and for their different reasons, petitioned the Security Council for its withdrawal. No solution was in prospect. The United States could not withdraw until she had established a government satisfactory to herself; yet any such government was bound to be regarded as her puppet and would require her assistance—even military support—to sustain it in power. The situation in the Dominican Republic remained unpropitious; so, in consequence, did the outlook for the inter-American system.

Meanwhile, the Dominican crisis has highlighted some of the cardinal features of the inter-American system. In the first place, it well illustrates United States domination of the system and the extent to which its fortunes are dependent upon her policies. The vast disparity of power between the 'One' and the 'Twenty' (or, rather, nineteen with the exclusion of Cuba) is underlined by the ability of the United States to violate the most fundamental principle of the inter-American system and then not merely escape open censure but even receive a substantial measure of endorsement of her action.

Yet, if the Dominican crisis demonstrates United States power, it also shows the limitations within which she can exercise it. In spite of the deployment of considerable military strength, it has so far proved impossible for her to impose a political solution upon the Dominican

Republic. She deemed it expedient to turn to the inter-American system for assistance in establishing an acceptable government in Santo Domingo; and in the OAS she was able to obtain only the bare minimum votes necessary for a formal multilateralization of the moves she has been making to gain her objective. She has failed to secure the creation of a truly inter-American peace force.

The Dominican crisis shows also the role the inter-American system plays in United States foreign policy: to support and not replace the unilateral Monroe Doctrine. Some observers have seen in the intervention confirmation that United States Latin American policy has hardened under President Johnson. But it must be recalled that Mr Kennedy warned the Latin Americans after the abortive invasion of Cuba that should they 'fail to meet their commitments against outside Communist penetration' the United States would not hesitate to act unilaterally.[10] Even when failing to make a show of prior consultation, however, the Johnson administration swiftly sought hemispheric support of its policy once this had been put into effect. Indeed, in spite of her cavalier treatment of the inter-American system, the Dominican crisis demonstrates its value to the United States. The 'legitimacy of multilateralization' is of great importance in sustaining her self-image; in staving off criticism of her intervention as aggression comparable with that of which she has consistently accused the communists; and in limiting the role of the United Nations in hemispheric affairs.

At the same time, the Dominican crisis has underlined United States dissatisfaction with the inter-American system as an instrument of her anti-communist policy. Although more blatant, her intervention in Santo Domingo is comparable with the overthrow of Arbenz in Guatemala in 1954 and the invasion of Cuba in 1961:[11] occasions when she acted unilaterally after failing to obtain adequate support from the inter-American system. The United States has criticized the OAS for acting too slowly and its machinery as being too cumbersome to meet an urgent crisis.

This criticism is partly justified, but the truth is that the Latin Americans do not regard the inter-American system as an instrument for furnishing swift endorsement of United States policies. Rather they look to it to impose a measure of restraint upon their powerful

[10] See above, p. 24.
[11] Moreover, it can hardly be doubted that, as in the cases of Guatemala and Cuba, the Central Intelligence Agency has been active in Santo Domingo, furthering the United States policy of favouring the military junta.

neighbour: to maintain the principle of non-intervention. Many do not accept the United States position on the Cold War, and reject the idea of the OAS as an anti-communist alliance. They believe, not without justification, that the United States is inclined to view any movement for substantial social reform as communist-inspired, and they are extremely reluctant to give OAS support to what would in practice be action by the United States. They tend to be more afraid of United States policy to meet the Soviet challenge than of any threat from communism itself. The Dominican intervention has confirmed their fear.

A positive indication of their attitude has been the re-emergence of a group of Latin American countries openly refusing to support the United States anti-communist policy. Mexico, isolated after the Ninth Meeting of Consultation, is still able, by virtue of her internal stability, to resist United States pressures; her former associates at Punta del Este, Argentina and Brazil, are too weak internally to do so. Peru, a leading supporter of measures against Castro at the Eighth Meeting of Consultation, but now under a somewhat more progressive government, deplored the United States intervention in Santo Domingo. Venezuela, for some time a main target of communist subversion, also refused to support the United States. Of the others, Chile's opposition is ominous. The administration of President Eduardo Frei had been hailed as just the type of Latin American government needed to bring about orderly reform and make a success of the Alliance for Progress.[12] But Frei has proved a severe critic of the OAS, and a firm supporter of Latin American unity and closer ties between Latin America and Europe.[13] The case of Chile illustrates the broad truth that unrepresentative governments in Latin America generally have been the most ready to co-operate with the United States; while progressive leaders in the region are coming increasingly to seek to strengthen bonds between the Latin American countries themselves and with other areas of the world. This has important implications for the inter-American system in the long-term.

[12] See above, pp. 186–7.
[13] President Frei visited a number of West European countries in July 1965. It is of interest that at the end of his visit to France he and General de Gaulle (who severely criticized United States intervention in the Dominican Republic) issued a communiqué stating that 'Relations between nations must be based on the principles of nonintervention in internal affairs and the right of peoples to manage their own affairs'. Quoted in Herbert L. Matthews, 'Latin America: Misunderstanding in the O.A.S.', *NYT*, internat. ed., 27 July 1965.

Some Latin American countries, and notably Mexico, favour United Nations precedence over the OAS as a means of lessening United States domination in hemispheric affairs. The Dominican crisis is not without significance for the relationship between the two international organizations. Although—because of United States influence—the Security Council was not able (at least up to July 1965) substantially to influence events in the Dominican Republic, there was greater reluctance among its members than hitherto to accept her contention that the matter should be left to the regional body. The Security Council insisted upon debating developments in the Dominican Republic; both the Dominican factions—and Cuba as an interested party—were given a hearing; and the United Nations Secretary General sent his representative to the scene of the struggle. One of the Latin American countries represented on the Security Council not only criticized United States intervention, but also strongly supported United Nations concern with the crisis. Ironically, as already noted, both sides in the Dominican conflict appealed to the Security Council for the withdrawal of the inter-American peace force.

Within the inter-American system, the Dominican crisis is significant, above all, in its implications for the principle of non-intervention so clearly violated by United States action. This study has shown something of the difficulties inherent in implementing this principle as well as in reconciling it with other objectives of the inter-American system. It has also shown how Latin American concern to uphold the principle of non-intervention has been mainly responsible for thwarting United States efforts to promote collective action to meet the challenge from international communism. 'Non-intervention' has always been directed primarily against the policies of the United States, and it is not surprising she has come to consider it 'obsolete' in the present situation. Today the United States opposes strict adherence to the principle of non-intervention as conflicting with the furtherance of the exercise of representative democracy.

But United States concern for representative democracy in Latin America is a facet of her anti-communist policy. There has been no serious question of her intervening in the case of the many right-wing military coups, from which, of course, this policy generally has benefited. It is only when her own concept of democracy, closely identified with private, capitalistic enterprise, is threatened by communism that she has felt impelled to demand collective action to defend it. Specifically, her policy is aimed at the Castro government of Cuba, which she accuses of imposing a totalitarian régime upon its people behind the shield of non-intervention.

The Dominican crisis is closely linked with the Cuban problem. The United States intervened to prevent a 'second Cuba' and accused 'Castroists' of being active in directing the uprising against the junta. The links between United States policies towards the Dominican Republic and Cuba since 1960 have already been shown in this study. Undoubtedly, the United States has endeavoured to establish in the case of the Dominican Republic precedents which could later be applied to Cuba. OAS supervision of elections in the Dominican Republic, which she favours, and the creation of a permanent peace force could (if achieved) prove valuable such precedents should favourable circumstances arise. The United States is far from reconciled to the continued existence of the Castro government; indeed the next logical step from a successful operation in the Dominican Republic would be direct action to bring about its overthrow. Such a possibility is a threat hanging over inter-American relations.

However, in July 1965 the Dominican intervention could not be described as in any sense a success. It was a severe setback to the inter-American system and a deeply humiliating experience for Latin Americans, for whom an important function of the system is to mitigate (by at least the appearance of prior consultation) the inevitable subordination of their interests to those of the United States. It is ironical that there was to have been held in the previous May the Second Special Inter-American Conference primarily to discuss ways of strengthening the inter-American system. Because of the Dominican crisis the conference was postponed first until August and then November. Only the greater setback of a further postponement made it imperative to hold it. But the crucial issues would have to be avoided. Otherwise there would be a sharp clash between those (supporting the United States) who urged measures to strengthen the 'peace-keeping machinery' of the OAS and those more concerned over 'intervention'. In short there would be raised the embarrassing question: to serve whose interests should the inter-American system be strengthened? For the Dominican crisis has confirmed the absence of a true community of interests between the United States and the countries of Latin America.

The Dominican crisis has re-emphasized what the Cuban problem had already demonstrated: that the issue of communism divides rather than unites the members of the inter-American system. The OAS has been quite unable to agree upon a common policy to meet the communist challenge let alone put it into swift operation. The United States has failed to carry her southern neighbours with her on this issue in spite of all the pressures her power and wealth enable her to bring to bear upon them. At the same time her efforts to do so have encouraged reactions in Latin America which make a long-term answer to the communist challenge much more difficult. She has strengthened the military and those groups opposed to changes which she herself has declared are necessary in Latin America, and has yet further alienated more progressive elements upon whose co-operation the long-term answer depends.[14] For even if she desired to do so, it is beyond the power of the United States to maintain anti-communist but unrepresentative governments in Latin America indefinitely.

The Organization of American States can be strengthened only as a body in which Latin American governments are genuinely consulted on the vital issues of the hemisphere and may hope to have influence on the decisions taken. United States efforts to make it a more effective instrument to combat communism will only weaken it; especially if these efforts take the form of unilateral action designed to force the hands of the other members. The immediate future of the inter-American system depends mainly upon what lessons the United States learns from her current Dominican experience. If she is going to treat all revolts against military juntas or other Latin American dictatorships as 'wars of liberation' and part of a world-wide communist conspiracy the prospects for the inter-American system are gloomy indeed.

In July 1965 United States foreign policy is emphasizing a military response to the communist challenge. This is shown, above all, by her increasing commitment in Vietnam. It has been suggested that the Pentagon rather than the State Department pressed for the despatch of the marines into the Dominican Republic.[15] Until this emphasis is changed—at least in the Latin American policy of the United States—the inter-American system has little hope of recovering from the severe blow it has received from the Dominican crisis.

[14] United States intervention in the Dominican Republic thus has dealt a heavy blow to the Alliance for Progress.

[15] See Henry Raymont, 'Latin America and the Pentagon Approach', *NYT*, internat. ed., 9 July 1965.

Select Bibliography

PRIMARY SOURCES

I. INTER-AMERICAN RELATIONS

Burr, Robert N., and Roland D. Hussey. *Documents on Inter-American Cooperation*. Vol. I, *1810–1881*; Vol. II, *1881–1948*. Philadelphia, Univ. of Pennsylvania Press, 1955.

Eisenhower, Milton S. 'United States–Latin American Relations: Report to the President', *DSB*, xxix/752 (23 Nov. 1953), pp. 695–717.

—— 'United States–Latin American Relations, 1953–1958: Report to the President', *DSB*, xl/1021 (19 Jan. 1959), pp. 89–105.

Gantenbein, James W., ed. *The Evolution of our Latin-American Policy: a Documentary Record*. New York, Columbia UP, 1950.

Manning, William R., ed. *Diplomatic Correspondence of the United States: Inter-American Affairs, 1831–1860*. 12 vols. Washington, Carnegie Endowment for Internat. Peace, 1932–9.

Stebbins, Richard P., ed. *Documents on American Foreign Relations, 1962*. New York, Council on Foreign Relations, 1963.

US Dept of State. 'Alianza para Progreso: Address by President Kennedy and Text of Message to Congress', *DSB*, xliv/1136 (3 Apr. 1961), pp. 471–8.

—— *The Castro Regime in Cuba*. Mimeo, Aug. 1961.

—— *Consultation among the American Republics with Respect to the Argentine Situation: Memorandum of the United States Government February 1946*.

—— *Foreign Relations of the United States, Diplomatic Papers. 1861–.* (Title varies.)

—— *Inter-American Efforts to Relieve International Tensions in the Western Hemisphere 1959–1960*. 1962.

—— *Intervention of International Communism in Guatemala*. 1954.

—— 'The Lesson of Cuba: Address by President Kennedy', *DSB*, xliv/1141 (8 May 1961), pp. 659–61.

—— 'Letter from President Dwight D. Eisenhower to President Juscelino Kubitschek, June 5 1958', *DSB*, xxxviii/992 (30 June 1958), pp. 1090–1.

—— 'Letter from President Juscelino Kubitschek to President Dwight D. Eisenhower, May 28 1958', ibid. p. 1091.

—— Bureau of Public Services. *Cuba*. Dept of State publ. 7171. 1961.

US Senate, 88th Congress, 1st session. *Events in United States–Cuban Relations. A Chronology 1957–1963 prepared by the Dept of State for the Committee on Foreign Relations, 29 Jan. 1963.* 1963.

2. INTER-AMERICAN CONFERENCES AND MEETINGS OF CONSULTATION [1]

The International Conferences of American States, 1889–1928, ed. James Brown Scott. New York, Carnegie Endowment, 1931.
—— *First Supplement, 1933–1940.* Washington, Carnegie Endowment, 1940.
—— *Second Supplement, 1942–1954.* PAU, 1958.

International American Conference (Washington, 1889–90). *Reports of Committees and Discussions Thereon: Revised under the direction of the Executive Committee by order of the Conference, adopted March 7 1890.* Washington, 1890.
—— *Rapport adressé au Gouvernement d'Haiti par Mr Hannibal Price Délégué à la Conférence Internationale Américaine tenue à Washington, du 2 Octobre 1889 au 19 avril 1890.* New York, 1890.
Third International American Conference (Rio de Janeiro, 1906). *Minutes, Resolutions, Documents.* Rio de Janeiro, Imprensa Nacional. 1907.
—— *Report of the Delegates of the United States.* 1907.
Fifth International Conference of American States (Santiago de Chile, 1923). *Actas de las sesiones de las comisiones de la Conferencia.* Santiago de Chile, Imprenta Universitaria 1923?.
—— *Records of the United States Delegation.* US National Archives.
—— *Report of the Delegates of the United States of America.* 1924.
—— *Verbatim Record of the Plenary Sessions.* Santiago de Chile, Imprenta Universitaria, 1923.
Sixth International Conference of American States (Havana, 1928). *Diario de la Sexta Conferencia Internacional Americana.* Havana, 1928.
—— *Minutes and Reports of Committees.* 2 pts. Havana, 1928.
—— *La participación de México en la Sexta Conferencia Internacional Americana: informe general de la delegación de México.* México, D.F., Secr. de Rel. Ext., 1928.
—— *Report of the Delegates of the United States of America.* 1928.
Seventh International Conference of American States (Montevideo, 1933). *Minutes and Antecedents with General Index.* Montevideo, 1933.
Eighth International Conference of American States (Lima, 1938). *Minutes of the Plenary Sessions.* Lima, 1938.

---

[1] Each group of conferences or meetings is arranged in chronological order. Reports by national delegations appear under the conference or meeting to which they refer. All published reports by US delegations are issued by the Department of State.

Ninth International Conference of American States (Bogotá, 1948). *Actas y documentos.* 7 vols. Bogotá, Min. de Rel. Ext., 1953–4.

—— *Project of Organic Pact of the Inter-American System, Submitted to the Ninth International Conference of American States by resolution of the Governing Board of the Pan American Union, February 4, 1948.* Doc. CB-10-E. Washington, 1948.

—— *La República Argentina en la IX Conferencia Internacional Americana.* Buenos Aires, Min. de Rel. Ext. y Culto, 1949.

—— *México en la IX Conferencia Internacional Americana.* México, D.F., Secr. de Rel. Ext., 1948.

—— *Report of the Delegation of the United States of America with Related Documents.* Washington, 1948.

Tenth Inter-American Conference (Caracas, 1954). *Diario de la Décima Conferencia Interamericana.* Caracas, 1954.

—— *Documents of the Plenary Sessions.* SP-1 to SP-56. Caracas, 1954.

—— *Report of the Delegation of the United States of America with Related Documents.* 1955.

Inter-American Conference for the Maintenance of Peace (Buenos Aires, 1936). *Informe de la Delegación de México.* México, D.F., DAAP, 1938.

—— *Proceedings (Stenographic Reports).* Buenos Aires, Imprenta del Congreso Nacional, 1937.

—— *Report of the Delegation of the United States of America.* 1937.

Inter-American Conference on Problems of War and Peace (México, D.F., 1945). *Diario de la Conferencia Interamericana sobre Problemas de la Guerra y de la Paz.* México, D.F., 1945.

—— *Report of the Delegation of the United States of America.* 1946.

Inter-American Conference for the Maintenance of Continental Peace and Security (Petropolis, Brazil, 1947). *Report of the Delegation of the United States of America.* 1948.

First Special Inter-American Conference (Washington, 1964). *Documentos de la Conferencia.* OEA/Ser. E/XII. 1 (español). 1964.

—— *Final Act.* OEA/Ser. C/I. 12 (English). 1964.

Fourth Meeting of Consultation (Washington, 1951). *Proceedings.* PAU, 1951.

Fifth Meeting of Consultation (Santiago de Chile, 1959). *Actas y documentos.* OEA/Ser. F/III. 5 (español). 1961.

—— *Final Act.* OEA/Ser. C/II. 5 (English). 1960.

Sixth Meeting of Consultation (San José, Costa Rica, 1960). *Actas y documentos.* OEA/Ser. F/III. 6 (español). 1961.

—— *Final Act.* OEA/Ser. C/II. 6 (English). 1960.

Seventh Meeting of Consultation (San José, Costa Rica, 1960). *Actas y documentos.* OEA/Ser. F/III. 7 (español). 1961.

—— *Final Act.* OEA/Ser. C/II. 7 (English). 1960.

Eighth Meeting of Consultation (Punta del Este, Uruguay, 1962). *Actas y documentos.* OEA/Ser. F/III. 8 (español). 1963.

—— *Background Memorandum on the Convocation of the Meeting.* OEA/Ser. F/II. 8, Doc. 2 (English). Corr. 2 Jan. 1962 (Original: Spanish).

—— *Final Act.* OEA/Ser. C/II. 8 (English). 1962.

—— US Senate, 87th Congress, 2nd Session. *Punta del Este Conference, Jan. 1962: Report of Senators Wayne Morse and Bourke B. Hickenlooper to the Committee on Foreign Relations, March 1962.* 1962.

Ninth Meeting of Consultation (Washington, 1964). *Documentos de la Reunión.* OEA/Ser. F/II. 9 (español). 1964.

—— *Final Act.* OEA/Ser. C/II. 9 (English). 1964.

—— *Report of the Investigating Committee appointed by the Council of the Organization of American States, acting provisionally as Organ of Consultation.* OEA/Ser. G/IV, C-i-658 (English), 18 Feb. 1964 (Original: Spanish).

3. Documents of the Pan American Union and OAS Official Records

International Bureau of the American Republics. *Minutes of the Executive Committee.* 2 vols, covering the period from 1 Apr. 1896 to 6 May 1901.

Pan American Union. Governing Board. *Minutes.* 52 vols, covering the period from 25 Jan. 1911 to 17 Mar. 1948.

—— *Conferencias especializadas interamericanas: compilación de datos.* Washington, 1964 (?).

—— *Inter-American Peace Treaties and Conventions.* OEA/Ser. X/2 (English). Washington, 1961.

—— *Inter-American Treaty of Reciprocal Assistance: Applications* (vol. I *1948–1959;* vol. II *1960–1964*), Washington, 1964.

—— *"Operation Pan America" and the Work of the Committee of 21: Basic documents and reports, August 1958–August 1960.* OEA/Ser. X/3.1.1 (English), 15 Aug. 1960.

OAS. Council. *Actas de las sesiones,* C-a-1–354 (18 May 1948–30 Dec. 1959); OEA/Ser. G/II, C-a-355 (20 Jan. 1960).

—— *Lista de los documentos publicados con relación a la situación entre la República Dominicana y Haiti.* OEA/Ser. G/VI, C/INF-246 Rev. 2, 15 Oct. 1964.

—— *Report on the Alliance for Progress, presented by Senator Juscelino*

Kubitschek, *former President of Brazil.* OEA/Ser. G/V, C-d-1102 (English), 15 June 1963 (Original: Portuguese).
—— *Report on the Alliance for Progress, presented by Dr Alberto Lleras, former President of Colombia.* Ibid. C-d-1103 (English), 15 June 1963 (Original: Spanish).
——— *Report on the cancellation of convocations of the Organ of Consultation in cases of the application of the Inter-American Treaty of Reciprocal Assistance, submitted by the Committee on Regulations and Procedure.* OEA/Ser. G/IV, C-i-672 (English) Rev. 4, 17 June 1964 (Original: Spanish).
—— *Report on the results of the Second Inquiry on the Establishment of an Inter-American Court of Justice, submitted by the Committee on Juridical-Political Affairs.* Ibid. C-i-688 (English) Rev., 25 Nov. 1964 (Original: Spanish).
—— *Statement by the Committee of the Council of the Organization of American States acting provisionally as Organ of Consultation (Situation between Haiti and the Dominican Republic).* OEA/Ser. G/V, C-d-1281 (English), 15 Dec. 1964 (Original: Spanish).
—— *Strengthening the Inter-American System: Statement by the Secretary General, Dr. José A. Mora.* Ibid. C-d-1258 (English) Corr., 15 Oct. 1964 (Original: Spanish).

Emergency Advisory Committee for Political Defense. *Annual Report submitted to the Governments of the American Republics, July 1943, with an Appendix containing the Recommendations approved from April 15 1942 to July 15 1943.* Montevideo, 1943.
—— *Second Annual Report submitted to the Governments of the American Republics, July 15 1943–October 15 1944, with an Appendix containing the Recommendations approved during this period and other Documents.* Montevideo, 1944.
Inter-American Commission on Human Rights. *Report on the Situation of Political Prisoners and their Relatives in Cuba.* OEA/Ser. L/V/II. 7, Doc. 4 (English), 17 May 1963 (Original: Spanish).
—— *Report on the Situation regarding Human Rights in the Dominican Republic.* OEA/Ser. L/V/II. 4, Doc. 32 (English), 22 May 1962 (Original: Spanish).
Inter-American Cultural Council. *Third Meeting of the Inter-American Cultural Council, San Juan, Puerto Rico, November 22–December 2 1959: Final Act.* OEA/Ser. C/V. 3 (English).
Inter-American Economic and Social Council. *Alliance for Progress: Official Documents Emanating from the Special Meeting of the Inter-American Economic and Social Council at the Ministerial Level, held in Punta del Este, Uruguay, from August 5 to 17, 1961.* OEA/Ser. H/XII. 1 (English). 1961.

—— *The Alliance for Progress: its First Year, 1961–1962. First report on the progress of economic and social development in Latin America and prospects for the future.* Washington, 1963.

—— *The Alliance for Progress: its Second Year 1962–1963. Second report on the progress of economic and social development in Latin America and prospects for the future.* Washington, 1964.

—— *First Annual Meeting at the Ministerial Level, held in México, D.F., from October 22 to 27, 1962: Final Report.* OEA/Ser. H/XII. 4 (English).

—— *Final Report of the Second Annual Meeting at the Ministerial Level, held in São Paulo, Brazil, November 11 to 16, 1963 (provisional version).* OEA/Ser. H/X. 4, CIES/580 (English), 16 Nov. 1963 (Original: Spanish).

—— *Third Annual Meeting at the Ministerial Level, held in Lima, Peru, from December 5 to 11, 1964.* OEA/Ser. H/XII. 9 (English). 1964.

Inter-American Juridical Committee. *Contribution of the American Continent to the Principles of International Law that Govern the Responsibility of the State.* OEA/Ser. I/VI. 2, CIJ-61 (English), Jan. 1962.

—— *Instrument Relating to Violations of the Principle of Nonintervention.* Doc. CIJ-51 (English), Feb. 1959.

—— *Opinion on the Legal Aspects of the Draft Declaration on Nonintervention presented by the Mexican Delegation.* OEA/Ser. I/VI. 2, CIJ-58 (English), Feb. 1961.

—— *Opinion on the Scope of the Powers of the Council of the Organization of American States.* OEA/Ser. I/VI. 2, CIJ-59 (English), Mar. 1961.

Inter-American Peace Committee. *Report of the Inter-American Peace Committee on the Controversy between Guatemala, Honduras, and Nicaragua.* Doc. CIP-131/54.

—— *Report to the Seventh Meeting of Consultation of Ministers of Foreign Affairs.* OEA/Ser. F/II. 7 (English) Doc. 6 (English), 5 Aug. 1960 (Original: Spanish).

—— *Report to the Eighth Meeting of Consultation of Ministers of Foreign Affairs, 1962.* OEA/Ser. L/III, CIP/1/62 (English).

—— *Special Report on the Relationship between Violations of Human Rights or the Non-Exercise of Representative Democracy and the Political Tensions that affect the Peace of the Hemisphere.* Doc. CIP-2-60 (English), 14 Apr. 1960 (Original: Spanish).

International Commission of Jurists. *Sessions held at Rio de Janeiro, Brazil, April 18th to May 20th 1927, Public International Law: Projects to be submitted for the Consideration of the Sixth International Conference of American States.* Washington, 1927.

Special Committee to Study the Formulation of New Measures for Economic Cooperation, Second Meeting (Buenos Aires, April 1959).

352 The Inter-American System

Address by Major Dr Fidel Castro Ruz, Head of the Cuban Delegation, at the Sixth Plenary Session held on 2 May, 1959. CECE/II-40 (English), 2 May 1959 (Original: Spanish).

—— Third Meeting (Bogotá, 1960). *Act of Bogotá: Measures for Social Improvement and Economic Development within the Framework of Operation Pan America.* Washington, 1961.

Special Consultative Committee on Security. *Report on the Work Done during its Third Regular Meeting, November 16 to December 11, 1964.* OEA/Ser. L/X/II.7, 11 Dec. 1964 (Original: Spanish).

SECONDARY SOURCES

1. INTER-AMERICAN RELATIONS

Alexander, Robert J. *Communism in Latin America.* New Brunswick, N.J., Rutgers UP, 1957.

Alvarez, Alejandro. *The Monroe Doctrine: its Importance in the International Life of the States of the New World.* New York, Carnegie Endowment, 1924.

Arévalo, Juan José. *The Shark and the Sardines.* New York, 1961.

Beale, Howard K. *Theodore Roosevelt and the Rise of America to World Power.* Baltimore, Johns Hopkins Press, 1956.

Bemis, Samuel Flagg. *John Quincy Adams and the Foundations of American Foreign Policy.* New York, 1949.

—— *The Latin American Policy of the United States: an Historical Interpretation.* New York, 1943.

Berle, Adolf A. *Latin America—Diplomacy and Reality.* New York, Council on Foreign Relations, 1962.

Bosch, Juan. 'Trujillo: Problema de América', *Combate* (San José, Costa Rica), i/5 (Mar.–Apr. 1959), pp. 9–13.

Cline, Howard F. *The United States and Mexico.* New York, 1963.

Dávila, Carlos. *We of the Americas.* New York, 1949.

Dozer, Donald Marquand. *Are We Good Neighbors?: Three Decades of Inter-American Relations, 1930–1960.* Gainesville, Univ. of Florida Press, 1959.

Duggan, Laurence. *The Americas: the Search for Hemisphere Security.* New York, 1949.

Eisenhower, Milton S. *The Wine is Bitter: the United States and Latin America.* New York, 1963.

Garcia Robles, Alfonso. 'Las relaciones diplomáticas entre México y el Brasil', *For. Int.*, iv/3 (Jan.–Mar. 1964), pp. 347–78.

Hanson, Simon G. 'The End of the Good-Partner Policy', *IAEA*, xiv/1 (Summer 1960), pp. 65–92.

Haring, Clarence H. *South America Looks at the United States.* New York, 1928.

Hull, Cordell. *The Memoirs of Cordell Hull.* 2 vols. New York, 1948.

Humphreys, Robin A. *The Evolution of Modern Latin America.* Oxford, Clarendon Press, 1946.

Ireland, Gordon. *Boundaries, Possessions, and Conflicts in Central and North America and the Caribbean.* Cambridge, Mass., Harvard UP, 1941.

—— *Boundaries, Possessions, and Conflicts in South America.* Cambridge, Mass., Harvard UP, 1938.

Langer, William L., and S. Everett Gleason. *The Challenge to Isolation, 1937–1940.* New York, Council on Foreign Relations, 1952.

—— *The Undeclared War, 1940–1941.* New York, Council on Foreign Relations, 1953.

Lieuwen, Edwin. *Arms and Politics in Latin America.* New York, Council on Foreign Relations, 1961.

—— 'Neo-Militarism in Latin America: the Kennedy Administration's Inadequate Response', *IAEA*, xvi/4 (Spring 1963), pp. 11–19.

Link, Arthur S. *Woodrow Wilson and the Progressive Era, 1910–1917.* London, 1954.

Madariaga, Salvador de. *Latin America between the Eagle and the Bear.* London, 1962.

Matthews, Herbert L., ed. *The United States and Latin America.* New York, The American Assembly, Columbia Univ., 1959; 2nd ed. Englewood Cliffs, N.J., 1963.

Mejía-Palacio, Jorge. 'Why an Economic Conference?', *Américas*, ix/7 (July 1957), pp. 2–6.

Munro, Dana G. *Intervention and Dollar Diplomacy in the Caribbean, 1900–1921.* Princeton, N.J., Princeton UP, 1964.

Nerval, Gaston, *pseud. Autopsy of the Monroe Doctrine: The Strange Story of Inter-American Relations.* New York, 1934.

Palmer, Thomas W., Jr. *Search for a Latin American Policy.* Gainesville, Univ. of Florida Press, 1957.

Pendle, George. 'Latin America', in RIIA, *Survey, 1953.* London, 1956, pp. 325–85.

Perkins, Dexter. *A History of the Monroe Doctrine.* Boston, Mass., 1955.

Pike, Frederick B. 'Can We Slow Our Loss of Latin America?', *IAEA*, xv/1 (Summer 1961), pp. 3–29.

Quigg, Philip W. 'Latin America: a Broad-Brush Appraisal', *For. Aff.* xlii/3 (Apr. 1964), pp. 399–412.

Quintanilla, Luis. 'La política internacional de la Revolución Mexicana', *For. Int.*, v/1 (July–Sept. 1964), pp. 1–26.

Rippy, J. Fred. *Globe and Hemisphere: Latin America's Place in the Postwar Foreign Relations of the United States.* Chicago, 1958.

Rodrígues, José Honório. 'Nueva actitud exterior del Brasil', *For. Int.*, ii/3 (Jan.–Mar. 1962), pp. 408–22.

Ronning, C. Neale. *Law and Politics in Inter-American Diplomacy.* New York, 1963.

Royal Institute of International Affairs. *Survey of International Affairs, 1925.* Vol. II. London, 1928; also the volumes for *1927* (1929), *1933* (1934) *1936* (1937), and *1947–8* (1952).

Smith, Robert Freeman. 'The United States and Latin-American Revolutions', *JIAS*, iv/1 (Jan. 1962), pp. 89–104.

Spykman, Nicholas John. *America's Strategy in World Politics: the United States and the Balance of Power.* New York, 1942.

Stebbins, Richard P. *The United States in World Affairs, 1951.* New York, Council on Foreign Relations, 1952; also the volumes for *1958* (1959), *1961* (1962), *1962* (1963), and *1963* (1964).

Stuart, Graham H. *Latin America and the United States.* New York, 1955.

Szulc, Tad. *The Winds of Revolution: Latin America Today—and Tomorrow.* New York, 1963.

Tannenbaum, Frank. 'The United States and Latin America', *Pol. Sci. Q.,* lxxvi/2 (June 1961), pp. 161–80.

Ugarte, Manuel. *The Destiny of a Continent.* New York, 1925.

Van Alstyne, R. W. *The Rising American Empire.* Oxford, Blackwell, 1960.

Welles, Sumner. *Where Are We Heading?* New York, 1946.

Whitaker, Arthur P., ed. *Inter-American Affairs: an Annual Survey, 1941–1945.* 5 vols. New York, Columbia UP, 1942–6.

Wright, Theodore P., Jr. 'Free Elections in the Latin American Policy of the United States', *Pol. Sci. Q.,* lxxiv/1 (Mar. 1959), pp. 89–112.

Wythe, George. *The United States and Inter-American Relations: a Contemporary Appraisal.* Gainesville, Univ. of Florida Press, 1964.

2. PAN AMERICANISM

Bornholdt, Laura. 'The Abbé de Pradt and the Monroe Doctrine', *HAHR,* xxiv/2 (May 1944), pp. 201–21.

Caicedo Castilla, José Joaquín. *El panamericanismo.* Buenos Aires, 1961.

Cuevas Cancino, Francisco. *Del Congreso de Panamá a la Conferencia de Caracas, 1826–1954: el genio de Bolívar a través de la historia de las relaciones interamericanas.* 2 vols. Caracas, 1955.

Gómez Robledo, Antonio. *Idea y experiencia de América.* México, D.F., Fondo de Cultura Económica, 1958.

Inman, Samuel Guy. *Problems in Pan Americanism.* New York, 1925.

Lockey, Joseph Byrne. *Essays in Pan-Americanism.* Berkeley, Univ. of California Press, 1939.

—— *Pan-Americanism: its Beginnings.* New York, 1926.

Martínez, Ricardo A. *De Bolívar a Dulles: el panamericanismo, doctrina y práctica imperialista.* México, D.F., 1959.

Reynolds, T. H., ed. *The Progress of Pan-Americanism: a Historical Survey of Latin-American Opinion.* Washington, 1942.

Whitaker, Arthur P. *The Western Hemisphere Idea: its Rise and Decline.* Ithaca, Cornell UP, 1954.

Yepes, J. M. *Del Congreso de Panamá a la Conferencia de Caracas, 1826–1954: el genio de Bolívar a través de la historia de las relaciones interamericanas.* 2 vols. Caracas, 1955.

3. THE INTER-AMERICAN SYSTEM: GENERAL

Anglin, Douglas G. 'United States Opposition to Canadian Membership in the Pan American Union: a Canadian View', *Int. Org.*, xv/1 (Winter 1961), pp. 1–20.

Ball, M. Margaret. 'Issue for the Americas: Non-Intervention v. Human Rights and the Preservation of Democratic Institutions', *Int. Org.*, xv/1 (Winter 1961), pp. 21–37.

—— *The Problem of Inter-American Organization.* Palo Alto, Calif., Stanford UP, 1944.

Bastert, Russell H., 'A New Approach to the Origins of Blaine's Pan American Policy', *HAHR*, xxxix/3 (Aug. 1959), pp. 375–412.

Dreier, John C. 'The Council of the OAS: Performance and Potential', *JIAS*, v/3 (July 1963), pp. 297–312.

—— *The Organization of American States and the Hemisphere Crisis.* New York, Council on Foreign Relations, 1962.

—— 'The Organization of American States and United States Policy', *Int. Org.*, xvii/1 (Winter 1963), pp. 36–53.

Facio, Gonzalo J. 'Impulso democrático al sistema interamericano', *Combate*, ii/10 (May–June 1960), pp. 48–56.

Fenwick, Charles G. *The Organization of American States: the Inter-American Regional System.* Washington, 1963.

Fernández-Shaw, Félix. *La Organización de los Estados Americanos (O.E.A.): una nueva visión de América.* Madrid, 1963.

Gómez Robledo, Antonio. 'El Tratado de Río', *For. Int.*, i/1 (July–Sept. 1960), pp. 47–81.

Humphrey, John P. *The Inter-American System: a Canadian View.* Toronto, 1942.

Inman, Samuel Guy. *Building an Inter-American Neighborhood.* New York, National Peace Conference, 1937.

Kelchner, Warren H. 'The Development of the Pan American Union', *B. PAU*, lxiv/4 (Apr. 1930), pp. 332–49.

Kunz, Josef L. 'The Inter-American Treaty of Reciprocal Assistance', *AJIL*, xlii/1 (Jan. 1948), pp. 111–20.

Lockwood, John E. 'The Economic Agreement of Bogotá', *AJIL*, xlii/3 (July 1948), pp. 611–20.

Macdonald, R. St J. 'The Organization of American States in Action', *Univ. of Toronto Law Journal*, xv/2 (1964), pp. 359–429.

Manger, William. *Pan America in Crisis: the Future of the OAS*. Washington, 1961.

Mecham, J. Lloyd. *The United States and Inter-American Security, 1889–1960*. Austin, Univ. of Texas Press, 1961.

Northwestern Univ., Dept of Political Science. 'The Organization of American States', in United States 86th Congress, 2nd Session, Senate, Doc. No. 125, *United States–Latin American Relations, Compilation of Studies prepared under the direction of the Subcommittee on American Republics Affairs of the Committee on Foreign Relations*. 1960, pp. 183–275.

Quintanilla, Luis. 'La convivencia Americana', *Cuadernos Americanos* (México, D.F.), cxxi/2 (Mar.–Apr. 1962), pp. 79–90.

Rodríguez Larreta, Eduardo. 'El derecho a la intervención colectiva', *Combate*, ii/7 (July–Aug. 1959), pp. 23–26.

Slater, Jerome. 'The United States, the Organization of American States, and the Dominican Republic 1961–1963', *Int. Org.*, xviii/2 (Spring 1964), pp. 268–91.

Thomas, Ann Van Wynen, and A. J. Thomas, Jr. *The Organization of American States*. Dallas, Southern Methodist Univ. Press, 1963.

Wells, Henry. 'The OAS and the Dominican Elections', *Orbis*, vii/1 (Spring 1963), pp. 150–63.

Whitaker, Arthur P. 'The Organisation of American States', *The Year Book of World Affairs 1959*. London Inst. of World Affairs, 1959, pp. 115–39.

4. THE INTER-AMERICAN CONFERENCES AND MEETINGS OF CONSULTATION

Bernstein Carabantes, Enrique. 'Punta del Este y las erróneas interpretaciones de un tratado', *For. Int.*, ii/4 (Apr.–June 1962), pp. 518–34.

Connell-Smith, Gordon. 'The Future of the Organization of American States: Significance of the Punta del Este Conference', *The World Today*, xviii/3 (Mar. 1962), pp. 112–20.

Dávila, Carlos. 'The Montevideo Conference: Antecedents and Accomplishments', *Int. Concil.*, no. 300 (May 1934), pp. 121–58.

Enríquez, Luis. 'A Latin Looks at Chapultepec', *The Inter-American*, iv/4 (Apr. 1945), pp. 16–17.

Gómez Robledo, Antonio. 'La crisis actual del sistema interamericano: primera parte', *For. Int.*, iii/1 (July–Sept. 1962), pp. 25–61.

—— 'La crisis actual del sistema interamericano: segunda parte', *For. Int.*, iii/2 (Oct.–Dec. 1962), pp. 176–208.

Kunz, Josef L. 'The Inter-American Conference on Problems of War and Peace at Mexico City and the Problem of the Reorganization of the Inter-American System', *AJIL*, xxxix/3 (July 1945), pp. 527–33.

McGann, Thomas F. 'Argentina at the First Pan American Conference', *IAEA*, i/2 (Sept. 1947), pp. 21–53.

—— *Argentina, the United States, and the Inter-American System, 1880–1914.* Cambridge, Mass., Harvard UP, 1957.

Popper, David H. 'The Rio de Janeiro Conference of 1942', *Foreign Policy Reports*, xviii/3 (15 Apr. 1942), pp. 26–35.

Rippy, J. Fred, and Alfred Tischendorf. 'The San José Conference of American Foreign Ministers', *IAEA*, xiv/3 (Winter 1960), pp. 59–72.

Ronning, C. Neale. *Punta del Este: the Limits of Collective Security in a Troubled Hemisphere.* New York, Carnegie Endowment, 1963.

Sanders, William. 'The Organization of American States: Summary of the Conclusions of the Ninth International Conference of American States, Bogotá, Colombia, March 30–May 2, 1948', *Int. Concil.*, no. 442 (June 1948), pp. 383–417.

Scott, James Brown. 'The Sixth International Conference of American States, held at Habana, January 16–February 20, 1928: a Survey', *Int. Concil.*, no. 241 (June 1928), pp. 275–349.

Welles, Sumner. *Seven Major Decisions.* London, 1951.

Whitaker, Arthur P. 'Cuba's Intervention in Venezuela: a Test of the OAS', *Orbis*, viii/3 (Autumn 1964), pp. 511–36.

—— 'Rio and Bogotá: Pan American Perspective', *IAEA*, i/3 (Dec. 1947), pp. 23–44.

Willner, Ann Ruth. 'Case Study in Frustration: Latin America and Economic Issues at Post-War Inter-American Conferences', *IAEA*, ii/4 (Spring 1949), pp. 29–44.

5. THE INTER-AMERICAN SYSTEM AND THE WORLD COMMUNITY

Brown, Philip Marshall. 'The Monroe Doctrine and the League of Nations', *AJIL*, xiv/1 & 2 (Jan. & Apr. 1920), pp. 207–10.

Canyes, Manuel. *The Organization of American States and the United Nations.* 6th ed. PAU, Washington, 1963.

Castañeda, Jorge. *Mexico and the United Nations.* New York, prepared for the Colegio de México and the Carnegie Endowment, 1958.

—— 'The Underdeveloped Nations and the Development of International Law', *Int. Org.*, xv/1 (Winter 1961), pp. 38–48.

Claude, Inis L., Jr. 'The OAS, the UN, and the United States', *Int. Concil.*, no. 547 (Mar. 1964).

Duggan, Stephen P. 'Latin America, the League, and the United States', *For. Aff.*, xii/2 (Jan. 1934), pp. 281–93.

Furniss, Edgar S., Jr. 'The United States, the Inter-American System and the United Nations', *Pol. Sci. Q.*, lxv/3 (Sept. 1950), pp. 415–30.

Houston, John A. *Latin America in the United Nations*. New York, 1956.

Humphreys, Robin. 'The Pan American System and the United Nations', *International Affairs*, xxii/1 (Jan. 1946), pp. 75–84.

Kelchner, Warren H. *Latin American Relations with the League of Nations*. Boston, Mass., World Peace Foundation, 1930.

Russell, Ruth B., and Jeanette E. Muther. *A History of the United Nations Charter: The Role of the United States, 1940–1945*. Washington, Brookings Institution, 1958.

Thomas, Ann Van Wynen, and A. J. Thomas, Jr. *Non-Intervention: the Law and its Import in the Americas*. Dallas, Southern Methodist Univ. Press, 1956.

Uruguayan Institute of International Law. *Uruguay and the United Nations*. New York, 1958.

Vandenberg, Arthur H., Jr, ed. *The Private Papers of Senator Vandenberg*. Boston, Mass., 1952.

6. The Good Neighbour Policy

Cronon, E. David. 'Interpreting the New Good Neighbor Policy: the Cuban Crisis of 1933', *HAHR*, xxxix/4 (Nov. 1959), pp. 538–67.

—— *Josephus Daniels in Mexico*. Madison, Univ. of Wisconsin Press, 1960.

Cuevas Cancino, Francisco. *Roosevelt y la buena vecindad*. Mexico, D. F., Fondo de Cultura Económica, 1954.

DeConde, Alexander. *Herbert Hoover's Latin-American Policy*. Palo Alto, Stanford Univ. Press, 1951.

Guerrant, Edward O. *Roosevelt's Good Neighbor Policy*. Albuquerque, Univ. of New Mexico Press, 1950.

Inman, Samuel Guy. 'The Rise and Fall of the Good Neighbor Policy', *Current History*, xxxii/188 (Apr. 1957), pp. 193–9.

Roosevelt, Franklin D. 'Our Foreign Policy: a Democratic View', *For. Aff.*, vi/4 (July 1928), pp. 573–86.

Welles, Sumner. *The Time for Decision*. New York, 1944.

Wood, Bryce. 'The Department of State and the Non-National Interest: the Cases of Argentine Meat and Paraguayan Tea', *IAEA*, xv/2 (Autumn 1961), pp. 3–32.

—— 'External Restraints on the Good Neighbor Policy', *IAEA*, xvi/2 (Autumn 1962), pp. 3–24.

—— *The Making of the Good Neighbor Policy*. New York, Columbia Univ. Press, 1961.

7. THE GUATEMALAN AFFAIR

James, Daniel. *Red Design for the Americas: Guatemalan Prelude*. New York, 1954.

Taylor, Philip B., Jr. 'The Guatemalan Affair: a Critique of United States Foreign Policy', *American Political Science Review*, l/3 (Sept. 1956), pp. 787–806.

Toriello, Guillermo. *La Batalla de Guatemala*. México, 1955.

8. THE CUBAN CRISIS

Chayes, Abram. 'Law and the Quarantine of Cuba', *For. Aff.*, xli/3 (Apr. 1963), pp. 550–7.

Draper, Theodore. *Castro's Revolution: Myths and Realities*. New York, 1962.

Duff, Katharine. 'Relations between Cuba and the United States (1898–1934)', RIIA, *Survey*, 1933. London, 1934, pp. 361–93.

Hilton, Ronald. 'Castrophobia in the United States', *The Year Book of World Affairs 1964*. London Inst. of World Affairs, 1964, pp. 56–72.

Smith, Robert F. *The United States and Cuba: Business and Diplomacy, 1917–1960*. New York, 1960.

Teichert, Pedro C. M. 'Latin America and the Socio-Economic Impact of the Cuban Revolution', *JIAS*, iv/1 (Jan. 1962), pp. 105–20.

Tondel, Lyman M., Jr, ed. *The Inter-American Security System and the Cuban Crisis*. Dobbs Ferry, NY, 1964.

Wright, Quincy. 'The Cuban Quarantine', *AJIL*, lvii/3 (July 1963), pp. 546–65.

9. THE ALLIANCE FOR PROGRESS AND ECONOMIC INTEGRATION IN LATIN AMERICA

Anderson, Margaret I. 'New Era for the Alliance: the Inter-American Committee on the Alliance for Progress', *Américas*, xvi/6 (June 1964), pp. 1–7.

Dell, Sidney. *A Latin American Common Market?* London, OUP for RIIA, 1966.

Dreier, John C., ed. *The Alliance for Progress: Problems and Perspectives*. Baltimore, Johns Hopkins Press, 1962.

Gordon, Lincoln. *A New Deal for Latin America: the Alliance for Progress*. Cambridge, Mass., Harvard UP, 1963.

Hirschman, Albert O., ed. *Latin American Issues: Essays and Comments*. New York, Twentieth Century Fund, 1961.

Huelin, David. 'Economic Integration in Latin America: Progress and Problems', *International Affairs*, xl/3 (July 1964), pp. 430–9.

—— 'Latin America's development crisis', *The World Today*, xix/9 (Sept. 1963), pp. 407–14.

Johnson, John J. *Political Change in Latin America: the Emergence of the Middle Sectors*. Palo Alto, Calif., Stanford UP, 1958.

Lleras Camargo, Alberto. 'The Alliance for Progress: Aims, Distortions, Obstacles', *For. Aff.*, xlii/1 (Oct. 1963), pp. 25–37.

Manger, William, ed. *The Alliance for Progress: a Critical Appraisal*. Washington, 1963.

Parkinson, F. 'The Alliance for Progress', *The Year Book of World Affairs, 1964*. London Inst. of World Affairs, 1964, pp. 96–127.

Urquidi, Víctor L. *The Challenge of Development in Latin America*. New York, 1964.

—— *Free Trade and Economic Integration in Latin America*. Berkeley and Los Angeles, Univ. of California Press, 1962.

Véliz, Claudio, 'Obstacles to reform in Latin America', *The World Today*, xix/1 (Jan. 1963), pp. 18–29.

—— ed. *Obstacles to Change in Latin America*. London, OUP for RIIA, 1965.

Wionczek, Miguel S. 'Latin American Free Trade Association', *Int. Concil.* no. 551 (Jan. 1965).

Index

BB